POLITICAL LIFE *in the* WAKE *of the* PLANTATION

sovereignty, witnessing, repair

DEBORAH A. THOMAS

Library of Congress Cataloging-in-Publication Data
Names: Thomas, Deborah A., [date] author.
Title: Political life in the wake of the plantation : sovereignty,
witnessing, repair / Deborah A. Thomas.
Description: Durham : Duke University Press, 2019. |
Includes bibliographical references and index.
Identifiers: LCCN 2019010890 (print)
LCCN 2019016272 (ebook)
ISBN 9781478007449 (ebook)
ISBN 9781478006015 (hardcover : alk. paper)
ISBN 9781478006695 (pbk. : alk. paper)
Subjects: LCSH: Jamaica—Politics and government—1962– | Social
justice—Jamaica—History. | Jamaica—History—1962– | Political
violence—Jamaica—History. | Rastafari movement—Jamaica. |
Civil rights—Jamaica—History. | Sovereignty.
Classification: LCC F1887 (ebook) | LCC F1887 .T466 2019 (print) |
DDC 972.9206—dc23
LC record available at https://lccn.loc.gov/2019010890

Cover art: Caskets of victims of the violence in Kingston, 2010.
Photograph by Ratiba Hamzaoui/AFP/Getty.

Duke University Press gratefully acknowledges the University
of Pennsylvania, which provided funds toward the publication
of this book.

for Connie

Generations come and generations go, but the earth remains forever. The sun rises and the sun sets, and hurries back to where it rises. The wind blows to the south and turns to the north; round and round it goes, ever returning on its course. All streams flow into the sea, yet the sea is never full. To the place the streams come from, there they return again. All things are wearisome, more than one can say. The eye never has enough of seeing, nor the ear its fill of hearing. What has been will be again, what has been done will be done again; there is nothing new under the sun. Is there anything of which one can say, "Look! This is something new"? It was here already, long ago; it was here before our time. No one remembers the former generations, and even those yet to come will not be remembered by those who follow them.

—Ecclesiastes 1: 4–11 (New International Version)

Contents

Galleries appear after chapter 1 and after chapter 2

Preface

DURING THE WEEK OF 24 MAY 2010, MEMBERS OF THE POLICE FORCE and the army entered the West Kingston community of Tivoli Gardens to apprehend Christopher "Dudus" Coke, who had been ordered for extradition to stand trial in the United States on gun- and drug-running charges. In August 2009 when the United States issued the extradition request for Coke, Bruce Golding, then Prime Minister, leader of the Jamaica Labour Party *and* member of Parliament for Tivoli Gardens, argued against the extradition on the procedural grounds that the evidence against Coke was obtained by wiretapping, which is illegal under Jamaican law. But by the third week in May 2010, under pressure from Parliament and the U.S. government, Golding announced to the nation on television that he had authorized the attorney-general to sign the extradition order. This led to a standoff between the security forces that had to find Coke, and many of Coke's supporters who were bent on protecting him at any cost. By the end of the week, Coke had not yet been found and at least seventy-five civilians were officially recognized as having been killed (the number community members give is closer to two hundred). The government established a curfew for Tivoli Gardens, and residents were forced to show passes when leaving or entering. Most movement in or out of the community was effectively stopped, which meant that many people were unable to work, to go to school, to shop for food, or to go about the ordinary routines of their lives. This continued until 22 June, when Coke was detained and subsequently extradited.[1]

Despite the immediate activities of various civil society organizations, it took almost three years for the Office of the Public Defender to submit an interim report to Parliament regarding the conduct of the security forces. The Commission of Enquiry that was called for by the Public Defender's Report of April 2014 finally got under way in December of that year and submitted its report to Parliament in June 2016, but the full scope of political violence in Jamaica has not been publicly aired or accounted for.

THESE ARE THE EVENTS THAT WERE THE IMPULSE FOR THIS BOOK. Yet this project did not begin as a book. This project began as a sort of visual ethnography, an attempt to bear witness, with all its attendant complexities and complications.[2] Deanne Bell, a Jamaican psychologist now teaching at Nottingham Trent University, had attended a screening at New York University (NYU) of the film that John Jackson, Junior "Gabu" Wedderburn, and I directed called *Bad Friday: Rastafari after Coral Gardens* (2011). That film documented the 1963 Coral Gardens "incident"—members of the Rastafari community call it a massacre—a moment just after independence when the Jamaican government rounded up, jailed and tortured hundreds of Rastafarians as the result of a land dispute. This "incident" was largely forgotten by most Jamaicans outside of a handful of Rastafari activists in western Jamaica who worked tirelessly to bring it into public consciousness. Despite these efforts, Coral Gardens was not reliably remembered even among Rastafari, especially the youth. This was partly because the events at Coral Gardens would have been difficult to assimilate within a triumphalist nationalist narrative of ever increasing freedoms and respect for black political activism. To create the film, therefore, we worked with members of the community to track down elders who had experienced that persecution, and we contextualized their narratives within the broader dynamics of the political and social hegemonies of the time, such as a visceral fear of Rastafari and other forms of black consciousness.

Our first screening of *Bad Friday* was on Friday, 21 April 2011, at the annual commemoration of the events, to a rapt audience of Rastafari and fellow travelers. After that, the documentary had its official premiere at the Bob Marley Museum in Kingston, and it screened at film festivals internationally, on college campuses across North America and the Caribbean, and on public television in Jamaica.[3] The Public Defender's Office in Jamaica pursued a reparations case based on the "incident," and the western extension campus of the University of the West Indies in Montego Bay developed a digital archive of Coral Gardens that includes our interviews as well as testimonies from additional police and civilians who were part of or witnessed the events of that week. *Bad Friday* now runs on a constant loop in the National Gallery of Jamaica and Institute of Jamaica's western branch in the Rastafari exhibit, and on 4 April 2017, Prime Minister Andrew Holness officially apologized to the Rastafari community and outlined a number of reparative benefits for those who were affected, including land and a trust fund (Cross 2017). An event that was all but lost to public consciousness has within the past five years become part of the national historical terrain.

This has been possible because the position of Rastafari vis-à-vis the Jamaican state is much changed since the early 1960s. In the early years Rastafari marked the limits of citizenship in independent Jamaica. They were seen as a threat to the consolidation of the new nation because they did not accept the authority of the Jamaican political leadership (instead seeing Africa as "home"); they did not subscribe to capitalist economic and social development models; and they attempted to turn the normalized hierarchies of color and class on their heads through both linguistic and ideological reconstruction. Now, Jamaica is known all over the world because of Rastafari and reggae music, and though some Rastafari maintain an opposition to political participation, newer organized groups have sought to create relationships with the state in order to advocate for their interests *within* the Jamaican polity via both local and transnational institutional fora. Consequently, the scale of Rastafari's impact and critical intervention, both locally and transnationally, has intensified to the extent that elements of the community's language, worldview, and day-to-day practice have become part of the nation's performance of itself. It is Rastafari, in other words, that is largely responsible for the growth of black pride and consciousness in Jamaica, and that has put Jamaica on the map globally, and particularly throughout the postcolonial world.

Coral Gardens has also been able to capture sympathetic public attention because we are now more than fifty years on from the incident—most of the police who were directly involved have either passed on or "repented" in one way or another, and while some of the families who were influential in the persecution of Rastafari in that area at that time are still active in the community, the general will of the population has changed. It was possible to create this archive in the first decade of the twenty-first century, therefore, because while the question of racial equality remains open-ended, significant transformations had occurred globally that no longer render Rastafari a threat to citizenship and nationalist integrity. This is not as obviously the case when we turn our lens to the extradition of Christopher Coke from Tivoli Gardens, for reasons that should become clearer in these pages.

After the *Bad Friday* screening at NYU, Deanne approached me and Junior about creating something similar addressing the state of emergency in 2010, a film or other visual work that would provide a platform for people in Tivoli Gardens and surrounding communities to talk about their experiences during the week of 24 May and to publicly name and memorialize loved ones they lost. Initially, I resisted. *Bad Friday*, I argued, was possible because of the long-standing ties we had to the community and the relationships we were able to create with individuals who had already been attempting to document the elders' stories. It was also possible because the situation was no longer "hot," as it were, not part of the overarching and ongoing oppositions that have characterized political life in independent Jamaica. Not having any ties to, or contacts within, Tivoli, and the sense of being in the thick of things regarding the still unresolved events of 2010 seemed to mitigate against doing anything there. Deanne persisted, however, and with the help of a few key figures including the American journalist Mattathias Schwartz, who generously connected us with the people with whom he had worked most closely in order to write his *New Yorker* article "A Massacre in Jamaica" (2011), we began our project together in early 2012.

Over the intervening years, we recorded about thirty oral histories in a friend's music studio, and we amassed a variety of additional materials, including the footage from the U.S. drone that was overhead during the operation (again, due to Schwartz's generosity), archival film and stills of the community itself, photography (both portraits of our interviewees and pictures taken by community youth during a workshop we ran with students from the University of Pennsylvania in August 2013), additional video from a guided walk through the community in January 2014, and emails and cables between personnel within the U.S. Consulate in Kingston and their counterparts in Washington, DC. And on several occasions, we convened the people who shared their experiences with us to show them drafts of our work in order to receive feedback, and to make sure we were walking the fine line they asked us to when we began working with them, a line that reflects their negotiation of dual power structures—that of the state and that of the Coke family. There was an immediacy to our work with residents in West Kingston, one that operated quite differently from the temporal frame that contextualized *Bad Friday*.

Both projects, however, stand as attempts to witness and to archive state violence, and to give some sense of how the practices and performances of state sovereignty—and the attempts to create life alongside, through, and in opposition to them—have changed over time. The sphere of the visual offers different affordances than academic prose. In visual work, we are able to proximately juxtapose divergent scales, perspectives, and times. And the affective engagements we have sought to reflect and generate through the production and editing decisions that we have made, as well as the dynamics of the present that condition these decisions, are sometimes difficult to capture or represent through language.[4]

Moreover, these engagements are stubbornly both unpredictable and aspirational, and our visual work seeks willfully to accept this indeterminacy, while also attempting to awaken some sort of recognition of the domains in which we, as producers and consumers of events and their representations, are complicit. This textual account extends and engages our visual process, and the complexities of archiving violence through this process, via the sort of transmediation Christine Walley has written about. For Walley (2015: 624), using multiple media in ethnographic practice can offer new and potentially more diverse spaces for engagement as well as "possibilities for expanded dialogue in an increasingly unequal era." Here, the term "transmedia" is coined not to evoke the use of multiple media platforms in research and dissemination, nor to highlight processes of adaptation from one medium to another, but to extend "ethnographic narratives across media forms, with each component making a unique contribution to the whole" (Walley 2015: 624) in ways that might encourage more robust conversations about ethnography as process, relationship, and representation.

Following this, our visual, sonic, and textual work ideally would be "read" together, with each speaking to the gaps in the other without necessarily seeking to resolve them into one seamless story. This kind of transmedial reading might ultimately also do more justice to the media worlds and digital nonlinearities linking us to our interlocutors (Ginsburg et al. 2002; Jackson 2004), helping us to rethink the social relations of ethnographic time and space in our research, writing, and extratextual practice. Ultimately, for me, the story I relate in these pages about making life in and through violence—institutionalized and imagined, past and present—spans multiple temporal and spatial frames, and requires attention to both embodied and cognitive modes of analysis. The archives that can generate these modes of apprehension and analysis, however, are different for different periods, and thus the process of evidence gathering requires another way of looking, the kind of "parallax effect" Faye Ginsburg (1995) advocated for many years ago, the different vision enabled by a change of position. My ultimate hope is that these changes of position might also allow us to understand revolution in a different register, one in which archiving and repair are allied projects.

Introduction

HUMANNESS *in the*
WAKE *of the* PLANTATION

WHAT DOES IT MEAN TO BE HUMAN—POLITICALLY—IN THE WAKE
of the plantation? How have people confronted the unpredictable afterlives
of colonialism and slavery, nationalism and state formation in ways that perform not only a material but also an affective transformation? What forms
of community and expectation are produced in and through violence? What
does modern sovereignty *feel* like? These questions have been haunting me
over the past twelve years during which I have been developing archives of
the relationships between sovereignty and violence in Jamaica.[1] My specific
obsessions have had to do with the temporal regimes to which postcolonial
sovereignty projects have been tethered. I have wanted to know how these
regimes have conditioned the affective states through which sovereignty projects are enacted and experienced and how they have shaped the complex processes of subjectivity within a modernity whose foundational infrastructures
were imperialism, colonization, and plantation-based slavery. I have been interested in what Sylvia Wynter identified as a constitutive tension between
the dominant logic of the plantation—a logic that undergirds *all* modern
sovereignty projects—and its internal threat, the (often millennial) spaces
within which enslaved people maintained a conception of themselves as human rather than as property.[2] It is this tension that would ultimately shape
the relationship between the national and the popular in struggles over sov-

ereignty, and it is this tension that becomes legible by ethnographically attending both to moments of exceptional violence and to the realm of everyday practice.

My aim throughout this text is to bear witness to these dynamics in the kind of quiet and quotidian way Tina Campt (2017: 32) has identified as a modality of refusal, the "nimble and strategic practices that undermine the categories of the dominant." Witnessing, as implied here, is neither straightforward nor unmediated; rather, it is ambivalent and relationally complex.[3] My agenda in these pages will be to juxtapose assemblages of archives—visual, oral-historical, colonial, and postcolonial—in order to think through the relations they bring into being among the psychic, material, prophetic, and political dimensions of sovereignty; the broader historical and geopolitical entanglements they make visible; and the possibilities they generate for a redefinition of human recognition.

The form of witnessing that interests me—one I am calling Witnessing 2.0—is not the witnessing of human rights organizations or of public tribunals such as Truth and Reconciliation Commissions (TRCs), which are limited in and through their relationships to the categories through which they are mobilized, such as human rights and reconciliation.[4] Witnessing 2.0 is, instead, an embodied practice. It is the kind of "co-performative witnessing" for which Dwight Conquergood consistently advocated—a commitment to "shared temporality, bodies on the line, soundscapes of power, dialogic interanimation, political action, and matters of the heart" (quoted in Madison 2007: 827).[5] It makes visible the ways affects operate in multiple temporalities and across levels of consciousness, and is thus closer to the form of witnessing described by Barbie Zelizer (1998, 2002), in which it is a moral practice that involves assuming responsibility for contemporary events. This is what Sue Tait (2011) has referred to as "bearing witness," distinguishing it from "eyewitnessing" by emphasizing its affective dimensions beyond visuality, thereby destabilizing the ocular-centrism that has facilitated imperialism.[6] Tait (2011: 1221) argues that "bearing witness exceeds seeing, and this excess lies in what it means to *perform responsibility*," what Avery Gordon (2008) has elaborated as response-ability.

By focusing on the extent to which one recognizes the various ways we are implicated in the processes we address, Witnessing 2.0 both produces intimacies through the development of affective archives and reveals the ways we maintain the conjunctures of power within which we live. Because the technologies through which we witness potentially exceed these conjunctures, however, Witnessing 2.0 offers us windows into what Walter Benjamin (2005: 510) called the "tiny spark of contingency," that spark that might produce something unexpected and that might reformulate the ground of the human outside of modernist binaries.[7] It is a practice of *recognition* and *love* that destabilizes the boundaries between self and other, knowing and feeling, complicity and accountability. Witnessing 2.0 can therefore ultimately produce the internal shifts in consciousness that radiate from one to another in unexpected and necessarily nonlinear ways, and that lead to lasting, world-changing transformations. What I argue throughout this text is that we must cultivate archives through attentive embodied care in order to recognize and respond to the psychic and sociopolitical dynamics in which we are complicit, and therefore to generate the ability to be response-able, to ourselves and to others.

NEW WORLD PLANTATIONS, IT HAS BEEN EXTENSIVELY ARGUED, PRO-vided the basis for modern social and economic arrangements, not only in the Western Hemisphere but everywhere.[8] Contemporary claims and complaints regarding humanness in the Caribbean are therefore being made within a modernity generated through the movement of Europe (with Africa, conscripted) toward the Americas and the establishment of new forms of genocidal violence as the basis of a changing transnational capitalist political economy. Fifteenth- and sixteenth-century mercantilism inaugurated material, religious, political-philosophical, scientific, and ideological processes that indelibly linked the "New World" and the "Old" in a common project of defining modern humanity in racial terms. The "settling" of the New World saw the delineation of racial hierarchy in the language of the potentiality for Christian conversion, a delineation that then became institutionalized during the sixteenth and seventeenth centuries by Inquisition tribunals (see, e.g., Silverblatt 2004; Wynter 2003). It also saw the twin transformative processes of racial fixing (of diverse African peoples into *negros* and diverse indigenous New World populations into *indios*) and racial flexibility (the various configurations of creolization, transculturation, and hybridity that emerged [see Whitten 2007]). These were processes that became institutionalized through particular extractive labor regimes and constellations of citizenship and subjectivity that excluded non-European groups from the category human (Buck-Morss 2000, 2009; Fischer 2015; Mbembe 2003; Wynter 2003). The initial racialized elaborations of what it means to be human would be subsequently mobilized to serve late nineteenth-century projects of indirect imperial rule throughout Africa and South Asia, as well as the emergent imperialist project of the United States.[9] Modern, liberal democratic political arrangements have been designed to hide these ontological processes; they have disguised the dehumanization of foundational racism through the conceptual framework of perfectibility.

Anticolonial and nationalist projects sought to interrogate, critique, and ultimately revise these originary delineations of the relationships among personhood, value, and political legibility through the development of new forms of community cultural consciousness, if not always substantially new economic arrangements. Indeed, the elaboration of continuities between imperial and nationalist modalities of governance has been a critical focus for these scholars, including attention—in the case of New World societies—to the ongoing forms of violence that have been enacted against black bodies.[10] While many anthropologists have offered brilliant and trenchant critiques of the diverse vectors of nationalist governance and subject formation, I have also felt we have sometimes stopped just short of the more sensory dimensions of sovereignty, leaving us largely unable to answer other, also pertinent questions.[11] This is, in part, because much of this work—inspired by Michel Foucault and Giorgio Agamben—has often failed to take into account the ways what Alex Weheliye (2014: 4) has called "racializing assemblages" are foundational, rather than incidental, to modern delineations of humans, not-quite-humans, and nonhumans. As Wynter (2003) reminds us, the making of the figure of "the poor" and the figure of "the black" are not different processes (as is commonly articulated through assertions such as, "In Jamaica it's not like in the United States; for us the problem is class, not race"). Both these makings, instead, are really one and the same, the recognition (and overrepresentation) of the European as "Man" and therefore human.

What analyses of "bare life" seem to disavow is exactly this: that race *always* prefigures notions of what it means to be a human—and, potentially, a citizen—and thus also what it *feels* like to be a problem, especially once political normativity is marked by liberal rights-oriented participatory democracy (Ramos-Zayas 2012). If we do not account for the ways Afro-descended people find themselves as objects in the midst of other objects, ontologically impossible without violence and exiled from the human relation, then we cannot fully account for subjectivity's discursive entanglements. And if blackness cannot stand on its own as humanity, but must always be recognized through, by, or vis-à-vis whiteness, then liberal governance can only ever perpetuate affective "double consciousness," the need to see oneself through the lens of imperial binaries.[12]

This would be the Afro-pessimist line, and it is a theoretically powerful one, moving beyond political economy and engaging the psychic foundations of the modern world as antiblack (Hartman 1997; Sexton 2007, 2011; Spillers 1987; Wilderson 2008, 2010). This mode of theorizing importantly points to the limitations of both our analytics and our strategies, as it offers a logic whereby the slave relation transcends time and space, perpetuating the impossibility of Black Presence in a context where "whiteness is not only always Presence, but also absolute perspectivity" (Wilderson 2008: 98). Like all logics, Afro-pessimism is (as Claude Lévi-Strauss would have said) "good to think with," but, of course, logics must be understood as contingent. They can exist in the world only as engagements, always in motion, always entertaining the possibility of human action.

This forces a return to my original question: Within this context, what has it meant to be a human capable of acting politically in and on the world? And how do we bear witness to these enactments? If we agree that sovereignty is best understood as dynamic practice, and that therefore there is no static constellation to which "it" refers, then we must think of it as performed and thus embodied (Biehl 2005; Fassin 2008, 2012; Fassin and Rechtman 2009; Hansen and Stepputat 2006; Stevenson 2014; Ticktin 2006, 2011), as constituted both from "below," as it were, and from "above."[13] As performance, sovereignty is also a mode of address and thus requires acknowledgment from an audience for whom the performance must be legible (Masco 2014; Rutherford 2012a).[14] If all social projects that are not forcefully imposed "must be affective in order to be effective," as William Mazzarella (2009: 299) has argued, then our ethnographic attention must be attuned to the production, reception, and circulation of these affective fields.

Focusing ethnographically on the relation between affect and sovereignty offers a number of important affordances, the first of which has to do with the emergence of the body on the stage of critical thinking, not just as the raw material of management, but also as a way of knowing, both publicly and intimately. This body is not private but is instead social, relational, and historical, and its unconscious is therefore also fully historically and culturally situated.[15] Exploring the constitution of the political subject not primarily through nationalism or through state- (and extra-state-)driven processes of subjectification, but through the cultivation of embodied affects that are shaped by the particular temporal conjunctures in which they emerge, enables us to interrogate the ways political affects can transcend the context of their emergence, allowing them to appear and resurface unpredictably. It can thus unbind sovereignty not only from territory, and therefore from the political centrality of the independent nation-state, but also from the teleologies of linear, progressive time.[16] What an affective approach to sovereignty gives us, then, is a better sense of what Danilyn Rutherford (2016: 287) has called "the embodied experience of a world in motion, the atmospherics of an age." These embodied atmospherics are the nonideological dimensions of hailing and the aspects of relation that arrive without always explicitly calling attention to themselves, creating a sensibility of community that disturbs both the spatial and the temporal dimensions of the nation-state through the particular forms of mediation that bring them into being.[17] They are grounded in particular historical materialities; they are generated through particular technologies; and they produce temporally specific expressions, with different effects in different periods.

In thinking through how the "Tivoli Incursion" came to be possible, I have been interested in cultivating an "archive of affect." This is Gayle Wald's phrase, one she mobilizes to understand the late 1960s and early 1970s television variety show *Soul!* as both a reflection of contemporary realities and an embodiment of dreams for a "black is beautiful" future (Wald 2015: 8). Archiving, here, is not oriented toward the past and its preservation or toward creating sites of pure memory or history. As Michel-Rolph Trouillot (1995) has taught us, archiving produces absences and forgetting as New World knowledge formations as often as it suggests new possibilities for social and political relations.[18] In the case Wald investigates, these relations are generated through popular cultural expression, but in our case they emerge through our collection of images, sounds, and narratives of state violence (see also Iton 2008). Nadia Ellis (2016) has called the elaboration of possibility generated by this kind of archival practice "improvisation," an embodied affective register through which African diasporic people enact survival under conditions of unpredictability and multiple forms of sovereign violence.

An archive of affect is not quite a counter-archive—or, perhaps, it would be more accurate to suggest that an archive of affect is not beholden to the nationalist and masculinist discursive frames that often contextualize counter-archives (Ellis 2015). Those documentation practices and social movements that have taken the space of the nation-state as their primary mobilizing rubric have accomplished many critical goals, but they ultimately have failed to complexly historicize our conceptualization of social and political processes and therefore have enabled the perpetuation of the "culture of violence" and "culture of poverty" tropes, as well as the patterns of exclusion that characterized the colonial period.[19] An archive of affect, however, opens a space of potentiality, one that might catalyze new possibilities for seeing connections previously unexamined and for reordering our ontological taken-for-granteds, such as time and space, politics and justice, and the very terrain of humanism itself (Reid-Pharr 2016; Wynter 2003). In making this argument, I am not suggesting there is some romantic and miraculous sphere of political action outside significatory processes and machineries. Instead, I am suggesting that the unpredictability of affect, and subsequently its power, lies in its simultaneous operation at the cognitive, mediated level and at a more visceral level (Mazzarella 2009). We constitute ourselves through political activity in the everyday, both at the level of consciousness and at the level of embodiment. Assembling archives of affect thus should tell us something about how the sphere of the political has been imagined and felt at various junctures and about the kinds of politics that are possible at these junctures.

Archives of affect, because they are nonlinear and thus unobligated to the teleologies of liberalism, can also shift the politics of reparations away from discretely local and legally verifiable events and toward the long and slow processes undermining our ability to forge social and political community together. They can urge us to be more skeptical about nationalist narratives of perfectibility whereby we triumph over past prejudices and injustices through a force of will and commitment to moral right, instead encouraging us to train our vision more pointedly to transnational geopolitical and sociocultural spheres and to the messiness of sovereignty at different moments. They address an audience that extends beyond the juridical limitations of the nation-state, thereby encouraging demands for a more comprehensive form of justice. At the same time, by inspiring us to see and hear differently, archives of affect can help us to focus on the everyday ways people innovate life without constantly projecting today's struggle into a future redemption. And because they are, in the end, technologies of deep recognition, they can cultivate a sense of mutuality that not only exposes complicity but also demands collective accountability.

MY LAUNCHING PAD FOR THESE INVESTIGATIONS IS THE CARIBBEAN, and specifically Jamaica, where the pressing questions always seem to come back, in one way or another, to how the society came to be so saturated with violence, and how to end it. In the Caribbean, the history of plantation development and the transatlantic slave trade has meant that there has been no straightforward relationship among territoriality, nativeness, and nationalist governance. Moreover, in Jamaica, as elsewhere in the British West Indies, the reckoning of land rights, norms regarding the organization of political authority, and conflicts among subgroups developed in relation not to originary land rights but to a context, at least prior to the nineteenth century, in which the planter class wielded considerable political influence within Parliament and absolute authority locally, and in which indigenous peoples have been conceptually disappeared (S. Jackson 2012).

In his classic *The Sociology of Slavery*, Orlando Patterson argued that the primary characteristic of Jamaican slave society was absenteeism. "This element was central to the whole social order," he wrote, "and was in some way related to almost every other aspect of the society" (Patterson 1967: 33). For Patterson, the consequences of absenteeism were legion: it evacuated Jamaican society of potential leaders within all sectors of society and therefore resulted in a Legislative Council populated by individuals whose "poverty and inefficiency [was] a matter of public notoriety"; who had "no respect" and "no influence"; and who therefore severely diminished the character and efficacy of public office (Governor Marquis de Sligo, quoted in Patterson 1967: 38). It prevented the development of a proper educational system, which meant that even planters and their children—save the wealthiest— remained semiliterate, and it "led to a complete breakdown of religion and morality among the resident whites" (Patterson 1967: 40), with clergymen themselves among the most profligate; this occasioned a breakdown of the institutions of marriage and the family. Most of all, absenteeism meant that the majority of estate profits were repatriated to England rather than reinvested locally, which "was disastrous for an economy so heavily dependent on foreign supplies" (Patterson 1967: 44). Absenteeism thus produced a "loosely integrated" society within which there were no significant institutions to create or reinforce laws.

Furthermore, Patterson points out, for more than 125 years after initial British colonization of the island in 1655, there were no comprehensive slave codes, and despite the passage of a Slave Act in 1696, the relationships between masters and slaves were governed by customs rather than laws. This meant that while masters typically enjoyed absolute legal power, slaves also were able to extract certain rights—most importantly, in relation to the cultivation of provision grounds, which became a much more expansive practice than what had originally been legislated by Slave Acts in both 1696 and 1788. While these grounds have typically been understood as essential to the production of foodstuffs to sell in the market (and therefore to the attainment of cash), and while they were crucial for the development and maintenance of religious and social practices outside the reach of the plantation, customary stewardship of provision grounds also "weakened slave resistance to white power," as Trevor Burnard (2004: 169) has reminded us:

> On the one hand, the tendency of slaves to engage in capitalist market-oriented activity worked, in the long run, against the logic of plantation slavery because it reduced slaves' dependence on the bounty of the master and thus reduced his control over him. On the other hand, private property and market exchange fractured slave communities. Disputes over property and property-related crimes opened fissures within slave ranks. Confronting attacks on slave prop-

erty rights from outside often healed these fissures, but it also often weakened the black community as a whole.

Making this relation between autonomy and cooptation even more complex is Burnard's assertion that whites (as estate owners, managers, and overseers) were slaves' only protection against the praedial larceny of other slaves. As a result, potential solidarities were further strained: "When a thief was from within a slave community, slaves could humiliate or ostracize the violator of group norms. But when a thief came from outside the closed society of the plantation, slaves had little option other than to turn to their masters, who alone had recourse to the law and the authority to apprehend and punish slaves, wherever they came from" (Burnard 2004: 165). Whites, here, embodied the law, and slaves, as property, had no inherent rights unto themselves; therefore, any legal action on their behalf had to be undertaken by their masters. Nevertheless, the customary agreements masters entered into with slaves ensured the smooth functioning of the plantation system. Moreover, after 1717, masters were also able to protect their more "valuable slaves" from prosecution for crimes as outlined by an act "'for the more effectual Punishment of Crime by Slaves.'"[20] Slaves, by contrast, entered into competitive arrangements with other slaves as custodians of property, and though they developed collective interests in the preservation of their economic and, arguably, sociocultural resources, this "communal solidarity was limited and territorially defined" (Burnard 2004: 170).

I have argued elsewhere that we could read in these dynamics the beginnings of a system of patronage and clientelism, albeit an unstable one, in which political authority was not only racialized but also tied to territorially rooted patterns of protection that ultimately encouraged alliances between the powerful and those they exploited and undermined alliances among the exploited themselves (Thomas 2011). In an interview with David Scott, Orlando Patterson made a similar claim, arguing that "there's a clear pattern of continuity between the instability of slavery and the plantation belt that . . . sometimes permeated the peasant area, and then fed right into the urban slums" (Scott 2013: 161). Indeed, patron-clientelism would become the defining characteristic of a political system that features what have come to be known in the contemporary period as "garrison" communities. In Jamaica, thus, a nexus of customary rights related to land use and heritability, and forms of patronage and clientelistic loyalty, forged the ground on which and mechanisms through which nationalist citizenship claims developed in the twentieth century.[21] What I want to highlight here is that just as the plantation was foundational to modern economic production and labor organization, it was this phenomenon that also shaped the infrastructures, practices, and processes of politics during the post-Emancipation period and within postcolonial New World nation-states.[22]

In Jamaica, the political economy of modern citizenship was, by the mid-twentieth century, defined through participation in the trade union movement. This broad movement ultimately became politicized via the formation of oppositional political parties: the People's National Party (PNP) in 1938 and the Jamaica Labour Party (JLP) in 1941, each connected to a union—initially the Trades Union Congress (after 1943) and ultimately the National Workers' Union (after 1952) and the Bustamante Industrial Trade Union (BITU), respectively. From the earliest moments, conflicts between unions were also partisan conflicts over territory, especially in downtown Kingston, and these conflicts were often violent. In response to a question from the political scientist, activist, and politician Trevor Munroe regarding street fighting during union conflicts in the 1940s, Richard Hart, whom we will come to know better in chapter 3, remembered that "whole streets changed the composition of tenants living in a particular area, because if you were a PNP man you couldn't live in certain areas." He explained, "You had PNP yards and JLP yards; and you had PNP streets and JLP streets developing. And only then, when the forces had reached that level . . . did the state—in classic Engelsian terms—intervene to preserve peace between the contending factions and did the police begin coming out" (Munroe 1990: 120).

Since power in this context was personalized, ultimately grounded within the charisma and patronage of one or another leader (Munroe 1972; Sives 2010), allegiances to union leaders—and therefore to political parties—were generally understood to be transmitted through the family, the community, and the workplace. Clientelistic networks, however, were not limited to those operating within the domains of organized political party activism with working-class Jamaicans; they also included those within the fields of education, business, journalism, and community development who could trade information, skills, and contacts with their counterparts in politics (Edie 1994; Stone 1980). This solidified divisions within the working class, and the hegemony of colonial class relations and patterns of leadership was secured in such a way that working-class Jamaicans would "continue support of a basically middle-class political order long after this support would have appeared unjustified on any calculation of social returns" (Munroe 1972: 92; see also Gonsalves 1977; Sives 2010; Thame 2011).

Beginning with universal suffrage in 1944 and culminating in independence in 1962, as government power grew it became more centralized, which further eroded the ability of working-class people to make decisions that would improve their political, economic, and social circumstances, even at the level of local government (Senior 1972). This situation was exacerbated by an intensification of partisanship in the distribution of state resources. While this became a feature of politics in the 1940s, it had become institutionalized with respect to labor by the 1950s and housing by the 1960s. The distribution of seasonal farm work tickets, for example, was by 1955 known to operate on a partisan basis. Consider the example, documented by Munroe, of a woman who registered for a job with the Government Employment Bureau and was asked what constituency she lived in: "I was told that I would have to be a member of some PNP group before they would help me to find a job. To make sure I wouldn't lie to them they told me to get a note from the Chairman of whatever Group I Joined" (letter in *The Star*, cited in Munroe 1972: 92). That this was party policy is evident from the 1959 PNP Group Leaders Training Course pamphlet Munroe cites, which laid out the following policy: "See that PNP people get work. . . . [O]f every ten, make it six PNP and four JLP," and "PNP hard core workers should be provided for" (Munroe 1972: 92).

By 1966, when the JLP was in power and some factions of organized U.S. labor were pressuring the American government to shut down the Farm Labour Programme, this kind of partisanship related to employment continued in the guise of assisting farm workers vis-à-vis U.S. unions. In a letter to his father, Norman Manley, who was then the leader of the opposition, Michael Manley, the island supervisor and first vice-president of the National Workers Union (NWU), explained that their "great friend in the American Labour Movement called Nick Zonarich" had advised him that he convinced the U.S. unions to organize West Indian farm workers rather than advocate for their removal. As a result, the younger Manley proposed that representatives from the NWU meet recommended farm workers from the PNP before they departed for the United States in order to "put them in a frame of mind to expect to be organized by representatives of the American Trade Union Movement." He added that the NWU and the PNP leadership agreed that their policy was to cooperate with the AFL-CIO, and that they did not "wish to include the Ministry of Labour and the BITU in such an exercise, but would prefer to help through the efforts of the NWU."[23] The full significance of this request will become clear in chapter 3, but I relate this correspondence here in order to show how political partisanship in Jamaica also took on a transnational dimension and was entangled with foreign institutional bodies. Of course, this has been true not only in relation to labor organizing, but also with respect to Jamaica's involvement in the international trades in drugs and arms, which, though a feature of political struggles during the 1960s, emerged more strongly in the 1970s and 1980s.[24]

By the 1967 elections, patronage (in terms of housing and jobs) was explicitly wielded as a political weapon, as government-constructed property by then constituted 40 percent or more of housing stock in downtown constituencies (Clarke 2006b). With continued patronage dependent on continued loyalty, the partisan system's most explicit manifestation was through the construction of housing schemes that were made available to people on the basis of party membership. While the colonial government had been involved in the construction of housing developments that solidified particular political allegiances in the aftermath of hurricanes and other disasters (Robotham 2003), and while the PNP had proposed a project of slum clearance and housing construction in 1961, it was the removal of squatters from Western Kingston and the subsequent construction of Tivoli Gardens that solidified the links among housing, territory, and political party. In 1963, 932 families comprising 3,658 people were removed from the Foreshore Road area in Western Kingston, and the destruction of their dwellings began on 2 October to enable Phase I of the Tivoli Gardens scheme (Sives 2010: 65). Additional evictions beginning in mid-February and continuing until mid-July 1966, displacing about two thousand people, led to the replacement of left-leaning "Back O' Wall" with Phases II and III of Tivoli Gardens. By mid-August, political gang warfare had surged, and in October, the JLP had declared a state of emergency that lasted until after the 1967 elections (Gray 1991). Following the completion of Tivoli Gardens, which remains (with Denham Town) the JLP's stronghold in downtown Kingston, the PNP government constructed additional housing for its supporters. The garrisonization of downtown Kingston was further reinforced by the abandonment of downtown spaces by Jamaican elites and middle-class professionals (Carnegie 2014; Robotham 2003).

Contemporary garrisons—of which Tivoli Gardens is considered the perfect example—are thus territorially rooted homogeneous voting communities in which political support is exchanged for contracts and other social welfare benefits.[25] As in the past, these exchanges have been institutionalized, and even codified as part of general procedures for the distribution of paid work and social services among constituencies downtown, with the vote-benefits nexus mediated through the relationship between the politician and a local "don." This relationship, however, has not been static (Sives 2010). It became part of a more general ideological struggle during the 1970s, and it subsequently transformed as the elaboration of the transnational trades in cocaine and weapons supplanted a previously smaller-scale trafficking in ganja. This has strengthened the role of dons vis-à-vis politicians, as dons' increasing involvement in both illicit and legitimate businesses has provided politicians with financial support, in addition to the military support offered during election periods (Harriott 2004; Samuels 2011). This is also what has perpetuated a kind of permanent war in which Kingston figures centrally as a spatially, racially, and politically polarized place, both discursively and symbolically, and it is what has brought garrison dons to the attention of the U.S. government.

What were thus made legible in 2010 were the various scales at which and through which the garrison operates. In other words, the garrison doesn't merely denote a physical space—one that is simultaneously local, national, and global—but also evokes an affective disposition encompassing the requirement of submission to a set of dictating norms and forms of violence that include the suspension of critical consciousness, the simultaneous denigration of blackness and its celebration in popular culture, the violent policing of movement, and the need to appeal to a "leader" for the provision of basic requirements. This is why other modalities of organizing political life and social development—such as Rastafari, the People's Freedom Movement, or the Black Power movement, all of which are discussed in these pages—are seen and subdued as threats, not only to Jamaican sovereignty and U.S. hegemony, but also to the worldview that positions black bodies as the instruments of profit, both economic and political, for others.

Again, what undergirds my arguments throughout this text is the assertion that these contemporary manifestations of garrison politics are grounded in a system of political authority on sugar estates oriented toward loyalty to a powerful figure and reliance on that figure for work, benefits, and protection. There is, in other words, a certain kind of global historical priorness that we should attribute to political organization in postcolonial New World societies, one that has to do with the infrastructures, practices, and processes of politics in which the plantation-based racialized categories of human, not quite human, and nonhuman remain foundational to nationalist sovereignty, despite material transformations in the position of black, "brown," and white Jamaicans (Hanchard 1999).[26]

We would also do well to remember that in Jamaica and elsewhere, the consolidation of plantation-based, rather than peasant-based, agriculture only deepened with the intensified penetration of the United States in the late nineteenth century. While in Puerto Rico, Cuba, and the Dominican Republic plantations heralded an intensified investment in sugar, in Jamaica it was banana production that became more vertically integrated into an export-oriented plantation system monopolized by the Boston Fruit Company (later to become the United Fruit Company), despite the origins of this industry in small-scale peasant production by black Jamaicans (Holt 1992).

Tensions regarding a deepening U.S. influence over the Jamaican economy extended to the political realm after the 1907 earthquake in Kingston, in the wake of which then Governor James Alexander Swettenham was recalled to Britain because he refused the assistance of a contingent of U.S. Marines who had arrived on a rescue mission. By World War II (with the Destroyers for Bases Agreement), and in its aftermath (with the establishment of the Anglo-Caribbean Commission), the United States had a significant foothold in Jamaican economic, political, and sociocultural life, and this foothold only deepened throughout the twentieth century and into the twenty-first with the militarization of drug policy (see Tate 2015). The United States was therefore fundamental to the reorganization of sovereignty in Jamaica after World War II, and intelligence gathering and labor mobilizing were the critical institutional spheres of this reorganization. I have much more to say about these processes throughout this book, but I outline them here in order to lay the groundwork for apprehending the multiplicity of sovereignties in which Jamaicans are imbricated and to which Jamaicans have responded in different ways at different times. In Tivoli Gardens, certainly, there have been multiple sovereignties at play, and the different scales at which they have operated—sometimes in collaboration and sometimes not—give us windows into the affective sociopolitical fields in which people attempt to make life.

IF WE CONCEDE THAT SEIZING STATE POWER IS BOTH AN ACT OF SELF-determination and an act of sovereign violence, then we are able to grasp the inherently contradictory nature of revolution, and we are in a position to take seriously Maziki Thame's (2011: 76) argument that "the postcolonial experience produces violence that in and of itself is related to processes of liberation." Drawing from Anglophone Caribbean scholarship attending to the relevance of Fanonian views of revolution to formerly British West Indian countries, Thame explores the gendered, racialized, and class dimensions of Caribbean nationalisms. Her argument is that within a configuration in which "middle class and professional men came to assume power over the nation and have maintained their dominance over other, weaker men and over women in general," the Caribbean state became an agent of this subject position (Thame 2011: 77). The relationships among gendered class, kinship norms, and nationalist respectability have been discussed elsewhere at length, but what is important here is Thame's contention that where full personhood and citizenship remain in question for black working-class Jamaicans, working-class men are criminalized, singled out for exceptional treatment by the state.[27] Violence against poor Jamaicans thus became normalized "as a feature of elite consensus around the establishment of a social order that rendered poor Blacks also demeaned" (Thame 2011: 79). The violence Thame is pinpointing is not only the violence of party politics and the racialized patterns of structural violence that have become normative throughout the Americas; it is also an everyday violence that permeates encounters with middle-class people, agents of the state, and each other. The garrison, for Thame (2011: 81), is the extension of this violence and is "a symbol of conquest and specifically of middle class dominance over the poor through the party mechanism," one that seeps into every other dimension of social organization and interaction, locally and transnationally.[28]

Frantz Fanon's point about revolutionary violence is that it turns the norms of society on their head; it purges colonial degradation and allows for the reclamation of personhood and the realization of meaningful social and economic transformation. But what kind of liberation could Fanon's cleansing and humanizing violence bring within this context, one in which the response to alienation from the nationalist state has been "violence, disorder and indiscipline though not necessarily of a revolutionary nature" (Thame 2011: 84)? Thame points out that for scholars such as Anthony Bogues, Obika Gray, Anthony Harriott, and Brian Meeks, violence in postcolonial Jamaica has been an "act of empowerment" and a "means to visibility" (Thame 2011: 84). "Through their competition and collaboration with the state in the use of violence," Thame (2011: 86) writes, "segments of the urban poor become empowered." Violence, in this frame, is a route to recognition, but one that has primarily been expressed and received (or rejected) through the very masculinism that undergirds the postcolonial order. I come back to questions of visibility in chapter 1, and I have much more to say about recognition in the coda, but the important question here is that if violence in postcolonial Jamaica has at its base "a masculinist understanding of empowerment—the imposition upon another as the basis for establishing one's humanity" (Thame 2011: 88)—does this allow for the development of new political, social, economic, and ethical logics? For Thame (2011: 89), what is required is "a new focus on the meaning of liberation, which seeks to deconstruct a decolonization steeped in men's desire for power," and to simultaneously transform the "institutions of alienation and domination that became features of the postcolonial state."

Here is the crux of an important insight into why earlier models of political liberation have been exhausted. If we must confront what David Scott (1999: 14) has argued over the past two decades is a crisis in the "coherence of the secular-modern project," then in what new ways might we rethink the limits of postcolonial sovereignty and its flawed models for sociopolitical change? How might we expose the incompatibility of decoloniality and liberalism without falling into what Wynter has called "simplistic easy radicalisms" (Scott 2000: 158)?

Within anthropology, the critique of liberalism has tended to center on the liberalism of Locke, Kant, and other framers of the Enlightenment-oriented modern state institutions that ultimately would come to operate through a focus on private property, market relations, and developmentalism.[29] It has not typically turned its critical lens toward the Romanticist strands of liberalism, in part—perhaps—because these are the strands that are more common fodder for anthropological research, the "cargo cults" and millennial movements critical of abstract rationalism and capitalist modernity we have striven to make legible, even inevitable, given configurations of inequality. While we have deconstructed the utopias envisioned through these movements, we have respected them, even sometimes rescuing them from the sense that Romanticism tends inescapably toward fascism, totalitarianism, and similarly reactionary programs. A Weberian tradition of anti-Enlightenment romanticism, however, is one that has been central to many successful social transformation projects, not just extremely conservative ones, in large measure due to the affective (as opposed to secular-rational) *force* of its movements, a force that is often circulated through the figure of a charismatic leader.[30]

Michael Löwy and Robert Sayre have advocated for a reconsideration of Romanticism. In *Romanticism against the Tide of Modernity* (2001), they argue that the critical force and clarity of Romanticism lies in its exposure of "the blindness of the ideologies of progress . . . the unthought of bourgeois thought" (Löwy and Sayre 2001: 250). Their argument is that Romanticism can be both revolutionary and counterrevolutionary, undergirding movements with vastly discrepant ends. What is common to all, however, is a "value on life, love, hope, freedom and joy, as well as creativity" (Löwy and Sayre 2001: 8), and a rejection of the Enlightenment's abstract rationalism, as well as the stultifying reification—defined here as "the dehumanization of human life, the transforming of human relations into relations among things, inert objects" (Löwy and Sayre 2001: 20)—accompanying the move to global capitalism. Where most locate Romanticism as emerging in the wake of the French Revolution as the result of disillusionment with the bourgeoisie that seized power, Löwy and Sayre (2001:20) track it back to the early eighteenth century and an emergent disillusionment with the spread of capitalism. They argue that in pushing a critique of capitalist modernity, "the Romantic view constitutes modernity's self-criticism."

Throughout their text, Löwy and Sayre chart a typology of Romanticisms, differentiating among Restitutionist, Conservative, Fascistic, Resigned,

Reformist, and Revolutionary or Utopian Romanticisms (which for them would include Jacobin-Democratic Romanticism), and distinguishing further among the English, French, and German varieties of each. It is that last category of Romanticism that contains some interesting bedfellows. Karl Marx and Friedrich Engels appear among the Utopian Romanticists, as do Nikolai Bukharin and Joseph Stalin, E. P. Thompson, and the Frankfurt School. Löwy and Sayre (2001: 214) also argue that surrealism was the twentieth-century movement that most "brought the Romantic aspiration to reenchant the world to the peak of its expression and that most radically embodied romanticism's revolutionary dimension." And, of course, it was surrealism, and later situationism, that inspired Aimé Césaire and Fanon, in part because it was a way to rethink form, but also because it reimagined the relationships among past, present, and future and eschewed the binary dualisms of self and other, mind and body, and so on.

While Löwy and Sayre do not tether their grounding of Romanticism in anticapitalism to imperialism and the colonization of the Americas at all, if we understand modernity as the ground upon which our degradation as non- or not-quite-humans is realized, then we should be able to see the appeal and purchase of an anti-modern critique of reification within settings characterized by colonization and plantation slavery. It is true, in other words, that aspects of Romanticism have been central to the contemporary rightward shifts throughout the Americas and Europe. But it is also true that they have undergirded powerful social movements—such as Rastafari—that have gone the furthest to critique the liberal, capitalist status quo and the progressive teleologies of developmentalism. I want to suggest, therefore, that we reformulate the "problem" of postcolonial sovereignty in terms of an ongoing struggle between two versions of liberal social change: secular-rational versus Romanticist, or, in other language, pragmatists versus poets. In this reformulation, the power of institutional transformation would probably rest in the modern secular liberal revolutionary framework, and the power of affective attachment would probably stay with the Germanic framework, in both its exclusionary and inclusive guises.

In Jamaica, this would look like a struggle for revolutionary social change between the progressive left—a formation I would take to include the various Marxist and Black Power groups that came to occupy the political landscape after universal suffrage in 1944, but perhaps most stridently in the late 1960s and early 1970s—and the prophetic left, a formation that would encompass Rastafari, but also Ethiopianism and earlier redemptive religious movements such as Bedwardism, as well as secular-prophetic hybrid movements such as Garveyism. Of course, these two formations, especially during the late 1960s and early 1970s, did not exist within a nationalist vacuum and were not necessarily mutually exclusive. At particular moments and within particular contexts, there were significant points of overlap, and sometimes collaboration. At other times, there were significant disconnects. These formations, as well, have existed within a broader political economy in which the region is increasingly dominated by U.S. economic interest, and it is this broader context that shapes the breaking of old regimes, the institutionalizing of new ones, and the devastation attending their collapse.[31]

For the progressive left, the bourgeois rights achieved through liberal revolutions are important, meaningful, and deserving of more profound elaboration through the "strong and slow boring of hard boards," as Max Weber (1946) famously defined politics. This is an approach that "criticizes the present in the name of certain modern values . . . while calling on modernity to surpass itself, to accomplish its own evolution" (Löwy and Sayre 2001: 28). And it is one that works from the messy and difficult here and now rather than envisioning a utopian past or future. It attempts to forge alliances among the positions of actually existing people, with all their actually existing flaws, in order to produce actually existing change through control of the state. For them, Romanticist movements are important but cannot ultimately play a leading role on the stage of revolutionary change. However, within our actually existing contexts, I would argue that it is Romanticist movements that have consistently produced meaningful and lasting transformations in people's understanding of the world and their place in it, and therefore of their internal worlds and intersubjective relations, in part because they do not respect the boundaries of the territorial state. Theorizing sovereignty in relation to questions of affect, therefore, forces us to generate more complex accounts of the historical and social relations through which notions of sovereignty are produced, experienced, and circulated across time and space. And it encourages us to more fully appreciate the complexity of how visions of the present, the future, and social change are inhabited and expressed in extremely complex and often contradictory ways by people who are operating in networks that encompass many scales simultaneously.

Let me return to Thame's claim that corruption, middle-class dominance, and the criminalization of black, working-class men and women in Jamaica can be dismantled only by displacing men's desire for power from the center of political thought and action. While Weberian conceptualizations of politics and revolution do much to help us take seriously the affective states that constitute notions of politics and community, it is true that they do not necessarily move us outside the broader frame of masculinism. However, neither, as we have seen, does the secular rationalism of the progressive left. What Thame is proposing is a kind of feminist solution, one that makes visible other kinds of struggle and action, typically led by women. This is a solution that doesn't rely on charismatic leadership and that involves collaboration among diverse stakeholders. This is, indeed, her own program of research, and it is a critically important one.

What I want to propose is another kind of feminist solution, not as an alternative but as a way to walk alongside Thame. It is a solution grounded in Witnessing 2.0, a quotidian practice of watching, listening, and feeling that is relational and profoundly intersubjective.[32] This solution is geared toward (1) taking seriously embodied ways of knowing and understanding in an effort to (2) track the long-term entanglements that have produced and sustained the binaries structuring our modern world so that we find ways to (3) undo dualistic modalities of thinking and acting in order to (4) generate meaningful forms of repair. In the coda, I argue that this repair must be generated through the "real love" (J. Jackson 2005) of deep recognition.

WHILE THIS BOOK BEGINS WITH A DISCUSSION OF THE EVENTS OF May 2010 in Tivoli Gardens, it travels successively back in time in order to flesh out some of the ways we might understand the various entanglements that helped us arrive at that moment, and the affects that might be understood to characterize it, as well as the other moments I explore. I argue that the worlds of West Kingston in 2010, of southern Clarendon during the late 1960s and early 1970s, and of Jamaica as a whole through the long 1950s are characterized by different affective sociopolitical fields. By this, I mean to explore affect in much the same way that some scholars of migration in the 1980s and 1990s understood the movement across territorial boundaries as generating a transnational sociocultural field (see, e.g., Basch et al. 1994; Glick Schiller et al. 1992; Sutton and Chaney 1987). The original proponents of transnationalism within anthropology were attuned to the importance of history, not merely in terms of how the past appeared in the present, but as a circulating discursive field that made evident the long-term geopolitical and economic entanglements that shaped migratory streams and the specific sociocultural patterns and processes that emerged in relation to these streams at particular moments. Affective sociopolitical fields, like transnational sociocultural fields, circulate. And because they raise questions about the sense of temporality that undergirds the broader geopolitical and epistemological dimensions of their production, I suggest that identifying them not only responds to the forms of racism that produced the ideological terrain of the post-contact New World but also encourages us to renew, revive, reconstruct, and represent our histories in order to rethink our present.

My discussion of the narratives we collected from residents of Tivoli Gardens, and of the forms of evidence given at the West Kingston Commission of Enquiry, suggests that the dominant affective register of neoliberalism is *doubt*; my treatment of Claudius Henry and his International Peacemakers' Association as it flourished and then declined between 1966 and 1986 leads to an exegesis of an affective field of *expectancy*; and my discussion of the ways Rastafari and communism became conjoined during the height of the Cold War, and of U.S. intervention into the trade union movement after the expulsion of the radical wing of the People's National Party in 1952, is shot through with *paranoia*. I show that doubt and paranoia are "kissing cousins," but where doubt references a diffuse sense of uncertainty, paranoia has a clear, if unpredictable, object. Expectancy, however, emerges as a moment of rapprochement between the secular-rational vision and the prophetic vision, one that is produced within a context in which an increasingly leftist PNP, active within the Non-Aligned Movement internationally, controlled the state. This moment was subsequently dismantled when the PNP was removed from power.

If archives of affect are produced in and through particular sociopolitical affective fields, then they also generate particular technologies through which we experience, confront, and interpret these fields.[33] These technologies also sediment over time and in relation to fields that have come before, thereby generating our contemporary landscape of the political. For the context I am describing here, doubt produces technologies of *misrecognition*, the result of obfuscation, denial, and the maintenance of public secrets. Expectancy produces technologies of *prophetic waiting*, a waiting in which the end is never the end because it was foretold from the beginning.[34] Paranoia, finally, produces technologies of *surveillance* and *conspiracy*; friends turn against friends, and what you see is never what you get.[35] Where doubt and paranoia short-circuit the future, focus on the present, and evacuate the past, expectancy generates new worlds for the future. Each of these affective sociopolitical fields is therefore tied not only to the temporal materialities that contextualize it, but also to different versions of social and political change. In other words, the fields are shared across social and political boundaries, but their experience is particular as a result of these boundaries. Moreover, the generational sedimentation of these fields and the time maps they index is key to reflecting not only on what sovereignty has felt like during the moments under consideration, but also on the ways the affective fields, once established, become available for reactivation, as it were, thus transcending their context of origin, something I discuss more in chapter 2.

While the chapters that follow focus on the periods I have outlined here, the interludes between the chapters outline three other moments. These moments are related, but in rhizomic rather than causal ways. They concern twentieth-century entanglements in Jamaica among colonial and nationalist governments, U.S. foreign policy, prominent local capitalists, external observers, a nationalist development-oriented middle class, and the trade in ganja and other drugs. Together—though again, nonlinearly—these moments also give a sense of the conditions that set the stage for the 2010 state of emergency in West Kingston. The assemblage of these moments also creates a story about how entanglements change over time, and one that is therefore about the dissolution of (British) imperialism and the shifting vectors of (American) empire. It tells us about what kinds of political imagination are possible—whether diasporic, Pan-African, or nonaligned—at different temporal junctures. The interludes also give a sense of what it has meant for others to bear witness, and specifically of how outsiders to Jamaican society bore witness to the public secrets that characterized the periods in which they found themselves in Jamaica. As such, they reveal how certain places—Jamaica, in this case—become central to knowledge production about the important questions of their day. In the interludes, Jamaica emerges as critical not only in relation to the transition from British to American hegemony throughout the Western Hemisphere, but also to the development of a perception of insecurity in the United States, one that was generated by circulations of drugs, communism, and black radicalism, but also by spies, money, and diplomats.

REFLECTING ON WHAT HE TERMED THE "DISMAL" STATE OF RECORD-keeping and maintenance in Jamaica, Anthony Harriott once suggested to me that "the attitude to history is indicative of the attitude to accountability."[36] This, ultimately, speaks to the ethical impulses of this project and the questions that frame the coda: How are we complicit in sovereign violence? To whom are we accountable? What are our obligations? And what might real liberation feel like?

Chapter 1

DOUBT

WE ARE WALKING WITH ANNETTE, OR, RATHER, WE ARE WALKING behind Annette. She has agreed to lead us through Tivoli Gardens so that our cinematographer can shoot street scenes. We are making a film that is designed to provide a platform for people to talk about what happened to them the week of 24 May 2010 and to publicly name and memorialize loved ones they lost when the security forces penetrated Tivoli Gardens to capture and extradite Christopher "Dudus" Coke. We have left the community proper and are walking in the informal settlement area that sits on land owned by the National Works Agency, which, despite its name change years ago, community members still call the Public Works Department (PWD). The first time we did a walk-through of the community in early 2013, community members living on the other side of the wall from the PWD dump told us they smelled what they thought were bodies burning during the state of emergency. Now, we are passing what looks like an empty field, with some patchy grass growing. Annette tells us that the soldiers dug up the land during the state of emergency, looking for weapons. "Did they find any?" we asked. She said no. Chineyman, who is also walking with us, added, "Dem didn't found any at the time."

A little further down, the land is owned by the Jamaica Railway Corporation, and we pass what was known as "Rasta City." We see what looks like the first row of blocks, foundations for concrete houses. Behind them are make-shift houses made from panels, doors that clearly had earlier incarnations, corrugated tin, and pallets, sometimes colorfully painted. Pink, yellow, and green. These dwellings have replaced others that were blasted down, bombed during the incursion. Chineyman points and explains, "All a dem house you see here, all a dem house did burn down."

The anthropologist Don Robotham (2003) once dubbed Kingston a "wounded city," the result of the growth of urban colonial ghettos in the late nineteenth century and their transformation into garrison communities during the mid-twentieth. Wounds leave scars, the material traces of violent encounters such as the pockmarked walls, burned-out stairwells, and broken windows that now dot the edificial landscape of Tivoli Gardens. But wounds can also remain invisible, like police action now covered by patchy grass or like colorful pallets serving as fences for new, precarious dwellings. Or like missing persons, the result of death or exile. Or like heartache. In her musings on the relationships between diasporic longing and belonging and queerness, Nadia Ellis (2015: 77) has argued that "Tivoli Gardens represents a diasporic terri-tory of soul. It is located within a nation and yet is extravagantly its own. . . . [It] is constituted, and I mean this more than metaphorically, by memories of the dead." I am interested in what these wounds and memories tell us about the unique constellation of post-Emancipation political developments in Ja-maica. What insights do they give us regarding the more general parameters of governance that map the geospatial contours of Kingston's sociopolitical and economic entanglements? How might we consider them an archive, not merely of the material traces of the performance of sovereignty, but also of the immaterial and affective dimensions of its experience, of what sovereignty feels like?

As we move through this chapter, I outline the relationships between twenty-first-century sovereignty and doubt. I explore how the technologies of visuality (which is not only about sight, but also about knowing) and tes-timony (which is not only about narrative, but also about sound) help us to bear witness to the phenomena that animate these questions and to generate some insights into the themes that emerged within the narratives we recorded with West Kingston community residents: a looping sense of temporality and racial reckoning (does a policeman forcing young men to dance and sing un-der conditions of extreme duress know he is evoking memories of the Middle Passage?); a difficult-to-parse relationship between surveillance and witness-ing (can a U.S. drone corroborate survivors' accounts of violent actions by lo-cal police and military, representatives of the government that requested the drone in the first place?); a complex chain of multiscalar political entanglements (is our appreciation of politics one that always accounts for the various overt and covert dimensions of U.S. interest?); a sense of trauma that is social rather than individual, and in which the loss of language is also a general condition of vision (are narrative silences and occlusions evidence of a desire for opacity or a socialized response to danger?); and, a profound perception of misrecognition (can non-garrison dwellers apprehend Tivoli Gardens residents as human beings in the fullest sense?). I argue in these pages that the affective sphere of doubt undergirds and produces these thematic phenomena at the beginning of the twenty-first century, as it also produces the conditions of their relating.

Doubt is both a pervasive condition of contemporary sovereignty and an experience produced through specific interactions across the spatial, racial, gendered, and classed reckonings of the uptown-downtown sociogeographic divide in Jamaica. Doubt strangles the imagination, both of those who are afforded privileges generated by this divide and of those who are continually, consistently denied them. It creates ambiguity and stifles our ability to enact creative, proactive solutions to contemporary problems. It therefore generates political paralysis, not merely because of the purported absence of alternatives to neoliberal sociopolitical economy, but also because of a contemporary resonance with earlier moments within the Caribbean. Doubt, therefore, also has a temporal dimension. The immediate past and near future are both evacuated, creating a kind of suspended time that is neither linear nor circular, neither palimpsestic nor repeating, but neither necessarily the kind of "cruddy" endurance Elizabeth Povinelli (2011) writes about.[1]

While doubt perpetuates particular taboos, it also has the potential to undermine public secrets as they come to light when surveillance archives are brought into the haze of day. Doubt is thus what sovereignty feels like in Jamaica at the beginning of the twenty-first century. It is this affective state that destabilizes the sovereignty of knowing that provided the basis for the Enlightenment drive toward classification and management, but that also creates perpetual insecurity about what it means to be human within a context still shaped by these originary drives. As a result, doubt demands that we ask questions about complicity, accountability, obligation, and futurity, and these are the questions sovereign violence should ultimately produce.

IF YOU WERE A MALE YOUTH IN TIVOLI GARDENS THE WEEK OF 24 May 2010, you likely experienced something like what Shawn Bowen went through. Shawn, thirty-three years old at the time and living in West Kingston with his child's mother and their one-year-old, was picked up three days into the state of emergency. On that day, his gate was kicked in. He picked up his son and went to the door, where he met a soldier who ordered all who were inside to come out of the house. Shawn, his child's mother, and his son joined the others who lived in the yard outside. They were all told to kneel. Shawn was instructed to put his son on the ground, but because the baby couldn't stand on his own, he refused. The policeman used his gun to hit Shawn on his back, so he gave his son to his child's mother to hold. The soldiers then went into the house and swept the pots off the stove, all the while antagonizing Shawn and the other men.

Along with the others, Shawn was taken to one of the roadblocks closing the entrances to Tivoli Gardens and was ordered to empty the sandbags that had been placed there by Coke's supporters. A truck pulled up, and the men were instructed to climb in the back. They were taken to the Denham Town primary school, where their hands were tied behind their backs, and they were herded into the bathroom. By that time, Shawn told us, he felt they were going to be killed—"executed" was the word he used. No one knew where they were; they were tied together; they were in the dark in a bathroom. "Bwoy," he thought, "mama a go miss a son now." The men were held for about three hours in the bathroom, and when another truck drove up, they were counted off and told to get in the back, twenty-five to thirty at a time. They were taken to another location, where they joined additional men. As they walked into the premises, Shawn noticed soldiers on top of the buildings with masks covering their faces—looking up at them earned him several smacks across his back with a piece of wood—and he saw men lined up "neat in a row" on their knees. After about six or seven hours at that location, another truck came, and they were told to get in. Shawn pled with one of the officers in the truck with them, asking where the truck would be taking them: "Me woulda like fi ask you if a dead we a go dead" (I want to know if we are going to be killed). The officer said no, if they had not yet been killed, they were not going to be. At that point, the truck turned into the parking lot for the National Arena, where, Shawn said, he saw three thousand or four thousand men, including a number of people he knew, as well as young teenage boys. He was kept there for several days "for processing," during which time he was unable to sleep or bathe. "So you can imagine the smell," he said.

"Chineyman," twenty-eight at the time of the incursion, had sent his two small sons, at the time one and three years old, out of the community prior to that Monday. He had also attempted to send away his little brother Dashan, who had just turned twenty-one, but instead of going to his grandmother's house in Portmore, as promised, Dashan stayed in Tivoli Gardens. Chineyman himself also stayed in the community, in part because of his business, but perhaps more importantly because his mother would not leave. Because Chineyman was taken away, held like Shawn and other men in various locations for the duration of the operation, he didn't find out that his little brother had been killed by the security forces until he was released, days later. By Chineyman's account, Dashan was a Christian and a well-respected youth within his high school, one who "never hold a gun from him born . . . a just straight bookwork." What he eventually found out was that his brother had been killed execution-style, on his knees, with his stepfather (who was also killed).[2] Their mother couldn't find Dashan's body for some time, but eventually the police showed her images of the dead on a laptop, and despite the decomposed state of many of the bodies, she eventually identified her son based on a tattoo she knew he had.

If you were a woman with children in Tivoli Gardens during the incursion, you might have had an experience like Claudette Morgan's on that Monday morning of 24 May. That day, Claudette got up and made breakfast, doing her normal chores around the house. She was waiting in the doorway with a friend who had planned to leave the community. Her friend lived close to Dudus's headquarters, but because he didn't want to return there, he stayed at Claudette's when his ride out didn't show, joining the family and friends who had begun to congregate. Claudette remembered hearing shots intermittently, "like a baby [labor] pain where it comes on and then stop." When she saw the helicopter come almost in front of the door to her house, she and her friend quickly slid backward into the house and pushed the settee to block the door. By then, it was after 10:00 AM, and everyone went into the kitchen behind the thicker concrete-block walls. They wanted to watch the news at noon to see what was happening and how it was being reported, but the cable power had been cut. Her husband and their older son crawled upstairs to get an antenna for the television set, but snipers on the roof across the street saw the movement and began firing at the house. They did not emerge from the house until Thursday.

During those long four days, thirteen people occupied their kitchen. Claudette prepared food every day, but no one could eat—"We just barely take like a mouthful and that was it because shots fired nonstop, nonstop. . . . [I]t was like we're in Vietnam." She said she felt weak, "not only me but all the women," but in fact it was she who took the phone calls alerting them about who had been killed. It was she who made sure everyone "bungled up" underneath the table so no one would get shot. It was she who looked through the window and saw the police throw one of her friend's dead sons into the back of a truck and drive away, and it was she who could identify the policemen because she knew the men's voices. But, she said, "Me terrify, man. So terrify. It terrible bad." She was sure they were going to die.

Annette, too, was sure they were going to die. She had returned the Saturday evening before the incursion from a church retreat in the country and saw the military trucks congregating near the harbor. On the Monday as the gunfire intensified, she called all of her siblings to tell them how to handle the situation. "They didn't grow in the community," she said, so she advised them to stay low and out of range. "Unless somebody directly come into the house, dem cyaan dead." Her sister Pet was on the way to church because she didn't feel comfortable staying at her house; Annette argued with Pet and told her to stay put at home. Some moments later, she received a call from a friend telling her that Pet had been shot on the corner of North Street and Chestnut Lane. Annette didn't believe it. She wanted to see for herself. But she couldn't leave her apartment because the police and soldiers were going house to house, searching. She sat in the dark with her twenty-one-year-old son, listening. "Yu a go dead, yu know," Annette told him. When they kick in our door, she said, "just know seh, wi a go dead." Eventually they heard the knock and let the soldiers in. They entered the apartment cursing, asking who was there, and Annette's son stood up with his hands up. The soldiers asked for their phones, put a gun in her son's back, and walked through the house with him in front as a shield. Then they gave Annette back the phones and told her to leave the door open after they left. Another set of soldiers and police arrived a while later and started searching the apartments again, but the soldier who had already been inside Annette's apartment told him the building was clear. Annette's sister's body stayed in the road for three days; by the time Annette went to identify Pet from the photographs the police had taken, Pet's stomach was completely distended; her skin was yellow and stripped off from having been in the hot sun; and she didn't have any hair on her head. One of Annette's sons, a mortician, assured her that "they would fix her up."

CHINEYMAN'S BROTHER, ANNETTE'S SISTER, THEY DIED "INNA" THE incursion, not "during" the incursion, or "because of" the incursion, but "inna" the incursion. If an incursion is, according to Merriam-Webster, a "sudden invasion or attack; an act of entering a place or area that is controlled by an enemy," then to be "inna" it suggests both immediacy (a seemingly unmediated experience) and duration (an ongoing and collective condition). Anyone familiar with garrison politics in Jamaica would know that this wasn't the first time the military and police entered, or attempted to enter, Tivoli Gardens by force. In May 1997, a joint battalion fought community gunmen for three days before retreating; four persons were killed, including a six-year-old boy who had been jumping on a bed, and the security forces were forced to retreat. And in July 2001, security forces attempted again to enter the community to recover guns and drugs. This time the death toll was twenty-seven (including a policeman and soldier). In both cases, no one was found criminally responsible for the deaths, a relative commonplace within a country with one of the highest extrajudicial killing rates in the world.[3]

Transformations of policing in Jamaica have typically occurred in response to instances of black rebellion.[4] The first attempt to establish a permanent all-island police force was made in 1832, the year following the general strikes organized by slaves that occurred during the Christmas holidays in 1831. What began as a peaceful protest was met with reprisals by the colonial government and the military forces. This, in turn, radicalized the slaves, who responded by burning down cane fields and great houses. This became the Baptist War, the largest slave rebellion in Jamaica, and it provided the ultimate impetus for the abolition of slavery throughout the British West Indies, but not before hundreds of enslaved persons were killed.

It was not until the 1865 Morant Bay Rebellion, however, that the Jamaica Constabulary Force (JCF) was established. In October of that year, several hundred land-starved black men and women marched to the courthouse in Morant Bay to protest their excruciating economic conditions. They were met by a poorly organized militia that opened fire on the crowd, killing several of them. When the Governor was made aware of the march, he sent troops to hunt down the protestors; more than four hundred black Jamaicans were directly killed by soldiers; 350 more were arrested and later executed; and hundreds were subjected to corporal punishment. Local elected political representatives used the experience of Morant Bay to vote themselves out of direct political participation, opting instead for Crown Colony rule, a form of governance by which British territories overseas exist directly under authority of the Crown.

It should be (but ultimately isn't) shocking that the fear of black Jamaicans acting politically in their own interests would prompt local elites to willingly give up representative politics in a context in which the rights of English citizens, including the right to make laws, was afforded to Jamaicans who were not enslaved as early as 1662, and where these same local political bodies often articulated nationalist sensibilities. Nevertheless, Crown Colony rule held in Jamaica without significant constitutional change until 1944, the date that saw universal adult suffrage become law. As political parties were developing locally, there was some concern on the part of the colonial government that officers within the police forces were becoming associated with either the People's National Party (PNP) or the Jamaica Labour Party (JLP), and were therefore developing a degree of partisanship that would influence the ways they carried out their policing duties. In fact, Jamaica was singled out within the West Indies as a place where officers should not be sent for instruction because "earlier experiences had shown that they came away with a political consciousness and bias which tends to prejudice an impartial performance of the duties required within a disciplined Police Force."[5]

In the postindependence period, the pattern of institutionalizing security in response to black Jamaicans' expressions of discontent, and the emergent concern regarding partisan policing, continued. The first joint police-military operation was undertaken in response to the Coral Gardens incident, a series of events that took place over Easter weekend in 1963 during which a Rastafarian who was involved in a land dispute near the Rose Hall plantation organized some of his friends to avenge the estate manager's attempt to run him off the property he was cultivating.[6] While searching for their targets, the group burned down a gas station and killed a bystander, then killed two additional police. The Prime Minister capitalized on the paranoia regarding Rastafari at that time and sent police from all over the island to Montego Bay, asking that civilians also join the police to hunt down every Rastafari they could find. Hundreds were rounded up and jailed; some were tortured; and at least eight were killed. This event precipitated the establishment of mandatory minimum sentencing laws for possession of small amounts of marijuana (on the books until only recently) and added to the anti-Rastafarian sentiments held not only by upper- and middle-class Jamaicans, but also by many poor Jamaicans. This link between the police and the military eventually led to the development of a Joint Command system, "for use in emergencies" (Lacey 1977: 113). And everyone watching the West Kingston Commission of Enquiry during April 2015 would have been reminded by former Commissioner of Police Owen Ellington that the JCF, though a civil police force, is organized and trained along military lines, and thus also contains paramilitary elements.[7]

After Jamaica's independence from Britain in 1962, the United States also took on a stronger role in the development and maintenance of the local police and military forces by providing funds through the Military Assistance Program and by training and equipping personnel through the Safety Program of the U.S. Agency for International Development (USAID) (Lacey 1977: 153). In June 1963, Jamaica and the United States signed a defense pact through which the United States would provide equipment—including weaponry and communications technology—to the Coast Guard Unit and

Air Wing of the Jamaica Defence Force (JDF). Between 1964 and 1967, $1.1 million in U.S. funds was dedicated to the Jamaican military (Lacey 1977: 153). In fact, when the Coral Gardens incident took place, it was an American aircraft that flew an injured policeman from Montego Bay to Kingston, and there were four additional American jets supporting this aircraft (Lacey 1977: 154). By the mid-1960s, U.S. aid was shifting to the police force. In July 1966, the Prime Minister received $200,000 from USAID to assist in the modernization of the JCF with respect to training, technology, identification procedures, "and patrol techniques, including aerial and sea patrols" (Lacey 1977: 155), and by late 1967, seven JCF officers had taken a four-month course at the Washington International Police Academy. In 1969, the Public Safety Program was inaugurated, which provided an additional $90,000 to finance the participation of fifteen Jamaican police officers in special training sessions with the police and U.S. Federal Bureau of Investigation.[8] In assessing the impact of this assistance, political scientist Terry Lacey (1977: 155) concludes, "In the context of an overall United States aid programme of $49.1 million between 1953 and 1967, of which $40.6 million was committed after independence ($22.6 million in loans and $18 million in grants), the United States spent after 1962 and up to 1969 about $1.4 million in aid to the Jamaican security forces." This amount constituted almost 8 percent of post-1962 U.S. aid to Jamaica, a figure that likely does not account for the total expenditures of the Central Intelligence Agency and Drug Enforcement Administration (DEA). Of course, the United States was not alone in providing financial and technical support to the Jamaican security forces after independence; the United Kingdom and Canada also continued to supply the JCF and JDF with military cooperation and other forms of exchange.

That there has long been conflict between the police and those residing in garrison communities is well known. Lacey has argued that throughout the 1960s, relations between police and politicians deteriorated, and that this deterioration contributed to a high level of political violence, especially during election periods. At the time, politicians were seen as more allied to the military than to the police force, and thus, Lacey (1977: 122) argues, the police unleashed their dissatisfaction "not against the political masters they despised but against the 'criminal class' which certain politicians had mobilized for political warfare." In other words, the police took out their own political frustrations on the downtown denizens who were being mobilized (and militarized) by political parties, not on the party politicians themselves. In May 1967, Prime Minister Hugh Shearer gave a speech that was interpreted as giving a free hand for police to "get tough" (Lacey 1977: 138), not only with criminals, but also with others who were seen as constituting a threat to the government and the security forces. Following the speech, police shootings (and, in particular, fatal police shootings) increased significantly. Shearer thus successfully mobilized the police force against the combined forces of politically oriented gangs, Rastafari, and the second wave of leftists and advocates for Black Power, thereby solidifying these groups as a threat within the context of intensifying U.S. concern.[9]

Since 1983, as one pillar of Ronald Reagan's War on Drugs and to promote more general bilateral cooperation with respect to drug and illegal arms trafficking, the government of Jamaica also developed an extradition treaty with the U.S. government. This treaty, which went into effect in 1991, was the first within the Caribbean region. It provides for the mutual extradition of any individual committing (or conspiring to commit) an extraditable offense, defined as an offense "punishable under the laws of both Contracting Parties by imprisonment or other form of detention for a period of more than one year or by any greater punishment."[10] As with other post–Cold War multilateral agreements such as the 2011 Caribbean Basin Security Initiative, many in the region see this treaty not as a guarantor of reciprocity and equality between and among nations, but as another domain through which the United States is able to assert influence and ignore the constitutional rights of Jamaicans and therefore engage in economic and political bullying.

Since 1994, the government of Jamaica has successfully facilitated the extradition of twenty-seven persons from Jamaica to stand trial in the United States (Haughton 2014), but the indictment in August 2009 of Christopher "Dudus" Coke—charged with conspiracy to distribute marijuana, cocaine, and firearms as the leader of the "Shower Posse" and the "Presidential Click" gangs—precipitated the political scandals and military battles that eventually forced Prime Minister Bruce Golding to step down.[11] Golding, who was also the member of Parliament for Tivoli Gardens, the community for which Coke was the "don," did not agree to sign the extradition order until May 2010, at which point attempts were made by law enforcement to arrest Coke and by Coke's supporters to thwart these attempts. Thus was the stage set for the battles that began in earnest early in the morning of 24 May, when, under a limited state of emergency, the JCF and JDF jointly penetrated the community of Tivoli Gardens.

This is part of the long history that made it possible for Kingstonians to wake up on 24 May 2010 with a U.S. drone overhead. I was in Barbados at the time and was following the Twitter stream along with other Jamaicans at the Caribbean Studies Association conference. "Does anyone else see a plane overhead?" "What is that white plane?" people were asking. "Is that a U.S. plane over downtown Kingston?"

Jamaica's minister of national security at the time, Dwight Nelson, went on television to deny that there was a U.S. plane providing surveillance imagery, a statement Prime Minister Golding subsequently had to refute. Golding admitted before the nation that there had, in fact, been a drone overhead and that he had requested this through diplomatic channels in the U.S. Embassy. Yet Golding maintained, even during questioning in February 2015 before the Commission that was convened to probe the West Kingston events of May and June 2010, that he had requested assistance from the U.S. government on the afternoon of Tuesday, 25 May, and that he had imagined this assistance would come in the form of satellite imagery, not a drone. However, a confidential email from Isaiah Parnell, then the U.S. attaché stationed within the embassy, shows that actors within the Jamaican government requested assistance from the United States much earlier. At 8:04 AM on Wednesday, 19 May, Parnell wrote to Julissa Reynoso, then the State Department's deputy assistant secretary in the Bureau of Western Hemisphere Affairs, informing her that he had approved "a GOJ [government of Jamaica] request to provide DEA surveillance tracking support over the neighborhood in which we think Coke is hiding out." He continued, "This support will include the use of a Department of Homeland Security aircraft flying unseen over the area with tracking and surveillance equipment."[12] There is no way in which we can construe this occurrence—either the drone or the circumstances under which it was requested, accommodated, and later denied—as exceptional. Yet the conditions that created it are far from transparent, and they have long, entangled histories.

OPERATION GARDEN PARISH, THE JDF'S CODE NAME FOR ITS OPERAtion, took place in two stages. The first, largely under the auspices of the army, entailed overpowering Coke's supporters and creating the conditions to enter the community, and the second (largely under the auspices of the police) entailed a house-to-house search for gunmen and weapons, what former Police Commissioner Owen Ellington described at the Commission of Enquiry as "disarming the community." During the first week of the Commission of Enquiry, those Tivoli Gardens residents who gave evidence publicly were continually questioned by lawyers for the JCF and JDF about how they knew the people they were blaming for terrorizing them were police, how they knew they were soldiers. Of course, they answered, because they were wearing uniforms, fatigues, bulletproof vests, sometimes masks. They were carrying the kind of weaponry that police and soldiers carry. I was one of the many during that first week who felt that this line of questioning was outrageous, but the question remained for me: why did the lawyers keep pursuing it? During the second sitting of the Commission, in February 2015, their purpose became clearer as Deborah Martin, the attorney for the JCF, led Ellington through his evidence.

On 19 February 2014, Martin interrupted Ellington's narrative testimony regarding the resistance "criminal elements" within Tivoli Gardens were mounting in the days that preceded the joint security forces operation to introduce two sets of photos: pre-op and post-op. These photos, she said, were taken by "persons connected to the security forces," and as the slideshow began, Martin asked Ellington to describe what we were seeing. Here are examples of what he said about the photos taken prior to the operation:

— These are "examples of implements used to effect barricades of streets in Tivoli Gardens."
— "Additional barricades, with barbed wire fencing around it."
— "Barricades which prevents access by members of the security forces and prevents citizens who wish to leave the community . . . from leaving."
— These slides show persons "blockading the area, setting up explosive devices to kill or injure security forces personnel, and by extension to kill or injure civilian citizens from the community, and uh, you know, creating positions from which the criminal elements could shoot from the police while taking cover behind these solid objects."
— "This is a street on the outskirt of the community where they have created what we regard as a firing position, using the sandbags as a kind of buffer."
— "This is another observation post, which could then double up as a firing position. If you look, you'll see the guys using night vision goggles."
— "This is a slide of an individual wearing what appears to be a ballistic vest, which citizens in the community could mistake for the police, a citizen in the community seeing this without more could believe it's a police officer because the vest looks exactly like those worn by the police."

Martin then showed a video clip and asked Ellington to "explain to us what we are seeing." He responded:

First the erection of the sandbag position, which . . . then becomes a firing position for the gunmen, the use of telescopic lens, so they can get line of sight on targets at standoff position, and, um, the guy actually testing his sights, lining up his rifle in a good position so that he can shoot with accuracy when he's ready. And the second person there is almost like being able to spot targets for him and indicate to him where to fire.

Ellington then described what a second video would reveal:

> We are about to look at a video with young men loading sandbags on a balcony and creating a gun port inside of it, and I think [these are] the premises where we also have a young lady with a baby in her hand, illustrating the danger that the criminals subjected the community to during the period. . . . [T]hey actually took over the homes of the citizens to erect barricades. . . . Some of these individuals may not have come from the community; they may have been imported gunmen.

Ellington also presented photographs of the days before the incursion started: of the protesters on 20 May, after the extradition order was signed; of the Darling Street police station on fire on 23 May; and of a burned-out police car in Hannah Town, a neighboring West Kingston community. He continued by stating that prior to 23 May, these slides and videos were presented during the cabinet brief, where they informed political representatives of the "deteriorating security situation" and "expressed the urgency of an operational response," making it clear that the police felt they needed support from the army within the context of a limited state of emergency.

Ellington was also asked to describe the attacks on police elsewhere on the island, which he did, and to outline the objectives for moving into "the center of influence" for these other attacks, Tivoli Gardens. He was also asked to respond to many allegations made by community members during their statements in front of the Commission, as well as to describe the police force's activities after they had gained control over the community. Finally, he was asked to show the visual evidence of what their searches revealed—115 guns, tons of ammunition, grenades, Molotov cocktails, and ballistic vests. About the vests, Ellington said:

> These are some ballistic vests which were recovered during the operation, and they include some previously worn by members of the police force which were stolen when the criminals invaded the police station at Darling Street. And we also have at least one ballistic vest worn by members of the Jamaica Defence Force, two? It looks like two. . . . You will have a situation like this where there are vests in storage for off-duty persons, those who were on duty may have fled with theirs . . . , and so when the criminals looted they would have found material like this . . . in Tivoli Gardens and Denham Town.

On 20 February, the slideshow continued, and Ellington continued to explain what was going on in the images, this one of a gas cylinder in a roadblock:

This is a propane gas cylinder which was affixed with explosives, and there was also electric cord, electric wire, connected to it which, upon examination, and there were several of these, we found that they led into buildings and at the end of them were plugs which could be plugged into a wall socket which would then set off this explosive. These were mainly embedded in the barricades and along footpaths which the criminal elements anticipated that the security forces would use in their march into Tivoli Gardens. . . . This is being disarmed by trained individuals.

Ellington continued to describe what was signified by the images: drains that were actually tunnels through which criminals escaped, bombs, soldiers recovering bullets from a bag of flour, and, finally, a video of the shallow grave gunmen ordered a policeman, who was subsequently set afire, to dig for himself. Ellington denied any extrajudicial killings or abuse of civilians' rights; he denied the allegation that the weapons found in Tivoli Gardens actually came from a large JCF stockpile; he denied that members of the JCF wore masks during the operation but said that "nothing prevents someone from tying on a bandana or something if they are seeking to avoid impurities in the air," and he denied allegations of police swabbing civilians' hands, checking for gunpowder. *police abusing authority*.

On 14 April, as the hearings continued, Ellington also testified that, although it wasn't brought to his attention at the time, in the days leading up to 24 May a stash of illegal guns had arrived in Jamaica via the Vernamfield airfield in Clarendon (originally an airstrip built by the U.S. Air Force as part of the Bases for Destroyers Agreement during World War II; it was closed in 1949). In fact, said Ellington, after the attempt by the security forces to enter Tivoli Gardens in 2001 (during which, you remember, twenty-seven community residents were killed), the Shower Posse or Presidential Click gangs—the transnational organizations that Coke ran—had begun to stockpile weapons, making "significant investments in an arsenal of weapons that included 50-calibre rifles, shoulder-mounted weapons, as well as explosives" (Barrett 2015). For Ellington, this represented a significant shift in how criminal organizations were arming themselves because these were group-target weapons, and this made the Presidential Click a "nontraditional, insurgency level" threat, a "challenge to the sovereignty of the state" like none other he had seen during his thirty-four-year career as a policeman. The assistance of the JDF, therefore, was "critical to the resolution of the threat." Finally, Ellington claimed not to have known about the earlier request by the Jamaican government to the U.S. government for assistance in the form of a surveillance drone and said that he had not seen any of the footage from the drone. If he had, he might have seen snipers on rooftops and police shooting at buildings, just as community members recalled during their testimony in December.[13]

Now, even when community members wouldn't say so publicly, there is generally no doubt about what the security forces—and, by extension, the broader community—were facing.[14] During the Commission of Enquiry, Major-General Stewart Saunders, chief of the Defence Staff of the JDF, gave evidence corroborating Ellington's slideshow. He cited intelligence reports that fortified barriers were being built at the entrances to the community and that they were booby-trapped with explosives and defended by gunmen carrying high-power weapons. The reports also revealed that gunmen were regularly on patrol throughout the community, and sentries were placed at strategic locations. Intelligence confirmed that a number of ex-military personnel were in the community, including at least one person who had served in Iraq with the U.S. Armed Forces providing critically important expertise. Lieutenant-Colonel Mahatma Williams added that high-rise residential buildings were used as strategic points of resistance against the security forces, and an extensive early warning system was discovered in a house at 15 Dee Cee Avenue that included a number of large televisions showing closed-circuit surveillance-camera footage of the entire community, especially its approaches.

For Williams and others, the preparations being made by gunmen who supported Coke "resembled urban warfare" (Government of Jamaica 2016: 124). And "urban warfare" of this sort is exactly the kind of military action we should expect in the future, according to David Kilcullen, former chief strategist in the Office of the Coordinator for Counterterrorism at the U.S. State Department and former senior adviser on counterinsurgency to General David Petraeus. Kilcullen has argued that four contemporary processes—population growth, urbanization, littoralization, and connectedness—will have an enormous impact on how threats to national security are organized and addressed moving into the future. He uses the 2010 West Kingston incursion, and garrison politics more generally, to illustrate what he sees as one of the important innovations in warfare moving forward: what he calls "competitive control" (Kilcullen 2013: 96), the phenomenon of non-state armed groups developing loyal constituencies by manipulating and mobilizing populations. Of course, one expects that police and military in Jamaica were already only too aware of the transitions Kilcullen outlines, most particularly the transnational development of protection rackets that create a "symbiotic relationship" (Kilcullen 2013: 100) between governments and non-state armed groups.[15]

In this regard, the effects of Ellington's testimony were twofold. First, his evidence invited doubt. Maybe the people who testified to being terrorized by police and soldiers were really seeing criminals in stolen ballistic vests. Maybe the gunshots they were hearing were fired by Coke's supporters, and not by members of the JCF and JDF. Maybe they were "duped," as Diane Nelson (2009) would say, caught up in powers beyond their control. The second effect of Ellington's testimony is equally pernicious. By the time those watching the Commission of Enquiry reached the end of the images, the videos, and the descriptions of what was happening in West Kingston and across the whole island, they would have forgotten that Tivoli Gardens community members had told harrowing stories about abuse at the hands of the security forces in December. And even if these stories were remembered, their tellers now would have become pawns trapped between two forces—the criminals and the police—rather than agents in their own right, attempting to survive an onslaught. Clearly, the intention of Ellington's testimony (and of that of other members of the security forces who also appeared in front of the Commission to give evidence) was to justify the actions of the police because they were protecting "innocents" from criminals and the Jamaican state from an insurgent force, but the overall effect also froze residents in time, as victims rather than individuals who have learned over the years how to negotiate the complex set of realities facing them and their families. Their own witnessing had thus failed to generate the sense of accountability I am claiming is the goal of Witnessing 2.0.

IF DOUBT IS THE AFFECTIVE REGISTER BEING CULTIVATED BY REPRESENTATIVES of the security forces, residents of Tivoli Gardens experience this doubt within the context of an expected recurrence of war between representatives of the state and supporters of the don. They signal this by their use of the words "norm" and "normally." Take, for example, the following statement by Donald Reid, a man in his sixties who has lived in downtown Kingston his whole life, mostly in Tivoli Gardens: "We have gone through a lot. People have been dying by the security force for years, it's not new. . . . [I]t just come in like a *norm* right now to the people. But this one was worse, you understand?" Everton Morgan, Claudette's husband, agreed: "What took place in May 2010 was far far more greater than what had happened before. We did not have that type of gunfire and aggression from the security force, and it wasn't actually so deep into the community. It was more like on the outskirts of Tivoli Gardens. But this time everything actually took place inside of Tivoli Gardens and that was something we were seeing for the very first time." Claudette corroborated Everton's remarks, noting that in 2001 and 1997, the gunfire was mainly located on the edges of Tivoli Gardens, "because they [the supporters of the don] *normally* would block the road. . . . So this time, they thought that that they would, you know, overcome the cops by blocking the road, building a bigger barrier, but it was way different. . . . So that is why we get it so hard." What accounted for this difference, in their estimation? "Remember this is an extradition case," Chineyman said. "Dis is something between the U.S. and Jamaica. Wha did go on back then, that is more like, me woulda say, politics." Jacqueline Gordon, one of the women who spent those four days under Everton's table, expressed the same sense of causality: "I was one of the persons saying that this one would be different, 'cause my neighbor and I was talking, and I tell her that this one is not going to be like *normal*. Cause the U.S. is involved in this one and they want the man . . . because *normally* we run outside and peep, and we look, and we run in and, understand? But this time we couldn't even move inside the house to go and have a bath." Even the security forces, when giving evidence at the West Kingston Commission of Enquiry, used the term "normal." The Commissioners stated, "It is not unusual for communities affected by gang violence to erect barricades to prevent drive-by shootings or other forms of indiscriminate armed attack" (Government of Jamaica 2016: 121). However, they noted that one of the innovations of 2010 was that these barricades "were higher than *normal* and obstructed visibility into the community" (Government of Jamaica 2016: 124, emphasis added).

Sovereign violence here has a constancy about it; it produces a sense of familiar expectations. But it also shifts in relation to the specific entanglements that might characterize moments in its duration. Where once violence would have been produced mainly through the channels of political partisanship that pitted PNP supporters against those of the JLP, after the 1980s crack boom it took on another set of turfs that, while still politically partisan, were also primarily economic, which means that loyalties could shift and power struggles both multiplied and fragmented.

Violence would also have been experienced differently by those living at the edges of the community (often those in the apartment towers) and those deeper inside (mainly those in two-story row houses). This speaks to a structural variation within garrison communities, communities that are most regularly discussed as if they are homogeneous. This kind of variation, as well as the ties community members talk about linking them to other communities within Kingston, throughout the country, and in the diaspora challenge the flattening that happens within both policy-oriented and popular discourse. This is significant because policy making typically pivots on the ideas that these are monolithic communities defined by a cultural "orientation" that is unassimilable to the normative mainstream. In Jamaica, this orientation has been articulated through the discursive framework of a "culture of violence" that has emerged as the result of historical experiences of slavery, colonialism, and patron-clientalistic partisan politics.[16] This purported cultural difference is seen to be rooted in a lack of social ties to the world beyond the ghetto or the garrison. Garrison dwellers' lack of cultural capital, in other words, is related to a lack of social capital, and this becomes a self-perpetuating system. John Jackson (2001, 2005) has shown us that within similar U.S. contexts, it is decidedly not the case that inner-city African Americans live in a cordoned-off world; instead, they negotiate their own marginalized position vis-à-vis affective and material ties to other classed experiences, networks, and forms of sociability. And in Jamaica, it has long been shown that urban dwellers maintain important ties to rural areas through the circulation of food, children, and capital. A view of garrison residents as homogeneous, therefore, is clearly untenable.

self-perpetuat.

Community residents' narratives of the violence they experienced also suggest a more general sense of continuity between the past and the present, between the slavery and post-Emancipation periods, between colonial and independent governance. We see echoes of this, for example, when Shawn tells us about a policemen taunting him and the other men who were rounded up, saying that since "passa passa"—a popular street dance formerly held every Wednesday on the main road bordering Tivoli Gardens—would not be held that evening, the men would have to enact it for the police, then and there. "So right now we had to fall in with some clapping," Shawn remembered. "'Cause is like a stage show we have to provide for these guys now. The humiliation that we under right now, we had to perform a stage show for them, clapping, singing, falling in, who a DJ haffi DJ and all dem ting there."

Hearing this in the studio, I gasped and looked at Deanne, who was seated on the floor to my right. My mind went immediately to that canonical image of the slave ship during the Middle Passage. Shawn's recollection prompted us to position the men tied to one another and moved from place to place under threat of the gun in an affective and material relationship with the slaves brought on deck during the Middle Passage to play music, dance, and be "exercised," or those on plantations who were ordered to entertain whites. Time moved, but circumstances hadn't entirely changed. We see the same forms of humiliation; we hear the same connotations regarding the value of their personhood. The "normal," therefore, must be understood as an awareness of the ordinary and shifting ways violence has been organized at various scales—within the garrison, between the garrison and the state, between the garrison and the transnational processes within which it is embedded and from which it profits, and between the state and the multilateral institutions to which it is held accountable. It has to do with the priorness of transnational black subordination, with the foundationality of blackness as a technology of ontological abjection undergirding modern notions of humanity and sovereignty, as this is experienced in dynamic ways over time. The "normal" creates embodied memories that are relived in the present, affective archives that continuously circulate the past in the present. The garrison, thus, is not merely a Jamaican phenomenon but an American phenomenon more broadly.[17]

WE ARE IN MY FRIEND MIKIE'S STUDIO ON DEANERY ROAD RECORDing community members' narratives for the film. It is our hope that by filming people outside Tivoli Gardens we might reduce the visual noise that sometimes seems to dampen some audiences' ability to hear. One of the musicians hanging out at the studio calls his nephew to say he needs to come and tell his story. This is how we met Shawn, who was there within an hour. We put him in front of the camera, and he told us the sequence of events I reproduced earlier. Somewhere along his odyssey, Shawn remembers a soldier picking on him in particular because at that time he was using bleaching cream. "I had a little skin tone, being brown," he explained, and the soldier told him he didn't like how he looked, that he should kill him for looking (at him) that way.[18] Shawn's friends beside him told him to "just easy and 'low him, mek him talk, don't look 'pon him."

Where many have interpreted skin bleaching as a sign of racial self-hatred, some critical scholars have also read it as a form of satirical performance and play that has emerged through popular culture (Brown-Glaude 2007). Krista Thompson (2015: 2) has theorized bleaching as a visual technology designed to aid in the process of representation. Interested in how popular visual culture provides a way for people, in her words, to "reflect on, represent, and recast their relationship to the modern, the past, the commodity, the global, the diasporic, and the national," she argues that the technologies of vernacular photography facilitate a "spectacular visibility," one that demands a new form of participation in black public spheres across diasporic locations (Thompson 2015: 10). For her, bleachers lighten their skin in order "to be representable" (Thompson 2015: 22) on film, a technology whose color balance was originally calibrated in relation to whiteness and was not sufficiently sensitive to accurately recognize the subtleties of darker skin tones (Azoulay 2008).

The derision related to bleaching is often most heatedly expressed by black middle-class Jamaicans, yet in Jamaica race and color are not ordinarily rec-

[handwritten margin note: almost killed for bleach]

ognized as important factors in analyses of the structural configuration of the garrison, despite their centrality to cultural and political struggles since the nineteenth century.[19] Instead, racial reckoning has usually been invoked in relation to the common popular ideology that class is the primary structuring principle within Jamaican society. The anthropologist Jack Alexander (1977), for example, long ago reported that middle-class Jamaicans reckoned their genealogies in relation to a common origin story featuring a nonlegal union between a white male master and a black female slave that produced illegitimate "brown" offspring who held a middling status between master and slave, and therefore who also represented a kind of indigeneity, being neither fully British nor fully African. Alexander argued that in the inaugural moment of this story, class, status, and race were directly correlated, but the story achieved mythic status beyond the inaugural moment because it was seen to have operational value for the society as a whole, explaining not only the past but also the present and future. This understanding of race and its relationship to the foundational racial narratives of Jamaican society, passed down from generation to generation and institutionalized through the educational system, housing, employment, politics, religion, and patterns of sociality (Austin 1984), "thus establishes the historical rootedness of the society and its members' place in it" (Alexander 1977: 432). In this way, citizenship became expressed through creole multiraciality, which was the dominant mid-twentieth-century ideology of middle-class nationalists.

While my own earlier research showed that public definitions of cultural citizenship have, since the late 1990s, tended more toward centering blackness over brownness (Thomas 2004), and while Charles Carnegie (1996) has poignantly demonstrated the popular taken-for-granted relation between observable blackness and Jamaican-ness, narratives like Shawn's show how these earlier reckonings of racial origin continue to structure the value placed on racial and cultural practices seen as connected to lower-class black people. This is because, as we must insistently remind, the patterns of racism that structured modern capitalism's development through New World plantation-based slave production continue to provide the parameters for what it means to be human today (Ferreira da Silva 2007; Mignolo 2001; Robinson [1983] 2000; Wynter 2003). Race, as the organizing principle of modern capitalist production and labor regimes, thus always prefigures modern notions of what it means to be a human and, potentially, a citizen; it disciplines us into the hierarchies of value and personhood that attach to particular bodies.[20] Of course, the forms of this disciplining change over time based on the technologies and processes that are available at any given moment.[21] Yet what Christina Sharpe (2016: 15) has called "living in the wake" — of the ship, of death, of grief, of consciousness—requires that we understand that we are "living the historically and geographically dis/continuous but always present and endlessly reinvigorated brutality in, and on, our bodies while even as that terror is visited on our bodies the realities of that terror are erased."

People often doubt whether systemic racism is a factor when the person enacting violence against a black body is also black. What Shawn's narrative should allow us to understand is that "race" is not something certain bodies possess but a historical and structural process of value differentiation, even within majority-black countries with representative political leadership. We should not imagine that this phenomenon is limited to Jamaica. In her analysis of antiblack state violence in Bahia, Christen Smith (2016a: 14) argues, "Not only do police officers and death-squad agents identify black people when they enact violence on the black body, but they also *produce* blackness through these acts," even as they themselves are identified as black. Race, here, is not an "elective identity marker" but a historical, structural, and relational experience (Smith 2016a: 14). This experience, of course, is grounded in local landscapes of power and aspiration, themselves structured by the specific colonial histories that imbue these landscapes with significance.

Shawn's narrative should thus draw our attention to the ways race is felt, made, and made relevant through relational practice (M'Charek 2013). Here I do not mean to evoke only the kind of interpellation insisted on by the phrase "Look, a Negro!" those hailings that undergird what it *feels* like to be a problem, to have the need for "second sight," moments rooted in a black-white binary.[22] Raciality is not merely produced through the visual apprehension of familiar differences but is built interactively, intersubjectively, and dynamically in relation to other humans, landscapes, and objects.[23] This is what imbues it with affect, and it is what generates the performative moments of racial violence.[24] I am belaboring these points here, dwelling in them a little longer than might seem necessary, in order to drive home the argument that the garrison is a racially saturated space of relationality among a range of differently situated actors, including the security forces, even in their absence.

Before Tivoli, there was Back O'Wall, the slum, a place of political radicalism, the grounding of Rastafari, the home of rural migrants to Kingston who brought with them their emergent, syncretized religious practices. Back O'Wall was a space that for nationalists remained woefully and stubbornly ungovernable. For others, it was a scourge of insistently antimodern black illegibility. While it was the PNP government under Chief Minister Norman Manley that initiated plans to transform the slums of West Kingston, the change in government just before independence in 1962 meant that the JLP would implement the waves of slum clearance that would lead to the creation of Tivoli Gardens under the leadership of Minister of Development and Housing Edward Seaga.[25]

For those who cut their teeth on the black nationalisms of the late 1960s Black Power movements, Seaga's bulldozing of Back O' Wall and his construction of Tivoli Gardens would have represented an aborted process of racial consciousness. For these nationalists, Seaga, a Lebanese Jamaican who looks "white," created with Tivoli Gardens a self-hating black population by transferring the reverence for British whiteness to "Syrian" whiteness, thus interrupting a process of black sociopolitical and spiritual liberation that was occurring there and elsewhere in West Kingston at the time within Rastafari camps and through other groups committed to forms of critical black consciousness.[26] Representatives of the security forces, themselves members of an emergent black middle class, might also have seen this continued colonially inspired reverence as an affront to their class position and racial consciousness, and this could have fed into their approach to people in Tivoli Gardens—both garrison hard-liners and bystanders—during the state of emergency.

Before the incursion, Shawn was in the music business, selling CDs during dances and occasionally working as a selector for a sound system. The months following the incursion saw Shawn in a self-imposed exile from Tivoli Gardens. During this period, beyond regular visits from his baby-mother and his son, what kept him afloat materially and emotionally was the Japanese expatriate community in Kingston. They looked after him, he said, thus situating himself within a transnational network of young Japanese men and women who travel to Jamaica to participate in the very popular cultural practices that are often derided locally, those related to dancehall. These youth move alongside downtown denizens, seeking out the blinding video light of the dancehall. This light, turning again to Thompson, constitutes one of many practices of black popular cultural hypervisibility whose excess not only creates an "afterimage" that produces an embodied memory in the face of disappearance or invisibility, but also potentially reconfigures the surveillant or categorizing functions of the visual archive of black people globally (see also Campt 2017).

WE ARE WATCHING A DRAFT OF THE FILM WITH SOME OF THE COMmunity members whose narratives populate it. We want to make sure they feel comfortable with the direction we're moving in and with what they said. It is the first time they are seeing the footage recorded by the U.S. drone that was overhead during the operation. Some mix of anxiety and awe fills the room as they watch, from a perspective that at times is as far as two-and-a-half miles above them, what they experienced cowering under somebody's dining room table, taking turns crawling to the bathroom, unable to eat or sleep. We acquired the footage from the journalist Mattathias Schwartz, who wrote the original exposé of the "Incursion" for the *New Yorker* (2011) and who worked with a Yale Law clinic to petition the U.S. government through the Freedom of Information Act for any materials related to the operation, including drone footage. He posted some of what was released—footage until approximately 3:00 PM on 24 May, which is when community members state the most horrible assaults began—and sent a copy of everything to me.

"Woy, you caught something there," Annette says as she watches soldiers run along the side of a building. They watch as the police, small as ants, run alongside the bulldozers and tanks rolling down the street and clearing roadblocks. They see the snipers (or are they gunmen?) on the rooftops, the soldier bending down, picking up something from the ground—a spent shell? —and pocketing it. They see the flames and smoke from an explosion. For those who gave evidence at the Commission of Enquiry, these are some of the very things they told the lawyers, lawyers who then questioned whether they themselves saw these things, who doubted whether they could say for sure it was snipers—and not gunmen—on the rooftops, whether there were really mortars dropped in "civilian" residential areas of the community.

In his essay "The Sound of Terror: Phenomenology of a Drone Strike" (2013), Nasser Hussain traces the history of the relationship between wars fought through air power and visual technologies. For him, as for many post-structuralists, the aerial cinemascopic perspective—the bird's-eye view—produces something different from our normative on-the-ground viewpoint, something purportedly more comprehensive and panoramic. However, because satellite imagery, like all visual technology, is never transparent, these images are no less partial and must often be interpreted for publics (Herscher 2014; Kaplan 2018; Stein 2017).[27] Moreover, while in some contexts people on the ground might be able to hear, or even sense, the drone overhead—an endless buzzing that reminds them that a strike is always possible, producing a kind of "anticipatory trauma" (Hussain 2013)—in this case no real-time sound accompanies the visual footage itself, save that of the internal movement of the camera, a grating repetitive shriek that after hours and hours of viewing had lulled me into its rhythm, becoming the score behind my movements for days after. While the footage from the U.S. drone corroborated aspects of community members' experiences, thereby disturbing an easy relation between surveillance technology and antiblackness (Browne 2015), it also disallowed any participation in the visual field it rendered and therefore denied the possibility of "returning the gaze" (Hussain 2013).

What does it mean for drone footage to be a tool for bearing witness, to become part of an archive oriented toward producing a kind of affective recognition?[28] What are the effects of this within a context in which the region as a whole, as well as the people who populate it, has been visually archived according to the old civilizational hierarchies of anthropological evolutionism? For planters, travel writers, and tourism promoters, the region has been portrayed as "natural landscape," "untouched" by the human labor early observers erased from view (Sheller 2002; Thompson 2015). It has been both "picturesque" and "playground," "virgin" and "teeming with natives," "seductive" and "sensational," all terms that erase the foundational violence of plantation slavery and colonial (under-)development and instead pathologize, romanticize, and categorize both the landscape and the people. Given the complex dynamics at play with respect to visuality in relation to black folk in diaspora, therefore, one of the important questions we, among so many others, have had to face has to do with how we document violence—literally, metaphorically, and symbolically—without reinscribing the violence of archival practice through the very process of bearing witness (Hartman 1997).

One way to walk this fine line is by focusing on the realm of the everyday. An emphasis on quotidian, non-eventful practice informs many of the scholars interpreting photographic documentation and circulation within both the intimate spheres of family and the public spheres of exceptional violence (Baer 2002; Campt 2012; Hirsch 1997). This emphasis also provides a mechanism through which the exceptional and spectacular can be incorporated within the everyday (Das 2007; Taylor 2003), creating the grounds for what Ariella Azoulay (2008) has called a "civil contract," an *affective* framework, rather than a legal or political one, designed to make visible the various complicities that shape the sociocultural and political-economic quotidian spheres in which exceptionally violent events become possible. For Azoulay (2008: 130), watching—rather than looking at—photographs becomes an exercise in citizenship instead of one of empathy or compassion, an exercise that is imminent in relationships among the photographer, the photographed, and the material technology of the camera and that "begins to sketch the contours of the spectator's responsibility toward what is visible." Tina Campt (2017) has pushed these points further and in relation to vernacular photographic documentation in the African diaspora. Her argument is that we must not only watch images, but also *listen* to them. By doing so, we do not just disturb the equation of vision with knowledge; we also more closely engage the quotidian affective registers through which we might glean alternative readings of past, present, and future among Afro-diasporic populations.

Part of our intention with the experimental documentary project has been just this: to bring into being a different ethical register focusing on the quotidian expectations and experiences of social and political personhood within the garrison of Tivoli Gardens and to create a different kind of visual archive from that which is more generally publicly available (on YouTube, for example). By this, I mean that most visual representations of garrison communities such as Tivoli Gardens foreground the sensationalist dimensions of poverty and political violence, becoming a kind of "ghetto porn."[29] This has had two important effects, the first of which is that the violence that occurs in these communities is seen as episodic and culturally derived rather than the result of structural and institutionalized political decisions taken over time. The second, related effect is that most Kingstonians (and Jamaicans more generally) who do not live in downtown garrisons doubt that people who do are fully human and therefore capable of imagining an alternative future. Indeed, a phrase we commonly hear in the process of telling others in Jamaica about what we are doing, even those who have a long history of political progressivism, has been, "There are no innocents in Tivoli," meaning that Tivoli Gardens denizens are always already saturated by criminality, "involved" in ongoing political and turf wars. For those articulating this sentiment, the actions of the security forces during the May 2010 incursion were ultimately legitimate, if also examples of extrajudicial violence. The other archives produced by the state during and in the wake of the "Incursion"—the de facto census of the youth who eventually ended up at the National Stadium, photographed, fingerprinted, named, and attached to a physical address; the so-called Book of the Dead, the online album of unidentified bodies in various states of decomposition that were perused at the police station by family members hoping to locate lost loved ones—were necessary, both in terms of making a previously unruly landscape legible to the institutions of the state and in relation to the need to identify and bring some kind of closure to the mass of civilians directly affected by the joint police-military action.[30]

As a response to these hegemonic forms of visuality, and in line with our efforts at Witnessing 2.0, we recorded community residents' narratives and shot still portraits against a stark white background. We did this in order to encourage viewers to focus on their words and their faces; to attempt to generate intimacy, acknowledgment, and recognition; to open a space for a more profound, if fleeting, intersubjectivity. Our intention was not, in other words, to generate trauma testimonies; it was, instead, to develop a dynamic and relational affective space in which the trauma of exceptional violence was deeply contextualized at many levels of scale and in which the entanglements among these different levels of scale remained as open and unresolved questions rather than pat narratives.

IN THE RECORDING STUDIO, MANY PEOPLE TALKED ABOUT HOW THE community smelled during the incursion. They said bodies were thrown in mass graves in the May Pen Cemetery; that they were left to fester on the street in the hot sun; that they were burned in the dump. Nadine told us that when she was called to identify her nephew Sheldon—one of the two nephews she had raised who was killed in the incursion—she could barely recognize him. His body was burned so badly the police had to ask her whether he had any "marks." "Him have a cut on him left foot," she said, "him have a chipped teeth, and 'pon him right side, him have a birthmark." This is how she identified her nephew. On the Thursday of the incursion, outsiders came to distribute food and water. As people emerged from their homes, they saw blood everywhere, bodies wrapped in sheets. "The place did smell right up," one woman remembered, squinging up her nose. The rain that fell later in the week helped, she offered, but you could still see the blood, and you couldn't avoid the stench.

WE HAVE WALKED BACK INTO THE COMMUNITY PROPER THROUGH the hole in the outside walls, and we pass a park, the one with the fountain that seems iconic within archival footage of Tivoli Gardens. We ask about the park, and Annette lights up. "Let me give you a likkle bit about the ambience," she says. "Mr. Seaga used to walk here with people with your color skin, every week." Here she is clearly referring to Deanne and me, not to Junior or Varun, and probably not to the (white American) students and cinematographer I have brought from the United States. "Uptown" people within the taken-for-granted social landscape of Kingston. "You see dem a pass through the community with cameras, too," she continued. She painted a picture for us: the fountain flowing, the daylight filtered through tree branches, the sea breeze blowing, people sitting and kissing on the benches. Deanne teased her about the kissing part, and she said she was too young at the time to be on the bench. She used to pass by with her friends on the way to church and "see something a gwaan," knowing it would lead to something more.

We run into Joan McCarthy in front of the park. She had been too shaken up to come into the recording studio with us and talk about her experiences "inna" the incursion in 2013, but she did ultimately give evidence in front of the West Kingston Commission of Enquiry in December 2014.[31] Joan's grandnephew and "son-in-law" were killed in her house, both shot as she waited downstairs on the verandah when the police took them back in the house to continue the search. She watched as the police came back downstairs, dragging a body wrapped in a bloody bedsheet. She begins telling us this, and Annette takes over, remembering that she could hear her grandnephew telling the police, with a Yankee accent, "My people's is in the States, my mom is in the States." Because he was a "foreigner," Annette said, he didn't know to beg for his life. He never should have died, Joan said; he had been due to fly out that April.

ONE OF THE MOST STRIKING PATTERNS WITHIN THE NARRATIVES we have archived is the fact that, with only one exception, community members did not say Christopher Coke's name. They ducked and parried. They referred to him as "that man," "the man they were looking for," "the one they wanted to extradite." Publicly, according to evidence given during the December hearings of the Commission of Enquiry, only a very few saw the roadblocks going up; no one saw anyone shooting at anyone; no one personally knew "Dudus," though they knew of him; and no one had personal knowledge of any of his intimidating or illegal activity, only of the extensive good he did for the community. No one participated in the marches protesting the signing of the extradition order, and no one knew "they" were building bombs and stockpiling weapons.[32] In fact, no one had even seen a gun. The Commissioners remarked on this "code of silence," lamenting the fact that it meant people were still concerned about their safety, even five years after the events. In our interviews, we were given clear parameters (by community members themselves, who are negotiating dual power structures—that of the state and that of the don system) for what could and could not be asked, and what community residents should or should not say (or what we should edit out if they did say something they shouldn't), in order for everybody (including ourselves) to remain safe. By this logic, saying Dudus's name out loud positions one as either loyalist or snitch, and everybody in Jamaica knows that "*informa fi dead*."

We might, as anthropologists, understand this phenomenon in relation to the concepts of "taboo" or "ritual avoidance." The conventional thinking here would be that if the taboo is breached, the status quo is shattered, power is unmasked, normal hierarchies are upturned, and the danger of (embodied) violence ensues for everyone.[33] Yet my feeling is that this phenomenon in Tivoli Gardens is part of a broader set of entanglements that form the basis of Jamaica's "public secret," something Michael Taussig (1999: 5) defined many years ago as *that which is generally known, but cannot be articulated.* In this case, the dominant—and related—elements of the public secret are (1) the amassing of weapons by criminal gangs involved in the transnational trafficking in drugs and arms; and (2) the protection of these gangs by local politicians and, to a degree and in particular moments, by agents of the U.S. government. In our interviews (though more often during off-camera conversations) these elements are spelled out, though not necessarily in obvious ways. People recounted what they saw in terms of preparations "the guys" were making prior to the commencement of the operation: the roadblocks that were being built; the intermittent gunfire meant to keep people in their homes; the looting; the building of bombs and the burning of police stations; the prevention of people from leaving or coming back. They spoke about the salience of U.S. involvement "this time," and wondered about the "tension between Kingston and Washington." They explained that the police and army were at war with criminals, and they acknowledged the importance of having a police presence remain after the state of emergency. Some even said that Dudus himself was responsible for the massacre because he chose not to turn himself in.

For Taussig (1999: 3), what is key to the power of the public secret is that it is never fully unveiled or revealed; rather, it is "presenced" through moments of partial exposure. Though public secrets circulate, they are never absolutely consumed—multilayered and full of gaps, they cannot be fully mapped, categorized, or identified. Thus, as Joseph Masco (2014) has argued for a post-9/11 U.S. context, they produce increasingly narrowly defined, non-collective, and indirect forms of political action. The public secrets that were obliquely revealed in community residents' narratives, or through the Commission of Enquiry, therefore constitute strategic prohibitions that in daily, non-eventful ways identify presences through absences, involvement through avoidance. It is also the case that doubt presences, but it does so without illuminating.

ANNETTE CALLS THE EVENTS OF MAY 2010 A "MASSACRE" RATHER than the more sanitized "incursion." She remembers going to a post-incursion grief counseling session in early June that had been organized by the Citizen and Security Justice Programme run through the Ministry of National Security. There she told people she had been glad about Keith Clarke's death. Keith Clarke was an upper St. Andrew accountant and brother of the former PNP minister Claude Clarke. He was killed in the middle of the night on 27

May by the security forces, shot twenty-one times in front of his wife and daughter, sixteen times in his back. He was thought to be harboring Coke, who had close ties to a prominent businessman who lived nearby. There was intense public uproar over Clarke's murder, happening as it did to a member of a well-known family in a wealthy "uptown" neighborhood. Annette's mention of Clarke was strategic, because, as she said, "if it never happen outside of Tivoli Garden, nobody wouldn't believe." Nobody would believe the security forces could act with such impunity.

This impunity was publicly brought into view when, during the Commission of Enquiry, Commissioners discussed the use of mortars with members of the command structure of the JDF (Police Commissioner Ellington testified that he was not informed of the intention to use mortars). Major-General Stewart Saunders pointed out that on previous occasions in the community, gunmen used women and children as human shields. As a result, he deployed mortars in order to "create a different sound in the operational area" (Government of Jamaica 2016: 156). By this, he meant that the mortars—thirty-seven were fired in what he understood to be three open areas—would keep women and children behind doors and would allow troops greater access to the affected areas. For Saunders, the mortars actually saved lives. "They had the desired effect," he continued. "They created some disorientation and we never suffered many injuries and fatalities" (Government of Jamaica 2016: 156). This statement, of course, is not entirely true, as mortars were fired not only in open fields, but also inside the community itself. The Commissioners condemned their explosion within Tivoli Gardens as "a serious error of judgment," arguing that the use of mortars was "reckless and wholly disproportionate to the threats offered by gunmen" (Government of Jamaica 2016: 332). The Commissioners also condemned what they saw as a general impersonal callousness for human life in the theater of operation. Here examples abound, but I will relate one that appeared in the Commissioners' report. Collette Robinson gave evidence about having been shot in her left bicep and trying to get to the hospital. "On my way to the hospital," she said, "a soldier stopped me and asked me where I was going. I told him to the hospital. He said, 'Go back down. Go dead.' I went back home. I heard that if anyone got injured, call a particular number. This was on the news. I called the number but no one came at all. I stayed in the house" (Government of Jamaica 2016: 160). Robinson eventually tried again, and a different soldier put her in an ambulance to get to the hospital for treatment.

In addition, the Commissioners explicitly questioned both the JCF and the JDF on their treatment and evidence regarding dead bodies—whether or not they were seen, whether or not they were picked up, whether or not they were taken to Kingston Public Hospital, whether their locations were recorded—and on a number of points found their "evidence untrustworthy" (Government of Jamaica 2016: 294), leading them to cite several officers, including the assistant commissioner of police, for dereliction of duty. The Commissioners were incredulous that even within a week after the operation began, "'none of the venues of alleged killings at Ground Zero were being treated as . . . potential crime scenes'" (Government of Jamaica 2016: 404), and that while the JCF expended a total of 1,516 round of ammunition, according to ballistics experts, "only 36 spent casings were recovered and submitted from Tivoli for analysis" (Government of Jamaica 2016: 451). Relatedly, they found the small number of firearms recovered in Tivoli Gardens—115 by the end of June 2010—was a "troubling feature of the evidence of the security forces" given the extensive firepower unleashed by the military and police, leading the Commissioners to doubt their assertions:

> We are asked to accept, on the evidence, that there were approximately 300 gunmen in Tivoli Gardens and Denham Town, yet by 28 May only 28 firearms were recovered. . . . With respect to Tivoli Gardens, the main target of the security forces, the number count of firearms recovered reveals a disconcerting deficit. By 26 May, the JDF recovered only 6 firearms; no firearms were found on any of the 19 persons whose deaths we report in Chapter 9. (Government of Jamaica 2016: 115–16)[34]

Finally, the Commissioners criticized the detentions. They argued:

> On the evidence adduced, considerable doubt is cast upon the claim that the purpose of detention was the protection of citizens. We find, on a balance of probabilities, that the purposes of detention were to make the area of operation safe for the security forces who remained there from the afternoon throughout the night of 24 May and to facilitate the processing of young men who were present in Tivoli Gardens at the time of the operation. The detentions were made AFTER various areas had been pacified or after high intensity violence had subsided or ceased. [Chief of Police] Ellington's assertion that detentions occurred "as we battled criminals on the ground" is at variance with other credible evidence. (Government of Jamaica 2016: 162)

For the Commissioners, the detentions were thus arbitrary and disproportionate to the situation at hand; while approximately four thousand persons were detained, only 148 were not released (Government of Jamaica 2016: 167).

WE ARE PASSING MARJORIE'S HOUSE. THE SUN IS BLAZING IN BE-
tween the fronds of the banana trees in the tiny garden plot to the right of
her house, creating light shards in the camera's image of her front door. These
are the same banana trees that sheltered her two sons as they were shot and
killed by the security forces. Marjorie has told us this story several times, but
it was her cadence and pacing the first time that struck me. Here is what she
told us in February 2013:

> I went to bed, me and my two sons, all of us, my two sons and my twin daugh-
> ter. That was the Monday. The soldiers, the police came in, and we went to
> bed, and a lot of gun firing. And we wake up the Tuesday morning, they wake
> me up, soldiers wake me up, knocked on the door and I wake up, and I opened
> the door and let them in. So they asked, "Who and who living here?" I told
> them, "My daddy which is blind, my two sons and my twin daughter, and my-
> self." They say I must send all the male out, and I said that's my two, it's only
> my sons, my two sons, so they took them out. So I asked them what they go-
> ing to do with them and they say they're, um, them going question them. So I
> watched them take them across the road, put them to kneel down. I was stand-
> ing at the gate. They were trying to get me back inside the house but I keep
> standing at the door 'cause I wanted to see what they were going to do with
> them. So they take them across the road, and they kneel down.

Here her voice broke, but she regained composure quickly:

> And then they were forcing me to come inside. I saw when they take my
> seventeen-year-old son and place him in the sidewalk, and I don't know what,
> I didn't hear what he was saying to one of the policeman, but he use his gun
> and lick him in his jaw. When I see is like the jaw twist one side and he were
> crying so they, I keep calling, I start, they did cry, and them say I must go back
> inside. So when I go back inside I just standing at the gate, they say "Go inside,
> go inside!" And I still didn't want to go, and I went in and they start, they come
> again and say, "Marjorie, go inside! Go inside, lady, go inside!" And I went in-
> side, and I keep on looking through the window, draw the curtain and keep
> looking, but they were telling me not to look, not to look, but I keep look-
> ing. And I see when they were carrying the two of them across the road. The
> twenty-year-old one was on his right side, the right side, and the seventeen-
> year-old on his left side and they were, keep, begging him, you can see they
> were talking talking, and they were crying with eye water coming down at their
> eye and they take them beside my house. I live at 25 and they take them to 23,
> and when I look, I was looking through the window and I could see there was a
> flowers garden there, and they put them to lay down there. The seventeen-year

old was on the right hand side and the big one was at the left hand side. And I keep hearing the seventeen-year old one crying, "Mummy, mummy, mummy, mummy, mummy!" And I couldn't answer 'cause there were, they keep coming, a lot of them was inside the house, the yard, and they had them over there. And I remove from the window one of the time and I hear when the seventeen-year-old say, "Mummy, they kill Pooksie." They kill Pooksie, and I went to my daddy and were crying and they hear the crying inside there. But it not shortly after, they kill the first one and shortly after I didn't hear nothing more of Fernando, that was the seventeen-year-old one. And but I went, I hear the gunshots them go off inside the yard, just beside me. So I went upstairs, I run upstairs, and I carry my daughter, the one that born last, which is Diane, and when I went up there, I climb on my daddy bed head, and I saw them pulling the twenty-year-old one, pulling the twenty-year-old one, and throwing him in the truck. But I didn't see when they removed the seventeen-year-old, but I know he was dead, 'cause I don't hear him calling for "mummy mummy" again.

In three minutes and twenty-one seconds, Marjorie narrated the execution of her two sons.[35] Her tone throughout, save the one moment when her voice caught, recalled the monotonous whir of a propeller, pushing us on through murky water to the silence at the end. Fernando announces the death of his brother and then suffers the same fate, and we know this not because we see the police shoot him, but because we no longer hear him crying out for his mother. The chaos of the scene is embodied in its telling. Marjorie's narrative is full of repetitions and of the hurried filling in of seemingly unnecessary expository details. Some of these are evident in the transcription: "they were telling me not to look, not to look, but I keep looking"; "I said that's my two, it's only my sons, my two sons"; "I carry my daughter, the one that born last, which is Diane." Other repetitions are surrounded by halting un-worded tics. In part, these are the result of her (likely unconscious but effortful) attempt to render her story in a lexicon and structure closer to English than patois, due to the formality of the setting and to her assessment of the class and educational level of her audience, both those of us who were actually present and those she imagined might be listening in the future.

After her sons were killed, Marjorie tells us, the police went back into the house demanding everyone's phones. At this point, Marjorie's father became frightened and told the police they didn't have any phones; they didn't take any pictures. "We didn't even take off their badge numbers," Marjorie remembered. She said the police wore masks on their faces but that one of them took it off, and she saw his face. "I know him very, very good," she said. "I tell Mr. Witter, Mr. Earl Witter, I see him face. And he had two rings on these finger." At the time, Witter was Jamaica's public defender and he, accompanied by a number of other representatives of government and nongovernmental organizations, walked through Tivoli Gardens a few days into the "incursion" at the request of the human rights activists and former Prime Minister Edward Seaga. While there, the team observed what was going on and distributed snacks and water.[36] This would have been when Marjorie told him about the policeman—a policeman she still sees from time to time in the community.[37]

Immediately after the week of 24 May, Marjorie received a number of visitors. "I had a lot of friends pass," she said. "I'm fairly well beknown in the area, and the MP of the area he came and visit me, which is the Prime Minister, that was Mr. Bruce Golding, he came and looked for me, and um, along with other of his colleagues, came there." Repetition again. Apparently, this team visited everyone who lost loved ones, everyone whose houses were bombed down or shot up. She said that when they came to see her, she was so angry—"outraging" was the word she used—she started "going on behaving bad." They asked her why she didn't leave the community when she could, why she didn't get on the bus.

What Marjorie's interlocutors were referring to were the buses that were sent to the main roads bordering the community on the Sunday before the security forces entered Tivoli Gardens. Radio and television stations had issued broadcasts encouraging "law-abiding citizens" to get on the buses and leave the community, but many hesitated to do so.[38] Not one person we interviewed attempted to go on a bus. In part, this was because, they said, they didn't know where the buses were going or what they would need for the journey—doubt, again. Moreover, they didn't want to bear the stigma associated with leaving the community in such circumstances. On other occasions when people left the community, their houses were broken into and ransacked. And on this occasion, they also heard that those who attempted to leave were being shot at.[39] Several people also evoked the Green Bay Massacre in January 1978, when fourteen political activists from another downtown community were promised employment and taken away in a van, only to be ambushed by members of the Military Intelligence Unit (a covert branch of the JDF). Five of the men were shot dead, and the others scattered, but there has never been a thorough inquiry into the matter, and the PNP government, in power at the time, denied responsibility. Marjorie didn't leave because she couldn't abandon her bedridden father or her daughters. They told her she should nevertheless have sent her two sons away.

After we spoke again later that year, Marjorie leaned over to me and said, with the tenor of a confession, "They blame me." I realized she was talking about her daughters, and as she began weeping quietly, I further realized she meant that they blamed her for their brothers' deaths because she didn't send them out of the community before that fateful Monday. "Diane always say, 'Why yu neva leave, why yu neva leave?'" Marjorie cried, and then, resigned, rhetorically responded, "Diane, I just don't know." Diane and Diana were too frightened to stay in the house alone after the state of emergency, and Marjorie couldn't guarantee that her father or her brother would always be available to be with them, so Marjorie moved them to "the country" with a family member. "They keep traumatize and getting fussy," she said. When we asked whether she thought her daughters would ever return to Kingston, she shook her head and said,

> No, they don't want to, they want to come and visit and then leave, because they say when they are there, too much memory is there. They seeing their brother friends and it just remind them, and because a lot of police they always drive up and down. When we are in the country where we are living you see less police, in Tivoli you always see them, even if you go to the market to shop, downtown, uptown, anywhere, everywhere you go you always seeing them, but in the country you hardly see them.

Diane and Diana also came into the recording studio to share their experiences with us. Diane spoke for her sister the entire time we were all together. She apologized (unnecessarily) for her sister's silence, and said they still hear the gunshots in their heads.

Marjorie's tone was urgent but measured, as if through her voice she could stem the tide of the agonizing madness of watching the police attack her two sons and ultimately listening to their last words. Marjorie Hinds's voice, however, could not keep the madness concealed. Hinds, who was injured when one of the mortars exploded (Schwartz 2011), and whose fiancé was killed during the incursion, still suffers pain from the shrapnel lodged in her arm. She has lost not only her mobility and her man (and thus the father of one of her children), but also her livelihood, since the security forces wrecked her dry goods shop:

> All a mi documents, everyting me lose, mi house mash up, mi shop mash up, everything me lose. My money, mi baby father come down fi buy mi house and mi cyar, everyting me lose, I don't see back nuttin at all. And mi shop, dem break mi shop, dem buss up gun shot inna the fridge, dem tear down mi ceiling, and right here now mi pickney dem dey yah, me a suffer dem right now, me nah have nobody fi gi me nuttin. . . . Me a suffer until to the day. Me have the kids dem, me haffi try fi find it for myself, mi sickly, mi haffi all go a doc-

tor . . . fi help me out. . . . So me cyaan work for the rest of my life, so me ask fi help. And although me still cyaan get no help, until today mi pickney fi go back a school and me nuh have no money fi buy a back to school ting. Me was a independent woman, whatever mi take come from mi shop, mi baby father used to send money for me every Monday, mi pickney would go a school, me coulda help people, supply them kids and stuff like that. . . . [Them] bust mi face, foot, my bottom it burn up, whole a my bottom spoil up, me couldn't wear panty for four months, haffi walk without panty because my bottom was burning up. I was a, bwoy, I was a vegetable, yu come and look on me and you a cry because the bomb mash me up real bad. And it bring back to the stage, to this day, and me thank God for Jesus, right now me have the kids dem, me haffi try with dem, normally me woulda dun buy the back to school thing but me just ask God to get a help fi take care a dem. Because me was an independent woman, me have everything for my comfort. I never used to beg nobody, I used to help people, give them money, because I had a shop, and mi baby father used to send me money every Monday morning, from Western Union, and mi kids dem gone collect money and me coulda help people who couldn't help themself. And give them money. And nobody know what can happen to them in life, it always a gift.

Marjorie Hinds's tone was frantic, her despair evident. As it happens, her voice reminded me of an elderly lady I used to care for sometimes when I was a nurse's aide at a geriatric psychiatric facility. This lady had been diagnosed with catatonic schizophrenia and, like so many of the patients there who had had their first psychotic break before advances in psychotropic medicine, she had been lobotomized and spent the rest of her life in institutions. She sat constantly with her mantra—"I'm dying, I'm dying, I'm dying, I'm dying, I'm dying . . ."—sometimes louder, sometimes softer, sometimes almost inaudible, but constant nonetheless. It was this same insistent urgency that came back to me listening to Marjorie Hinds.[40]

Marjorie Williams's measured cadence—both for us and publicly in front of the Commission of Enquiry—and Marjorie Hinds's frenetic and repetitive pleading stand as different expressions of the register of trauma. For linguistic anthropologists, register has been defined as a "*repertoire* that is associated, culture-internally, with particular social practices and with people who engage in such practices" (Agha 2004: 24). The pragmatic effects of register have to do with the ways we understand identity, how we parse the dynamics of social relationships, and, therefore, how we understand the organization of formal practices, such as rituals, as well as how we recognize, reproduce, and contest the hierarchies they index. As historical formations themselves, registers might also therefore be seen as diagnostic of particular geopolitical and socioeconomic configurations, such as those through which the normativities of relation and value are continually reproduced, without necessarily being immediately available for metalinguistic perception. Remember, for example, Shawn Bowen's comment regarding the humiliation of having to entertain the policemen during his long ordeal of detention. Shawn did not himself invoke the slave ship, yet in relating that experience, he evoked its palimpsestual specter, and thus the exceptions that were foundational to liberal modernity. In this way, his narrative encourages us to dispense with the notion that modern temporality is linear and to discard the idea that we shed these relations of expropriation and displacement as time moves progressively forward (Thomas 2016).

If we are to understand Marjorie Williams's and Marjorie Hinds's narrative voices as expressions of a trauma register, we must also then destabilize the idea that trauma is centrally expressed through the loss of language. Trauma scholars have tended to frame the temporal ruptures and recurrences we hear in these narratives primarily in psychoanalytic terms, in which the individual inability to fully speak one's pain reflects a trauma neither processed nor fully buried and therefore always prone to resurfacing in relation to new provocations (see, e.g., Caruth 1995; Felman and Laub 1992). However, if we think through these ruptures and repetitions as social and historical, rather than individual, we are drawn more fully into the orbit of what sovereignty—colonial and nationalist—feels like. If Shawn's narrative register brought into being the durational traumatic violence of Western colonization and the transatlantic slave trade, those of Marjorie and Marjorie reflect the impossibility of black mothering in the wake of the plantation, what Smith (2016b: 31) has called the "sequelae" of black motherhood, "the gendered, reverberating, deadly effects of state terror that infect the affective communities of the dead."[41] This is not to say that there are not individual silences in the narratives we have collected; it is, instead, to argue that silences can become strategic technologies through which we are invited to confront collectively held public secrets, to name and recognize the sociohistorical entanglements that complexly create our relational present. This recognition mandates a "something to be done" (Gordon 2008) that is social rather than a focus primarily on individual expressions of grief that must be overcome through the therapeutic restoration of language.[42]

Frantz Fanon's attention to colonial madness in *The Wretched of the Earth* (1963) is instructive here.[43] He famously asserted that mental pathology under colonial rule was "the direct product of oppression" (Fanon 1963: 251), the result not of innate inferiority but of the brutality of colonial domination and the configuration of the colonized as object. "Because it is a systematic negation of the other person and a furious determination to deny the other person all attributes of humanity," he wrote, "colonialism forces the people it dominates to ask themselves the question constantly: In reality, who am I?" (Fanon 1963: 250). For Fanon, as is well known, the solution to this problem— both the problem of subjectivity and the problem of colonial domination— was armed resistance.[44] Yet reading the all-too-often overlooked case studies included at the end of *Wretched*, we come to understand that, of course, this resolution is not so simple. Think, for example, of Case No. 2 of Series A, the survivor of an ambush in his village during which houses were burned down, women were beaten, and the men who were not successful in running away were corralled and shot at point-blank range. The patient "refused to have anyone behind him," Fanon explains, and when brought to the hospital, he attacked nurses, doctors, and other patients. Aggressive and anxious for the first month or so, this patient eventually calmed down and "asked to be let out in order to learn a trade that would be compatible with his disability" (Fanon 1963: 261). Or remember Case No. 1 of Series B, in which two teenage Algerians murdered their European playmate. The thirteen-year-old boy recounts the incident this way: "We weren't a bit cross with him. Every Thursday we used to go and play with catapults together, on the hill above the village. He was a good friend of ours. He usn't to go to school anymore because he wanted to be a mason like his father. One day we decided to kill him, because the Europeans want to kill all the Arabs" (Fanon 1963: 270–71). Fanon does not give us the denouement of this case, only the conversation he has with the boys during which they continue to assert no immediate "motive" for killing their friend beyond the vague sense of retribution for an earlier massacre in which French militia murdered forty men in Rivet. "'In your opinion, what should we have done?'" one of the boys asks Fanon:

> "I don't know. But you are a child and what is happening concerns grown-up people."
>   "But they kill children too, . . ."
>   "That is no reason for killing your friend."
>   "Well, kill him I did. Now you can do what you like."
>   "Had your friend done anything to harm you?"
>   "Not a thing."
>   "Well?"
>   "Well, there you are." (Fanon 1963: 272)

Needless to say, these wounds do not easily heal, not because the trauma of individual experience isn't resolved, but, again, because the social and political infrastructures that generated the originary trauma of Western liberalism and its exclusions have sedimented. They have become "normal."

Whereas for Fanon, colonial madness could be outrun by collective nationalist struggle, others have seen political potential in madness itself, not merely as a diagnostic but also as a mechanism for care and a strategy for articulating grievance in registers that are not easily defined in juridical terms.[45] I am thinking here of Ann Cvetkovich's (2003) seminal intervention regarding trauma and archives. Her claim was that trauma, because of its simultaneous ephemerality and structural-historical situatedness, "demands an unusual archive" (Cvetkovich 2003: 7), and that this archive produces certain affects that might become foundational to new forms of public culture. With this, she meant to trouble conventional distinctions between political and emotional life, as well as those between political economy and psychoanalysis, instead suggesting that trauma should be thought of as "a dimension of co-constituted affective and social (economic and political) experience" (Cvetkovich 2003: 43). The terrain of this new public culture is far from settled, however, and in fact should not be settled, since to settle it would be to fall into the deterministic traps, or even the hopeful redemptive ones (see Hartman 2008), that tended to characterize early approaches to witnessing. That is, by giving voice to suffering in the presence of a sympathetic witness (the aid worker, the anthropologist, the documentary-film maker), language, and therefore the potential to self-actualize, would be restored.[46]

It is not enough, however, to merely shift our gaze from the individual to the social and historical in relation to the trauma of eventful violence. Truth and Reconciliation Commissions, for example, as well as other kinds of historical memory projects, have made witnessing a kind of collective therapeutic process in which compassion, rather than justice, becomes the dominant public responsibility (Fassin 2008; Fassin and Rechtman 2009; Trouillot 2000). This is Carlota McAllister's (2013: 95) argument, one she develops in the process of seeking other kinds of affective relations between "those who testify and those who hear testimony." Working in postwar Guatemala, McAllister turns away from therapeutic norms of testimony and toward accounts of how her interlocutors initially came to revolutionary consciousness, thus overcoming the political silences often reproduced through normative conventions of testimony and attuning herself to a form of listening that requires "learning not only how to ask new questions but also to refrain from demanding answers" (McAllister 2013: 12).

Leaving narratives open-ended, I would add, also allows space for listeners to explore their own accountability for and complicity within the situation at hand. Remember Azoulay's "contract," developed intersubjectively and in relation to both the technology capturing it and the particularities of historical and geopolitical context. This is a line of reasoning I pick up more fully in the coda. For now, I want to simply argue that bearing witness to a mother's madness can also represent an opportunity for us to imagine a response to grief and trauma that requires neither isolation nor ultimate resolution into grievance, but one that instead allows us to recognize those responses grounded in care and mutuality, the response-ability of Witnessing 2.0 (Williams 2016; Cheng 2001; see also Ralph 2015). Even the Commissioners, when Marjorie Hinds gave evidence publicly at the enquiry, asserted the need to "treat this witness with caution," given her "special circumstances" and as a form of "taking care" with her. They did not allow her to be cross-examined.

ANNETTE IS VIEWING A DRAFT OF THE FILM WITH US, AND SHE watches herself walking. Pointing. Turning. The camera is behind her, tracking her movements beside the empty field, down Bustamante Highway. She is watching herself from behind, and at one point she turns to face the camera. In the street that day, I remember, she turned because she was concerned that some of our crew had splintered off, and she wanted to make sure we all stayed together. In the room watching, though, she started. I asked her what was wrong, and she said she thought she had been watching her sister walking, that it wasn't until she turned that she realized she was watching herself. This is surprising, given everything Annette has said about her sister—that she was significantly more petite than Annette is; that even though she did domestic work, she always looked pulled together and wore "spiky heels" in and out of the community; and that, as Annette once said, "she don' talk like me, she talk standard." But in that moment, watching the film, she saw her sister in her body. She didn't recognize herself.

If what doubt-full sovereignty feels like in Tivoli Gardens is a kind of misrecognition—and here I mean to evoke misrecognition in its most capacious sense, one that incorporates not only the difficulties of making oneself as human, but also the resistance to identifying the geopolitical and psychic infrastructures of modernity itself—then we must ask questions about the kinds of recognition that might be possible, even desirable, within garrison Jamaica. One of the most striking patterns within the narratives we archived was the fact that with few exceptions, when we asked what community residents thought could and should happen to change their situations, beyond the Commission of Enquiry (about which most community members were, not surprisingly, skeptical), they seemed unable to articulate any kind of transformative program, instead leaving it obliquely up to the next generation or making vague mention of education or jobs programs.[47] This was not striking because we were looking to them for the next emancipatory political vision, or because we were seeing in them the potential vanguard of "resistance" that would finally transform the organization of the state. It was striking because it constructed a future evacuated of the *"prophetic redemptive tradition"* I discuss in the next chapter, a tradition that has been so foundational to alternative visions of sovereignty and belonging. We could see the "Tivoli Incursion," then, as marking the end of a particular version of revolutionary political possibility throughout the region.[48]

Political scientist Rupert Lewis (2012: 39) has argued that the state of emergency and eventual extradition of Christopher Coke tells us something about "the subjective dimensions of political life and the changing socioracial constitution of political parties in Jamaica." By "subjective dimensions," Lewis means the complex interpersonal relationships that shape politics, complexities that others might understand as affective dimensions. If it is true that about 60 percent of urban constituencies are fully or partially garrisoned (Harriott 2008), then, Lewis argues, what happened in 2010 was really the first major "assault" on the system of garrison politics, an attempt to reclaim Tivoli Gardens within a national political and juridical system. While through the decades the political and parallel garrison leaderships have used the state system to generate employment and housing within specific downtown communities, "under this structuring of politics, the Jamaican people saw their material, social, personal, and human life freedoms eroded" (Lewis 2012: 43). For Lewis, the real postcolonial crisis rests upon the fact that both political parties in Jamaica have become little more than election machines and don't have a philosophical agenda other than gaining control of the state, which means that the focus has been on expediency rather than on long-term planning and development goals. The political agenda, in this formulation, should therefore be rooted in an attempt to fundamentally reform political parties.

That there has been weak civil and political will toward this end is at the center of Anthony Harriott's assessment of Jamaica's crime problem. For Harriott (2009: 24), one of the Commissioners for the West Kingston Commission of Enquiry and a well-known criminologist retired from the University of the West Indies, organized crime is "at the center of gravity of the Jamaican crime problem"; it corrupts and corrodes and promotes a culture of silence. In a lecture sponsored by the GraceKennedy Foundation, Harriott argued that the first imperative in relation to decreasing crime and violence in Jamaican society would be the active imposition, by the state, of a cessation of violence in high-violence communities. For the state to reclaim a monopoly over the use of force, he proposed, it would have to arrest violence entrepreneurs, not the many "thousands of individuals who are annually caught up in conflict violence, that is, not-for-profit violence" (Harriott 2009: 69). In other words, real change would have to be rooted in the destabilization of networks that perpetuate organized crime first through the seizure of resources, including financial contributions to political parties, and second by mainstreaming impoverished urban communities through the creation of legal and viable opportunity structures. Combined with a program of police reform, correctional services modernization, social crime prevention, and the development of a legitimate opportunity structure and alternative forms of dispute resolution, Harriott argued, the Jamaican state might reassert itself in communities such as Tivoli Gardens in transformative, rather than punitive, ways. Many of these points are echoed by members of the Peace Management Initiative, the civil society organization established in 2001 to work toward gang demobilization, the de-escalation of violence, conflict mediation, and the development of economic pathways for youth alternatives to working with local dons (Hutchinson 2016). As they have argued, people saw "great value in the termination of the state-within-state status of Tivoli Gardens" (Hutchinson 2016: 33), which doesn't, of course, mean that they condoned the means by which this happened.

Dismantling the infrastructural scaffolding of garrison politics was also one of the main recommendations of the Commission of Enquiry, alongside the provision of counseling services; the compensation of victims for property damage, wrongful death, and injuries; the reform of the JDF and JCF; and a public apology by the state in Parliament "to the people of West Kingston and Jamaica as a whole *for the excesses* of the security forces during the operation" (Government of Jamaica 2016: 478).[49] External observers from the Economic Commission for Latin America and the Caribbean (ECLAC) who were brought in to assess the socioeconomic effects of the events of May 2010 emphasized economic mainstreaming. They suggested conducting a benchmarking analysis; developing an economic cluster around food and dry goods, vending, music, and sports; elaborating social welfare programs and establishing a micro-credit facility for households headed by women; reducing stigma and the associated discrimination that results in social exclusion; and using "the creativity of the people to generate cultural heritage products that can be offered as additional tourism products utilizing the creativity of the population in dance, theatre, food and the music history of the communities should be the outcome of the process of revitalization" (ECLAC 2010: 55). In this way, communities affected by garrison violence, and in particular Tivoli Gardens, could be "functionally integrated" into Jamaican society (ECLAC 2010: 54).[50]

While the recommendations from these various organs differ in their details and their priorities, as well as in the directionality of their approaches (with some emphasizing work from the ground up and others suggesting reforms from the top down), all of them ground recognition in concrete policy changes related to the organization and practice of political economy. That this is a crucially important yet extraordinarily difficult program goes without saying. However, what is not addressed explicitly in these recommendations is the broader "condition of our condition," the psychic and affective dimensions of the afterlives of colonial madness and the contemporary experience of sedimented violence.[51] Attention to this sphere is not usually plausible (or even desirable) in governmental and juridical reports, and it requires different archives, such as those we might find in popular cultural production.[52]

Yet this attention is key to the real realignments of sovereignty that must happen. What I mean to argue is that we must also *formally* recognize the following: just as slavery was foundational to the development of modern capitalism in the New World, as well as to liberal notions of governance and private property and their imbrication within geographies of race and gender, the garrison is foundational to institutionalized political modernity in Jamaica. If racial slavery within the context of mercantile and, later, industrial capitalism is what transformed notions of personhood, value, and time reckoning in the Americas, then garrison politics is what has transformed the experience of citizenship in postcolonial Jamaica. The point I am trying to make is that the exceptionality of the garrison is actually constitutive of politics in Jamaica, not just in downtown Kingston—though residents there may feel it the most keenly—but everywhere.

If we were to think about the 2010 state of emergency as a kind of "revolution," therefore, it would be one to end politics as usual (Lewis 2012). This would mean, of course, to upend the foundations upon which and the mechanisms through which liberal democratic nationalism was built and actualized in Jamaica. However, in many ways, the "incursion" was seen by many—including some who live in Tivoli Gardens—as a necessary response to a revolution that had already happened. The scaffolding of patron-clientelism had already been significantly bent not only by the general climate of neoliberalism, but also by Dudus himself, who, more than any don before him, operated independently of politicians, united dons across Jamaica and transnationally (even in some cases across political parties), and created opportunities within *private* enterprise for himself and others. This is decidedly *not* the revolution imagined by mid-twentieth century nationalists or by postindependence leftists.

This revolution, instead, instantiates the contemporary reorganization of sovereignty and brings to light the new affective mechanisms through which governance occurs. If sovereign state formation in the British West Indies was originally built on a developmentalist alliance among peasants, political parties, and unions who channeled (coopted, for some observers) the energy of the regionwide workers' strikes during the late 1930s into a legible anticolonial struggle, and if this alliance was eventually destabilized in places like Jamaica by the adoption of economic development policies that ultimately maintained dependence and by the emergence of garrison politics writ large, where the emphasis was on loyalty not to party or principle but to individual leaders (both politicians and strongmen), what we are now seeing is an attempt to dismantle the garrison system without truly exposing the transnational entanglements and geopolitical machinations that have facilitated the wealth, privileges, and protections that have made this kind of system possible over the many years. This suggests that we must reorient our approach to both sovereignty and repair. I have more to say about repair in the coda, but for now I will just propose that the effects of violence must be measured not merely in terms of numbers (of persons dead, of dwellings razed) but vis-à-vis the structural, qualitative, and affective dimensions of experience in order to challenge the ontological notions of temporality, causality, and mutual responsibility that have become naturalized.[53] "Looming behind each singular loss and even the aggregate of genocide," Nelson (2015: 103) writes in her analysis of the possibility of reparation (or the lack thereof) after genocide, "is an older colonial imbalance, so that there can never be a fully adequate repair. Things cannot, not ever, go back to how they were. . . . But you also cannot, not ever, give up on something that might be called justice."

WE ARE SITTING AT HELLSHIRE BEACH EATING FISH AND FESTIVAL, talking with two of the people from Tivoli Gardens who helped us recruit participants for the film. We are asking them who they see as the film's primary audience. "Uptown people," they say. "Human rights people." They want the film to screen at festivals so that people see it and pressure the Jamaican government to be accountable for what happened. They want it to air on local television so that people can "know." They want to be seen as human beings, not as criminals or potential criminals. We promise to do our best, and we will certainly strive for these goals. But we have additional agendas. What we want to cultivate through the visual project is what Pierre Bourdieu (1994: 2) famously called a more "radical doubt," an "imperative to submit to radical questioning all the presuppositions inscribed in the reality to be thought and in the very thought of the analyst." What could we do, we wondered, to call the taken-for-granteds into question? To encourage a deep historical interrogation of the realities in which we find ourselves? To create a space in which people—especially liberal, middle-class Jamaicans—feel uncomfortable with and personally implicated within the narratives and analyses they encounter in the film?

In her consideration of the case of Argentina during the "Dirty War," Avery Gordon (2008: 133) argues that the middle class was forced out of its complacency by the Madres de Plaza de Mayo, who shamed them into doing something. Middle-class consciousness, for Gordon, "always has something else on its mind: the bills, the errands, the car, the house, the petty tyrannies of administrators, colleagues, relatives—its seemingly absolute advantages and disadvantages. This is a class-consciousness that escapes real public civic life because it is tired or busy or what can you do about it anyway?" What would it mean for middle-class people to imagine a reality in which the basis for our humanity is recognition by and through the garrison dweller? What other forms of political possibility might this bring into being?

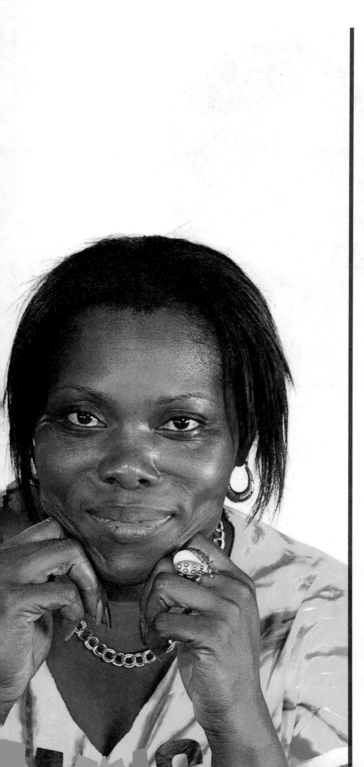

ANDREA SMIKLE

Born at Victoria Jubilee Hospital, 20 September 1966

Andrea's whole family lived in Tivoli Gardens. At the time of the incursion, she had a stall in the market where she sold snacks, rum, and beer. She is the mother of two sons and two daughters. Her elder daughter was seven months pregnant during the incursion, and her two sons were taken out of the house by the police on Tuesday morning. They didn't return until Friday, and she almost didn't recognize them.

Photograph by Varun Baker, 24 × 36 in., on display in Bearing Witness: Four Days in West Kingston, *Penn Museum of Archaeology and Anthropology, November 2017–December 2019.*

ANNETTE IRVING
Born at home in Tivoli Gardens in 1972

Annette attended Tivoli Gardens High School. At school, she enjoyed medicine, physics, and biology, and she had wanted to become a doctor. She is active in her church and has worked with national and multilateral organizations like Jamaicans for Justice and UNIFEM (United Nations Development Fund for Women) on projects to benefit the community. Her younger sister was killed during the incursion as she attempted to seek refuge at her church.

Photograph by Varun Baker, 24 × 36 in., on display in Bearing Witness: Four Days in West Kingston, *Penn Museum of Archaeology and Anthropology, November 2017–December 2019.*

CHRISTOPHER JONES
Born in Williamsfield, St. Catherine, 17 December 1972

Christopher went to live with his father in the Java area of Tivoli Gardens at age fifteen. A follower of Rastafari, he eventually became involved in a downtown arts movement called Roktowa, which he described as "artists without borders."

Photograph by Varun Baker, 24 × 36 in., on display in Bearing Witness: Four Days in West Kingston, *Penn Museum of Archaeology and Anthropology, November 2017–December 2019.*

CLAUDETTE AND RASHID MORGAN

Both born at Kingston Jubilee Hospital; Rashid born on 11 March 1997

During Claudette's early years, she lived in Trench Town, Kingston,
before migrating to Canada with her father and stepmother. At age
thirteen, she returned to Jamaica and went to live with her grandmother
in Tivoli Gardens. Along with her husband Everton, she hosted thirteen
people in her house during the incursion, among them four of her
children. Her son, Rashid, said that during the incursion everyone was
feeling fear and pain. When the policemen came into their house, he
thought it was his time to die.

Photograph by Varun Baker, 24 × 36 in., on display in Bearing Witness: Four Days
in West Kingston, *Penn Museum of Archaeology and Anthropology, November
2017–December 2019.*

CLAUDETTE MINTO AND SUDEKA ALDRED
Claudette was born at Victoria Jubilee Hospital, 26 May 1966

An orphan, Claudette arrived in Tivoli Gardens at the age of thirteen to live with her uncle's wife. She lives with the neighbor she grew up with, her daughters, and one cousin. Everyone else in her family left the community after the incursion. Like many others, she spent the four days of the incursion under a table in her house with several other people.

Photograph by Varun Baker, 24 × 36 in., on display in Bearing Witness: Four Days in West Kingston, *Penn Museum of Archaeology and Anthropology, November 2017–December 2019.*

DENISE DYER

Born at Jubilee Hospital, 17 December 1965

Denise grew up in Trench Town, Kingston, and then moved to Rema (another "garrison" community) to live with her grand-aunt. She has since moved back to Trench Town with her six children. On the day the incursion started, she was following what was happening on the radio and television, worried about her sister, Claudette Morgan. She felt that the money that was spent on the Commission of Enquiry that investigated the incursion would have been better spent if it had been distributed to the victims' families.

Photograph by Varun Baker, 24 × 36 in., on display in Bearing Witness: Four Days in West Kingston, *Penn Museum of Archaeology and Anthropology, November 2017–December 2019.*

DONALD "SEXY" REID
Born in West Kingston,
2 June 1958

Donald moved between
different communities
in West Kingston while
growing up. He was a
vendor in Oxford Mall. He
was taken along with many
of the young men rounded
up during the incursion, but
he said he didn't get beaten
as badly because he was "age-
able" (not a young man).
He says that in Jamaica,
everything is about politics.
"There's no truth, no rights."

Photograph by Varun Baker,
24 × 36 in., on display in Bearing
Witness: Four Days in West
Kingston, *Penn Museum of*
Archaeology and Anthropology,
November 2017–December 2019.

ERROL "SKIPPER" BLANCHETT
Born 4 December 1947

Skipper grew up in West Kingston, which was the central gathering place for Rastafari at the time. His family was offered a house in Tivoli Gardens when it was constructed, but they declined. "I wanted to live a free life," he explained. Skipper said he thought the majority of people who died in 2010 were innocent, because the people who were involved with "tribal war" left the community before the security forces came in. He lost a nephew during the incursion.

Photograph by Varun Baker, 24 × 36 in., on display in Bearing Witness: Four Days in West Kingston, *Penn Museum of Archaeology and Anthropology, November 2017–December 2019.*

EVERTON BARNETT
Born in St. Elizabeth in 1970

At the time of the incursion, Everton had lived in Tivoli Gardens for almost twenty years, working various jobs and driving a taxi. During the incursion, he watched from across the street as soldiers shot from the rooftop in the direction of his child's mother, who had their three-year-old daughter in her arms. Now, every time his daughter hears a loud noise, she wets herself.

Photograph by Varun Baker, 24 × 36 in., on display in Bearing Witness: Four Days in West Kingston, *Penn Museum of Archaeology and Anthropology, November 2017–December 2019.*

EVERTON MORGAN
*Born in Clarendon, 18
October 1970*

Everton moved to Kingston
at age nineteen, where he
met his wife, Claudette.
He is an avid cricket lover
and often referees matches.
At one point during the
incursion, he tried to crawl
upstairs to get a television
antenna, so they could
learn from the news what
was going on outside, but
soldiers saw movement
and began firing into the
house. When interviewed,
he said that the government
should have gone about the
extradition in a way that
didn't jeopardize so many
civilians.

*Photograph by Varun Baker,
24 × 36 in., on display in* Bearing
Witness: Four Days in West
Kingston, *Penn Museum of
Archaeology and Anthropology,
November 2017–December 2019.*

JACQUELINE GORDON AND RODRICKA BAILEY
Jacqueline was born at Jubilee Hospital, 18 October 1967; Rodricka was born on 8 June 1999

Jacqueline lived in Denham Town until she was six and then moved to Tivoli Gardens with her sister after their mother died. She mentioned that toward the end of the four days, the community smelled really terrible. They thought they smelled smoke coming from the cemetery. They assumed the security forces were burning bodies. Rodricka was attending high school at the time of the interview. She feels people don't like to talk about the incursion much and that it's better "to just keep happy and try to forget it."

Photograph by Varun Baker, 24 × 36 in., on display in Bearing Witness: Four Days in West Kingston, *Penn Museum of Archaeology and Anthropology, November 2017–December 2019.*

MARJORIE HINDS
Born at Victoria Jubilee
Hospital, 18 March 1973

Marjorie lived in Tivoli her
whole life, and in the Java
section of the community
for seventeen years with
her child's father Mickey
Freeman, who had been
working in construction
at the new U.S. Embassy
but was killed during the
incursion. She herself was
injured from the shrapnel
from a mortar that the
security forces dropped in
the community and spent
several weeks in the hospital
with terrible burns.

Photograph by Varun Baker,
24 × 36 in., on display in Bearing
Witness: Four Days in West
Kingston, *Penn Museum of*
Archaeology and Anthropology,
November 2017–December 2019.

MARJORIE WILLIAMS AND DAUGHTERS DIANE
AND DIANA BARNES
*Marjorie was born in Kingston, 14 November 1961; her twins were born
at Jubilee Hospital in 1997*

Marjorie moved to the area that is now Tivoli Gardens at age three.
She attended St. Alban's Primary School and then graduated from
Tivoli Gardens High School. When her kids were younger, she worked
seasonally in Cayman doing housekeeping work in hotels. Her two sons
were killed, execution-style, outside her house on the second day of the
incursion. Since that time, the twins have been living in central Jamaica,
as they didn't feel they could stay in Tivoli Gardens.

Photograph by Varun Baker, 24 × 36 in., on display in Bearing Witness: Four Days
in West Kingston, *Penn Museum of Archaeology and Anthropology, November
2017–December 2019.*

MAXINE LOVE
AND DAUGHTER
AALIYAH LEVY

*Maxine was born at Victoria
Jubilee Hospital, 30 October
1973; Aaliyah was born in
downtown Kingston, 2 June
1989*

Maxine grew up in Tivoli
Gardens and went to Tivoli
Gardens High School. She
received her certificate
in cosmetology from a
community college. Aaliyah
is asthmatic, and became ill
during the incursion while
they were huddled with
their neighbors. After the
incursion, they stayed with
Maxine's sister for three
weeks before going back to
Tivoli Gardens. Maxine's
children did not want to
go back.

*Photograph by Varun Baker,
24 × 36 in., on display in* Bearing
Witness: Four Days in West
Kingston, *Penn Museum of
Archaeology and Anthropology,
November 2017–December 2019.*

NADINE SUTHERLAND
*Born at Jubilee Hospital,
20 June 1968*

Nadine lived on Maxfield
Avenue with her mother
until she was thirteen
years old, when she moved
to Tivoli Gardens with
her grandmother. At the
time of the incursion, she
was working at a fishing
manufacturer in Kingston,
but when interviewed she
had just been laid off from
a job at Kingston Public
Hospital. She had lost a
son during a previous state
action in Tivoli Gardens,
and during the incursion her
two nephews were killed.
One of her nephews was
almost unrecognizable, his
body was burned so badly.

*Photograph by Varun Baker,
24 × 36 in., on display in* Bearing
Witness: Four Days in West
Kingston, *Penn Museum of
Archaeology and Anthropology,
November 2017–December 2019.*

ORANDO "CHINEYMAN"
PAGE AND SONS
*Born at the Kingston Public
Hospital, 6 September 1981*

Orando has spent his entire
life in Tivoli Gardens. He
loves music and works
sometimes for the Live Up
record label. He also runs
a shop with his mother
and screens movies in the
community for the children.
His little brother, Dashan
Page, was killed during the
incursion, execution-style,
in the arms of his stepfather,
who was also killed.

*Photograph by Varun Baker,
24 × 36 in., on display in* Bearing
Witness: Four Days in West
Kingston, *Penn Museum of
Archaeology and Anthropology,
November 2017–December 2019.*

PATRICIA ROBINSON
Born in Kingston,
12 November 1967

Patricia grew up in Tivoli
Gardens. She lives with
three of her four children
and an uncle. During the
incursion, she heard mortars
exploding and the house
shook. She was afraid for
her three boys, but because
her uncle was also in the
house, her sons "didn't really
get that kind of harassment"
when the police came in.
Her aunt was shot in her
arm and her niece in the
foot from stray bullets that
came into their house, but
she didn't lose anyone who
was close family.

Photograph by Varun Baker,
24 × 36 in., on display in Bearing
Witness: Four Days in West
Kingston, *Penn Museum of*
Archaeology and Anthropology,
November 2017–December 2019.

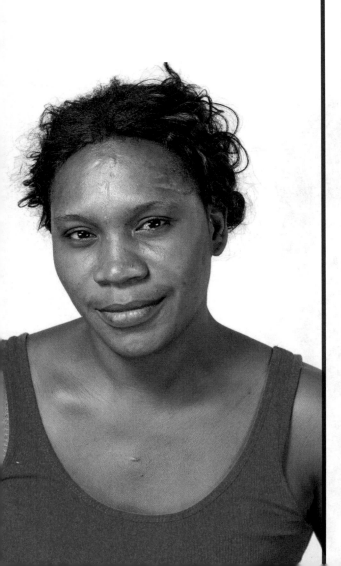

SHARON WARREN

*Born at Victoria Jubilee
Hospital, 5 May 1982*

Sharon grew up in Tivoli
Gardens. In school, she
liked math and running.
When the incursion started,
she had a three-month-old
infant. She watched as
police and soldiers came
into the community. The
next day, her best friend
called for her help because
her child's father had been
shot and she needed to get
him to a hospital. Sharon
helped her find a pushcart
and they tried to push him
out of the community to
get to Kingston Public
Hospital.

*Photograph by Varun Baker,
24 × 36 in., on display in* Bearing
Witness: Four Days in West
Kingston, *Penn Museum of
Archaeology and Anthropology,
November 2017–December 2019.*

SHAWN BOWEN
Born 8 December 1979

Shawn has lived in Tivoli Gardens his whole life. He had a CD stand and a CD shop at the time of the incursion, businesses that kept his son and girlfriend afloat. After his odyssey during the incursion, he stayed in "in exile" from Tivoli Gardens for several months, during which time it was a community of Japanese expatriates—dancehall aficionados who knew him from his work in the music business—who kept his spirits up.

Photograph by Varun Baker, 24 × 36 in., on display in Bearing Witness: Four Days in West Kingston, *Penn Museum of Archaeology and Anthropology, November 2017–December 2019.*

SUNIL MORGAN
Born at Kiwanis Medical Center, 10 February 1992

Sunil grew up in Tivoli Gardens. He was eighteen years old at the time of the incursion, but when interviewed he was working at a clothing store in Kingston. During the incursion, as he heard the security forces coming closer and closer to his house, he wondered whether they would come in and kill him and his whole family. He tried to keep calm, and because he was with his father, he felt safer. He said he had to keep a "strong heart."

Photograph by Varun Baker, 24 × 36 in., on display in Bearing Witness: Four Days in West Kingston, *Penn Museum of Archaeology and Anthropology, November 2017–December 2019.*

Interrogating Imperialism

CERTAIN HISTORICAL PERIODS HAVE BEEN MARKED BY A PROLIFER-
ation of visitors to Jamaica and the rest of the Caribbean. As the testing
ground for British colonial policy in the region, and as the location of efforts
to enact new forms of freedom, Jamaica loomed large in the Atlantic imagination (Holt 1992). The moment immediately after Emancipation (1838),
for example, saw missionaries and government functionaries alike traveling
to the Caribbean from Great Britain and the United States to see the results
of the "Great Experiment" (see, e.g., Bigelow 1851; Philippo 1843). Toward
the end of the nineteenth century and the beginning of the twentieth, English visitors again arrived, interested in the prospects (or lack thereof) for
free trade and economic modernization. This is not only how we get James
Anthony Froude's racist screed *The English in the West Indies; or, The Bow of
Ulysses* (1897) and *Froudacity* (1889), John Jacob Thomas's response to it, but
also how we meet other observers who were interested in emergent avenues
for the "upliftment" of black populations in the aftermath of slavery, such
as Elizabeth Pullen Berry, then a fellow of the Anthropological Institute of
Great Britain and Ireland.[1] What is particularly important for our story here
is that as Americans came to be convinced of their Manifest Destiny after the
Spanish-Cuban-American War, not only westward but also across the seas,

they began traveling to the West Indies and publishing travelogues that outlined their assessments of the new empire growing up quickly around them.

Jamaican political scientist James Carnegie, writing about political developments during the early twentieth century, noted that Jamaicans came to resent what he called the "knocking" of their country by observers. He argued that "those most often 'guilty' of this habit were American writers in sophisticated and intellectual magazines" (Carnegie 1973: 152). For Carnegie, the "chief 'knocker'" in the first decades of the twentieth century was Harry Franck. Franck's *Roaming through the West Indies* (1920) is an account of a more than six months' journey throughout the Caribbean, in which he included Cuba and Puerto Rico as "our" West Indies, as well as the southern United States, which were just as exotic to him as the Caribbean. Franck was someone who had traveled extensively throughout Latin America, and he often compared what he was seeing in the Caribbean with similar phenomena occurring in countries such as Bolivia, Brazil, Colombia, and Venezuela. In his twenty-page chapter about Jamaica, Franck called Kingston "the most disappointing town in the West Indies"; it is "a negro slum," he writes, "spreading for miles over a dusty plain" (Franck 1920: 404). For Franck, Kingston was the height of insolence, petty crime, disease, degeneracy, delinquency, and loose manners; even the white officials were "slow, antiquated, [and] precedence-ridden," in striking contrast, he argued, "to the young and bustling, if sometimes poorly informed rulers of our own dependencies" (Franck 1920: 407). Despite the obvious racism of his assessments, Franck did manage to excoriate the British for land scarcity among laborers, as well as an underdeveloped public education system. For him, the future of the West Indies lay with America. This was a view that was also expressed by some of the Jamaicans he met on his journey, both white and black, and it became cause for consternation after World War II, when there was talk of forgiving Britain's war debt to the United States by annexing its colonies.

Not surprisingly, Franck's writings spurred both a defensive Jamaican pride and an increased anti-American sentiment that was unmitigated by more balanced assessments of Jamaica, such as the one written by Raymond Buell in 1931 for *Opportunity* magazine and later reprinted in the *Daily Gleaner*, Jamaica's newspaper of record.[2] Buell's somewhat Romanticist take on the Caribbean—in his words, the "American Mediterranean" (Buell 1931: 136)—betrayed a commitment to the narrative of racial harmony espoused by many writers at the time who compared American systems of racial apartheid unfavorably with what they saw as more fluid arrangements in the West Indies.[3] For Buell (1931: 137), Jamaicans seemed "unusually contented" and "remarkably loyal to the Crown," and thus uninterested, Marcus Garvey notwithstanding, in any form of self-determination. U.S. agribusiness was the culprit for Buell, and Jamaica, for him, stood in a much better position than Puerto Rico or Cuba "simply because the economy of the island is based not upon the single crop of sugar produced by foreign plantations, but upon diversified agriculture—bananas, sugar, coffee, pimento—much of which is in the hands of the peasant farmer" (Buell 1931: 138). Jamaican peasants, in Buell's view, were beneficiaries not only of the land-reform programs that had been undertaken, but also of the general lushness of the island, which for him meant that "nobody goes without food" (Buell 1931: 139).

Buell's argument here is reminiscent of Lord Sydney Olivier's. Olivier, a Fabian socialist and advocate of communal landownership, was the Governor of Jamaica on three occasions in the first decade of the twentieth century. Olivier entered the West India Department of the Colonial Office in April 1882, so he had a more than fifty-year relationship with Jamaica by the time he published *Jamaica: The Blessed Island* (1936), as well as a long liberal history as an advocate of land reform and retreat from empire. His own entrance into Jamaica followed an extended period of debate within British intellectual and political circles regarding the role of colonial government in an era of emergent free trade. This debate made bedfellows of Christian conservatives and apologists for slavery such as Thomas Carlyle, who asserted that black people's purported cultural and religious inferiority justified the continuation of strong colonial rule, and liberal observers such as Anthony Trollope, whose belief in empire was grounded in the sense that formerly enslaved people lacked both nationalism and race pride (see Carlyle 1849; Trollope 1859). Both of these positions were supported by the evolutionary science of the time, including Darwinism and the notions of racial fitness that would grow from it. The Morant Bay Rebellion and Governor Edward John Eyre's recall to England, however, changed the terms of this debate, and a new school of thought emerged, led by people such as John Stuart Mill and W. P. Livingstone, that was directed toward social reform and state intervention (Rich 1988). It was this liberal line that inspired Olivier as he began his career in the Colonial Office.

In his own analysis of the possibilities for a post-plantation future, Olivier was convinced that advancement in the West Indies lay in the support of peasant production, and he indicted the colonial government for not attending to the development needs of freedpeople.[4] Indeed, he saw British "mismanagement" during the immediate post-Emancipation period as the primary cause of the 1865 Morant Bay Rebellion and the subsequent establishment of Crown Colony rule. Throughout *The Blessed Island*, Olivier argued for the breakup of large estates that were not being actively cultivated and for the establishment of a Land Department that could redistribute these properties; he described small settler agricultural production and advocated for more attention to public work, public health, transportation, and development; he spoke glowingly about advancements in secondary school education; and he discussed "Conjugal Habits" in relatively sensitive and empathetic terms. He also put forward his opposition to the United Fruit Company's exploitation of peasant-based banana production, as well as his support for the loosening of Crown Colony rule and the establishment of a local Executive Council. And although Olivier did not explicitly name Franck, *The Blessed Island* also stood as a rebuke to that sort of sensationalist assessment of the West Indies in general, and of Jamaica in particular. In this regard, it is worth quoting a passage from the book at length:

> Taken at her best, Jamaica is a smallish Island community of proprietors of extensive estates engaged in agriculture and stock-breeding, and many thousand small working landowners, tenants and labourers similarly employed, together with the shopkeepers, dealers, transport workers, tradesmen, artisans and unskilled wage-workers that do their daily business, and with as many clergymen, lawyers, doctors, professional men and schoolmasters as can find occupation in ministering to their less elementary needs. It is easy to think of the kind of people such citizens in such small communities anywhere tend to be. Most outsiders who will look at a book about a West Indian Island would probably be more attracted by a sensational description of Hayti, where negroes are understood, in common repute, to have developed their own racial character and congenial civilization, and, in the outcome, to find the crowning ecstasy of their souls in sacrificing babies to devils. That is exciting. That is the stuff for a popular book of travel. How often have not Jamaicans encountered the scribbling visitor, eager for copy, who questioned them under his breath about Obeah and Voodoo, romantically clinging to the illusion that some thrill may still be attainable by the explorer of the sordid blackmailing quackery that masquerades in dark corners in the rags of African magic, or anxious to catch the atmosphere of romantic Creole passion, as if that of Clapham were not now ardent enough for the most daring of novelists. (Olivier 1936: 6)

For Lord Olivier (1936: 10), Jamaica was to be viewed as peaceful and prosperous relative to other imperial territories and as "the leading case and the most convincing example of how the problems of mixed racial communities can be most happily solved." His was not a laissez-faire liberalism, which, as the result of the turn-of-the-century events in South Africa, he understood as "leading to racial segregation and the polarization of white and black economic classes" (Rich 1988: 222). Jamaica in particular, and the West Indies generally, was possessed of a racial "balance" that justified "benevolent colonial administration as opposed to a market-oriented one" (Rich 1988: 222). In Olivier's eagerness for others also to recognize the importance of this distinction, he invited William Macmillan, a Scottish-born South African historian, to visit Jamaica and the West Indies more broadly. Olivier knew Macmillan was working on a book about development possibilities on the African continent and suggested that the West Indies would provide a model for the newer African colonies to emulate.

Macmillan, whose family moved from Scotland to South Africa when he was six years old, had a family history of colonial service. He was educated in Stellenbosch until 1903, when he received one of the first Rhodes Scholarships to Oxford, where he read history at Merton College (Macmillan 1985). After some years studying for the ministry of the Free Church of Scotland in Europe, he returned to South Africa, where he was appointed to a lectureship in history and economics at Rhodes College in Grahamstown. In 1917, he took up a professorship at what would become the University of the Witwatersrand, where he built the History Department. The founder of liberal historiography, Macmillan was opposed to the notion that two "civilizations" existed in South Africa and was the first to argue that South African "Natives"—and, by extension, race relations more generally—should not be studied in isolation from the broader political and socioeconomic context. It is important to remember that Macmillan was arguing these points within an intellectual climate that increasingly looked to the disciplines of psychology and anthropology to provide explanations for black inferiority in the lead-up to the formal establishment of apartheid. By the early 1930s, Macmillan had been pushed out of Wits due to his anti-segregation stance and his belief that history should be directed toward political action (Murray 2013).[5] At that point, his research interests were drawn to the wider problem of colonial development in Africa as a whole, and he decided he "would be in a more helpful field in the Colonial Empire than struggling to make any impression at all on those in control in South Africa" (Macmillan and Macmillan 2008: 122). After a research tour in East Africa in 1930, he began working on the book *Africa Emergent*, a draft of which was completed in the fall of 1934 (Macmillan 1980).

By this time, Macmillan had received the invitation from Olivier, and he decided to add a comparative dimension to his African explorations. Jesse Jones, Director of the Phelps-Stokes Institute in South Africa, granted Macmillan funds to visit the Negro colleges of the American South, and there he awaited word from the Carnegie Corporation, from which he had requested additional monies to tour the West Indies. Though skeptical of Macmillan's political leanings, F. P. Keppel, the secretary-general of the Carnegie Corporation at the time, awarded him $1,000 for a social and economic report on the West Indies, in which he was to make no mention about the state of education, colonial administration, or race relations (Macmillan 1985: 53). Thus, Macmillan set off for the United States, arriving in October 1934.

Macmillan's second wife, Mona, has given us the most comprehensive account of his journey, drawing from letters he sent her while traveling. However, I was also fortunate to meet with Hugh Macmillan, an Africanist historian and William Macmillan's son, who generously gave me access to his father's notes and letters from his trip to Jamaica, and who made it possible for me to see his mother's diaries from their later year in Jamaica at the Bodleian Library in Oxford.[6] Mona writes that Macmillan "had not been very happy in the atmosphere of the American South" (Macmillan 1980: 209), though his meetings with Booker T. Washington and leaders of the New Deal effort confirmed some of his own beliefs regarding development in Africa. He left the United States with some relief, assuming that in the British colonial West Indies he would be on more familiar ground. In Jamaica, his first stop, however, she reports that "he was surprised to find an older type of colonial world, dominated by local vested interests" (Macmillan 1980: 209).

While in Kingston, Macmillan met with Governor Sir Edward Denham, as well as with Acting Colonial Secretary William D. Battershill, and other administrators, including the director of agriculture and the secretary of the Agricultural Society. He also met with the education superintendent; members of the Parish Council, Legislative Council, and Health Office; and business leaders, including A. R. Farquharson, who was then the head of Jamaica Banana Producers. Macmillan interviewed Norman Manley, who, like many others at the time, was preoccupied with attempts by Banana Producers, the local trade organization consisting of small-scale banana cultivators, to break the monopoly the United Fruit Company held over the industry. And he met with Theo McKay (Claude McKay's brother) and Marcus Garvey, whom he found intelligent, critical of Banana Producers, bitter about the Legislative Council, and in possession of a "long memory for grievances also against planters."[7]

As he traveled across the islands, Macmillan was appalled by the conditions of poverty and apathy in each of the islands he visited. "In the West Indies," he wrote, "as in newer colonies, the slender annual total of imports and exports, the condition of the dependent peoples, as also the precarious existence of those Europeans who persevere as planters or settlers, tell a tale of poverty so profound as to give little warrant for the assumption that colonies are a source of great profit to the possessing country either as outlets for population, as vents for goods, or even as sources of cheap raw materials" (Macmillan [1936] 1938: 25). He found that the isolation of islands from one another resulted in a conservatism that maintained traditional hierarchies of privilege and met new ideas "with suspicion or active hostility" (Macmillan [1936] 1938: 45). "These islands sleep!" he wrote to his wife, and though he was impressed by the industriousness of the peasantry—"They really do produce their own food, and a fair variety of export crops"—he found estate-based agricultural production particularly backward, with planters uninterested in scientific improvements and land reform "still only an aim, not an achievement" (Macmillan [1936] 1938: 81). Macmillan was particularly distressed by the state of colonial administration, which he felt was autocratic, inefficient, "selfish," and "more wholly brainless often than in Africa."[8] "This is not good Britain," he wrote, "the conventional comfort of the British tropics is very trying. . . . Intelligent people seem to have to hide their light under gallons of drink and bushels of blather about sweeps and racing. . . . This place is a chance for a rare Governor, but His Excellency is even lonelier than in Africa."[9] Macmillan continued with his critique of colonial governance in a letter to his wife, written from Mandeville:

> This place forces readjustment of our ideas—what *is* civilization? What do we want? Stirring up problems of which even the few malcontents here are unconscious? Living is easier than anywhere (even West Coast [of Africa])—existence anyhow—the people are fairly happy? But most ill mannered on the whole: administration is bad, but a lot of it jobbed by their own wealthier people, the planters using the "haves" among the blacks to keep things smooth and easy for (considerable) property; peasant holdings are many, and available but it's bad government, no model (as Leys would like to think)—there are "masses" miserably poor and unambitious, touts and beggars, and bad country housing: typhoid and no water supplies . . . and in Kingston filthy slums well out of sight and out of mind, but plenty of people drifting in to fill them and to live goodness knows how. It is, as I think I said, the eighteenth century. . . . No inconvenient intellectual life, lots of horse racing and polo and cricket, no real "Bolshies" to stir them up—some anxiety about hurricanes and banana prices, and how much better it might be. There is as much warning as direct help for Africa.[10]

As Macmillan was getting ready to leave, he wrote from King's House that what he saw in Jamaica was "cruder exploitation than any in Africa merely because there is more wealth," and that it was clear to him that in the "older colonies" the white planter was the primary problem for development.[11]

From Jamaica, Macmillan traveled to Trinidad, where he again was struck "by the inefficiency of estates run by inexpert agriculturalists" (Macmillan 1980: 212), and from Trinidad, he went to Grenada, St. Vincent, and Barbados. In a letter dated 21 February 1935, he wrote about Barbados that he encountered "the best agriculture anyone could want, every acre tilled—over 1,000 people to the square mile, yet sheer eighteenth century paternal slavery. Intelligent, shockingly poor people, no radicals, too little discontent and the filthiest town I've seen in the British or any world" (Macmillan 1980: 213). He was to go from Barbados to Antigua, but by then labor strikes had started in St. Kitts, so he was redirected there. In Saint Kitts, which did not boast the kind of peasantry Macmillan had encountered elsewhere in the West Indies, he was happy to find "a more politically aware proletariat composed of workers returned from employment in America" (Macmillan 1980: 214). There, he wrote, "discontent is hopeful" (Macmillan 1980: 214). In St. Lucia and Montserrat, Macmillan found land tenure to be "chaotic," more akin to sharecropping in the U.S. South, and this solidified his commitment to developing peasant proprietorship. Mona reports that "he came home in a mood of righteous indignation" and immediately delved into writing his report before finishing *Africa Emergent*. He completed the book in October 1935, and it appeared in spring 1936 as *Warning from the West Indies*. The title was his publisher's choice; despite his own use of the term "warning" in his letters, he had wanted Faber to change it to "lesson."

While granting that "race relations" were relatively harmonious, Macmillan displeased Olivier by reporting that the intransigence of planters, coupled with the failure of the Crown Colony imperial government "to carry its burden of responsibility for the unrepresented masses," provided no positive example for African colonial development (Macmillan [1936] 1938: 63). Indeed, his argument was that poverty, hunger, and the lack of provisions for public health, education, and infrastructure prevented the development of political consciousness among the masses of the population.[12] Of course, this argument was to be proved wrong when, after the book's original publication, labor riots broke out across the British West Indies. This occurrence—"unthinkable" for Macmillan at the time—prompted him to write a new preface for the 1938 Penguin paperback edition.[13] This time, he asserted that what happened in the West Indies was a "warning of what we are to expect in other parts of the Empire unless our responsibilities come to be deliberately accepted."[14] Macmillan would go on to write an even more trenchant tract critiquing imperial neglect and supporting the move toward self-government for the colonies as World War II began (see Macmillan 1941).

Not surprisingly, *Warning* was not favorably received by local government administrators in Jamaica upon its original publication. From Mona's perspective, Lord Olivier was devastated, "even hurt at such a slur on his cherished islands, and the apparent rejection of peasants as a sovereign remedy" (Macmillan 1980: 216). F. P. Keppel sent a copy of the book to the Colonial Office, and it was then circulated to a range of under-secretaries and advisers for comments, which were extensive in their criticism (Macmillan 1980: 216). Nevertheless, Macmillan's original recommendations were reiterated by the Royal Commission of Enquiry led by Lord Moyne, which had been sent to investigate the causes of the riots. They centered on extending and augmenting the Colonial Development Act of 1929 through which funds were allocated throughout the empire for projects that would support general welfare in the West Indies, and this became a model for the kind of "development" that would emerge as the backbone of the emergent move toward self-government, Macmillan's ultimate end game. It also became a model for a more centralized and interventionist Colonial Office.

Mona Macmillan, in her own exegesis of her husband's contribution to a shift in colonial policy, argued that "he was interested in finding new political methods which might meet the need for self-expression and self-determination of the oppressed people with whom he was concerned; and he saw that better social conditions would not come about without planning by governments, and government planning was still suspect as a socialist idea" (Macmillan 1985: 74). Indeed, as a result of the riots in the West Indies, in the late 1930s the new colonial secretary, Malcolm MacDonald, engineered massive policy changes that ultimately would lead to political decolonization throughout Africa and the West Indies. As the historian John Flint (1989: 213) has argued:

> The entire set of attitudes which had characterized policy in the 1920s began to be turned upside down within the Colonial Office. The policy of minimal government was abandoned; colonies were now to be developed with imperial financial aid; indirect rule came under mounting attack; settlers came to be regarded with increasing suspicion as potentially obstructive or even disloyal. Above all the Colonial Office, perhaps for the first time in its long history, began to consider itself as the head and ruler of its empire, where policy would be formulated and imposed. Officials now began to attempt the definition of a consistent policy of positive trusteeship, designed not to protect Africans from change, but to 'develop' them economically, socially and politically. The colonial service was expected to carry out a new colonial policy determined in London, not in the colonies.

These changes were attributed to the efforts of Macmillan in the West Indies and his commitment to a road to self-government through the eradication of poverty via social development initiatives. However, on the eve of self-government in Jamaica, another observer would show us the extent to which these processes remained incomplete.

Macmillan's inquiries were taking place just as Ethiopianism began to enjoy a revival as a result of Italy's invasion of Ethiopia in 1935, and right before Leonard Howell established his Rastafari commune at Pinnacle in 1940. Yet nowhere in *Warning* does Macmillan mention the emergent Ras Tafari, or a lingering Garveyism, despite his own interview with Garvey while in Jamaica. While Macmillan focused on the poverty of the black masses in Jamaica, and though he mentioned slums in western Kingston, he also would not yet have seen the massive urbanization and slum creation set into motion by declining agricultural production and the development of the bauxite industry. When Macmillan eventually returned to Jamaica in 1954 for a yearlong post as a visiting professor in the History Department at the University of the West Indies, he was suffering from advanced macular degeneration disorder, and therefore was unable to follow up on his earlier investigations.[15] This is where Katrin Norris enters our narrative.

FINDING HUGH MACMILLAN WAS RELATIVELY STRAIGHTFORWARD, as his email address appeared in his mother's memoir. Katrin Norris was much more difficult to track down. Nobody I asked seemed to know what had become of Norris after she published *Jamaica: The Search for an Identity* (1962). My first significant lead came from an old social column in the *Gleaner* written by Laura Tanna in February 2006. Tanna had been working on a memoir and contacted Norris at the request of her publisher in order to make sure her surname was spelled correctly. Tanna reminded her reading public that Norris had been a reporter for the *Daily Gleaner* in 1960 and 1961 on economic and political issues and that after her return to England, she published her book, studied at the Institute of Race Relations at the London School of Economics, and married Luke Joseph Fitzherbert. Tanna also reported that Norris (now Fitzherbert) had published a second book in 1967, titled *West Indian Children in London*, and that prior to her retirement she had started an educational charity designed to promote confidence and motivation in children who were, in the language of today, "at risk" and in danger of failing in school. "Sounds like we could use Katrin FitzHerbert back in Jamaican again!" Tanna (2006) concluded.

Once I found her right surname, a search called up her autobiography, *True to Both My Selves* (1997), which was the winner of the 1997 J. R. Ackerley Prize for Autobiography and was critically acclaimed by the *New Statesman*, the *Times Literary Supplement*, and the *Daily Telegraph*. *True* is an incredibly compelling narrative that traces Katrin's life and family history, beginning with her maternal grandmother Ethel, an Englishwoman who married a German who had migrated to London at seventeen in 1895. Together they maintained a barbershop at a time when the German community in London numbered upward of fifty thousand and when there was a thriving Anglo-German cultural life, despite growing anti-German sentiment. As World War I began, Katrin's grandfather was interned in the Islington Workhouse on Cornwallis Street in Holloway with four hundred other Germans, but after the first daytime German air raid on London in July 1917, the Cornwallis Street Workhouse was beset by intense anti-German riots. After the war ended in 1918, Germans were being deported, and their English wives were given the choice either to accompany them and never return or get a quickie divorce.

Katrin's grandmother decided to take their daughter, Elfreda, and move with her husband to Germany, which she had briefly visited some fifteen years before, initially settling in Luckenwalde, where his parents lived. There they maintained an oasis of English life within economically depressed and politically unstable surroundings. By the summer of 1931, Elfreda had fallen in love with a German soldier, Eberhard Thiele, whom she married within three months and with whom she had a son (Udo, born in 1933) and Katrin Olga Ethel Thiele (born in 1936).

Growing up in Berlin, Katrin found personal joy in living the emergent Nazi ideals not of race hatred but of unity and economic regeneration. At that point, she claims, it was unclear to her and her family (and, ostensibly, to many Germans) what Hitler's endgame was. By the time Katrin was four or five, her father had become a Nazi Party official, administering the Hitler Youth. Like many high up in the party, he was often away from home for months at a time. During the war, Katrin and her brother "shared the same wartime experiences as millions of German children: bombing, evacuation and, for the lucky ones of us, successful flight from the Russian advance" (Norris 1997: 2).

In 1943, Eberhard moved Elfreda and their children from Mahlsdorf to the first of several locations outside Berlin to avoid the bombing. In spring 1945, as disillusionment and desertion plagued Hitler's army, Katrin and her family were "liberated" by American soldiers. The Germans had lost the war, and Katrin's mother went to work for the Americans as a translator. Having not heard from Eberhard for several months, they were unsure of both his fate (it turned out he had been taken prisoner by the British) and his involvement in one of the last massacres of Polish Jews at Gardelegen (it turned out he was not). After Eberhard return clandestinely to visit his family, Elfreda sent him away, fearing that his presence would make the Americans think she had been hiding him all along. By then, photographs of concentration camps had begun to circulate, and Hitler and Nazism were taboo subjects. They did not see Eberhard again in Germany. In 1946, Elfreda was given the option by the liberating soldiers to be "repatriated" and to take her children with her back to England, and she took it. The problem was, Katrin had never been English, so reinventing herself as Kay Norris (her grandmother Ethel's maiden name) with English manners and English dispositions was an almost overwhelming task. In England she was to pretend she was a normal English girl, to avoid speaking German, and to avoid all mention of her father. Eventually, Katrin's mother returned to Germany and remarried, and Katrin, who by then had become a stellar student, stayed on in Cornwall as a boarder at her school. In the end, her mother, grandmother, and grandfather all returned to London, and Katrin, now properly Kay, began her studies at Oxford. While she had reconnected briefly with her father while in secondary school in England, it wasn't until 1956 that she spent a holiday with him in Canada, where he had relocated with his new wife and stepsons.

Fitzherbert's complex rendering of a childhood and father she adored, and of frequent separations from her grandparents and her mother for both personal and geopolitical reasons, is incredibly compelling. Take, for example, the following questions she was forced to ask herself upon repatriation and the forced forgetting of her German origins: "Could all the Nazis I had known—just about everyone I loved—really have been the loathsome brutes subsequently portrayed? Could all the Nazi ideals I had been taught to revere, notions like self-sacrifice and dedication to duty, really have been utterly vile?" (Norris 1997: 5).[16] Her experiences growing up would have given her an appreciation for the complexities and contingencies of life, love, and politics that she would eventually take with her to Jamaica. Obviously, this history stayed with her, as it was ultimately the reason I was able to finally track her down.

At a meeting of the Anglo-German Family History Society that was held on 14 December 2013, an Internet notice reported, Katrin gave a presentation about her autobiography. At the end of her remarks, she suggested that more awareness might be brought to the mistreatment of German immigrants in England at the onset of World War I through historical theater. Toward that end, she invited those present who might be interested in developing a play to meet with her so that they could get something together for the one-hundredth anniversary commemorations. And at the end of the notice, there it was. After months of dead ends and futile Internet searches, her email address and phone number were typed at the bottom of the flyer.

I'm sure I must have shrieked, but now I don't remember. Katrin graciously agreed to meet with me in her West London flat in November 2014, where she picked up her story.

Feeling that she had to leave England to sort out her complicated history and relationships for herself, Katrin took a research fellowship at Cornell University, which she started but didn't finish. Instead, she moved to New York City and started working at *Newsweek*. During a vacation with a friend in Barbados in 1960, she attended a performance of the University College of the West Indies Chorale. When she said she was amazed by its multiraciality, I asked her whether that had been her first time encountering black people. "No," she exclaimed. "We were liberated by black people!" The experience made her want to see Jamaica for herself, and *Newsweek* agreed to finance her voyage.

Katrin arrived in Kingston after ten days on a cargo ship, holding letters from prominent individuals in Barbados that helped her get a job at the *Daily Gleaner* as a reporter covering economics and politics. She wrote regularly about political meetings but didn't always get a byline. During this period, she also wrote critically about mechanization within the sugar industry. She also advocated for the development of a handicrafts industry in Jamaica within a context of intensified manufacturing and for greater interaction between tourists and ordinary Jamaicans within a context of emergent all-inclusive hotels.[17]

Her father, who was still living in Canada, suggested that since she was in Jamaica the whole family could meet in Cuba over the Christmas holidays. Upon her return, Katrin wrote under her own byline, laying out her experiences and assessments of Cuba's revolution. Arguing against the idea that Fidel Castro was a "Russian puppet," she outlined "his own brand of rather straight-forward socialism" over the course of several columns published in the *Sunday Gleaner*.[18] She extolled Cuba's new education policy, describing in exhilarated terms Castro's announcement of the "Year of Education" in front of the Ministry of Education to a crowd of "wildly cheering Cuban teachers and a thousand foreign guests."[19] She wrote in admiring language about their plan to eradicate illiteracy and went as far as to argue that Jamaica might consider adopting the Cuban practice of sending urban teachers to rural areas to build schools, organize villagers, and provide education not only in academics but also in the "basic rules of hygiene, nutrition, agriculture, [and] animal-care."[20]

Katrin also wrote about Cuba's economy and how Castro had sought to put "the little man first." Having visited a cooperative about a hundred miles outside Havana, she discussed new three-bedroom bungalows with modern kitchens and bathrooms that had been built for rural families, noting that the eighty-one-year-old woman she stayed with told her that it was the "first time in her life [she lived] in a house which didn't leak when it rained and which had a hard floor."[21] These homes, she explained, were purchased by peasants over a five- to ten-year period out of a percentage of their earnings and profit shares. It was not only rural housing that impressed Katrin, but also urban housing. When recounting that she had asked to see a slum district in Havana that she had heard about, she was told that it was "abandoned since the inhabitants had been moved to a new housing area."[22]

While Katrin noted that some shortages did exist, and while she reported the presence of a thriving black market in U.S. dollars, she also saw no signs of inflation and was impressed by the enormous mass support for Castro's policies. Commenting on the growing opposition to Cuba's revolution, both within Cuba and from Cubans in Miami, she argued that their "sabotage war" was "too disorganized . . . to provide the united opposition without which a civil war seems unlikely."[23] Overall, she felt that "Castro has something to defend" and argued that his "claim that his government has achieved more in two years than previous governments achieved in 50 years is not without some simple arithmetic facts to support it." While "Americans are being led to believe that Cubans are living in fear and terror," she wrote, the overwhelming majority of Cubans was behind Castro, "and they love their revolution, which has given the ordinary people a better life than they ever had before."[24]

As a result of these editorials, Katrin was courted by new friends: communists. She emphasized her own political naïveté with me, explaining that though she was sympathetic to the kinds of redistribution and development projects she saw under way in Cuba, she was not herself a communist. She had also not anticipated the attention she would receive either from the communists or from the government. She remembered that Frank Hill had invited her to dinner one evening and had gracefully told her she should stop writing editorials sympathetic to Castro's Cuba, and that she should drop her new communist friends. Otherwise, he said, she would get in trouble with the government.

One of Katrin's new friends was John Vickers, a trade unionist who in 1957 ran afoul of Michael Manley, then island supervisor and first vice-president of the National Workers Union (NWU), the union affiliated with the PNP after 1952. In *A Voice at the Workplace* [1975] 1991: 137), Manley describes Vickers as a "bright but unstable young man" who was developing a movement among a racially conscious vocal minority of bauxite workers at the Kirkvine works of Alumina Jamaica. According to Manley, Vickers "moved from the field of industrial relations to the question of race," and "all of a sudden, the Kirkvine works became a hot-bed of racial tension" (Manley [1975] 1991: 138). One evening, a valve burst in the factory, killing one of the Jamaican workers, and in the confusion that ensued Vickers ended up calling a strike. "From the union point of view, the strike was a disaster," Manley continued:

> First of all it was in flagrant breach of contract and had no clear focus which could lend it moral if not legal legitimacy. It was an explosion rather than a collective act further to a collective purpose and, as if that were not bad enough, it took place at a time when the market was bad and Alcan would have welcomed the excuse to shut down the plant for a few months to relieve pressure on storage space throughout the Alcan system. As a consequence, the union found itself in an impossible situation where it could not repudiate the strike, since that would have left the workers defenseless and might have led to the actual destruction of the union itself; at the same time it could not adopt the strike because this might prove the final provocation leading to a long plant shut-down. (Manley [1975] 1991: 138–39)

While Vickers pressured the NWU headquarters to make the strike official, he also made incendiary comments about the union generally, and about Manley personally, which turned the workers against Vickers. Manley was eventually able to regain control, securing a mandate from the workers to resume work and appointing an enquiry into the circumstances of the strike. The enquiry revealed "that the strike was not a sudden explosion but had in fact been quite elaborately planned from sometime before" (Manley [1975] 1991: 139), and that it was perhaps an attempt to move the NWU more to the left under Vickers's leadership. Manley remembers this incident as one of the unhappiest in his career, given that it "nearly broke up the bauxite workers' movement" (Manley [1975] 1991: 137).

Vickers was a hero to what we might deem a left-wing Black Power faction among the bauxite workers, but both his race-consciousness and his leftist tendencies troubled the Colonial Office, which identified him as someone who "might possibly have Communist connections."[25] As we will see in chapter 3, Vickers was indeed a sometime member of the People's Freedom Movement in the late 1950s.[26] The Colonial Office also corroborates Manley's accounting of these events, noting their own concern "that the Union had temporarily lost control of the workers" and that the cause of Vickers's unauthorized strike was "race relations."[27] This was alarming, as Governor Blackburne put it in a letter to Philip Rogers, assistant under-secretary responsible for Caribbean affairs in the Colonial Office, because "a Fulbright scholar had recently been in Jamaica to investigate the effect of industrialization," and his inquiry, which centered on Alumina Jamaica, "revealed a very unhappy state of affairs in regard to race relations."[28] It is not inconsequential that in August of the previous year there had also been concerns at Alumina Jamaica about workers who had attempted to form an Independent Mine Workers Union. Moreover, a few years prior to that attempt, Charles Millard of the U.S. steelworkers' union—whom we will meet again in chapter 3— proposed that workers should break away from the NWU and affiliate directly with U.S. Steel, a proposal that was rejected by the NWU and by the Caribbean organization of aluminum workers.[29] As we will see again in the next interlude, agitation related to the bauxite industry continually raised concerns for the Colonial Office and, later, for the U.S. State Department. Of course, concerns regarding the extent to which returns from the industry benefited ordinary Jamaicans were also central to Norris's account.

Union organizing was not the only capacity in which Vickers came to the attention of the Colonial Office, however. As part of a police crackdown on "subversive activities" in the country, the apartment he shared with Katrin was searched, and both Vickers and Norris were arrested for possession of "undesirable literature"—in this case, a number of books, pamphlets, notebooks, and other matter, as well as a copy of the *World Student News*, published by the International Union of Students, with a front-page article titled "Hands Off Cuba."[30] The charges were applied under the Undesirable Publications—Prohibition of Importation Law of 1954, which updated and made more restrictive the Undesirable Publications Act of 1940. This law reflected the growing anticommunism of the post-1952 Cold War, and it served to legitimate the raid and search of the dwellings of those involved in leftist movements and causes (Munroe 1992). Vickers and Norris were charged at the Half Way Tree Police Station and taken to jail. Katrin had vowed to write about this experience—the horrible conditions of the jails in which children were confined with adults and where incredible abuses regularly occurred. However, she said, she lasted only three or four hours, then was begging the *Gleaner* to bail her out. She and Vickers were scheduled to appear in court the following week, at which point their trial was set for 2 May 1961. After a postponement, the charges against Katrin were withdrawn, but Vickers stood trial on 16 May and was sentenced to pay a £10 fine and serve thirty days in prison.[31]

Katrin believed their apartment was searched because of an act of sabotage in one of the Esso oil tankers along the harbor. The tanker was jerry-rigged with a bomb that was to detonate the night British Prime Minister Harold Macmillan and his wife were due to arrive in Jamaica. Katrin's sense was that this sabotage was being unfairly pinned on her and, presumably, John, because police were looking for someone to blame. The Prime Minister's visit, and some protests associated with it, were reported in the 1 April 1961 issue of the *Daily Gleaner*, but the averted explosion was not. It does appear, however, in colonial intelligence records in a file regarding the security of explosives stores.

A report from the Jamaica Constabulary Force dated 5 April 1961, reads:

1   At about 0900 hours on 28 March 1961 a representative of Esso Standard Oil, Foreshore Road, reported to the Police that earlier that morning workmen had discovered that two tankers, one belonging to the Company and the other to the Jamaica Railway Corporation, had been damaged at the fuel loading point near the Installation.

2   An inspection of the scene showed that the undercarriage of both tankers had been damaged by explosives, and an unexploded home-made bomb was found under the high octane pipe some yards away from the tankers. The bomb was constructed of a 12" length of 2½" iron pipe cemented at both ends. From one end protruded a fuse to which was tied a piece of cloth. A small electric detonator was found in the vicinity.[32]

The Island Chemist inspected the bomb and reported that it was filled with dynamite. The report continues that on 4 April, another homemade bomb was found resting against a water main "on a girder beneath a bridge adjacent to the Water Commission Power Station at the foot of Red Hills, St. Andrew." And on 2 April, there was a report that "the detonator store at the Patrick Road Construction Company, Washington Drive, St. Andrew, had been broken into and the following items stolen—2,400 Electric Detonators; 1,300 ordinary Detonators."[33] It is most significant that explosives from the Patrick Road Construction Company were found at the headquarters of the African Reform Church at 76 Rosalie Avenue during the police raid of Reverend Claudius Henry's compound, something that Katrin wrote about with alarm in her book and something I discuss at some length in the next chapter.

For now, let us return to Katrin's story. During the period between the arrest and the trial she was being pressured to marry Vickers by people who were concerned that she might be deported if she didn't demonstrate significant ties to Jamaica. Katrin did end up marrying him but ultimately felt she had made the wrong decision. "I freaked out," she said, "and didn't know what to do so wasn't thinking clearly." The marriage tore her family apart, she said ruefully, and her mother's husband never forgave her "for marrying a black man."[34] At this point, she remembered, she felt disillusioned and betrayed, and she wanted to leave Jamaica. Her exit was duly noted by the Colonial Office, which received the following intelligence report:

Departure of Katrin VICKERS née Norris: Katrin Vickers, wife of John Vickers (monthly report for April 1961, para. 9 refers) left Jamaica for the United Kingdom on 27 September to join her husband. During her stay in Jamaica Mrs. Vickers was closely associated with leading PFM members, members of the Rastafarian cult and other security subjects, including Alfonso Herrera, the Cuban Consul.[35]

In England, Katrin was commissioned to write a book about her experiences, and this resulted in the publication of *Jamaica: The Search for Identity* just before independence in 1962. The book offers a scathing critique of post-Emancipation development and documents discontent with hegemonic versions of nationalism within both rural and inner-city areas. Asserting, like Macmillan, that no meaningful changes were undertaken after the abolition of slavery that would have benefited the lives of the majority population, she argued that "the slave's new freedom was very much a freedom to starve" (Norris 1962: 5). She picks up from Macmillan's analysis of the ways plantation-oriented political, economic, and sociocultural norms continued into the post-Emancipation period to describe postwar developments. She discusses the effects of the 1952 split in the PNP, the 1961 demise of federation, and the development of the bauxite and tourism industries.

Norris reserves her most forceful criticism for local political leadership, whom she saw as overly colonial in orientation. She contended that Jamaican nationalists were not sufficiently translating the country's economic resources into revenues that would boost the standard of living of the majority and argued that despite rapid economic development through tourism and the bauxite industry, extreme poverty persisted, which also resulted in extensive migration, both rural-to-urban and to Britain.[36] For Norris, the slums of West Kingston and the Rastafari living there were emblematic of the government's failures, the most obvious evidence of a disjuncture between the view of Jamaica projected to "outsiders" and the reality of living in the country during the late colonial moment. Most startling for her in this regard was the failed attempt in 1960 by the Rastafarian leader Claudius Henry and his followers to take over the Jamaican government and leave the country in Fidel Castro's hands as his community repatriated to Africa.

Countering the common sensibility of Jamaica as a multiracial paradise, Norris wrote, "Racial equality exists in Jamaica, but it is an equality on the white man's terms, based on the presupposition that the white man has agreed to tolerate the black man, rather than on a belief in the black man's equal rights." She continued, "Any suggestion that the Negro should be respected by the white man is in the Jamaican context interpreted as racism"

(Norris 1962: 93). What galled her was that this phenomenon went unnoticed by middle-class Jamaicans and white visitors, who, in her estimation, willfully chose not to see what she called the other side of Jamaica, happy instead to imagine that Jamaica's problems were due to the laziness and disorganization of poor black people. "If a more than usually inquisitive visitor were to drive round Kingston at night," she mused, "he might easily have come across a street-meeting several thousand strong," where he might see

> an agitator cursing the white man, cursing Jamaica, arousing frenzy in the mob with tales of Africa, with threats of "We will drive the white man into the sea"; . . . "Freedom" . . . "Africa yes! Jamaica No!" . . . "Remember Lumumba" . . . slogans in African dialects; in short, a harangue making little sense to an outsider. . . . Next day if he looked at a newspaper to see what it had all been about, the meeting would be unreported. (Norris 1962: 37)

Norris then turns her attention to Millard Johnson's People's Political Party, which contested the 1961 elections, and to Rastafari, for which she offers sympathetic exegeses, all the while discussing Jamaica's version of racism, in which, she argues, "black and white are not so much skin colours as attitudes" (Norris 1962: 64). She concludes the book by advocating for an agricultural development program in which Jamaica produces for consumption *and* for export, rather than relying on the importation of basic foodstuffs, and she calls for a tourism industry that doesn't cordon visitors off from the "real" Jamaica, and that is not geared only toward wealthy visitors. She presents the drive to migrate as a lack of faith in Jamaica, one that is also rooted in an educational system that positions Britain as the pinnacle of all things civilized. "If the welfare and preferences of the inarticulate masses were to become the main concern of the Government," she concludes, "it would be possible to build a stronger economy, a healthier society and a very individual culture" (Norris 1962: 92).[37]

For Norris, writing *The Search for an Identity* helped her process her time in Jamaica. She subsequently did two years of postgraduate work in anthropology at the London School of Economics under Raymond Firth, during which time she was awarded an Emslie Horniman Anthropological Scholarship in 1963 to support her fieldwork with West Indian children in state care. This work, an extraordinarily sensitive and compelling ethnography of the difficulties confronting childcare officers at state children's homes, was ultimately published as *West Indian Children in London* (1967). In it, a long discussion of West Indian family practices and gender norms feeds into an analysis of 150 case histories of West Indian or half–West Indian children in long-term care during the winter of 1964–65. Having also attempted to put some of her findings into action by working as an assistant care coordinator at a state home in Lewisham, and consonant with her assertion that anthropology should be useful, Norris outlines a number of insightful recommendations designed to assist childcare workers in understanding their clients and in providing them with the information and services they need in order to ensure the well-being of their children.[38]

In 1964, Katrin married Luke Jos Fitzherbert, a member of the peerage, and they raised two daughters—Kitty, who was born in England in April 1966, and Monica, who was born in Jamaica in 1968 and whom they adopted in 1974. Katrin did not continue within academia but dedicated the rest of her career to child welfare. She went on to create the National Pyramid Trust in the United Kingdom, which provided a framework for primary teachers to identify children at risk and develop effective preventive strategies. Her husband was also active in philanthropy and social change until January 2007, when they were both in a severe car accident that killed him instantly. A poster-size photograph of him was still hanging on her living room door when I visited with her.

AS OBSERVERS, MACMILLAN AND NORRIS (FITZHERBERT) HAD A NUM-ber of things in common. They both had the experience of feeling isolated from their particular "mainstreams" because of their very complex backgrounds. Norris (Fitzherbert) was born in Berlin and left at age ten to "return" to the United Kingdom and had the additional odd experience of having had to hide her identity from others; Macmillan was born in Scotland, and because of his missionary parents and more general imperial family circulations, moved to South Africa at age six. That they would both become writers and critics of multiracial societies they could stand outside of (racially, socially, and politically) while also living within them is perhaps not so unusual.

Both chronicle critical moments in Jamaica's colonial history, documenting important shifts in relation to colonial, then impending nationalist, governance. And both center their criticism of political life in the wake of the plantation on leadership—colonial and nationalist—while advocating for a more interventionist state that would attend to the social, health, and educational needs of the majority of the population. Secondarily, both express a distrust of American adventurism, represented in Macmillan's case by agribusiness in general and the United Fruit Company in particular, and in Norris's case by bauxite mining in general and in the North American aluminum companies in particular. For both of them in their own time, the political leadership, in holding on to colonial norms and plantation-oriented modes of production, had not served their constituencies, and the emergent economic patterns were not seen as being capable of providing substantial amelioration. The result, in each case, is racialized expressions of mass discontent, and though they themselves don't offer sympathetic recognition of workers or Rastafari per se, they *do* define the forms of discontent they see as important and emergent types of political consciousness, inevitable results of attempts to maintain the status quo.[39] Jamaica teaches both Macmillan and Norris (Fitzherbert) about the dangers of concentrating resources and power in ways that maintain the dynamics of the plantation; about the long-term social, economic, and psychic effects of inequality; and about their own place in relation to the processes and events taking place around them.

Chapter 2

EXPECTANCY

SITTING ON THE VERANDA WITH BROTHER RUDDY GORDON, ANY-
one can tell he is one of Green Bottom, Clarendon's respected elders. Everybody who passes hails him. I sat next to Ruddy on many occasions, but
on this particular day I was there to ask him about the Reverend Claudius
Henry's understanding of the relationship between political life and spiritual
life and how this shaped his ideas about development and governance after
his release from prison in 1966. In particular, I wanted to know how and why
Reverend Henry developed a relationship with Michael Manley just prior to
his election as Prime Minister in 1972, as well as how and why that relationship soured. Moreover, I was interested in knowing more about the bakery,
the business that formed the economic backbone of Henry's International
Peacemakers' Association until its collapse in the early 1980s.

My attention was drawn to the Reverend Claudius Henry because of his
position on violence—what started it and what would end it—within the
Jamaican political context. For Reverend Henry, violence could be overcome
only through the true realization of both material and spiritual development,
within a context of a tripartite governance structure that incorporated the
political, the economic, and the spiritual. For those familiar with Rastafarian
tenets, this would on some level reflect the philosophy of trinitarian leadership of prophet, priest, and king, but for Henry its manifestation would re-

quire the abolition of oppositional party politics and the joining together of secular political and spiritual leadership under the aegis of His Imperial Majesty (HIM) Emperor Haile Selassie. It is this union that would create God's Kingdom on Earth, and this Kingdom would be sustained through the collaborative work of the faithful in a variety of collective economic enterprises located on the Peacemakers' compound in Green Bottom. It is the failure of political leadership to come to terms with this spiritual mission, Reverend Henry would have contended, that has led to the delegitimation of the Peacemakers' vision and, therefore, to the destruction of its businesses and the scattering of its followers. However, the apparent diminution of Henry's movement should not, they would argue, be seen as failure. They have known all along, based on the teachings of Henry himself, that things would fall apart before the great reawakening, before God's Kingdom would be realized on earth, and before Jamaica would become the center of the universe, teaching the world about peace.

This is clearly the language of prophecy and is, of course, not limited to the International Peacemakers' Association. Anthony Bogues has argued that by the late nineteenth century, Afro-Caribbean subjects had developed "a *prophetic redemptive tradition* within the black radical political tradition," one that reordered the "symbolic universe of colonial rule" in their struggle to produce themselves as human within conditions of exploitation (Bogues 2002: 17, 20). What is compelling to me about this tradition, and about the Peacemakers as one iteration of it, is what it can tell us about the difference between a conceptualization of development as "progress" and one of development as prophecy—or, more broadly, between the progressive and Romantic versions of social change I outlined in the introduction.

While chapter 1 focused on the affective register of doubt as characterizing neoliberal sovereignty, this chapter moves us backward in time to the moment of developmentalism, itself characterized by the register of expectancy that was circulated through the technology of prophetic elaborations of history and the future. Where doubt seems to evacuate the temporal plane of the future, the expectancy undergirding both rational planning and prophetic realization figures the future as certain. Here, the present, rather than the future, is suspended—"timeless," for Vincent Crapanzano (2000)—as the secular and sacred faithful plan, implement, await, and endure.

It is not for nothing—and this brings us back to Maziki Thame's arguments I limned at the end of the introduction—that this planning, implementing, awaiting, and enduring have tended to coalesce in relation to charismatic (male) individuals. Within anti- and postcolonial Caribbean contexts, A. W. Singham (1968: 10) famously identified the "hero-crowd relationship" as the hegemonic modality of elite-mass sociopolitical relationships. For Singham (1968: 307), and for other political analysts who followed him, this relationship was rooted in the pathologies of colonialism, which he saw as producing authoritarianism on one end of the political spectrum and "anomie, rage, compulsion, and withdrawal" on the other. Despite the unmediated zeal and personalized loyalty that followers afforded their leaders, Singham argued, this organization of political praxis prevented the development of mass political education and, therefore, real participatory democracy in the immediate postindependence period.[1] Charisma, through this lens, might be the spark that lights political consciousness, but, in classically Weberian terms, once bureaucratized it becomes routinized, and while it might gain formal legitimacy, it loses its potentially progressive, generative force as it becomes mired in the day-to-day pragmatic management of political expectations.

Singham's analysis was famously rooted in his disillusionment with the shift in Eric Gairy's leadership of the trade union movement in Grenada from a position of radical anticolonial egalitarianism to an intensifying paranoia, corruption, and absolutism. By the time he became the nation's first independent Prime Minister in 1974, Gairy had sown the seeds for a disenchanted New Jewel Movement's seizure of the state in 1979 and its institutionalization of new and revolutionary frameworks for governance and development. Singham's disillusionment, therefore, and his assertion that the power of charisma leads to totalitarianism must be understood within the framework of mid-twentieth century anticolonial secular democracy. I am wondering, however, whether focusing on charisma in relation to prophetic leadership might give us another lens through which to apprehend the ways political expectancy has operated within the post-plantation Americas. In order to think through this question, I want to take a brief detour to another context—Indonesia—not to argue for an easy parallelism, but to explore the ways different conceptualizations of power shape people's attachment to political projects over time.

In his classic essays about political cultures in Indonesia, Benedict Anderson ([1990] 2006) sought to explain the differences between liberal/secular and traditional (pre-republican) Javanese notions of power in order to understand something about how we might apprehend the appeal of a figure such as Suharto in terms of the continuation of traditional notions of power within modern political relations. Anderson argued that Western (by which he meant Weberian) notions of power are grounded in four principles: abstraction, heterogeneity, limitlessness, and moral ambiguity. Power in secular, liberal democracies does not, he explained, exist independently of relationships; its sources lie in the dynamics of these relationships and the patterns of behavior that characterize them; its accumulation knows no boundaries; and because it indexes a relationship between human beings, it "is not inherently legitimate" (Anderson [1990] 2006: 22). Within traditional Javanese configurations, however, power existed independently of its users or deployers because it was concrete; it was "that intangible, mysterious, and divine energy which animates the universe" and was therefore constant (it neither expanded nor contracted; neither did it accumulate), and homogeneous ("all power is of the same type and has the same sources"); and it did not "raise the question of legitimacy" (Anderson [1990] 2006: 23). Within traditional contexts, power was expressed through *concentration*, meaning that "the most obvious sign of the man of Power is, quite consistently, his ability to concentrate: to focus his own inner Power, to absorb Power from the outside and to concentrate within himself apparently antagonistic opposites" (Anderson [1990] 2006: 28). Power, in this conception, acted "like a magnet," and its diminution indicated not only the loss of the ruler's power, but also "disorder in the natural world—floods, eruptions, and plagues," and "inappropriate modes of social behavior—threat, greed, and murder" (Anderson [1990] 2006: 33). Within this context, Anderson argued, rule was experienced as highly personalistic. "Proximity to the ruler, rather than formal rank, is the key to power in such a state," he wrote, and the irrelevance of notions of social contract and mutual obligations has important implications for how we understand the role of charisma in relation to political and social authority: "The charismatic leader has Power in much the same sense that the traditional rulers of Java had it. He is regarded as the center from which Power radiates, and the believer attaches himself to this Power, rather than submitting to it, as he might to rational-legal authority. The charismatic leader's Power is revealed rather than demonstrated" (Anderson [1990] 2006: 74).

Anderson elaborated this exegesis in order to point out a limitation within Weber's understanding of charisma, which was that by focusing on the social, economic, and political contexts in which charismatic leaders emerged, Weber did not pay enough attention to either the historical contexts in which people were embedded and through which they interpreted political processes or the cultural anthropological dimensions of leadership and authority. Tracking earlier notions of power and its circulation led Anderson to assert that charisma is not merely a modern index of rational-legal bureaucratic crisis but a phenomenon that precedes the spread of liberal rationalism and secularism, reappearing in modern political arrangements as a "permanent, routine, organizing principle of the state" (Anderson [1990] 2006: 76) rather than as a temporary resolution of crisis.[2] Ultimately, for him, this suggested that "all human societies at one time or another had had a *substantive* view of power as an emanation of the cosmic or divine; but that each culture had probably developed its own idiosyncratic diagnostic of this power" (Anderson [1990] 2006: 79).

I am not suggesting here that we adopt this universalism; nor am I purporting to draw easy lines between the conceptions of power that may have been operative in the societies from which African-descended populations in Jamaica originated and the prophetic attachments that have been evident among followers of Claudius Henry, Michael Manley, Edward Seaga, Christopher "Dudus" Coke, and others. I am, however, directing our attention to an important provocation, which is that the proximal attachment to immanent power has been central to transformative political movements and generated the affective sphere of expectancy. This sphere reaches beyond the legal and juridical realms of experience (the sense, for example, of what rights one might come to expect based on adherence to liberal democratic norms) and toward something more temporally durative and ongoing. I will have more to say later in the chapter about how the social dimensions of this expectancy have tended to obscure the normative gender and racial ideologies buttressing the crises that open the field for new charismatic leaders to emerge. What I want to emphasize here is that a tradition of charismatic prophecy frames the forms of political expectancy that shaped political engagement during the mid-twentieth century in part because it acknowledged the ways Jamaica's foundational social, economic, and political processes — those of plantation development, slavery, and white supremacy — still informed contemporary life.

By exploring the ways in which, and infrastructures through which, expectancy circulated among, through, and beyond the International Peacemakers in southern Clarendon during the late 1960s and 1970s, I am interested in bearing witness not only to the vision that was developed — one that was imagined as alternative to but aligned with the secular vision of various strands of the progressive left — but also to the way the collective work of bringing that vision into being created an affective sphere of praxis that, though rooted in a particular place and a particular time, nonetheless might ultimately transcend these in rhizomic, unpredictable ways. In other words, my exploration of the International Peacemakers is intended to help us to understand something about how social and political visions renew and reactivate even as their material iterations collapse. It also helps us see how these visions must always negotiate — only sometimes vanquishing — colonial and nationalist sovereignties and the forms of violence they perpetuate, through the liberal organization of partisan politics.

BROTHER RUDDY WAS BORN IN RED HILLS, ST. ANDREW, IN 1931, THE first child for his parents. His mother was a member of the Baptist church, and she used to take him there with her. The teacher took a liking to him and felt he was bright, so she moved him from the Basic School he was attending to the church primary school at an early age. As the years went on, Ruddy continued to advance beyond his age level, but when he was thirteen, his mother died, and he dropped out of school. "I became a bad bwoy," he said. "I start to do some bad things . . . pure gambling and ganja smoking all night." By the early 1950s, Ruddy found himself in Kingston, where he became attracted to the Rastafarian doctrine. He went to various branch meetings of the Ethiopian World Federation, on Spanish Town Road, in Coronation Market. "Any day I hear they were keeping a meeting," he said, "I was there. I was attracted to what they were saying. I saw more light into it than in the church." By the late 1950s, Ruddy was back in Red Hills, where he met Brother Slim, who became his best friend.

Brother Slim was born in 1925 and grew up in Ellen Street, Manchester, until he went out on his own and moved to Kingston. By 1949, he had sighted Rastafari, and because he was living in East Kingston, he became part of Count Ossie's group in Rockfort, which included Philmore Alvaranga and the other original members of the Mystic Revelation of Rastafari. Shortly thereafter, Slim relocated to Red Hills and met Ruddy there. "I found that he was a man of understanding," he remembered, "that we could reason together." At the time, Red Hills was an area where people from all over Kingston would quarry stones, and men who went there from lower St. Andrew started to tell Ruddy, Slim, and others about a preacher who was promoting a Back to Africa doctrine near Waltham Park Road, on Rosalie Avenue. But because he was a minister, Ruddy and Slim—who were already reasoning with youth in the area about Rastafari—weren't interested. "Looking back to the days of slavery," Slim explained, "we know what the religious system has done to us as a race of people." Nevertheless, one Sunday evening, Ruddy and two other men decided to go.

They arrived at 78 Rosalie Avenue to find Reverend Henry absent, so they caught a movie at the Carib Theatre—*The Ten Commandments*, as it turned out—and determined never to go back. Yet something tugged at Ruddy the following Sabbath, and he found himself at Rosalie Avenue, watching the Reverend preach from the rostrum. "I don't know if it was the Bible he was turning," Ruddy said, "but I see that man took his eye out the book and look on me so, and when him look on me so, him smile and put his head back in the book." Ruddy was startled by this and felt the Reverend was looking right through his face, telepathically chiding him for not appearing prior to that day. He listened, and because he was impressed by what he heard, he went back the following week. That second time, however, he was disappointed. "According to what he was saying to me," he explained, "is like he is showing me that him is God, not Haile Selassie, and me say no, him a talk foolishness, me nah go down back there." But the next week, the spirit tugged at Ruddy again, and he found himself back downtown in the Reverend's church. That week, he felt Reverend Henry speak directly to him. "What are you worrying yourself about?" he challenged. Stunned, Ruddy resolved not to question the Reverend again, "and from that day I took my seat, until now." Now he only had to convince his best friend Slim to come alongside him.

At that time, the Reverend was selling blue membership cards for a shilling, unless a person couldn't afford the shilling, in which case he would give the card away free. Ruddy bought one for himself and one for Slim. Five times he tried to give Slim the card, but Slim wouldn't take it. It wasn't until he saw one of the Reverend's pamphlets that Slim decided to give him a chance. The title of the pamphlet was "Standing in the Gap with Unquestionable Truth. Building God's Kingdom, a New Word of Righteousness, of Love, and of Everlasting Peace on Earth. Creation's Second Birth." For Slim, the "Reformed" in the organization's name at the time—the African Reformed Coptic Church of God—was key, as it represented "something you're going to build over," and in July 1959 he agreed to attend his first Sabbath service at Rosalie Avenue. "I listened to his preaching," Slim said, "and what he was saying was just the same thing as I was really saying, so I say well then this must be something." From that point both men became part of the Reverend's innermost circle, as did Brother Roy McHayle and several other men from Red Hills, Seivright Gardens, and Cockburn Pen. When the Reverend's son Ronald returned to Jamaica from the United States, these men also became part of his camp. Ronald had served in the U.S. Army during the Korean War and was planning to train men to take over "a certain colony" in Africa. This was the plan that was thwarted by the government raid in 1960.

IN JAMAICA, IF ONE KNOWS ANYTHING ABOUT REVEREND HENRY, ONE knows about his involvement with Edna Fisher, a very successful fish vendor and a key figure in the Ethiopian World Federation who had invited Henry to use her home at 78 Rosalie Avenue as his headquarters. One probably also knows about Henry's declaration of 5 October 1959 as "Decision Day," the day of massive repatriation to Africa for which he attracted upward of fifteen thousand persons, selling tickets for passage on ships that never arrived. Or one knows about the raids on his church at Rosalie Avenue and his son's compound in Red Hills in 1960, raids that resulted in the seizure of more than five thousand detonators, several sticks of dynamite, ammunition cartridges, a shotgun, a revolver, swords, clubs, batons and a spear, and a letter to Fidel Castro promising to leave Jamaica in his hands as they repatriated to cultivate their "own vine and fig tree" (Chevannes 1976). And one likely knows about Henry's conviction and imprisonment for treason that followed these raids and of the execution of his son alongside two of his (African American) comrades. This is the period of the Reverend's activity that has been of greatest interest to scholars, who have tended to position what has come to be known as the "Henry Rebellion" within a lineage of popular struggles against the status quo that made the question of racial equality central to a broader political struggle and that questioned the terms of liberal democracy through which "progress" was supposed to take place.

For example, Bogues (2002: 5) has argued that where Norman Manley understood politics as "the means by which to awaken the national spirit" and the "*product* of civilizing processes," with the ultimate goal of taking control of the state and cultivating a political consciousness that reflected liberal values related to self-government, Henry tapped into a long tradition of black struggle that did not have, as its core mission, the seizing of state power. Instead, by foregrounding the history of slavery and asserting black personhood, Henry's practices and teachings were "*performative political actions of the subaltern rooted in a prophetic political imagination*" (Bogues 2002: 19). Brian Meeks (2000: 34), as well, has viewed Henry's platform, and, in particular, the events of 1960, as "the ideological product of an alternative universe of resistance whose markers were the assertion of Africa, blackness, and revolution." This was a universe that denied "any notion of racial harmony as the norm in Jamaica," that understood Jamaica as "a place where black people are oppressed," and that conceptualized community in terms of Pan-Africanism rather than through Jamaican nationalism (Meeks 2000: 46). For these scholars, what has been important about the events surrounding Reverend Claudius Henry in 1959 and 1960 is the counterpoint they provided to the liberal creole nationalism that was about to become legitimated through the granting of formal independence in 1962.[3]

This was also the period of the Reverend's activity that was of most interest to the Colonial Office, which began soliciting reports on his movements as early as his return to Jamaica in 1957. One such report in April 1959 chronicles the weeklong convention that was held at 78 Rosalie Avenue and attended by hundreds of congregants, during which the Reverend announced that he "was chosen by God to deliver them out of bondage and lead them back to Africa." At this convention, the report continued, he also issued cards that would be used as passports and told his followers that he expected representatives from Africa and the United States to be at a meeting at Race Course on Emancipation Day that year.[4] Later reports indicate that the Reverend continued to hold meetings at Rosalie Avenue and that he had also begun preaching and distributing "passports" in the parishes of Clarendon, Manchester, and St. Mary.[5] In response to a petition the Reverend wrote to him in May 1959 asking for a meeting to discuss the possibilities of repatriation to Africa, Secretary of State Alan Lennox-Boyd drafted a letter to Governor Kenneth Blackburne, saying:

> I should be obliged if you would inform Mr. Henry that I have received his petition and have considered his request for an interview with Her Majesty's Government. There is no reason to believe that any of the countries in Africa would be willing to receive substantial numbers of persons from Jamaica, nor am I aware of any source of funds from which the cost of transportation could be met. Her Majesty's Government are therefore not prepared to arrange an interview to discuss a matter of this kind. . . . I should also be grateful if you would suggest to Mr. Henry that he refrain from the publication of statements suggesting that repatriation to Africa will be arranged, in view of the obviously impracticable nature of his plans.[6]

In June of that same year, when Governor Blackburne wrote to Lennox-Boyd for information about the Rastafari movement, Lennox-Boyd took the opportunity to differentiate the general movement from Henry's "agitation," arguing that "the Ras Tafari movement and the Reverend C. V. Henry have in common a platform to the extent that they both advocate a return to Africa for their followers in Jamaica; but whereas Mr. Henry is a charlatan who is preying on the simple people of Jamaica, the Ras Tafari movement has a definite historical background."[7] A year later, Governor Blackburne had occasion to reconsider this assessment. After the 1960 raid on the Reverend's compound in Red Hills, he reflected on the popular response to Henry's treason trial in an internal security report. "It is evident that, divided into several factions though it is, the Rastafarian movement represents a deep-seated malaise affecting, in a greater or lesser degree, perhaps as many as 50,000 of the population," he wrote. "Its susceptibility to exploitation by trouble-makers is also clear, as are signs that this exploitation has begun."[8]

The Colonial Office was not entirely unsympathetic to Rastafari—or perhaps it is more accurate to say that they understood Rastafari, and other related movements, as having grown out of the dire economic conditions in which most Jamaicans still found themselves on the eve of independence. In his report of November–December 1960, Governor Blackburne acknowledged that the threat to internal security posed by Rastafari and others had its roots "in the fact that too many of the population had been 'left behind' in the great upsurge of development of the past few years." Blackburne's almost poetic assessment of the inequalities attending the industrialization-by-invitation policy adopted by the local government is worth quoting at length:

> But, despite all the publicity attendant on the opening of every new factory, despite figures showing the growth in the national income, and despite a fantastic increase in the number of cars on the roads, a sizeable part of the population—particularly in Kingston—are still without jobs, without houses, and without prospects for the future. For many years this lower segment of the population has based its hopes on political promises at the times of election campaigns; but they now see the gap widening between themselves and the more fortunate members of the community, and they are beginning to lose hope. The sad fact is that the development of industry and the import of capital for housing and other development projects has not kept pace with the rapidly increasing population; and the number of unemployed increases rather than decreases. It is from the ranks of these underprivileged people that C. V. Henry gained such support for his "Back to Africa" movement; it is from these people that the Rastafarians are gaining recruits; and it is from these people that some minor incident could easily provoke a serious riot in Kingston at any time.[9]

Governor Blackburne here reiterated the position of sympathetic scholars such as Sylvia Wynter, albeit without the explicit critique of colonialism. Wynter (1960: 50) wrote, "The Voodoo Priest, the Prophet, the leader of a sect have always been the forerunners of rebellion and political change in Caribbean society.... [T]hese are all men who arose out of the same tensions and frustrations of unjust social systems. They spoke for the men apart, the disinherited."

While the earlier period of Reverend Henry's activity generated extensive interest, what has been less examined is what Henry and his followers built after he came out of prison in 1966 when he changed his views about the centrality of repatriation to the attainment of justice and personhood for black people in the West and instead focused on building "Africa in Jamaica" (Nettleford 1970: 101). It is this period that interests me most, as it allows us not only to formulate a conceptualization of development and governance that is alternative to—though in many ways allied with—liberal democratic state formation, but also to see it in action and to understand its long-term effects. Indeed, the affective fields generated by participation in Henry's later development experiment is what allows us to see movements such as Henry's as movements that can't "fail," despite claims to the contrary by both detractors and sympathetic observers. Indeed, it is the strength of the affective transformation undergone by those who participated in the movement that continues to shape their outlook on the contemporary period and that touches those with whom they come in contact. This is what was always so evident on Ruddy's veranda; this is the basis of how and why the prophetic tradition of black struggle is always available for resurrection, even by those who were not involved in the original movement; and this is what sovereignty *feels like* for those who have long been outside the dominant developmentalist paradigms elaborated by the colonial and nationalist states.

PEASANTRIES HAVE BECOME CENTRAL ANALYTIC VECTORS OF POST-Emancipation Caribbean development, and much of what we know about the structural position of peasantries is the result of ethnographic field research that was conducted in the 1950s and 1960s in Puerto Rico, Haiti, and Jamaica. Sidney Mintz's pioneering work positioned peasant production and marketing in relation to other modes of production—including, importantly, the plantation—both within and among Caribbean territories and vis-à-vis global transformations in capitalism. Mintz argued that in the more mountainous islands, "proto-peasantries" developed during slavery as the result, in Jamaica, of the system of provision-ground farming and internal marketing, a system with which planters did not interfere or regulate, even allowing slaves customary rights to bequeath the use of provision grounds to their descendants. After emancipation, these proto-peasantries became what he termed "reconstituted peasantries"—that is, they began as slaves and *became* peasants as "*a mode of response* to the plantation system and its connotations, and *a mode of resistance* to imposed styles of life" (Mintz [1974] 1989: 132–33).

Mintz's position on the question of the extent to which peasant practices constituted forms of resistance to the plantation regime, however, was nuanced. To those who were promulgating this emergent trend within West Indian scholarship, he responded that Caribbean populations "have not *generally* responded to the plantation regimen in terms of their class identity but along other dimensions of social affiliation" (Mintz [1974] 1989: 154), but that the significance of land to Caribbean people reflects an attempt to ground their identity as persons in a common commodity: "In these terms, the creation of peasantries was simultaneously an act of westernization and an act of resistance" (Mintz [1974] 1989: 203). In other words, while Mintz acknowledged that provision grounds and the internal marketing system— and, later, free villages—provided the ability to cultivate a degree of autonomy from the plantations, he did not see them as out-and-out "resistant." Neither did he see them as separate spheres, arguing against the idea that conflict was what characterized the relationship between plantations and peasantries. Instead, he wrote, "In the contemporary Caribbean these modes are in fact often cooperant, and individuals or even whole communities may maintain a peasant adaptation while engaging in part-time work on the plantations" (Mintz [1974] 1989: 133).

This insight regarding the complementarity of peasant and plantation production reiterates the argument William M. Macmillan made some two decades earlier in *Warning from the West Indies*.[10] After the West Indies–wide labor riots of the late 1930s, Macmillan's suggestion to extend and augment the 1929 Colonial Development Act, through which funds were allocated throughout the empire for projects that would support general welfare, was finally implemented, and in 1940 a more generous sum was made available, with an additional allocation specifically for the West Indies, as well as the appointment of a comptroller general of services. These new development and welfare schemes built on (and ultimately subsumed) the work of Jamaica Welfare, which was established in 1937 as the result of negotiations on behalf of striking banana workers between Norman Manley, who would become the leader of the People's National Party (PNP) at its founding in 1938, and Lorenzo Dow Baker, president of the Boston Fruit Company (which would become the United Fruit Company).[11] Jamaica Welfare was a cooperative, participatory social-development organization based on the principles of self-help, mass education, and community betterment. It was inspired by the cooperative movement in Europe and North America, and its Better Village Plan provided a model for other locations within the British Empire, including Pakistan and Uganda (Marier 1953). These were the initial mechanisms put in place in the 1940s, as a result of the global dislocations during the 1930s, that were geared toward development and state formation in rural Jamaica, with the longer-term project having to do with "preparing" people for eventual self-government. In this way, development also became a moral-political project.

The historical sociologist Michaeline Crichlow (2005) has located Jamaican state formation squarely within the public elaboration of this discourse of development aimed at rural peasants with a view toward transforming them into suitable citizens. She positions what she calls "smallholders" in relation to a "coincidence of various agendas, oppositional in some respects, which serves to produce more governable subjects via submission, consent, and participation" within a broader context of capitalist modernization and development, thereby framing development as mutually transformative of the state

and the people whom the state seeks to govern, rather than as merely oppositional or resistant (Crichlow 2005: 1). To do so, she tracks agricultural policy
from the post-Emancipation period to the present in order to show how, in
opposition to immediate post-Emancipation policies and taxation practices
that disproportionately threatened the livelihoods of peasants (in relation to
planters), the late colonial and early nationalist states in Jamaica presented
rural smallholders with a promise of development and sovereignty—as long
as they adhered to particular notions of respectability—through which they
could exercise their own citizenship and participate in a sense of a shared national project and, therefore, a nationalist identity.[12] This promise brought
together the interests of the nationalist elites of both political parties and
smallholders, giving all a stake in nation building while also politicizing the
lives of peasant producers by creating significant linkages between middle-
class political leaders and rural working people.

It is important to point out that while this may have been true for smallholders, it was not generally the case for peasants who did not own land and
who were, instead, casual laborers, that same constituency that circulated between rural and urban poverty after World War II. With the constitutional
changes beginning in 1944, this class might have been captured and politicized through a progressive worker-peasant alliance,[13] but progressive trade
union organizing on the left remained primarily urban in nature, and Bustamante's success with rural sugar workers was rooted in a "proprietary approach to trade unionism" (Hart 1989: 102), one that was more in line with
the "bread-and-butter" unionism that would come to dominate the labor
movement in the United States after the split between the American Federation of Labor and the Congress of Industrial Organizations. "The Communists," as Ken Post (1981: 2:542) has noted, "and to a large extent the PNP as
a whole, failed to penetrate that class [of landless peasants]. Insofar as any of
its members moved towards political protest, it was indirectly, through the
medium of Rastafarianism, and often then as migrants to urban centres."[14]

Crichlow goes on to demonstrate how politicized, democratically oriented
middle-class organizers lost control of the development project as the institutions through which they had worked—such as Jamaica Welfare—became
arms of an increasingly bureaucratized state. This sidelined the participatory
ethos that structured earlier interventions and generated instead a kind of dependence on the institutions of the state, now led by individuals handpicked
to carry out centralized development policy. Charles Carnegie has similarly
pointed out that the move from "the problem of the social" to the narrower
focus on constitutionalism from the 1940s forward resulted in a shift "from
the more broadly inclusive, disinterested and collaborative model of com-

munity development promoted through Jamaica Welfare to the more self-interested, partisan, competitive one of electoral politics" (Carnegie 2015).

These processes were occurring simultaneously with an enhanced focus on urban development, toward which end links were being forged between politicians and constituencies in downtown Kingston through the promise of housing and employment contracts in exchange for votes and loyalty—a loyalty that was increasingly enforced by violence, as outlined in the introduction. While these developments are largely postindependence ones, it is critical to remember that the initial linkages between middle-class political nationalists and rural peasants solidified a particular notion of the developmentalist state among diverse sectors of the society, which also meant that "those who opposed development and sociocultural policy found themselves unable to imagine alternatives to the structures through which the state had legitimated itself" (Crichlow 2005: 64).

This is so in part because, "for the Creole nationalist," as Bogues (2002: 25) has argued, "the space of the political was narrow and institutional."[15] This created a situation in which, among those who were antagonistic to the development models being propagated by the Jamaican state and its allied sectors, only Rastafari conceptualized development outside the orbit of a state structure. In 1959, for example, a group of Rastafari circulated a twenty-one-point document in which they outlined aspects of their political program, which included an analysis of white (and "brown-man") supremacy and their desire to destroy it, "thereby putting an end to economic exploitation and the social degradation of the black people," and that exhorted its readers thus: "Suffering black people of Jamaica, let us unite and set up a righteous government under the slogan of REPATRIATION AND POWER" (Munroe and Bertram 2006: 267). This reflected a political worldview that was grounded in a Pan-African ontological reordering of what it meant to be human and an understanding of how this was historically constructed and managed. The question, Bogues (2002: 26) continues, "was how to reorder that history and establish a new ground for African humanness." This was exactly Henry's project upon his release from prison in 1966.

It is key that the nationalist state's developmental focus left landless itinerant workers—both rural and urban—outside the primary scope of citizenship. These workers were not the independent stakeholders (via land) championed by the nationalist leadership, and after the labor riots they were typically managed (rather than cultivated) through union organization, as I show in chapter 3. These are precisely the people who were hailed by Henry's message, both within urban Kingston and St. Andrew and in Clarendon's sugar belt, and particularly the Vere plains. Indeed, we should not see these constituencies as distinct. Post reminds us not only that the peasantry was closely articulated with rural wage laborers throughout the post-Emancipation period, but also that it has been intimately linked to casual urban laborers since the beginning of World War II. This intimacy resulted in and derived from constant movement back and forth from impoverished rural districts to urban slums, a movement that ultimately forged the class basis for those who were attracted to Rastafari (Post 1981: 1:188), which, as Barry Chevannes (1981: 392) tells us, was the "dominant ideological force among the urban poor" by the 1950s.[16]

In the Vere section of Clarendon, where Henry established the International Peacemakers Association, the history is one of itinerant sugar workers eking out a living. The area became a stronghold for the Jamaica Labour Party (JLP) under the leadership first of Alexander Bustamante, after he abandoned his West Kingston constituency when the PNP became the dominant urban party, and later under Hugh Shearer during his period as Prime Minister. However, it is also true that the pro-socialist Sugar and Agricultural Workers Union (SAWU), which was founded in September 1953 by Richard Hart as an alternative to Ken Hill's Trade Union Congress, itself the left-leaning alternative to Bustamante's Industrial Trade Union, did very well in the area. Trevor Munroe (1992: 114) has noted that despite their history of JLP support, "sugar workers in the Vere plain of South Clarendon, Chief Minister Bustamante's political constituency, were among the strongest contributors to the SAWU." Vere's history as a sugar center and as a JLP constituency thus shaped both the composition of the group that ultimately would be attracted to Claudius Henry and Henry's own political vision and experiences.

CHRISTINE "LOVEY" GORDON WAS BORN 27 MAY 1933 IN CHARLES Town, St. Mary. At twelve, she left her grandmother's house in St. Mary to join her mother in the Kingston neighborhood of Cockburn Gardens, where she finished her schooling. In Kingston, she first began attending a Baptist church with her mother but became disillusioned with the established churches because, she said, "I heard this one was preaching against the other and that one preaching against the other . . . and I said I don't like that because is one God." She stopped attending church, but her daughter's father invited her to try the Wednesday night meetings of Rastafari at 78 Rosalie Avenue, where she had already been learning dressmaking. She attended for the first time on 25 March 1959, and as she listened to Reverend Henry, she wondered, "How this man talking like him is God?" and why he didn't seem afraid of the government. Like others I would interview later, Lovey felt that when the Reverend spoke, he was speaking directly to her, and her interest was piqued when he started talking about black history in Jamaica: "He talked some things about slavery that my grandmother told me because she know a bit about slavery, so I started to think, and I said my grandmother tell me so and so and so, and this man is talking the same thing, you know? And I got serious." Lovey continued to attend Reverend Henry's meetings despite her family's disapproval, and when her stepfather began to lock her out of the house, she slept at the homes of friends after meetings. In fact, it was when the Reverend said one evening, "Some of you when you leave your home and go to service here, when you leave your home them lock you out," that she was convinced of his power. "I said, wait, this man *is* God," and she became a regular presence every week:

> I found what I wanted, the truth. My grandmother told me some of them. A lot of things, about slavery what happened. . . . I remember one day she called me and said, come here child, this I want you to know. Our God is a king seated on the throne in Zion, this I want you to know. I said, mummy, what color is he? You know why I asked her? I keep on dreaming seeing God from I was about nine years old and he was a black man. And one of the time I dreamt, we were walking together, me and him, and we didn't talk, and I found out at the end of the dream that he was God and he was a black man.

For Lovey, that man was Reverend Claudius Henry.

Brother Burnett Hall also understood Claudius Henry as the true and living God. Brother Hall was born in Font Hill, St. Thomas, on 2 April 1933. He grew up with his mother and father and worked at many odd jobs "hard from twelve years old until this very moment at eighty-one." By the time he was in his mid-twenties, he had migrated to Kingston and was quarrying stone, but he didn't encounter Reverend Henry until the Kemp's Hill days. He became a tile maker and bread salesman when the Green Bottom compound became established. For Hall, "Him come in like God. . . . [T]here is no other man in the world like to him. I call him God because no man couldn't perform those things without him." Like many others, Hall recounted the miraculous things he saw Reverend Henry do, such as stopping the rain during a meeting he had called at Racecourse so his followers could hear his message without getting wet.

Lester Lindo was one of the Kingston faithful. Born on Molynes Road on 8 June 1929, he attended the Merl Grove primary school until his father died when he was seven. As he grew older, he started working as a mason and moved to Cockburn Pen, a center of black nationalist sentiment at the time, housing some foundational Garveyites, as well as some families who were involved in the Ethiopian World Federation.[17] Lindo became aware of Claudius Henry on Decision Day (5 October 1959), and at that point, he said, "Our heart turn to his word, and we acknowledge him as a right leader and follow his instructions . . . and walk in his footsteps." His sense was that Henry's message was one of righteousness and that he taught people to live with one another with true love, to obey his command so they could live together as one people. Eventually, Lindo moved from Kingston to Vere and did construction and masonry work at the compound.

Henry Hannum was also born in Kingston, in the Cockburn Pen area, on 7 August 1933. He grew up near Spanish Town Road and then in Harbour View, and he ultimately relocated to Vere. He never really went to church growing up, but when he arrived in the "sugar belt" and began working the dray cart at a sugarcane factory, he met Claudius Henry in Kemp's Hill and accepted the faith. Once in the community, he worked in the factory and the bakery.

Brother South was born 5 December 1929 in the northern part of Clarendon. As a child, he moved with his parents to May Pen, and then to Vere. He grew up going to a Baptist church with his five brothers and three sisters, but his father was a Revivalist. Brother South stopped going to school when the family moved to May Pen, and he worked as a mechanic and a cane cutter until he, in his formulation, "entered badness." In 1959, he heard that a Back to Africa meeting led by Claudius Henry was going to be held at Racecourse. "From the man get up and start talk," he said, "his doctrine reach my approval. That's why I'm here until now." What was stunning to him, Brother South said, was learning that he was "an African descendant, you learn that? You have idea of such?" For him, this was revolutionary because he felt he and his peers were "locked off of things," of particular knowledges and histories. He attended the Decision Day event on 5 October 1959, and was there "from the Monday until the Sunday, we leave and come home." He visited the Reverend in prison and was happy when Henry decided to move to Vere, "where we was." At that point, Brother South "came out of the cane world" and began working in the bakery.

Brother Clarence Benjamin also attended the Decision Day event. He was born on 15 October 1919 in Manchester and grew up with his mother. By his own admission, he was a "bad bwoy" and never finished primary school, but he was also prone to visions, the first of which he had when he was seven. As a youth, Benjamin worked selling ground provisions. He moved to town, sighted Rastafari, and began working in fish vending. Then he got typhoid fever and ended up moving to Vere. It was there, during the meeting at Racecourse, that he learned about Decision Day. He remembers thousands of people crowded inside and around the church at 78 Rosalie Avenue. He himself listened to the Reverend from his perch in a cherry tree in the yard, and he said that every time he glimpsed the Reverend, he would see "the shade of His Imperial Majesty." When Henry came out of prison, Benjamin was still professing the word of Rastafari, but when he heard Reverend Henry's speech at the Success Club and his invocation of Matthew 5, "Blessed are the peacemakers," he decided then and there that he would follow him. At that point, he trimmed his hair, and in 1970 he stopped working cane and went to work with the organization, doing "every Jesus ting, all the work that the organization carry," though primarily in the bakery and mixing concrete. For Brother Benjamin, "Reverend Henry is the last almighty prophet, the last body, that God Almighty could a find to come back inna. . . . [H]im is the Almighty God, the last father, the prince of peace."

Finally, Brother Kiddie, born in the Bayfield district of Vere in 1941, was the third of ten children for his mother and father, a contractor who migrated in the 1950s to England. When his father was able, he sent for his wife and the younger children. Kiddie remembered, "We the elder ones have to give the opportunity to the smaller ones, and they take them up to England and that was it." Kiddie had heard about Reverend Henry when he spoke at Racecourse in 1959 about his Back to Africa movement. At the time, he said, there were many people preaching this doctrine, but it was the Reverend's version that moved him most because he was helping "people to have a good knowledge of themselves, and at the time the government nuh want people to have no knowledge more than cane piece, and the political arena, and the churches." When the Reverend came out of prison, he was among the crowd at Success Club, and upon the move to Green Bottom from Kemp's Hill, Reverend Henry told Kiddie that God had chosen him to "build his Kingdom and to live in his Kingdom with him." Since then, Brother Kiddie has been one of the stalwarts. Initially he managed the farm, but some years after Henry died in 1986, he became—at the injunction of Henry's will—the caretaker for the compound. He lives there with his wife, Miss B, who was born 1 June 1955, in Trelawny but grew up in Vere, where both of her parents were followers of Reverend Henry. Miss B, however, didn't meet Henry until his release from prison, and she was part of the first class in the school— originally named the Ethiopian Peacemakers' School of Ancient Traditional Bible History—that was opened on the Green Bottom compound in 1968, with ninety students enrolled. Brother Douglas McHayle (known as Brother Dougie) was another member of that first class, having moved from Cockburn Gardens to Vere with his parents in 1968. His father, Roy McHayle, was one of Henry's staunchest followers and allies from the early days until 1974.

Chevannes's early fieldwork with members of Henry's group during the summers of 1969 and 1972 revealed that after Henry's imprisonment in 1960, many of his followers who had come from Vere returned home (Chevannes 1976: 280). Others, such as Slim, were on the run. "I had to be running up and down," he reflected, "couldn't settle, because the government was on our heels. I find myself living into town, and [then I had] to go back to the hills and keep hiding from them." Eventually, Slim ended up going to Kemp's Hill and living among the brethren there, and they began to build thatch huts and live communally on a piece of land owned by one of the members in of the group there. Other members mobilized to build a new church for the Reverend on Waltham Park Road because Edna Fisher's three-year imprisonment alongside Henry also caused her to lose the property at Rosalie Avenue. When Henry came out of prison, he rejoined Fisher at her new property on Charles Street, preached at the new Waltham Park Road church, and continued to develop the property in Kemp's Hill, to which he had moved by late 1967. Miss B, who grew up on the Peacemakers compound, remembered that "Reverend come and make the place civilized"—that he tore down the wattle-and-thatch houses to build block houses, built two water tanks, asphalted the road, and arranged for electrification.

As mentioned, when Henry emerged from prison, one of the major shifts in his doctrine was the rejection of repatriation, a rejection that fueled his mission to build the Kingdom in Jamaica. For those denizens of Vere who came to know Henry after the events of 1959 and 1960, this would not have signaled a significant shift. For those followers from the earlier days, however, this change of program would have been critical, particularly as it seemed to mark a distancing from other versions of Rastafari that were circulating at the time. For example, Brother Kiddie recalls that the injunction against smoking came from the Reverend while he was in prison, and that it was an attempt to stop community members from being harassed by police. Others remember Reverend Henry as someone who worked with Rastafari because those were the people drawn to his Back to Africa program, but that his real intent was to "reform" them, to "gather them in and change them."[18] At the first meeting held at the Success Club upon his release from prison, he told his followers to "cut off unoo hair, clean up unoo self," because they were not Rastafari, they were Peacemakers. And while some acknowledge a number of shared views—"Man is God and God is man, you know? And about our ancestors, them taking us from African down in slavery"—their overarching feeling, cultivated by Henry himself, was that Rastafari were not living "a clean life."[19]

While today it might sound jarring to hear someone like Sister Lovey say that the Peacemakers couldn't "join with Rastafari" because "dem tief, dem kill, dem lie," we must remember that by 1955 there were three major gangs in West Kingston, all of which were involved in various levels of theft, and all of which were in one way or another affiliated with or inspired by Rastafari (Chevannes 1981). In fact, Rastafari became the dominant ideological force in the urban slums after the purging of the socialist arm of the PNP in 1952, and by 1960, the dreadlocks had emerged as the leading faction within the movement. When Burnett Hall says that the Reverend preached "clean up and come" to the dreadlocks, we must also see this in relation to a longer-standing set of antagonisms among peasant and poor urban communities.[20] Of course, this perspective also alienated the dreadlocked constituency, who felt that "master couldn't lead them because him clean face."[21]

Further alienating those who adhered to a more traditional Rastafari philosophy was the Reverend's assertion that the vision that had led him to return to Jamaica after fourteen years in the United States also accorded to him the power of God. As Brother Ruddy remembered, when the Reverend asked the angel who was urging him to complete his mission in Jamaica for his "marching orders," the angel said, "All power is given to you both in heaven and on the earth; what you bound on earth is bound in heaven, and what you loose on earth is loose in Heaven. And God has given you a new name." Here, Ruddy is evoking two biblical references. The first is Matthew 18:18, which in the King James Version reads, "Verily I say unto you, Whatsoever ye shall bind on earth shall be bound in heaven: and whatsoever ye shall loose on earth shall be loosed in heaven." The second is from Isaiah 45, in which God gives his anointed the new name of Cyrus and empowers him, through his recognition of the Lord's unquestioned position as God of Israel, "to subdue nations before him; . . . [to] loose the loins of kings, to open before him the two leaved gates; and the gates shall not be shut." This is how Reverend Henry came to take on the name Cyrus, and, as Ruddy related, "That hard power didn't suit the dreadlocks, and that turned them away."

Dreadlocked Rastafari were not the only group hostile to Reverend Henry's mission during the Kemp's Hill period. The government also raided his compound in Kemp's Hill, as well as other branches of the Peacemakers, on at least four separate occasions in 1968 (23 January, 5 April, 5 May, 3 June). In late January, for example, 140 Jamaica Constabulary Force (JCF) officers supported by 150 Jamaica Defence Force soldiers raided the Kemp's Hill headquarters, the church at 75 Waltham Park Road, the house at Charles Street, the Port Morant branch of the church in St. Thomas, and the Brae's River branch in St. Elizabeth.[22] This combined force removed community members from their homes and gathered them outside, guarding them with rifles and bayonets while their homes were searched. They also dug out a deep pit on the property that the Reverend had been preparing for waste storage, searching for weapons but finding none. Residents who were there at the time remember this with particular amusement because as soldiers came out of the pit empty-handed and declared it empty, the Reverend told them it was not empty; instead, it was "full of air." These raids were extensive and frequent enough to capture the attention of the Jamaica Council for Human Rights (JCHR), which published a statement in the *Gleaner*.[23] In the statement, the JCHR expressed concern that the raids hadn't resulted in any criminal convictions, only in relatively minor charges against four persons for possession of banned literatures (in two cases), a breach of the Dangerous Drugs Law (in one case), and a breach of the gunpowder and explosives law. They also stated that the raids contravened two constitutional principles: "First the military forces should not be used against citizens in ordinary police operations where no real danger to the State is involved; secondly, the freedoms of conscience and assembly are the possession of all persons, however distasteful their doctrine or views might be to officialdom."[24] The JCHR concluded that these raids "constitute a serious assault on the fundamental rights of these persons and accordingly on the freedom of the whole nation" and worried that if the government and police were allowed "to select what religious bodies, or political groups are acceptable in the community and to destroy the meeting places and residences of those who do not meet with their approval, then we are set firmly on the precipitous road to dictatorship."[25]

It is unclear why Reverend Henry moved his followers to Green Bottom, but community members recall that he bought the various parcels of land from people sympathetic to the movement and amalgamated these to make up the current eight-acre compound. The first building he constructed on the new property was the school, which attended to children from all around the district and as far away as Rocky Point. In 1968, the school was opened with ninety children enrolled, all of whom received a free hot lunch during the course of the day, and many of whom eventually enjoyed free transportation to and from school via a minibus purchased for this purpose. The second building constructed was the church, and the third was the bakery. It was at Green Bottom where Reverend Henry further elaborated and disseminated his political vision.

I TAKE THREE PAMPHLETS—MEDIA THAT CIRCULATED THROUGH-out the community and among left-leaning sectors of the population as a whole—as my point of departure for bearing witness to Henry's concept of governance and its relation to the proliferation of violence in Jamaica. Henry released these pamphlets between the late 1960s and early 1970s, prior to the election of Michael Manley in 1972. The first, distributed on April 28, 1969, is titled simply "Violence in Jamaica." In it, Henry reveals his understanding of himself as "a prophet to Israel" and, as such, one "Branch of the Godhead." He writes that despite the fact that the PNP sentenced him to ten years of prison and hanged his son, and despite the efforts of the JLP to "retard my work of Love and the Building of God's Kingdom for the freedom of suffering humanity" (here he is referring to the raids), he sought to be in service to the government of Jamaica in order to solve the violence problem plaguing the country.

Henry's analysis of violence in Jamaica didn't differ substantially from the dominant secular version I have already outlined. However, in framing violence in relation to prophecy he provided a space for himself (as the leader of a community) to work with politicians in the establishment of "God's righteous Government in the earth," where "suffering humanity" would be offered "freedom of movement and peace of mind." In his formulation, it is the book of Hosea that explains why state violence begets communal violence: "Hear the word of the Lord, ye children of Israel: for the Lord hath a Controversy with the inhabitants of the Land, because there is no *Truth*, nor Mercy, nor Knowledge of God in the land. By *swearing*, and *Lying*, and *killing*, and *stealing*, and committing *adultery*, they break out, and blood toucheth blood." God turns his back on Jamaica because "the land is *full of bloody crimes* and the city is full of *violence*. Destruction cometh; (Soon) and they shall seek *Peace*, and there shall be none" (Ezekiel 7:22–25). At the moment of reckoning, it is the Kingdom of the New Creation International Peacemakers' Association that will be God's on earth, and Daniel 2:44 tells us that this Kingdom "will never be destroyed." Yet this is a Kingdom that for Henry required joint trusteeship with a political leader; in the words of 2 Samuel (3–4), this trusteeship would be "Just: ruling in the fear of God" and "as the tender grass springing up out of the earth by clear shining after rain."

This political leader, Reverend Henry elaborated in the second pamphlet, issued on 25 September 1969, three weeks after Norman Manley's death, was Michael Manley. In the pamphlet, Henry traced both a political and a biblical history that led him to this selection. The political history centered on Norman Manley's struggle to establish self-government in Jamaica, his emergence as chief minister in 1955, and his defeat during the elections just before independence in 1962 at the hands of supporters of the JLP who elected Alexander Bustamante as Jamaica's first Prime Minister. In the pamphlet, Henry positions this defeat as a usurpation of birthright, akin to Jacob's deception of his father, Isaac. Biblically, Henry legitimates Michael Manley's self-declaration as "Joshua" through reference to Solomon, who was charged with fulfilling the role his father could not and with finishing the work of "building God's Temple in Jerusalem." The election of Manley, in Henry's estimation, would "save Jamaica from the spreading wave of crimes and political violence, and give rest and peace to this troubled New Nation" by freeing Jamaica "from racial hate, political violence, and high society injustices, and victimization."

Henry's vision of the trinity godhead consisting of himself, Michael Manley, and Emperor Haile Selassie was given visual substance in the third pamphlet, "Surely Thy Rod and Thy Staff Shall Comfort Israel," printed on 10 November 1971. This trinity was to preside over a one-party state (thereby eliminating the partisan violence that plagues electoral politics). This state would "lead the People of Jamaica into Righteousness, Freedom and International Peace." For those Rastafari who were skeptical of involvement with "politricks," who wondered how politics and righteousness could work together, Henry wrote, "Political deliverance can only Come to the people of Jamaica through MICHAEL JOSHUA MANLEY and none other, according to Daniel's prophecy." Cooperation between himself as "ISRAEL'S GOD," Selassie as "KING OF KINGS OF ETHIOPIA," and Manley as the New World's Solomon would "build Jamaica a NEW JERUSALEM—THE HOLY CITY."

It was this last pamphlet that drew the attention of the Jamaica Council of Churches (JCC), which apprehended it as blasphemy and called a private meeting at which it determined that Manley would have to repudiate Claudius Henry and state that he had no prior knowledge of the pamphlet (Chevannes 1976). The pamphlet also ended up in the hands of the JLP, which publicized it by reprinting it in three advertisements condemning the reputed connection between the PNP and the Peacemakers that were published in the *Gleaner* just prior to the elections in late February 1972.[26] After the first two JLP advertisements were published, the JCC wrote a letter to the editor of the *Gleaner* condemning the Labour Party for "dragging the name of God into politics" (Chevannes 1976: 285) and revealing that Manley had already repudiated the pamphlet (Senior 1972). By doing so, the church body appeared to support the PNP just as Jamaicans were about to go to the polls. The PNP issued its own counter-advertisement on 26 February, arguing that "Jamaicans know" that the PNP hadn't been involved in any way in drafting, printing, or mailing the pamphlets. Moreover, the ad asserted that the PNP regarded the pamphlets as blasphemous and that the party's leaders wanted to "disassociate themselves from such senseless and deceitful political trickery," something they saw as a common tactic of the JLP during election campaigns as far back as 1944.[27]

In her retrospective analysis of the 1972 elections, Olive Senior (1972: 48) argued, "There is no question that the PNP was aware of the pamphlet long before Mr. Manley's repudiation of it, and that in recent years Henry had identified himself and had been identified with the PNP." She also suggested that the PNP "would not have repudiated the pamphlet if it had not been used against them by the JLP" (Senior 1972: 48), a cynicism that is shared by Robert Hill, who has argued that Michael Manley launched his career through Reverend Henry, that his search for credibility within the realm of black power militants was realized through his alliance with Henry, and that this alliance also bestowed on Manley a prophetic status: "They [the Peacemakers' band] used to go and open Michael's political meetings, the drumming was a big feature. And of course when the drums start to play, the nyabinghi drums, the message it's sending out is that this is a black man ting. So Michael got political legitimacy, symbolically communicated by the link with Reverend Henry."[28] Indeed, the impact of Henry's support was undeniable. Though Shearer maintained his South Clarendon constituency, he nevertheless won by only 343 votes, a far cry from his 2,965 vote majority in 1967 (Senior 1972: 69). Moreover, the PNP won handily in other Clarendon constituencies, dismantling the traditional JLP hold on the sugar belt. Brother Dougie, who, as I mentioned earlier, grew up in the community, remembered how exciting this was for the community because "it elevate Rasta to a certain status." He also asserted, "If Michael Manley never have Reverend beside him, he wouldn't have swept Manchester, St. Elizabeth, Westmoreland, Hanover. . . . He couldn't win in 1972."

It is important to point out that Manley was not the first political leader Henry solicited, and he would not be the last. Brother Ruddy maintained that Henry had always sought a political partner and that this search was based on Ezekiel 22:30, which in the King James translation states, "And I sought for a man among them, that should make up the hedge, and stand in the gap before me for the land, that I should not destroy it: but I found none." Remember that Henry's first pamphlet, the pamphlet that caught Slim's attention, was titled "Standing in the Gap." According to Ruddy, Henry first approached Norman Manley, which would seem ironic since it was under Norman Manley's leadership that Henry had been imprisoned and his son hanged. The elder Manley, however, did not take him on; for that reason, Henry turned to Alexander Bustamante (unsuccessfully), and then, when he was released from prison, to Shearer. Ruddy recounted that Henry wrote Shearer a long letter entreating him to join forces with him so they could "build a welfare organization in Jamaica second to none in the world." Shearer, Ruddy said, did not reply in writing but instead announced on the radio that when he sends policemen to the compound, "do not tell them anything about the Beatitudes," because they are quite clear on the differences between themselves and criminals just released from prison. Of course, the Beatitudes comment is a reference to the verse in the gospel of Matthew's fifth chapter that gave the Peacemakers their name.

Reverend Henry also cultivated relationships with various leftist groups who were active during the late 1960s. In part, these relationships were rooted in his emergent friendship with Walter Rodney, who met Henry while speaking at Garvey's shrine on the eighty-first anniversary of his birth (Lewis 1998). Rodney endeavored to take a number of young activists to the Peacemakers compound, including members of the New World Group and the Workers Liberation League. Indeed, Rodney was extraordinarily impressed by the Reverend's program of economic self-determination, and when he addressed the Peacemakers' congregation, he told them they "must hold up Kemp's Hill, because if Kemp's Hill go down, we will be going back into captivity for a hundred years."[29] It should not come as a surprise that Rodney's alliance with Henry was listed by Prime Minister Shearer as one of the reasons he was banned from reentering Jamaica in October 1968 after attending the writers' conference in Montreal (Lewis 2014). On 20 November 1968, on the heels of Rodney's deportation, Henry published a pamphlet that also made clear the influence of their friendship on the development of Henry's political philosophy. Titled "The New Creation International Peacemakers Association: I Am Black," the pamphlet outlines the failure of "White Gentile Nations" to achieve peace and attributes it to their inability to formulate peace in relation to the establishment of God's Kingdom in which the poor are valued. "At this stage," Henry wrote, "I must declare myself to all people, a Leader of *Black Power* for Peace, for righteousness, and for the Building of God's Kingdom, a New Creation of Love." After Rodney was returned to Guyana, some young leftists sought to maintain a relationship with Reverend Henry by providing professional resources related to law, business, and printing, but eventually these ties fizzled as Henry made the choice to support Michael Manley's PNP.[30]

After the relationship between Manley and Reverend Henry began to sour, about which I say more later, Henry also determined to approach Edward Seaga when he became the leader of the JLP in 1974. "He said, 'Ruddy, I am thinking seriously of giving Mr. Seaga a chance and see if he will be any better,'" Ruddy remembered, "'because if I don't give him a chance and anything happen, he is going to say if he had got the chance he would have done better.'" Ruddy recalled accompanying Reverend Henry to the JLP headquarters in Kingston to meet with Seaga, but unfortunately they chose a day when he was not in the office. His secretary assured the two men that Seaga would be eager to talk with them and asked that they set a date. The Reverend asked for 28 March, the day his son Ronald was hanged. "But when we left and come back," Ruddy laughed, "until this day we don't see anything from Mr. Seaga."

Finally, Reverend Henry developed ties with the Workers Party of Jamaica (WPJ) and even spoke at the party's inaugural conference in December 1978. As with Manley's campaign in 1971 and 1972, the Peacemaker drummers played at WPJ conventions. The Reverend's interest here was in having the WPJ help the Peacemakers find investors to assist in their various businesses, while for the WPJ the interest was in building a base for the party at a time that it was beginning to more fully appreciate "the role of black power and Rastafari in the movement against British colonialism and neocolonial relations."[31] This a bit of an ironic alliance, as Munroe—one of the leaders of the WPJ—was the son of Huntley Munroe, who had been the prosecuting lawyer during Henry's treason felony case and had therefore sent him to prison and his son to death. Moreover, it was an ideologically curious alliance, given Reverend Henry's sermon to his followers at Green Bottom on New Year's Eve moving into 1978. The sermon, excerpted in the *Gleaner*, outlined his mission for 1978 "to get out of Egypt and to work for the peace of God's Kingdom to return to Jamaica." Entering a new phase of his mission, therefore, he wrote

> I have been preaching to you for 19 years, telling you about God's Kingdom. Many have refused to listen but God Almighty has said in his word, "Because they received not the love of the truth that they might be saved, I will send them a strong delusion that they should believe a lie." That is why some people are seeking communism as a way out, but the only way to solve Jamaica's problems is by the establishment of God's new and righteous church. . . . Why does our leader have to go to Russia to seek help? Why does he have to go to Cuba to seek help to solve Jamaica's problems? Why is he so frantically calling upon the name of communists? Is it because he has refused to follow the instructions given to him by God? . . . I have heard the Prime Minister say that he is not a communist and never will be one. But it seems that he is looking for a shortcut. It will not work. If communism worked in other countries before this, it is not going to work in Jamaica because it is not of God's Kingdom. . . . [C]ommunism cannot repair the breach.[32]

The irony of the relationship between the Peacemakers and the WPJ is only heightened by community members' assertion that when the Reverend "comes back again," he already has selected "a man" to join him, and that this man is Trevor Munroe.

Not everyone in the Peacemakers organization understood or seriously re-flected on their leader's framing of the political. For the majority of Henry's followers, it wasn't the most central vector in their affective experience of the movement, with one significant exception. Most community members at-tributed Edna Fisher's death to political machination. Miss Edna was beloved within the community—a strong and fair woman, not only did she provide a space for the Reverend to build his Kingdom, but she also treated everyone in the community "like a mother." Having continued her fish vending and ini-tially developed the bakery, Miss Edna was the mastermind behind the Peace-makers' economic enterprises. On the day of her death in February 1970, she had gone to Rocky Point with one of the Peacemakers' drivers to buy fish. When they reached Freetown, she sent the driver on to Kingston and hopped in a minivan to return to Green Bottom. Shortly thereafter, a young man ran to the compound, and reported that she was lying in the road, having been strangled and thrown from the van. Ultimately, she died of a heart attack.

The story many tell is that this foul play was the result of the Peacemak-ers' campaigning for Manley prior to the 1972 elections, and of one incident in particular in which they had attached a portrait of Michael Manley to the front of one of their cars and driven right into Tivoli Gardens. People report-edly went out like gangbusters, saying, "A wha dis? ?! !" Miss Edna was said to have gotten out of the car and said, "A me Edna, see me here? Come kill me!" Because they knew her, they backed off, "but they were going to kill her," Ruddy said. Her death, therefore, was seen by many as retaliation by the JLP government. My own sense is that while this may indeed be true, Miss Edna's death may not have been directly caused by her boldness in Tivoli Gardens, as it is not clear that the Peacemakers began actively campaigning for Manley prior to 1971.[33] Others, stating how "controversial" her death was, wondered how anyone could have overpowered her, a "big and thick and powerful black woman" who "nearly reach 300 pounds," and so also wondered whether "Rev-erend did want to get her out of the way because she was too powerful, too overbearing.... [W]hen she make her decision, from she right, you can't talk to her."[34] This suspicion led some of the members to leave the community.

Whatever the motivations and actual circumstances, it is true that her death marked a key turning point within the organization. As one commu-nity member put it, "Reverend was a spiritual man and Sister Edna moved with the temporal,"[35] and her absence caused a level of disorganization within the businesses and the community in general. Because of this, Reverend Henry asked two of his children who had been working overseas—one in England and one in America—to return to Jamaica to help him. His son Bertram, who was born in Coleyville, Manchester, in 1937, acknowledged that business wasn't really his father's forte: "My father wasn't a businessman as such, you know? And he had all these people around him that was sort of operating the business, and he never go around and do any supervision you know, he had people 'round here and he was mostly up in his room and writing and having dialogues with the people around him." Bertram's mission, as he saw it, was to support his father by regularizing his accounting, yet he was constantly frustrated—as were some of the leftist activists who were engaged by Henry in the late 1960s to help him with business matters—by Henry's propensity to make business decisions (the realm of the "temporal") as a result of community needs (the realm of the "spiritual").

For those followers closest to Henry, however, his political vision *was* a significant aspect of his prophetic power, and of his ability to transform the relationship between politics and violence in Jamaica. This is how Brother Ruddy understood Henry's attempt to partner with a secular politician:

> A two-party system divides the people and it must create hatred. It must create hatred. And what they should have done is really turn the country into a republic and have one state. One party . . . but you can't have two party fighting against each other because . . . the poor man is just in the middle. . . . We want one government for everybody. . . . If you have a prophet to direct the state, then the government would be of God. So you wouldn't have no conflict.

Similarly, Brother Kiddie believed that Reverend got a vision from God while he was in prison that he was to work with a "man" (by this he meant a secular politician), to work together as "a Moses and a Joshua, one for the estate and one that could run the church." Kiddie continued that, therefore, when Henry heard Manley proclaim himself as "Joshua," he thought he had found that man. Most community members remember Manley being impressed by the community and say that he entreated Reverend Henry to tell him "how you manage to keep the people together, not only to gather them but to keep them together." Most also say that his inability to understand this was due to his tendency to lean on "book knowledge" rather than prophecy and righteousness. They argue that though the Reverend was laying out the vision of their partnership and the spiritual guidance he would enjoy as a result of it, Manley "never chose that part; he preferred to choose the system and the idea of his father" (again, the temporal over the spiritual).[36]

Those followers who understood the Reverend's political vision were also the followers who recited the injunctions the Reverend outlined to Manley: that after he won the elections, he should move Jamaica toward republican status and rename it the Republic of the Honorable Marcus Garvey, and that he should revise the constitution in a way that would benefit the poor rather than the rich and that would remove the Privy Council (the highest advisory council and court of the Queen's government), instead developing a local supreme court. Some also recall Manley saying that he couldn't do what was being asked of him because the United States would invade Jamaica and kill him, just as they did with Salvador Allende in Chile. Even when the Reverend told Manley to "look at Egypt, and how God protect Moses coming out of Egypt," Manley was unable to "protect the covenant" between himself and Reverend Henry; instead, he "waste away from every single Godly offer given unto him."[37] Their private disappointment with Manley's inability to combine forces with Reverend Henry was made public with Manley's disavowal in February 1972. At Manley's request, the Reverend met him at Pembroke Hall, St. Mary, where he was holding a pre-election political rally. There, Manley told Reverend Henry that the churches and the opposition were pressuring him because of the pamphlets and asked that he go back to Green Bottom without distributing any. He also told Henry that he was going to denounce him publicly, and a little before the election, he sent Dudley Thompson to the compound with a letter to sign acknowledging this disavowal. "And Reverend looked upon the letter, and read the letter," Ruddy related, "and in the letter it said, the Reverend Claudius Henry's doctrine is blasphemous, it's deceptious and misleading. And Reverend looked on Mr. Dudley Thompson and said, 'Mr. Dudley, I hate to do this, but if it will allow him to win, I will do it.' . . . Reverend signed it, but that was the end of Manley."

Others place "the end of Manley" after he won the election in 1972. Many recalled that at this point, Manley went to Reverend Henry and asked what he could do to advance his program since he had given such important support during the campaign. When the Reverend asked for land, Manley instead offered money. This was seen as an attempt at bribery, which extended the disillusionment with Manley that was already growing. As Brother Slim said, "That was where the cookie crumbled between the PNP and the Peacemakers."[38] For others, the cookie crumbled with Manley's appointment of Reverend Ashley Smith as his spiritual adviser; they saw this as Reverend Henry's rightful position and experienced the exclusion as a slight, both immediately after the 1972 elections and again in 1976 when Manley again sought Reverend Henry's help in the campaign process. Members of the community had also advocated for the Reverend to be appointed by Manley within the Ministry of Youth and Community Development "or in any Ministry which you think he can best exercise his God-given wisdom."[39] They based this request on their own support of him during the elections, as well as on the work Reverend Henry had already completed with them: "Sir, record will show that we the people of Vere were among the worst in the Jamaican Society, we were thieves, gamblers, bloodshedders and everything that was contrary to a civilized society. Today it can be proven that we are among the best in our society and this honorable credit goes to this honorable Gentleman, the Rev. Claudius Henry, the Repairer of the Breach."[40] I was unable to find any record of whether the Prime Minister responded to this correspondence.

For the true believers, however, the dissolution of Henry's relationship with Michael Manley was placed in the context of prophecy. Ruddy laughed, "As I tell you, Reverend knew every man inside out, me tell you that. You think Reverend didn't know Manley wasn't going to do the work that he wanted him to do?" As proof, Ruddy invoked the same "I Am Black" pamphlet of 1968 in which Henry wrote, "The whole World with the Leaders of Jamaica on their maiden five years Voyage of Independence are ripping their way like the titanic into their iceberg of 1972, Armageddon Destruction." He looked at me and reiterated: "He said Jamaica is heading for her iceberg, and will hit hers in 1972, but him put in Manley. So who gwine make Jamaica hit the iceberg?" For Ruddy and others, this was only the beginning of a process by which the great empires of the world would begin to crumble, leaving the Peacemakers standing as the true Kingdom of God.[41] They base this on their interpretation of Daniel 2: 44, which reads, "And in the days of these kings shall the God of heaven set up a kingdom, which shall never be destroyed: and the kingdom shall not be left to other people, but it shall break in pieces and consume all these kingdoms, and it shall stand for ever." This Kingdom, for Ruddy, would be built on God's law, and "it would be a system where everybody is being protected, everybody will be satisfied." As should be evident, Ruddy's conceptualization of good governance here is not one that outlines democracy along the tenets of liberal creole nationalist developmentalism but, rather, is grounded in the "protection" and "satisfaction" of people who have not previously enjoyed such principles. Of course, people in the Peacemakers' compound were "protected" and "satisfied" as a result of the Reverend's businesses. These businesses—in particular, the bakery—were critical to the day-to-day affective experience of sovereignty among the majority of the Reverend's followers. For people who had had nothing, building something collectively from which they could thrive was completely transformative.

CHEVANNES'S EARLY RESEARCH AMONG THE PEACEMAKERS FOUND that people were so attached to Reverend Henry, they were willing to work for little or nothing (Chevannes 1976). This was corroborated by my interviews some forty years later. They remembered that schoolchildren and workers had hot lunch every day, and there were shops, cow pens, hog pens, chicken pens, and a food farm that provided full employment for followers living on or near the compound. Indeed, my observation of Peacemakers' pay ledgers for 1973 and 1974 shows that an average of eighty to one hundred people were paid weekly (and National Insurance Scheme contributions were made for them). Brother Dougie estimates that the community's register in 1970 was up to twenty thousand, and of these individuals, approximately one thousand regularly attended Sabbath services in one of the church branches and worked on the compound or the farm in Sandy Bay.

Ruddy recalled that when the Reverend moved to Kemp's Hill, he left Kingston and moved, too. "We were building a Kingdom," he said emphatically. "Reverend couldn't pay us a salary at that young infant stage," [but we knew when things grew] he also step up with what he give us. And we were very comfortable." Slim agreed. "Reverend didn't have money to pay us, but we come together, we work together," he said, "and we work willingly." Slim remembered when the Peacemakers bought the block machine, a small one that only made one block at a time. With pride oozing out of every pore, he told me, "That place down there, as far as you see it, every block was made was made by these two hands." Burnett Hall similarly remembered making the tiles, and others spoke of cultivating the farm. But once the compound was fully constructed, most of the men in the community ended up working in one way or another with the bakery, as "Peacemakers bread" became the number-one enterprise.

The bakery began at Charles Street in Kingston after Miss Edna came out of prison in 1963. According to Ruddy, she started with "five pounds of flour and a little piece of yeast, and she was just baking into a kerosene stove, so you know it's not anything big. . . . Members [of Henry's group] would come in and buy, and probably a few people around Charles Street who knew her, because she was a very well beknown person." Slim gleefully corroborated Ruddy's account, adding, "We used to knead it with our hands, use rolling pin and knead the dough together. . . . [W]e used to carry it on our head." When the community moved to Kemp's Hill, the members built a brick oven to run the bakery on a larger scale. They also had a Bedford pickup truck and a Land Rover for which they built big wooden boxes to carry the bread out for delivery. Eventually they'd deliver bread all over Clarendon, as well as to Kingston and parts of St. Andrew. The bakery grew again when the Peacemakers relocated to Green Bottom, where they expanded to also bake bulla cake, Easter bun, and other sweets. Eventually they were running eight or nine vans delivering bread throughout Clarendon, Kingston and St. Andrew, St. Catherine, St. Ann, St. Elizabeth, and Manchester. Each van could carry two thousand loaves of bread a day, and, Ruddy remembered, when they packed the vans, "sometimes we haffi force the door to close it. . . . [T]he people, how they love the bread!" Ruddy himself preferred driving the St. Elizabeth route: "I would start at the foot of Spur Tree, near Gutters, and going right through to Peppers, and go straight through to Brae's Hill and come up to Balaclava, then turn back down and come back and go to Santa Cruz, and go all those shops in Santa Cruz to Bamboo and back."

Because Reverend Henry was not a member of the Master Bakers Association, the Peacemakers purchased flour and sugar through an arrangement with GraceKennedy Limited. They also produced their own milk and eggs, so although they were paying a higher rate for the flour, they were able to keep other costs low.[42] In the flush years of the Peacemakers' bakery, they received upward of sixty bags of flour a day, even during the periods of scarcity.[43] Indeed, during the 1970s, when many bakeries stopped making bulla cake because they could not break even, Reverend Henry continued to make them. "Not only to make them," remembered Bertram, his son who returned to Jamaica from England after Miss Edna died, "but he would put ginger and nutmeg in them." Henry was extravagant with his ingredients, also obtaining "wet sugar" and coconut in the Clarendon hills to make the Peacemakers' products special. And his bread, Bertram confided, also weighed more than other bread—a pound and a quarter rather than a pound—which meant he was selling bread more cheaply than other bakers, a fact that "got him in trouble" with other bakeries and the Master Bakers Association.

Not that the Peacemakers were preoccupied by this "trouble." Because they were dedicated to a "black power for peace" economic enterprise, they delivered to small community shops across the island, but not typically to the "Chiney shops" that dot most rural communities in Jamaica. In part, this is because since the 1950s the Chinese have had a monopoly on the major corporate bakeries in the country and therefore have supplied their own shops. But it was also part of a broader mission geared toward racial self-respect and economic self-determination. Ruddy related to me how one Chinese Jamaican baker visited the Peacemakers' compound to observe their process. At the end of the visit, he purportedly laughed, saying that he'd never make a profit if he produced bread the way the Peacemakers did. "He was looking the money," Ruddy explained, "but we were looking the quality for the people." Slim added, "The bakery did make us independent. Yes, we could manage our own economy, through the bakery. Because if you is in a system that you is fighting to overthrow, and you are depending on their economy, then you are not going to get through, but if you have your own economy, then you will be able to." For most Peacemakers, economic self-sufficiency also led to a more general satisfaction and sense of fulfillment. Brother South remembered the salad years of the bakery wistfully: "We had a nice time, very very nice time. . . . We worked all year when the bakery going on, and it was a very excellent, nice nice time." When asked what made it so nice, he responded, "The livity, the livity of us, you understand, one towards another, you live like brothers and sisters."

Chevannes's (1976) approach to the Henry movement frames it in relation to anthropological studies of millenarian movements. Importantly, he draws from Peter Worsley's reworking of Weber's concept of charisma within these movements to argue that "charisma is not a function merely of a single individual's strong personality and hard work but is created by a people in a very complex interaction process fostered primarily by the impoverished conditions of their lives" (Chevannes 1976: 271). Echoing Brother South, Chevannes (1976: 282) notes that the "followers place high value on the spirit of community which they share, that is, the feeling of being one and of working toward the singular goal of realizing externally what is first realized internally, namely the Kingdom. Both of these factors increase their sense of security which in turn feeds itself back into motivation and discipline." What Chevannes is emphasizing here is that the affective attachment to what could be seen as a millenarian project is generated socially and through daily practice. This insight allows for the possibility that it was not necessarily Henry's own force of personality that galvanized his followers, though he was celebrated as prophetic and all-knowing (and often as the omniscient God himself). Several politically leftist visitors to the compound during the late 1960s, in fact, have mentioned to me that they did *not* see Henry as particularly charismatic or as an especially strong preacher. Instead, it was the social dimension of collective participation, buttressed by economic self-sufficiency and a sense of being part of a mission that had as its goal something broader than national development, that created a lifelong spiritual transformation among Henry's followers. And this spiritual transformation outlived the material enterprises that generated it. This is why it is so important to consider the social and historical dimensions of charisma and how they can produce the affective attachments to sociopolitical movements that ensure their longevity. As Miss B put it, "The Peacemaker's purpose is to renew people to live, bring back the people knowledge." Even today.

"FROM SISTER EDNA DIED," MISS B REMARKED, "THAT'S WHEN THEY started to tief Reverend, started to take advantage of the organization." While Edna Fisher's death was in many ways catastrophic for the community, there are a number of other moments that we might also consider part of a more general set of challenges that began to undermine the Peacemakers' material success and, therefore, Henry's ability to keep the community together. In 1974, after four years of working with his father, Bertram Henry left Jamaica for New Haven, Connecticut. By then, Reverend Henry had married his third wife, Sadie Jackson (whom people called "Nurse"). "Now that he's married and have a wife," Bertram explained to me during one of our interviews, "you know things are going to change."[44] Bertram wasn't the only person wary of Nurse's influence on his father; Slim and many others within the community saw her as "an abomination to the organization." Bertram, however, also felt that "the people around [Reverend Henry] didn't want to accept me and Elaine," his sister, so they both left. By 1979, however, Bertram had returned again. At that point, Nurse had left, and the bakery had closed. GraceKennedy had stopped providing the compound with flour and other materials, and Reverend Henry told his bank manager that Bertram would be taking charge of the bakery. "The bank manager paid up GraceKennedy whatever was owed," Bertram stated, "and the bakery was started up again with two old bread vans. It was a hustle to keep it going, you know?" Bertram felt that his father's followers were worried he had returned to take the business and the property from them, and coming on the heels of the dissolution of his marriage to Nurse, whom many see as having bled Reverend Henry dry of everything he had, the Peacemakers were probably exceedingly sensitive about the input of outsiders. Bertram eventually concentrated on the business in Sandy Bay on another plot of land owned by his father, and in 1981 he left again for Florida, "because me and the people just couldn't get along."

Another moment. In 1972, the Reverend preached that he was the final prophet God sent to his people, and in 1974 he wrote a pamphlet in which he used a combination of Genesis 49:8–10, the story of Samuel and Saul, Jeremiah 13:18, and Ezekiel 21:26 to support the notion of his own divinity and his displacement of HIM Haile Selassie as "high priest" within the Trinity. The key passage here is Genesis 49:10, which in the King James Version reads, "The scepter shall not depart from Judah, or a lawgiver from between his feet, until Shiloh come; and unto him shall the gathering of the people be." Ruddy recalled, "When Reverend was writing this pamphlet now, he was saying that he was the coming of Shiloh, so HIM had to depart." This move was seen as blasphemous by many in the community (as well as by other Rastafari), and several people left as a result, including Brother Dougie's mother and, eventually, his father. Three months after this pamphlet was written, in September 1974, HIM Haile Selassie was deposed as the emperor of Ethiopia by a military coup. While Dougie's father, previously one of the closest people to the Reverend, was never able to come to terms with this split—indeed, after leaving the community he spent twenty years in Brooklyn, where he joined the Seventh Day Adventist church—Dougie himself has since come to an appreciation of what he feels Reverend was really trying to articulate.

After HIM's deposal, Dougie explained, the Reverend stated that "the Godhead shift from Ethiopia to Jamaica and he sit in that place," that "when the King move out of the way the Priest is in charge until another King is appointed." Brother Dougie believes that people misinterpreted these statements at the time because they were looking at God as an external force rather than seeing God within themselves, as HIM Selassie himself advocated. "His Majesty say if you have the God in you, you see it in me, because the God is within," Dougie continued, "and I go back to Reverend Henry's original statement [and] I realize this is what Reverend say in 1972, so it simply mean that man is God upon earth, and man attain God status by his life, his standard." Nevertheless, at the time it was "total tears and sadness" because people felt betrayed by what they saw as a change in position on the part of Reverend Henry, and the community's membership decreased by about half.

Yet another moment of dissolution. In 1977, it was reported that the government planned to seize Lebanon Farm, Reverend Henry's 168-acre property elsewhere in Clarendon. Bertram remembered, "They said it was idle land. It wasn't. He had a lot of cows, and once I visited him there, and he had about ten calves, just that week alone." Henry enlisted the support of sympathetic journalists to advocate for his cause. One of them, Ken Jones, published an article on 30 October under the byline "Special Reporter for the Gleaner" that pointed out the various ways in which the land had been improved by Henry and his followers, pointing to a chicken coop and cattle, as well as crops such as peas, peanuts, sweet potatoes, pumpkins, corn, sugar cane, and various grasses.[45] Jones's feeling was that Reverend Henry was being targeted because he had broken with the PNP government and had started making public statements against Norman Manley.[46] However, two earlier *Gleaner* articles also reveal that the Land Development and Utilization Commission had not, in fact, given notice that the entire property would be declared idle, and clarified that Henry's property had been inspected in June of that year. It was found that the area being cultivated in Seymour grass exceeded the ten-acre allotment for crops not deemed to improve land (of which this type of grass was one). Reverend Henry had apparently appeared with a lawyer at the time and date appointed in a letter sent to him to contest these charges and agreed to cultivate the area with a different type of grass. The article claims that this led to the matter being dropped by the commission.[47]

Another moment of dissolution. Throughout 1972 and early 1973, the

Peacemakers were building "Bethel," the house Henry constructed for himself and his wife that boasted a meeting room in which he kept the ark of the covenant and where he envisioned delegates from all over the world convening, as well as a guest suite reserved for HIM Haile Selassie. While the grand opening of the house was held on 28 April 1973, it was not until 16 April 1978 that it would appear in a photograph in the *Gleaner*, accompanying a column Reverend Henry contributed titled, "A New World Created in Man."[48] In the column, he warned that the Kingdom of God was near, that "judgment" had been upon Jamaica since 7 July 1977, and that he and God would be "purging" Jamaica "beginning Sabbath May 6th, 1978, before the rest of the nations." On 19 May, Henry was attacked in his home by three gunmen who broke in and beat him and his wife, sending him to the hospital for more than two months. In a later newspaper column, Henry used this incident as a prophecy that "God will be passing through earth within the next (17) seventeen months, in answering to the cry of the poor." Because of the imminent coming of the New World Order, he called for all guns to be turned in by 1 August 1978.[49]

Finally, the last moment of dissolution. With the change in government in 1980, companies began to slow the delivery of needed goods to the Peacemakers. Members of the community believe that Prime Minister Seaga ordered GraceKennedy to grant them ever smaller quotas of flour, for example. Brother Kiddie lamented, "When you can't get cement, you can't make block, you can't make tile." And, of course, without flour, you can't make bread. As the bakery declined, the community began to dissolve. "It was so embarrassing," Slim stated mournfully. "Because after so many years, we couldn't carry ourself. All of a sudden now, everything gone right down to nothing. Reverend couldn't even pay light bills." Miss B added, "If you saw the place when it was floating, you would never believe it could come like this." And when I asked Ruddy whether people began to lose faith, he responded, "Lose faith? Well, some would. Like in everything, everybody is not of one mind. . . . [T]hat's how it goes. Some will understand; some won't."

Those who understood were not daunted in their faith. Indeed, they knew the community's decline was the fulfillment of prophecy, necessary for the impending rebirth. As they tussled with Bertrand for full control of the property, and for the percentage of the Sandy Bay business profits that were earmarked by the Reverend (in his will) for its upkeep, they also knew that, as Ruddy put it, "The things that the Reverend Henry say should happen, most of them is gone through already." Slim added that the Reverend had told them "the end of this organization is going to come, [and] people are going to forget that such an organization did exist," but eventually "people will come to seek a vision of him" and the community would rise back up. Henry also outlined a number of events that would alert his followers that the Kingdom was near. Ruddy listed them: "He said he was going to give the PNP government a woman Prime Minister. You see Portia [Simpson-Miller] is there. He said he is going to put a black man in the White House in America. You see [Barack] Obama there. And he said that when these things happen, the greatest miracle that God has ever planned to perform on mankind is going to be performed right here." At that point, Ruddy continued, Vernamfield, the former area of land leased as an Air Force base by the United States during World War II, would have to be reopened to accommodate the number of people who would be traveling to Jamaica by air. Cars would line the roads to Green Bottom, and people would have to park and walk to the Peacemakers compound to see Jamaica become the center of God's Kingdom on Earth. For Henry, Ruddy remembered, the years just before his death were a "very serious period, and man better look up."

Reverend Henry died on 26 September 1986, at eighty-three. Today, only a handful of elderly stalwarts and the custodian of the compound and his family still live on the compound.[50] They continue to hold their Sabbath service, but with only about fifteen regulars, all in their sixties and seventies. More recently, however, Brother Kiddie's twenty-something son Nelson Mandela Thompson—so named because he was born on the day of Mandela's arrival in Jamaica after his own release from prison in 1991—has taken the mantle of leadership and attempted to revitalize the community. In a sermon he gave commemorating the fifty-fifth anniversary of Decision Day on 9 October 2014, he revealed his own prophetic revelation:

> When I was 17 years of age, I went to my bed one night, and in my sleep I had a dream, I heard a woman's voice calling my name, the woman's voice is calling my name, and I find myself walking from my house 'round to the shrine where the body of the leader and his wife rest, and the last time I answered that voice, I answered and it woke me out of my sleep, and when I realize there's a voice in my head that is telling me that it was Sister Edna that was calling me name, and I kept looking for her in that dream, I tried to understand, I know that I was getting a calling, and I'm trying to work out my purpose of calling, why my name was being called. I wasn't here in 1959, but I get my calling, I received my calling after so many years, I received my calling, and each and every day that I am here, I am trying to fulfill my calling.[51]

Mandela is determined to "give back to the community," and he has started a youth club toward this end. When asked what he thought might draw people to the faith now, he responded that the Reverend taught that this kind of proselytizing was no longer necessary. "I cannot convince a person to be part of the organization," he said. "What I can do is tell them about the organization . . . , and then they will have to look within themselves and make the comparison within their heart about the Peacemakers and the rest of Jamaica, and think if this is different from what they are already receiving."[52] After a period of fundraising, Mandela has also re-registered the Peace-Makers Association Limited as an incorporated company so that they can move forward with their other business and educational plans, which include potentially establishing the Peacemakers compound as a vocational training center under the aegis of the Heart Trust, and capitalizing on the current legalization of ganja by becoming a depository for farmers throughout the area. Until these efforts are realized, however, the stalwarts remain faithful to Claudius Henry's vision because they have seen other prophecies fulfilled. As Brother Kiddie told me in 2012, "We just continue."

IT IS THIS SENSE OF TIME AS DURATIVE THAT CONTRASTS SO STRIKingly with the hegemonic, state-driven, developmentalist framework that was intended to determine mid-twentieth-century notions of citizenship and sovereignty. If development is merely framed in relation to progress, and if by progress we mean the evolutionary Western narrative—whether liberal or Marxist—that positions universal humans along a continuum of belief and practice, with secular democratic self-realization (economically and politically) at the pinnacle, then we remain incapable of truly apprehending the actually existing ways people have sought to realize their aspirations. Evoking development in relation to prophecy, however, takes seriously Afro-Jamaicans' experiences of the disjunctures of Western liberal time and thus reveals a different relationship between the domains of the material and the spiritual, the political and the social. This, in turn, helps us to more sincerely appreciate the centrality of affect not only to everyday practice and the constitution of community, but also to the long-term visions and re-visions of alternative social and political organization. Remember Brother Ruddy's assertion, "We were building a Kingdom," and his association of democracy with protection and satisfaction, rather than with liberal tenets of rule of law, participatory and representative government, the separation of church and state, and the elaboration of individual human and civil rights. Ruddy's conceptualization of democracy shatters a notion of it as a transcendent category of rule and instead reflects a relational and historicized understanding of the effects of plantation slavery and imperialism on the constitution of political authority, economic development, and sociocultural personhood in

Jamaica and beyond. "Development" is thus apprehended not vis-à-vis progress toward a fuller realization of "democracy" within a secular, territorially bounded state, but, rather, in relation to the elaboration of black personhood and humanity globally. And self-realization is guaranteed not through the apprehension of rights, but through an ethical relational position that links individuals across differences of nation, class, and color not juridically but spiritually.

Consider, too, Brother Kiddie's description of his attraction to Henry as "a feeling in me," one that was shared by many in the district who were interested in the various versions of Back to Africa preaching, and one that he sought to spread. "If the Kingdom is in you," he said, "you will do everything to make somebody feel the way you feel." His "feeling," here, is exactly the sense of protection and satisfaction experienced by those working collectively toward a common spiritual goal (one that encompassed political and economic development, locally defined), and is therefore worth "continuing," as he noted.

Others have conceptualized continuation as endurance, emphasizing its "cruddiness" and its deadening "keeping on" of "bare life" over the more hopeful overcoming associated with Christian-inspired social movements.[53] In the context I have elaborated here, endurance is undergirded by *expectancy*, and hope, as Hiro Miyazaki (2004: 5) has noted, is a method "of radical temporal reorientation of knowledge." It is this sense of expectancy, this reframing of space, and this epistemological approach that prophetic approaches to temporality generates within Black Atlantic contexts. What is key here is that the temporality of prophecy ensures the certainty of redemption in a way that progressive time does not. Within secular, progressive development paradigms of both liberal and radical stripes, unexpected dislocations occur, global geopolitics change, and markets move. They leave behind myriad "if onlys." If only we had pursued X or Y strategy, rather than A or B. If only we had anticipated this or that external intervention, dislocation, brick wall, invasion. If only we had created additional alliances. If only "the people" had been more politicized. These "if onlys," in turn, generate the senses of nostalgia, the silences, the agonizing disappointments of political generations as they watch their visions crumble, their dreams deferred, obliterated, and, many times, forgotten.[54]

Prophetic time, by contrast, validates the expectancy of and faith in a future in a way that creates a sense of an already existing freedom rather than one that is always one or two steps away. Within a context in which the foundational realities have been racialized and civilizational genocide; export-oriented capitalist exploitation and commodification through mining and plantation development, slavery, and indentured labor; and various forms of trade-union-based nationalisms, what good is planning, allocating, and rationalizing when the question of what it means to be human has not been settled? Prophetic time offers an ontological alterity that does not rely on a condition of being prior, outside, or marginal but instead is rooted *in* the violence of modernity; in this way, it also authorizes an understanding of the persistence of Atlantic histories in the present. It focuses on the future, "but futures are projected out of construals made of or in relation to the present . . . [and] cannot be detached from the ways pasts are felt to be in or excluded from the present" (Munn 1992: 115; see also Trouillot 1995). The future, in this vision, rights past wrongs, includes past exclusions. Rather than seeing prophetic time as the evacuation of the "near-future" promised by developmentalism and planning (Guyer 2007), we might see it as an upending, a "dread history" (Hill 1983), a retelling of modernity's master narrative, and therefore a reconfiguration of the space and time of political action whereby the social order is reconfigured and the last finally become the first, the bottom becomes the top.

Remember James Snead's (1981: 148) classic reworking of Hegel and his assertion of the historicity of Africans: "Being there, the African is also always already there, or perhaps always there before, whereas the European is headed there or, better, not yet there." For the cinema studies scholar Kara Keeling (2005: 242), this reworking raises the possibility that "the African might be understood as that from which the movement of the European (the human) derives and black culture might be understood as the crucible for a European progressive culture that ultimately arrives at that which was already there before, black culture. The human unfolds in time, while the Black is internal to time—the Black haunts the human's past, present, and future." Black subjectivity, therefore, exists in nonchronological time, and moreover, Keeling (2005: 242) states, "European subjectivity arrives at black subjectivity under the pressure of post-structuralism." Here, the last becomes the first, not as the result of an objective universalist reordering but because of the insistence that no ordering stands outside the historical processes that generated capitalist modernity and its aftermaths.

Remember, too, that in the early days Rastafari promulgated a belief in the superiority of blacks over whites, announcing that

> black men were civilized when the white man was living in the caves of northern Europe. The throne of Ethiopia is older than the throne of King George. The white man says that black men are not good, but David, Solomon, and the Queen of Sheba were black. The knowledge black men have cannot be ob-

tained in college. They are born with the knowledge they possess because they have been with God from the beginning of Creation, and they have been with God everywhere. (Simpson 1955b: 169)[55]

Prophetic time not only reorganizes historical experience but also generates an epistemological frame within which all utterances and occurrences are interpreted as being directly related to the prophetic expectancy. As an example, recall Ruddy's interpretation of Prime Minister Hugh Shearer's "Beatitudes" speech. He and other astute observers within the community understood Shearer's invocation of Matthew's epistle as a direct response to Reverend Henry's solicitation of him as a political partner. Others in Jamaica at the time, however, would have interpreted Shearer's comments—part of a speech given to delegates representing policemen from across the island at the twenty-third annual Central Conference of the Police Federation on 11 May 1967—within the context of an attempt to improve the relationship between police and politicians, a relationship that had become "so antagonistic that it constituted by the late 1960s a major factor contributing to a high level of violence, impelling the police to lash out not against the political masters they despised but against the 'criminal class' which certain politicians had mobilized for political warfare" (Lacey 1977: 122). This was the backdrop for Shearer's speech, the exact words of which were, "The police had the full backing of the government in bringing violence to an end"; thus, "When it comes to handling crime in this country I do not expect any policeman, when he tackles a criminal, to recite any Beatitudes to him."[56] Members of the police force interpreted these words as sanction for becoming more aggressive with criminals, and indeed high levels of police violence were recorded in 1968 and 1969 (Lacey 1977: 122). Both constituencies, as it were—the general Jamaican population and the International Peacemakers Association—were searching for explanations for and deterrents to the intensifying violence they saw developing around them, violence they all understood as having political partisanship at its foundation. What led them to different conclusions were their divergent apprehensions of the relationships between political and spiritual economy, affect and temporality.

But they also had a different relationship to the space of the political. Where Reverend Henry would position Jamaica in relation to a global black humanity, any secular political partner he chose would have been concerned with the space of the nation-state. This brings us back to the issue of charisma and its temporal and spatial orientation. I have already referred to Chevannes's exhortation that we explore charisma as a social rather than individual category, an exhortation that further helps us to understand the dynamics of the forms of political practice that have (been actively) developed in Jamaica and in the broader Caribbean. Erica Edwards (2012) has also pushed us to see Weber's discursive framing of charisma as one that, grounded as it is in a "universalism" rooted in territorial European experiences, ignores the forms of violence that have undergirded transformative movements throughout the Americas. "Neither race, nor gender, nor sexuality, nor class, nor history," Edwards (2012: 14) writes, "are understood as significant independent variables in the canonical studies of charisma." For Edwards, this has led to a flattening of heterogeneous freedom struggles and to an elision of the ways they have challenged the social dynamics of capitalist modernity. At the same time, it has constructed charisma as a form of normative, masculinist political authority, thereby blinding us to other forms of political praxis and leadership.

On one hand, Edwards's assertions might be seen as why the political work of women within organizations such as the Peacemakers has been minimized or conceptualized as "support." Indeed, the full history of Miss Edna's ideological and practical contributions to the organization remains to be written. On the other hand, Edwards also leads us to reconsider the aims and ambitions of political work, as well as the audiences in whose name it is done. If prophetic expectancies disrupt linear, developmentalist conceptions of time, as well as territorially bounded understandings of the sphere for political action, then their appeal must lie in the ontological rearranging of the taken-for-granted relationship between "Man" and "Human" (Wynter 2003), in the realignment of blackness with self-determination, self-direction, value, and prescience. If, as I argue, the dominant affective experience of sovereignty during the 1970s was expectancy, then we learn from the Peacemakers that expectancy takes on different valences within different spheres. What does it mean to be human within developmentalist frames? To be perfectible, and therefore always measured against the ideals of Western liberalism. What does prophetic expectancy give us? Freedom, always and already.

I BEGAN THIS CHAPTER ON BROTHER RUDDY'S VERANDA, WHICH IS where we spent the bulk of our time together during the two years preceding his death in November 2013. I enjoyed our visits and debates immensely, debates that were often peppered with the meanings and resonance of particular biblical passages for the Peacemakers, and my sense was that this feeling was reciprocated. At that point, Ruddy was still attending Sabbath service, but he alternated weeks with his wife since they were taking care of her bedridden mother and couldn't leave her alone.

Ruddy was a charming and charismatic presence and a true intellectual. I often wondered why, if he had been so close to the Reverend, he hadn't been selected to lead the community after Henry died in 1986. After all, when younger activists and intellectuals based in Kingston visited the community in the late 1960s and in the first year or so of the 1970s, they reported that it was Ruddy, not the Reverend, who was leading Sabbath service; they saw Ruddy as Reverend Henry's lieutenant.[57] I asked Ruddy about this once. "You seem like you were really the closest to the Reverend," I said. "Yes," Ruddy answered, "he said nobody know his work as well as me." "So," I asked, "why didn't he leave you in charge of the community?" This is how Ruddy answered:

[Reverend Henry] realized something. Because he spake so highly of me, I was hated. Until now. Covetousness. When he was about to go, he called me and another brother by the name of Brother Shay. . . . He said to me, "Ruddy, do you know," him said, "do you know that I should have been gone away already and looking to come back now?" And we said, "Yes, sir?" "Yes, I should be gone. . . . But I can't find anybody to leave here." Him said, "Ruddy, it can't be you. If I leave you when I come back all I am going to see is filth and blood damp all the walls." . . . [But] he talk it and say is only Shay and Ruddy know what I want. Him said, "All that I give to Israel, Israel turn him back. . . . I don't know what to do. I can't leave you [in charge], and I can't leave you."

This, presumably, is why Brother Kiddie, faithful and loyal servant of the Reverend's message, became the caretaker of the compound.

During our last few visits together, Ruddy was becoming increasingly ill and seemed sometimes to be receiving visions. He would surprise me by becoming agitated, raising both hands in the air as if bestowing a prophecy of his own. In the end, I didn't understand what he was trying to say as he waved his strong and flexed arms, something about "these hands," and "destruction," and, not surprisingly, "the end."

"Whoever you give to this world, the world don't want." This is what Ruddy said the Reverend told him. Brother Kiddie and Miss B had never seemed too keen on the fact that I spent so much time with Ruddy. They didn't say so directly, but I could feel it. Then one Saturday when I had taken friends from Kingston and a few of my students from the University of Pennsylvania to Sabbath services, Miss B pulled out a pile of 8 × 10 photographs of the community dating as far back as 1967. As we looked through them, I noticed there were very few images of Ruddy. When Reverend was pictured with his closest lieutenants, Ruddy wasn't included. The bread vans, the ovens, the block factory—no Ruddy. For someone who was so central to the organization, I thought, it was odd that he wasn't more visible within the community's own archive.[58] Not long after, when I visited the compound again on my own, Brother Kiddie and Miss B sat me down purposefully. They told me what seemed at the time to be the most fantastic story about Brother Ruddy having been kicked out of the community by Reverend Henry. They said he had been embezzling from him, stealing money from the bread vans during his delivery route and trying to turn people against the Reverend. I listened, but I was skeptical.[59] Then Ruddy died.

Two years later while visiting with Brother Dougie, we heard more.[60] Dougie's father, Roy McHayle, had been one of the original members of Reverend Henry's group in Kingston, and thus also of the Peacemakers—and, recall, one of the faithful who were disillusioned by the Reverend's speech in 1974 and left the community. Dougie himself stayed away from the community for more than twenty years. He was bitter, he said, because he felt that his father never fully recovered not only from what he saw as a betrayal of the political and spiritual vision, but also from a personal disloyalty. His father, Dougie said, was second in command to the Reverend, but Ruddy engaged in a campaign to discredit him and in the process broke up the relationship between his father and mother. Dougie confessed that at one point he had planned to kill Ruddy because of this treachery; he even approached Ruddy to let him know his plan. But in the end he forgave him and left it alone. When he finally went back to the community in 1997, Dougie learned more. He said at that point he found out that the Reverend had kicked Ruddy out of the community because of "dishonesty, driving the van without authorization and misappropriation." But we had already heard this, so it wasn't what was surprising to us. Dougie also said that community members knew Ruddy was a registered member of the Bustamante Industrial Trade Union (BITU), which would have meant he was "a Labourite" (a JLP supporter) when the community had worked so hard to work with Manley's PNP government, and thus, that they felt he was "an agent." Brother Ruddy Gordon, a spy?

If it was true, he would not have been the first. At least one member of Ronald Henry's camp in Red Hills was informing the government about the activities of the Reverend and Ronald in 1959 and 1960, and it is alleged that he was the one—not Reverend Henry himself—who wrote the letter to Fidel Castro that was found during the raids in 1960. And even the most cursory perusal of the records held at the National Archives demonstrate that members of the Special Branch of the JCF were attending meetings of the Ethiopian World Federation and of each group of Rastafari throughout the island,

and were surveilling Claudius Henry (among other Rastafari). The threat of Rastafari—of the projects of self-determination, of the upending of white-supremacist ideology, of the decentering of the nation-state—was a threat to many actors with multiple (and sometimes divergent) agendas, at various levels of scale, and with multiple ramifications for the geopolitical horizons that developed most forcefully in the middle of the twentieth century.

Clarendon dwellings before Reverend Henry's release from prison, circa 1966. Photographer unknown.

From prison to reign. Reverend Henry comes out of prison, Success Club, Kingston, 1967. Photographer: Omroy Brown.

International Peacemakers Association leadership (Reverend Claudius Henry, center; Brother Ruddy, third from left) at the International Peacemakers compound in Clarendon, in front of the school, circa 1970. Photographer: Omroy Brown.

(*above*) Bethel, under construction, Clarendon, circa 1972–73. (*below*) Bethel, completed, Clarendon, April 1973. Photographer: Omroy Brown.

International Peacemakers Association Drum Brigade, marching in honor
of Michael Manley's visit to the community in Clarendon, circa 1972.
Photographer: Omroy Brown.

Outdoor service in Clarendon (Brother Kiddie on kete drum), circa 1972.
Photographer: Omroy Brown.

Service inside the Tabernacle, circa 1972–73. Photographer: Omroy Brown.

(*above*) Making tiles for the construction of the compound in Clarendon (Brother South on the left), circa 1967–68. (*below*) Tile display, circa 1967–68. Photographer: Omroy Brown.

Making cement blocks for construction of the compound in Clarendon, circa 1967–68. Photographer: Omroy Brown.

Kneading the Peacemakers' bread, circa 1967–68. Photographer: Omroy Brown.

Cooling the bread, circa 1967–68. Photographer: Omroy Brown.

Bagging the bread, circa 1967–68. Photographer: Omroy Brown.

The bread vans, circa 1967–68. Photographer: Omroy Brown.

(*above*) Preparing the farmland in Sandy Bay, Clarendon, late 1970s or early 1980s.
(*below*) Peacemakers' cattle in Sandy Bay, Clarendon, late 1970s or early 1980s.
Photographer unknown.

Edna Fisher's funeral procession, February 1973. Photographer: Omroy Brown.

The Ark of the Covenant, Edna Fisher's final resting place on the Peacemakers' compound, circa 1973. Photographer: Omroy Brown.

(*left*) Black Power for Peace, circa 1973. (*right*) Community gathering, circa 1973.
Photographer: Omroy Brown.

Israel's new creations, a baptism in 1982. Photographer unknown.

Michael Manley and Dudley Thompson visit the community prior to the 1972 elections. Photographer: Omroy Brown.

"GOD'S RIGHTEOUS KINGDOM"

CERTIFICATE OF MEMBERSHIP. "THE LEPERS GOVERNMENT."

FREE

From the Ancient and Mythical realm of Neptune Rex, Court of the Dawn, "The Rod and the Star" "Ensign" "Th ed, Gold and Green", with the morning star in the Centre.

Know all ye by these present that I .... *Rudolph Gordon*

And my family of..........

Address.......... *Red Hills   St Andrew*

re registered members of The African Reform Church of God in Christ, The first fruit House of Prayer. Foun and Pastor, Rev. C. V. Henry, R.B. with "The Seventh Emmanuel's Brethren", Administrating "The Lepers Governmen under the United Ethiopian Pilgrim's Pioneer Movement.
Pioneering Israel's scattered Children of African Origin back home to Africa, this year 1959, deadline date Oct. 5 This New Government is God's Righteous Kingdom of Everlasting Peace on Earth, "Creation's Second Birth." Holder of this Certificate is requested to visit the Headquarters at 78 Rosalie Ave., off Waltham Park Road, Au 1st 1959, for Our Emancipation Jubilee commencing 9 a.m. sharp. Please preserve this Certificate for removal. No p port will be necessary for those returning home to Africa. Bring this Certificate with you on August 1st., "Identification" We are sincerely, "The Seventh Emmanuel's Brethren" gathering Israel's Scattered Children removal, with our Leader, God's Appointed and Anointed Prophet, Rev. C. V. Henry, R.B.

Given this 2nd day of March 1959, in the year of the reign of His Imperial Majesty, 1st Emperor of Ethiopia, "Gods Elect." Haile Selassie. King of Kings and Lord of Lords. "Israel's Returned Messiah."

Brother Ruddy's original certificate, 1959.

Surely Thy Rod And Thy Staff Shall Comfort Israel

Rev C V Henry R.B.

Emperor Haile Selassie

Michael Manley

Moses And His Rod

The King And His Righteous Sceptre

Joshua And His Staff

We the Sons of God (Peacemakers) of whom the Bible declared saying, "Blessed are the Peacemakers for they shall be called the Children, or Sons of God. Matt. 5.9 Hereby desire at this time to make clear our intention to the people of Jamaica, and the General Public; Those at home and those abroad: Why: AS SONS OF GOD, we have Accepted; and are Supporting the Peoples National Party?

(1) We are convince, that God has given the Leader Joshua, a New Heart of Righteousness, also He has given Him Visions of Jamaica's last condition, and whereas no Leader can be Successful, without having Visions from God: "For where there is no Vision, the people perish". Prov. 29.18.

That is why Jamaica is drifting further and further in Crimes, because her Leaders have no Vision from God.

Therefore it is time that the people of Jamaica realize, that MICHAEL (JOSHUA) MANLEY are fighting for a Righteous, and just Cause, whereas to Establish a Righteous Government in Jamaica which will stamp out Crimes, and bring an end to Racial Hate, Political Violence, Hooliganism, Segregation, Discrimination, Victimization, Shooting, Killing and the Shedding of Innocent Blood.

Jamaica has become The Home of Murderers. "How is the Faithful City, become an Harlot?
It was full of Judgement; Righteousness lodged in it; But now Murderers. Isa. 1. 21.

It must be clearly Understood, that we THE SONS OF GOD, 'THE REPAIRER OF THE BREACH of the Nations, with Michael (Joshua) Manley, Leader of the Peoples National Party, with HIS IMPERIAL MAJESTY HAIL SELASSIE, are in Power and Authority to Lead the People of Jamaica into Righteousness, Freedom and International Peace.

This willnot be an easy fight: But we have Won already, because we have God fighting with us to Establish a New World Order, making PEACE in the earth, hence to us God said, "Thou art my battle axe and weapons of war; for with thee will I break in pieces the Nations, and with thee will I destroy kingdoms". Jer. 51. 20. Therefore we are not, coming to the nations, with Violence neither are we coming with Guns and Swords. But in the Power of God. "For the Weapons of our warfare are not Carnal, but mighty through God, to the pulling down of Strong holds". 2 Cor. 10. 4. (Even the Strong holds of Politics in Jamaica) which destroy the Moral of the Youths of this country with Legalized Gambling, and have Jamaica and her people to become like the rest of the Nations which know Not God.

The Bible said, "Righteousness Exalted a Nation, but Sin is a Reproach to any people."
Because of Bad Leadership, Jamaica has become the Victim of Destruction: To free Jamaica from Reproach of Sin, we must do the work of Reconstruction; in other words, Build Jamaica a NEW JERUSALEM, A HOLY CITY.

POLITICS AND RIGHTEOUSNESS

Some may say, "How can Politics and Righteousness work together, and how can the SONS OF GOD (PEACEMAKERS) Join up with the PEOPLE'S NATIONAL PARTY?
But it must first be understood that many were called but few were chosen. Therefore, we with them, and the Co-operation of ISRAEL'S GOD and KING OF KINGS OF ETHIOPIA, will easily Solve all Jamaica's Problems and bring back the former Peace we once enjoyed here in Jamaica. TOGETHER we will work to Build Jamaica a NEW JERUSALEM —THE HOLY CITY: A Paradise of Truth and Everlasting Peace.

DELIVERANCE THROUGH MICHAEL

Political deliverance can only Come to the people of Jamaica, through MICHAEL JOSHUA MANLEY and none other, according to Daniel's prophecy.
"And at that time shall Michael Stand up. (As He is now Standing to deliver the poor)

The Great Prince which Standeth for the Children of thy people: and there Shall be a time of Trouble, such as never was Since there was a Nation even to that same time: and at that time thy People, shall be delivered Every One that shall be found written in the Book". Dan 12. 1. So, make sure your names, are written in MICHAEL'S BOOK: Meaning 'VOTE' for Him, AS GOD'S APPOINTED LEADER.

We have Suffered Death, and Imprisonment, for this message of Truth, and No One came to Our Refuge, but Mr. MICHAEL MANLEY.
"But I will shew thee that which is noted in the Scripture of Truth and there is none that holdeth with me in these things, but Michael your Prince. Daniel. 10. 21.

We are,
Sincerely,
The Sons of God (Peacemakers)
With: Rev. C.V. Henry R.B.
Green Bottom Dist.,
Green park P.A.
May Pen
Clarendon Ja.
Nov., 10, 1971.

Printed by "Courier Press", Kingston 10.

The Trinity pamphlet, 1971.

THE TRINITY OF THE GODHEAD (PEACEMAKERS)
SURELY THE SCEPTRE, THY ROD AND STAFF OF POWER SHALL COMFORT ISRAEL AND BRING PEACE TO THE WARING WORLD

Emperor Haile Selassie, the King of Kings and Lords of Lords with His Righteous Sceptre.

"The Sceptre shall not depart from Judah nor a lawgiver from between His feet, until Shiloh (His Imperial Majesty) Come; and, unto Him shall the gathering of the people be." Gen. 49.10

This man is Israel's Returned Messiah, Bearing in His Righteous body the same Spirit which dwelleth in Jesus Christ, two thousand years ago. He has returned to Free the nations, and give Peace to all mankind; Therefore Jehovah has given Him A Kingdom, Second to None in the world, and has made Him Governor among the nations. "For the Kingdom is the Lord's: and He is the Governor among the nations". Psa. 22.28. This, all people should know, and learn to Respect. For God said, "A new thing will I do in the earth." Now the time has come; The perfect Ruler has Returned, and we are Building for Him A New Jerusalem, A Holy City of Truth, "Thus saith the Lord, I AM RETURNED unto Zion and will dwell in the midst of Jerusalem: and Jerusalem shall be Called A City of TRUTH".

Therefore we are building for Him, Here in Jamaica A Righteous Government of Peace, which shall be upon His shoulder.

"For unto us a child is born, unto us a son is given: and the Government shall be upon His shoulder: and His name shall be Called Wonderful, Counsellor The Mighty God, The Everlasting Father, The Prince of Peace." Isa. 9 6-7.

Rev. C.V. Henry R.B. (Repairer of the Breach)

Moses with His Rod of Iron. Jehovah, the God of Moses, has Appointed me to make Peace in the Earth, among the nations; For this Cause, I was made a prisoner, notwithstanding the humiliation and embarrassment which I have suffered for Righteousness, They have left me void of animosity, vindictiveness or hatred for anyone: Now the time for a change has Come. This change will be brought about by Moses, Joshua, and The King of Kings and Lord of Lords, "The Trinity of the God-head:"

This will be the greatest Religious event to take place on earth, since the beginning of the creation of God.

Therefore, I am Calling upon all nations, great and small to get together and make Peace among themselves, this year (1972), before Jehovah God begins to shake mightely the earth.

"See that ye refuse, not Him that speaketh. But now He hath promised, saying, yet once more I shake not the earth only, But also heaven." Heb. 12. 25-27.

Michael (Joshua) Manley The Man Appointed by God, to lead Israel into Canaan, and was Approved of by Israel's God. The King of Kings and Lord of Lord of Ethopia. Before handing him the Staff for Just Ruling, AS it is said of Him.

"The God of Israel said the Rock of Israel spake to me, He that Ruleth over men must be Just, ruling in the fear of God." 2 Samuel, 23.3.

There is no other man, in Jamaica found worthy as a Political Leader, to receive this Honourable Staff of Justice and Power, to lead the people of Jamaica into a Righteous Government of Peace with Security; As Prime Minister, But (Joshua).

Therefore as A Prophet of God, "The Repairer of the Breach", I declare Joshua, an Honest, Upright and Sincere Leader, Approved by God, to lead Jamaica, and Jamaicans into a New Government of Righteousness and Peace

I am therefore calling upon all Sincere people, whether of the Labour Party Government, or of the People's National Party; to give Joshua a fair chance, to prove himself a God-sent Leader, and we with him will build A New Jamaica; because we are all Isrealites and not only P.N.P's or J.L.P.'s every one in Jamaica today needs a change for a Righteous Government. "For when the Righteous are in authority, the People Rejoice, But when the Wicked beareth Rule the People Mourn". Pro. 29.2.

Are you an Isrealite? If you are, Then are we Sons of God (Peacemakers). Let not Politics separate us from the Kingdom of God, which we are now Building.

HIS IMPERIAL MAJESTY, MOSES AND JOSHUA «THE TRINITY OF THE GODHEAD» MAKING PEACE

REV. C. V. HENRY, R.B.,
GREENBOTTOM
GREEN PARK, MAY PEN
CLARENDON
JAN. 17, 1972

Printed by "Courier Press", Kingston 10.

The Trinity pamphlet, 1972.

25 South Camp Road
Kingston 16
Telephone: 82628

MICHAEL
MANLEY

14th June, 1971.

Rev. Claudius Henry,
Ground Bottom P.O.

Dear Rev.Henry :

Further to my letter regarding the Central Kingston
Annual Conference, please let me know whether it would
be possible to have The Peacemakers all day.

Kind regards.

Yours sincerely,

Michael

Correspondence with Michael Manley, June 1971.

OFFICE OF THE PRIME MINISTER

P.O. BOX 638,

KINGSTON, JAMAICA.

1st May, 1972.

Dear Rev. Henry,

Thank you for your letter of March 20, in which you raised the matter of Joseph Hay.

I have asked the Hon. Noel Silvera, Minister of Home Affairs and Justice to investigate.

I must apologise for the delay in replying but I have been deluged by mail and it has been quite a job to tackle.

Thank you for your prayers for me and my Government for, as you well know, we have a formidable task before us if we are, as you say in your letter, to govern "the people in Righteousness and to make Jamaica a paradise of Peace and Love".

My continued good wishes to you and your Brethren,

Yours sincerely,

Michael Manley
Prime Minister

Rev. C. V. Henry, R.B.,
President,
The International Peacemakers' Assoc.,
Green Bottom,
Green Park P.A.

Correspondence with Michael Manley, May 1972.

OFFICE OF THE PRIME MINISTER

24 EAST RACE COURSE

P.O. BOX 638

KINGSTON, JAMAICA

5th March, 19 73

Dear Reverend Henry,

Thank you very much for your letter of February 26th.

I am delighted to hear of the opening planned for
April 28th, and think that the picture of the house 'Bethel' is very
beautiful. My wife and I are very sorry that we will be unable to
attend because of a very important previous commitment. However,
we are arranging to be specially represented by Senator The Honourable
Dudley Thompson.

We will certainly do what we can to assist you in your
desire that His Imperial Majesty should be present.

With my warm regards,

Yours sincerely,

Michael Manley

The Rev.C.V. Henry,
The International Peacemakers Association,
Green Bottom,
May Pen

Correspondence with Michael Manley, March 1973.

OFFICE OF THE PRIME MINISTER
1 DEVON ROAD,
P.O. BOX 272,
KINGSTON 6, JAMAICA

January 8,   19 74

Dear Claudius,

I was delighted to hear that you have agreed to help Ruddy Lawson in his campaign and even more delighted to hear that you have already started to do so.

As you well know, Western St. Catherine, particularly the two Old Harbour Divisions, is very crucial in the parish to ensure that we control the Parish Council, so that you can easily see that your valuable help is extremely important.

I remember with great pleasure the recent lunch with you and the very important discussions which we had. It is a source of regret to me that because of the extreme pressure on my time I cannot meet with you as frequently as I would like to. I do hope that there will be an opportunity in the near future for us to have another such session.

Best of luck to you and Ruddy Lawson and God bless yo

Yours sincerely,

MICHAEL MANLEY

Rev. Claudius Henry,
Green Bottom,
May Pen P.O.,
CLARENDON

Correspondence with Michael Manley, January 1974.

Naming Names

JUST MONTHS PRIOR TO THE 1980 CHANGE IN GOVERNMENT IN BOTH Jamaica and the United States, and as the Cold War raged on Latin American and Caribbean soil, the American Louis Wolf "outed" fifteen Central Intelligence Agency (CIA) agents working undercover in the U.S. Embassy in Jamaica during a press conference held at the Pegasus Hotel in Kingston.[1] He accused the CIA of undermining the elected socialist government of Jamaica and supplied biographical information about the agents he named. The list of outed agents included Richard Kinsman, whom the *Covert Action Information Bulletin* (*CAIB*) had also previously identified as the chief of station in Jamaica.[2] The *Covert Action Information Bulletin* was a periodical Wolf founded in 1978 with Ellen Ray, Bill Schaap, and Philip Agee, the former CIA agent who had spent the better part of the 1960s working to subvert left-leaning movements throughout Latin America. Wolf's belief was that these agents were conducting operations in Jamaica on a similar scale, and with similar intentions, as had happened in Chile prior to the ousting of Salvador Allende in 1973. His agenda was, in part, to "name names," to identify those working under the cover of the U.S. State Department or the U.S. Agency for International Development (USAID) to thwart and discredit regimes seen as threatening to U.S. economic and geopolitical interests.

Three days after Wolf's press conference, the *New York Times* reported that Kinsman's Cherry Gardens home was attacked by gunmen in the middle of the night.[3] According to the reporter, three men opened fire from .45 caliber weapons on Kinsman's home from a distance of one hundred feet; twenty bullets hit the house, and two went through an open window. Kinsman's wife and children were not home at the time of the alleged attack, and Kinsman did not initially call the police, who were summoned the next morning by neighbors when Anne Williams, Richard Kinsman's household helper, found shells in the yard. He did, however, call the *Gleaner*. The article concluded by stating that Wolf had named Kinsman in a press conference earlier in the week as a CIA operative. For Wolf, the attack on Kinsman's home was a cover-up orchestrated by the CIA to build a case against Wolf's project of bringing covert action out of the shadows of night and into the light of day. Why was Kinsman's first move not to call the police but to notify the *Gleaner*? Why was his family conveniently not present? Why was no one ever arrested or charged? While we cannot fully know the answers to these questions, we do know that Wolf's press conference did ultimately result in new legislation regarding national security and the protection of agents' identities in the United States.

As with the attention to William Macmillan's and Katrin Norris's engagements with Jamaica in the first interlude, the purpose of the excavations presented here is to think through what a later outside observer might tell us about shifts in sovereignty during the postcolonial period and about Jamaica as a key site in relation to knowledge production about political economy and social life in the Western Hemisphere. Wolf's attention to Jamaica reveals a shift from the anticolonial moment's focus on land reform and development to the intensity of U.S. interest and surveillance during the height of Cold War empire building.

LOUIS WOLF, BORN ON HALLOWEEN 1940 TO A WELL-TO-DO BUSI-ness family in Philadelphia, was raised a Quaker. I met with him on 7 December 2014 in Washington, DC, where he has lived much of his adult life, and he described his political trajectory over coffee. Drafted in late 1963, he became a conscientious objector and joined the International Volunteer Services (IVS), a precursor to the Peace Corps. With the IVS, he worked in Sam Tao, Laos, teaching English to Hmong nurses working in a clinic at the end of the runway managed by Operation Brotherhood, a CIA proprietary. The clinic itself was treating people who were brought in on Air America, the CIA-owned airline, during the U.S. government's secret war against the Lao

Communist Party. From October 1964 to April 1967, Wolf also worked with peasants digging wells and cultivating rice, but "his anger grew as the daily barrage of napalm and B-52 blockbusters brought rural Laos into the war in Southeast Asia and blew off the map the villages [he] had worked to build."[4] He moved to the Philippines to do graduate study in international rural development, but he did not finish his degree because he became active in the antiwar movement there through an organization called Concerned Americans Abroad.

In the Philippines, Wolf co-founded an antiwar newspaper, *The Whig*, that "maybe had ten issues," he said, and was written by allies inside the Air Force who exposed covert activities on the part of the military. For example, his reporters wrote about the U.S. Air Force police who were running a death squad at Clark Air Base, which, he said, was the staging point for a lot of the bombing of Vietnam. Wolf stayed in the Philippines until 1972. He was arrested several times at the U.S. Embassy and once at Clark Air Base. He was taken to Philippines military headquarters, where he thought he would be tortured and put to death, but after five days he was released. He then traveled to London, where he spent five years working with the dispatch news service at the headquarters of Amnesty International, after which point he returned to Washington, DC.

In the inaugural issue of the *CAIB*, Wolf and the other editors explained their position on publicly naming covert operators. "We do not believe that one can separate the dirty work of the CIA from the people who perform it," they wrote:

> The exposure of past operations is valuable, but it is only half the job. How many times have we all heard the CIA, the FBI and others say, whenever a particularly nasty covert operation has been exposed, "Oh yes, but we don't do that anymore." We believe that they do, and that the same people are often involved.
>
> As a service to our readers, and to progressive people around the world, we will continue to expose high-ranking CIA officials whenever and wherever we find them.[5]

This mirrored the position of Philip Agee, whose book *Inside the Company* (1975) was geared toward exactly this kind of exposure. In a later essay, "Destabilization in Jamaica," he wrote, "By ripping away the CIA's mystery and secrecy, always a needed source of strength, and by laying bare its people and its operations, the socialists whom the CIA was trying to defeat gained in strength."[6]

Agee, born in July 1935, was recruited to the CIA in the late 1950s and began working in Latin America. After some years, he became disillusioned with the operations he and his colleagues were conducting and began publicly arguing that the work of the agency could not be separated from the general social and economic conditions of the countries in which they were operating. Agee came to feel that the CIA's training of police and military forces, as well as other forms of U.S. support, gave "the ruling minorities ever stronger tools to keep themselves in power and to retain their disproportionate share of national income." Moreover, he wrote, "Our operations to penetrate and suppress the extreme left also serve to strengthen the ruling minorities by eliminating the main danger to their power" (Agee 1975: 503). Agee thus came to the conclusion that the CIA was operating in the interests of American businesses rather than Latin American masses. This is the point at which he decided to begin exposing patterns of CIA operations and to work with revolutionary organizations to help give them the tools to defend themselves.

Agee exposed CIA plots to overthrow governments in Ecuador, Ghana, Guatemala, Guyana, Iran, Sudan, Syria, and Zaire between 1950 and 1975. In *Inside the Company,* he wrote about CIA efforts to bring in repressive regimes in Greece and to destabilize the Allende government in Chile, establishing instead a military junta that subsequently massacred tens of thousands of people. He revealed the CIA's involvement in the 1965 coup in Indonesia that removed Sukarno from power and led to the slaughter of at least 500,000 people; he uncovered the CIA-arranged assassination of the Dominican dictator Rafael Trujillo and its prevention of the return to power of the liberal Juan Bosch; and he exposed the CIA's funding and direction of the failed invasion of Cuba at the Bay of Pigs (Agee 1975: 8–9). On 16 November 1976, after his return from Jamaica, where he outed ten agents at a press conference, a deportation order was served requiring him to leave England. In 1978, he went back to Jamaica with Louis Wolf, Bill Schaap, and Ellen Ray, and they launched the *CAIB.*

THE COVER OF THE DECEMBER 1979–JANUARY 1980 SPECIAL ISSUE OF *CAIB* features a photograph of Michael Manley and the headline "Michael Manley: Under Attack Again." Several articles lay out the case for U.S. destabilization during Manley's second term as Prime Minister. Ellen Ray outlines the campaign of misinformation that accompanied the appointment of Ulises Estrada, the Cuban ambassador who arrived in Jamaica July 1979. She argues that spurious allegations by people outside Jamaica that Estrada was an intelligence officer only served to support Edward Seaga's claims that Cubans were, at the time, "infesting" Jamaica.[7] And Fred Landis, a Chilean-born American psychologist who did his doctorate on psychological war-fare and media ops in Chile in 1970–73, made the case for the replication in Jamaica of the CIA-sponsored media assault that helped to oust Allende in Chile.[8] Landis identifies how the Inter-American Press Association (IAPA) influenced reporting in the *Gleaner* in ways that were directed at influencing (and toppling) Manley's government.

The IAPA started at the instigation of the U.S. State Department through the American Society of Newspaper Editors in 1926 as the first Pan-American Congress of Journalists. During World War II, the association counteracted pro-Axis propaganda in Latin America, but, Landis argues, the IAPA's "stock theme" would develop later: "to warn that 'freedom of the press' is threatened in whichever corner of the world U.S. influence is on the decline."[9] Contend-ing that the list of IAPA presidents and board members reads like a roster of CIA agents, Landis dates IAPA influence on the *Gleaner* to 1968. "Consistent with the pattern of CIA-inspired destabilization efforts against the Jamai-can government, especially beginning in late 1975," he wrote, "Oliver Clarke, *Daily Gleaner* chairman and managing director, was duly promoted in 1976 to IAPA Executive Committee membership. The scale of anti-Manley propa-ganda in the *Gleaner's* pages escalated sharply."[10] Manley's government was positioned as a threat to freedom of the press; the links between Manley and Castro were emphasized; and difficulties in the economy were foregrounded.

The August–September 1980 issue of *CAIB* continues with its reporting on the negative media coverage of Manley, arguing that the *Gleaner* diatribes were "deliberately directed towards creating disaffection and mutiny within the security forces, openly encouraging the overthrow of the government."[11] The editors again compare the situation in Jamaica with the media to Chile, and they describe assassination attempts. These attempts on Manley's life were also the subject of an essay by Ernest Volkman and John Cummings that appeared in the December 1977 issue of *Penthouse*.

In that essay, Volkman and Cummings laid out a case for destabilization that began in 1974, after Manley announced he would follow a program of democratic socialism. At that point, they argued, Henry Kissinger (then the U.S. secretary of state) began lobbying President Gerald Ford to authorize a covert operation that would oust Manley and install a regime friendlier to the United States. They report that in the fall of 1975, Ford gave the order to CIA Director William Colby to "handle it" and conclude that when all was said and done, "The CIA was directly involved in at least three assas-sination attempts against . . . Michael Manley, Prime Minister of Jamaica."[12] They also note that Kissinger was angry that Michael Manley had welcomed a delegation from Angola and that he supported Cuba's military involvement there in the fight against South Africa. During a visit to Jamaica in December 1975, he urged Manley to back away from democratic socialism, from his friendship with Fidel Castro, and from his position of leadership within the International Bauxite Association (IBA). Despite continual denials of U.S. attempts to destabilize Manley's leadership, immediately after Kissinger's visit observers in Jamaica noticed an increase in the U.S. Embassy staff; Jamaica was denied a request for a $2.5 million loan from USAID; and, by early 1976, aluminum companies had begun to dump large quantities of bauxite on the world market to depress prices.[13]

Volkman and Cummings also argued that during that period, the United States began to capitalize on political violence and partisanship. "Shipments of guns and sophisticated communications equipment began to be smuggled into the island," they wrote. With the CIA gunrunning and the importation of CIA-trained Cuban exiles into Jamaica, violence escalated wildly in early 1976.[14] In May 1976, anti-Manley gunmen took over a tenement yard in Kingston and set it on fire, refusing to allow residents to leave, and by 19 June, Manley had announced a state of public emergency that lasted until after the elections. In September 1976, Agee visited Jamaica at the invitation of Dennis Daly, then chair of the Jamaican Council for Human Rights. Agee gave many public speeches during the two weeks of his trip, repeating the same themes during every radio and television program on which he appeared: "The American government, through the CIA and other agencies, seemed to be engaged in a broad campaign to squeeze the Jamaican economy and create popular discontent, and through propaganda and political violence to create such a climate of fear and tension that voters would turn to the conservative Jamaica Labor Party for relief."[15] During a press conference toward the end of his trip, Agee also named eleven covert CIA agents working in the U.S. Embassy, revealing their cover positions, their previous assignments, their local residences and telephone numbers, the types of cars they drove, and their license plate numbers. After his visit, "three of the eleven agents he named hurriedly left the country, but on the next flight down to Kingston, the CIA flew in five new agents."[16]

After Manley's reelection, according to Volkman and Cummings, the CIA reorganized its station in Jamaica to focus on economic discontent among middle- and upper-class Jamaicans. Agee recounts the continuation of U.S. pressure on Manley through Andrew Young and others, propaganda through the *Gleaner* and other media outlets, and the encouragement of sedition within the security forces.[17] Manley's speech in defense of the Cuban military presence in Africa during the Conference of Non-Aligned Nations in Havana in September 1979 prompted President Jimmy Carter to cancel some

$10 million in projected food aid for Jamaica. And a few weeks after Wolf's press conference, the former CIA officer John Stockwell—who had served in Vietnam and who was the chief of the CIA's secret intervention in the Angolan Civil War during 1975–76[18]—also conducted a speaking tour throughout Jamaica. "As with Landis and Wolf," Agee wrote, "Stockwell's trip . . . received wide media coverage and contributed substantially to the continuing efforts to expose American efforts to defeat Manley and the PNP."[19] On 4 November 1977, a cable was sent from the U.S. Embassy in Kingston to the U.S. State Department about Volkman and Cummings's story.[20] Not long after, Volkman, who had a thirteen-year history of reporting on national news for New York's *Newsday*, was reassigned to the Long Island aerospace beat.[21] How did the U.S. government get to the point of active destabilization and assassination attempts in Jamaica?

ON THE EVE OF JAMAICA'S INDEPENDENCE, U.S. VICE-PRESIDENT Lyndon B. Johnson was briefed on the importance of his attendance at the independence ceremonies. "Our political objectives with regard to Jamaica are the following," his briefing paper outlined:

1   To see independent Jamaica, through the maturity of its political leadership, become a stable, progressive, democratic state, friendly to the United States. Such a state, led by a responsible government, should be an example to other governments in the area and hence, become an element of stability in the Caribbean.

2   To encourage the present government to continue its resolute anti-Communist policy, with particular reference to neighboring Cuba.

3   To stimulate efforts on the part of Jamaica to widen and deepen its Caribbean inter-area arrangements, bearing in mind that the concept of a West Indies Federation is now dead.[22]

The problem with Jamaica, as the United States then saw it, was that the legacy of slavery created a negative association with hard work. Unemployment, illegitimacy, and overpopulation were also perennial U.S. government concerns. The U.S. government's strategy for the transition to independence (and therefore to the U.S. sphere of interest) thus was "to help Jamaica attain economic viability and to improve social conditions," and to move the country toward "full participation in the inter-American system through the OAS [Organization of American States]."[23]

Beginning in early 1967, the United States began paying greater attention to the details of Jamaican politics, in part because of increased violence leading up to and following the elections that resulted in a Jamaica Labour Party (JLP) victory under Donald Sangster. The 1967 elections also shifted the balance of political power in West Kingston from the People's National Party (PNP) to the JLP, as JLP candidates won a number of constituencies traditionally considered PNP areas. By 9 March 1967, telegrams from the U.S. Embassy to the Secretary of State were reporting on flare-ups of gang-based political violence in West Kingston that left several dead and numerous structures damaged by fires. They also noted that police moved a one hundred-man mobile reserve "into temporary encampment in Denham Town area of West Kingston."[24] U.S. personnel were clearly aware, as well, that politicians were involved in these emergent patterns of crime and violence: "In the warfare between political gangs preceding the elections, politicians issued arms to criminal elements supporting the respective gangs. Those elements began using the arms in criminal ventures. . . . Politicians seemed unable or unwilling to control those elements."[25]

Once Sangster became ill in late March 1967, the U.S. State Department began worrying about who would take over the JLP, with Hugh Shearer, Robert Lightbourne, and Edward Seaga emerging as the main candidates. State Department officials described Seaga as "coldly calculating as well as efficient" and stated, "Those who know him have no doubt that Seaga, if not assassinated beforehand, will eventually lead the JLP and the nation." At that point, however, they believed Seaga wanted to bide his time and build a power structure first.[26] They were concerned about losing Sangster, who was respected by both the JLP and the PNP, and having the party's leadership shift to "personalities" such as Seaga. They saw this as a "chilling prospect to a large number of 'thinking' Jamaicans," in part because of what they apprehended as Seaga's tendency toward "going-it-alone."[27] They argued that this inclination "derive[d] from the egotism, and the aggressiveness, deep in the Jamaican character. . . . Clearly a policy of this sort has unpleasant implications for the United States."[28]

Soon thereafter, the State Department also had the PNP leadership to wonder about as Norman Manley began to prepare for his retirement, which he formally announced in July 1969. Michael Manley was understood as the "leading candidate for the job," and at that point, U.S. intelligence assessed him as a pragmatic leader who would work to rejuvenate the party after the election loss that February. "With pragmatism in the saddle," Deputy Chief of Mission David Wilken wrote, "the exponents of doctrinaire socialist policies have faded quietly in the background." The problem, as U.S. officials saw it at the time, was that the PNP hadn't attracted as much young leadership as the JLP had, and that "there were better opportunities afforded by the loose personalistic structure of the JLP than by the well defined pyramid of the PNP organization."[29]

Of course, the principal motivating concern underlying U.S. interest in Jamaican politics was bauxite and alumina, of which Jamaica supplied 65 percent of U.S. imports, as well as other private U.S. investment in the country (which then totaled about $200 million but was projected to double). Jamaica's strategic location—in other words, its proximity to Cuba—was also a key factor in U.S. attention to its domestic stability and development progress.[30] American officials did not share the British view of Jamaica as a racially harmonious paradise. Instead, they worried about social tensions they understood as rooted in slavery and British imperialism, and they understood these tensions as deriving from "racial and economic disparities."[31] Because they felt racial tensions could lead to political unrest, they were attentive to the various forms of Black Power that were emerging in Jamaica and throughout the Caribbean, just as they were attentive to civil rights and Black Power struggles in the United States.[32]

For example, U.S. intelligence prepared long and detailed internal security reviews of Walter Rodney a couple months before the October 1968 protests of the Jamaican government's refusal to allow him to land upon return from the writer's conference in Montreal. These reviews outlined Rodney's education, political networks, and interactions with different groups of Rastafari, including Reverend Claudius Henry's Peacemakers. U.S. reviews of Rodney were skeptical about his ability to successfully mobilize Rastafari, however. They felt Reverend Henry was "probably being used by RODNEY merely to provide a ready made following and it is unlikely that he has any use for HENRY in any other respect, apart from his potential as a continuing source of annoyance to the Jamaican Government."[33] More generally, they reported that Rodney's "wooing" of Rastafari was "without success":

> They listen to his views and give him the respect due to a man of learning, but seem unwilling to accept him as a leader. Nevertheless, he continues to cultivate them. He is seeking support also from the underprivileged youth of Kingston. Recently he has sought the support of the "Vikings[,]" a gang of violent robbers, thieves and bully-boys active in Kingston and at one time 50 strong. . . . [The gang] has been used before to provide "strong arm boys" by aspiring politicians and it is probably this aspect of its proclivities which attracted ROD-NEY's attention. . . . He has also tried, so far without success, to arrange a meeting between the Vikings and C. V. HENRY.[34]

Broadly speaking, U.S. intelligence was well informed about the different active groups of left-leaning and racially conscious political and cultural organizations, both those based at the University of the West Indies and those rooted in communities near the university and downtown, and the State Department was interested in the extent to which communists and Black Power activists might come into greater alignment. "While Communism is not particularly significant in Jamaica and has never really gained much ground (partly due to the religious and agrarian conservative orientation of most Jamaicans and to their general suspicion of foreigners and alien ideologies)," one analysis revealed, "it is always possible that a black power apparatus could be taken advantage of by a Communist group. Dr. Munroe openly advocates communist revolution in Jamaica through black power."[35]

Racial and economic disparities were understood by U.S. intelligence to exacerbate political partisanship and therefore to lead to political violence. Just as U.S. officials were aware of the different organizations of black leftist mobilization, they were also well versed on the forms of political clientelism that were intensifying during that period, as is evident from the following analysis of political discrimination in employment: "Under the Seaga/Tavares system, no 'outsiders' can be employed on public works. Pressures are also being levied on the large employers to hire the 'proper' people . . . Traditionally, only 60–70 percent of the public jobs were reserved for the party faithfuls, but now the JLP is more methodical and ruthless in its approach to such problems."[36] U.S. policy objectives, therefore, were geared toward seeking Jamaican support for U.S. anticommunism positions in the region and beyond and toward ensuring the "steady evolution of Jamaican participation in the political, economic and social, and security institutions of the Western Hemisphere."[37] In 1967, these objectives would be met by continuing to facilitate Jamaican emigration to the United States, supporting the expansion of Jamaica's family-planning program, investigating the potential of increased royalties and taxes for bauxite, increasing earnings from tourism, helping with education programs, constructing ten thousand low-cost housing units, strengthening the Jamaica Constabulary Force through training in civil disturbance control and antiterrorist activities, helping to develop joint Jamaica Constabulary Force–Jamaica Defence Force internal security actions and surveillance systems, and developing the leadership to have "more awareness of the free world outside Jamaica, and of its modern ways, and more appreciation of how much the U.S. does to keep that world free and make it modern."[38] That these remained the core objectives of the United States regarding Jamaica until the early 1970s, and that this was primarily motivated by interest in bauxite and other economic investments, was made clear in communications between the U.S. Embassy in Jamaica and the State Department.[39]

As Guyana began moving toward nationalizing its bauxite industry, how-ever, concerns were raised by U.S. officials in Jamaica. While they felt that Prime Minister Shearer was willing to work with U.S.-owned bauxite com-panies, they also knew that Shearer and others in the Jamaican government felt that if Forbes Burnham were successful in obtaining a controlling inter-est in bauxite for the Guyanese government, Jamaica would be pressured to follow suit.[40] In July 1970, Ambassador Vincent de Roulet, whom Manley would later expel from Jamaica, proposed a renegotiation of the agreement between the Jamaican government and the American companies in order to permit greater equity in the industry for Jamaica and to "stave off a national-ization problem."[41] He further proposed that the State Department agree to fund Shearer's reelection campaign. Arguing that his continued leadership was in the United States' best interest, Shearer had asked the ambassador for something in the ballpark of a million to a million-and-a-half dollars.[42] Viron Vaky, the acting assistant secretary of state for inter-American affairs, advised Henry Kissinger, then the U.S. national security adviser, that this proposal should be rejected. He argued that "the implication that such aid could buy a bauxite arrangement is particularly dangerous," and that "there is no threat which would warrant this kind of delicate involvement or expense." While "Shearer may be friendly to the US," Vaky continued, "his likely election op-ponent does not appear to be a threat and CIA thinks it's a Tweedle-dee/ Tweedle-dum electoral prospect."[43]

Tweedle-Dum, in this case, was Michael Manley, and as the 1972 elections drew nearer, the U.S. State Department began considering the implications of a PNP win. A general intelligence report from the embassy informed the State Department that the PNP had absorbed several radical groups over the previous year, one of which was the International Peacemakers Associa-tion.[44] However, embassy officials were more concerned with criminal gangs of youth than they were with left-wing and Black Power groups, whose in-fluence they felt had declined. They reported that while the two parties had similar roots in the trade union movement, and while the differences be-tween them weren't overly stark to that point, the PNP tended to be more committed to ideologically driven planning, and the JLP lacked a strong po-litical philosophy and was more pragmatic in nature.[45] Nevertheless, U.S. of-ficials did not anticipate any major change of course, with the exception of a greater risk of the diplomatic recognition of Cuba. After his victory, Manley dispelled this concern by assuring the ambassador that he had no intention of establishing diplomatic or trading relations with Cuba until U.S. restrictions were no longer in effect.[46]

By the spring of 1974, therefore, U.S. intelligence officials felt they had good leverage in Jamaica, despite Manley's changed position on Cuba. "We appear to be in a strong position with respect to Jamaica," they wrote. "The country badly needs receipts from U.S. tourists, U.S. economic assistance, and the large U.S. market for its bauxite. Although the United States currently relies on Jamaica for about half its bauxite supply, interruption of this trade—either temporarily or for a protracted period—almost certainly would hurt the Jamaicans more than it would us."[47] By this time, Manley had begun agitating for a 51 percent share in mining and alumina facilities and a gradual repurchase by the Jamaican government of some of the 230,000 acres of bauxite-rich land that had been purchased by the American and Canadian companies. While officials within the U.S. State Department were especially alarmed by Manley's plan to build bauxite smelters, they were still convinced that "a specific threat of hostile action, however, probably would dissuade Jamaica from a strong nationalistic course."[48]

After Manley imposed a tax increase on the bauxite companies, tying it to the posted price of aluminum, Jamaica's bauxite revenues were projected to increase from $25 million to about $165 million.[49] Officials with the CIA believed the companies would accept Manley's demands because they would pass the increased cost to their clients and because they "would be highly reluctant to abandon all or even a significant share of their [$]850 million investment stake in Jamaica."[50] Manley's subsequent organization, with seven other bauxite-producing nations, of the IBA, however, was apprehended by U.S. government officials as a cartel along the lines of the Organization of Petroleum Exporting Countries (OPEC). The seven countries in the IBA—Jamaica, Guyana, Suriname, Guinea, Sierra Leone, Australia, and Yugoslavia—accounted for 75 percent of bauxite production globally and 68 percent of commercially exploitable reserves.[51] With Manley's announcement in November 1974 that Jamaica would follow a program of democratic socialism, both the bauxite companies and the U.S. government became less sanguine, and the CIA began reporting on Manley's "messianic commitment to bring about the social and economic assimilation of the black masses" which, they argued, had "pushed him steadily leftward."[52]

A March 1976 memo reported on Manley's conviction that the status quo in Jamaica had become untenable.[53] While State Department officials seem to have concurred on this point—giving as evidence "the attitudes of the new generation: the intelligent, educated young people are typically revolutionary radicals; many of the less fortunate, jobless and hopeless, expend their energies in criminal and violent action"[54]—they were concerned about Manley's personalistic style (and his "love for political rough and tumble"), and his "paternalistic political morality."[55] Intelligence agents saw Manley as capitalizing on left-leaning domestic and global developments but didn't believe he shared "the unalterable enmity his youthful advisers feel toward the US," and they felt that his "mind [was] not closed to a productive alliance with Washington."[56] They saw him as imperious and impatient, and therefore also vulnerable to pressure by those more radical than him. And they were concerned that his pursuit of egalitarianism "made him something of a moral crusader—who sees the world in terms of good and evil—rather than the wily, calculating politician. This messianic zeal makes him, like the ideologue, less pragmatic and hence less predictable."[57]

Of course, the U.S. government was also concerned about Manley's connections with Castro, about his creation of a self-defense force within the PNP after outbreaks of political violence in West Kingston in January 1976, about what they saw as his inability to "rein in" his Minister of Housing Anthony Spaulding, about his relationship with the left wing of the party, about the possibility that he would break the terms of agreement with the International Monetary Fund in the face of pressure from an increasingly economically depressed population, and about his lack of public denunciation of the accusations that the JLP was receiving CIA funds to overthrow his government.[58] U.S. representatives, however, do not seem to have responded to these concerns in one voice.

On one hand, in 1976 the embassy seemed to have been on board with what may have been part of a media-destabilization campaign, writing to the secretary of state that it had been "informally and confidentially approached for information on sources of assistance to Jamaica," including Cuba and the Soviet Union, in order to support a series of newspaper articles "designed to put into favorable perspective U.S. and other Western world assistance."[59] On the other hand, a 1978 USAID document argued that because Manley had "to deal with radical elements within Jamaica's political spectrum" and "maintain his credibility as a leader of the Southern bloc," he would sometimes take public positions that did not support immediate U.S. interests.[60] The author continued that these "tactical political requirements" should not "disturb the elements of our long-term assistance strategy when they merely irritate us, and do not threaten major U.S. interests.[61] By August 1980, however, the intense political violence between rival gunmen of the PNP and the JLP had become dire, and U.S. intelligence became focused on street warfare, the weapons trade, and anti-U.S. propaganda.[62] The 1980 elections, of course, were the bloodiest in Jamaica's history, with more than eight hundred people dying during the campaign season. This is the context into which Wolf walked in July 1980, and it is the context that continues to frame U.S. interest in political and drug warfare in Jamaica, as well as Tivoli Gardens community members' experience of this warfare.

PRIOR TO 1975, THERE WAS NOT MUCH PUBLIC INTEREST IN THE identification of undercover CIA officers. Until that time, the protection of national security information was covered through the National Security Act of 1947, which said:

> Whoever, having or having had authorized access to classified information that identifies a covert agent, intentionally discloses any information identifying such covert agent to any individual not authorized to receive classified information, knowing that the information disclosed so identifies such covert agent and that the United States is taking affirmative measures to conceal such covert agent's intelligence relationship to the United States, shall be fined under title 18, United States Code, or imprisoned not more than ten years, or both.[63]

However, as the Vietnam War came to a close and in the wake of the ousting of Chilean President Salvador Allende, a Select Committee to Study Governmental Operations with Respect to Intelligence Activities, headed by Senator Frank Church, was established to investigate U.S. government intervention overseas and, in particular, the role of the intelligence services.[64] The Church Committee placed the CIA under public scrutiny as never before. However, the exposures of Agee, Wolf, Stockwell, and others like them prompted the CIA to fight back. After Richard S. Welch, the CIA chief in Athens, Greece, was killed in front of his home, Lloyd Bentsen introduced new agent identities legislation in the Senate in 1975.[65] While the bill did not move very far at that point, interest in it was revived after the Kinsman kerfuffle in Jamaica.

On 2 February 1981, Senator John Chafee introduced S-391, a bill to amend the National Securities Act of 1947 to make it a crime to release the names of CIA agents working undercover, and on 23 September 1981, the House of Representatives passed the Intelligence Identities Protection Act by a vote of 354 to 56, with twenty-three abstentions. This led to the passage of Public Law 97-200 by the 97th Congress on 23 June 1982, which was signed into law by President Ronald Reagan. The new language put forward through this law criminalized the disclosure of information by persons "in course of a pattern of activities intended to identify and expose covert actions" [c].[66] The opposing votes in the House and the Senate were all democrats, among them Senators Joseph Biden, Gary Hart, and Daniel Patrick Moynihan, who took issue with the vagueness of the language. What would constitute a pattern? they wondered. And how would one glean intent? In an op-ed in the *Christian Science Monitor*, Biden criticized the proposed law as harmful to national security, not because it would allow for federal prosecution of those "who deliberately impair American intelligence operations," but because it could hinder "the efforts of legitimate journalists to expose any corruption, malfeasance, or ineptitude occurring in American intelligence agencies" [67] Remember the context for this concern: Watergate was brought to light by journalists, and journalists had also exposed U.S. covert actions in Brazil, Chile, the Congo, Cuba, and Guatemala, as well as operations such as MK-ULTRA and Operation Phoenix and a variety of assassination attempts.[68]

Wolf's own response to this law asked how the "intent" of journalists would be determined and whether a series of critical articles on the CIA would be considered a "pattern of activities"?[69] He, among others, pointed out that if journalists were prosecuted for researching or writing an article whose purpose were to disclose even one name, it would be a First Amendment violation. The proposed legislation thus constituted an attempt to pass an official secrets law. Others agreed with this argument. Joseph Lerner, editor of the *Washington Book Review*, wrote, "Although proponents of the bill insist that they only wish to punish 'non-mainstream' writers such as Louis Wolf, the language of the proposed law in no way distinguishes between so-called mainstream and non-mainstream journalists. Nor is there a constitutional way to do so."[70] Lerner also interviewed Wolf, asking why he thought CAIB was being singled out. Here is Wolf's response: "I can't believe that four people in a small office in the National Press Building in Washington, DC could be such a tremendous threat to an organization with a multibillion dollar budget, 30,000 employees, and the unlimited resources of the government. It is obvious that the CIA wants to widen the wall of secrecy that has always surrounded it since its inception in 1947."[71] Despite Wolf's conviction that the CIA must be accountable for what the organization does in the name of U.S. taxpayers, and his insistence that "as Americans, it is our right and duty to stand up and say this is wrong, particularly when it involves covert action around the globe," after the new law was passed, the editors of CAIB announced that, although they would continue reporting on the covert activities of the U.S. government abroad, they would have to stop naming the names of individual agents.[72]

Deemed threats to national security, Wolf and Agee suffered individual consequences for the work they did. Wolf was prevented from entering the United Kingdom, and Philip Agee's U.S. passport was revoked in December 1979 while he was in West Germany. Agee filed suit against the secretary of state in the U.S. District Court for Washington, DC, arguing that the revocation of his passport violated his Fifth Amendment right to criticize the government. He won on a technicality, but the case raised an important question that would eventually be taken up legislatively, which was the extent to which "the constitutional right of an American citizen to travel abroad must inevitably compete with the broad power of the national government in the international agreement" (Lessne 1981–82: 450). Agee eventually made his home in Cuba, dying there on 7 January 2008.

Wolf would continue his work through other fora. In the wake of demonstrations in Panama against the continued existence of the School of Americas in 2009, he testified in the Federal Court of Columbus, Georgia, pointing out that the school had trained more than 64,000 Latin American and Caribbean "soldiers in combat skills, sniper training, counter-insurgency techniques, use of advanced combat arms systems, commando tactics, and psychological operations."[73] The school was established in 1946 to train militaries throughout Latin America, but these militaries ultimately were turned on their own citizens rather than on external threats. Wolf also testified that the Office of Public Safety (OPS) was established in 1957 by the CIA "to do for foreign police personnel what the School of Americas did for the militaries in the southern hemisphere."[74] Working formally under the cover of USAID, he argued, the OPS trained more than a million police officers in a variety of techniques, including assassination (this operation was called Operation Phoenix).

The Intelligence Identities Protection Act (IIPA) hasn't been mobilized frequently, as the Espionage Act has a broader purview (Szilagyi 2010). In the twenty-first century, the act came back into more general consciousness when a journalist publicly identified Valerie Plame as a covert CIA officer in 2003. The only other time someone was charged under the IIPA was the 1985 prosecution of Sharon M. Scranage, a former CIA agent posted overseas who leaked the identities of certain CIA case officers to her boyfriend, Michael Soussoudis, who was a suspected Ghanaian intelligence agent (Szilagyi 2010: 2282). Scranage pleaded guilty, so courts have not been able to comment on the effectiveness of the IIPA.

IT IS NOT INSIGNIFICANT THAT WOLF'S PRESS CONFERENCE IN Kingston occurred as the drug trade and drug war were both intensifying through the transnationalization of alliances between governments, leaders within downtown "garrison" communities in Kingston, and regional traffickers. By the mid-1960s, the export of ganja to the United States was a multimillion-dollar-a-year business (Campbell 1987: 111), and by the early 1970s, the pressure was on Manley to stem this trade.[75]

After President Richard Nixon established the Drug Enforcement Agency (DEA) in 1973, the United States embarked on a massive program to eradicate supply, and in 1974, at the request of Manley and his Minister of Security Eli Matalon, the DEA implemented Operation Buccaneer, a program by which the agency would use military and paramilitary powers—both American and Jamaican—to disrupt the cultivation, merchandising, and smuggling of ganja (Campbell 1987: 113).

Operation Buccaneer was lauded by DEA officials and politicians alike as a huge success. By 14 December 1974, agents had seized 730,000 pounds of ganja, an additional 8,083 pounds of ganja seeds, sixty-five pounds of hashish, and twenty pounds of cocaine. They also confiscated eleven weapons, ten aircraft, seventeen vessels, and more than $143,000; arrested ninety-eight defendants; and destroyed more than five hundred acres of ganja (Sears 1975: 115). Operation Buccaneer also marked several "firsts: " It was the first time the DEA operated a fixed-base sea and air unit in a foreign country, at the invitation of that country; the first time it transported and installed an entire communications system; the first time the U.S. Coast Guard participated in a DEA operation, performing intelligence and interdiction functions; and the first time a foreign narcotics task force had the cooperation of the U.S. Department of State and U.S. Department of State Agriculture, USAID, the U.S. Embassy, the Coast Guard and Customs Service, and the Army, Navy, and Air Force (U.S. Government 1975: 440–41; see also Sears 1975; Vance 1975). Since that time, the United States has provided more counter-narcotics assistance to the government of Jamaica than to any other country in the Caribbean (Jones 2002: 125).

While Nixon's War on Drugs had originally focused on war veterans and substance abuse, and had included a comprehensive program for treating addiction, by the 1980s and 1990s the emphasis of the war had shifted to American security concerns, with funding for treatment programs falling by the wayside. The eradication of the drug trade has subsequently justified U.S. political and military intervention throughout the Western Hemisphere, and we might therefore see the U.S. involvement in the 2010 "Tivoli Incursion" as an attempt to enforce American drug policy. In her analysis of the 2010 events and their aftermath, Madeleine Bair (2011: 12) has argued that if we don't connect the story of Jamaican garrisons and the story of American drug use, "then America can continue to deny its responsibility" for the civil unrest in West Kingston and for the technologies through which it occurred.

It is exactly this kind of linking that Wolf was encouraging in the late 1970s and beyond.

WHILE WILLIAM MACMILLAN AND KATRIN NORRIS WERE REPORTing from Jamaica at the end of the British Empire, Wolf gives us insights regarding U.S. notions of national security and rights toward the end of the Cold War in the midst of American empire. Jamaica, here, emerges at the center of a number of perceived threats to internal security in the United States—drugs are one; communism is another; and, insofar as it might destabilize U.S. economic interests through its relationship with Marxist radicalism, black nationalism is another. What Jamaica teaches Wolf, and us via Wolf, is that U.S. political and military interest is never unitary and seamless; that different government agencies or officials can hold wildly different assessments regarding the parameters of necessary action and probable threat; that there is a certain predictability regarding the primacy of naked economic interest; and that there is no liberal democratic configuration in which rights are ontologically held. Instead, they are always contingent on economic and geopolitical strategic interest.

Chapter 3

PARANOIA

AS WE SAW IN CHAPTER 2, THE VARIOUS ITERATIONS OF RASTAFARI IN Jamaica have become emblematic of a radical rejection of the status quo, a classic Romanticist critique not only of capitalist Enlightenment—which, in the Caribbean, ended up taking the shape of plantation slavery—but also of mainstream anticolonialism, with nationalism instead being envisioned as the racist continuity of an oppression that began with the forced removal from Africa, and therefore producing the longing for return, physically and spiritually. This has been true even as a look through newspaper and colonial surveillance archives make it clear that contemporary peasants and workers in the communities surrounding Rastafari camps often expressed some degree of ambivalence regarding the practices they saw, heard, and experienced. Nevertheless, the dominant contemporary approach to Rastafari has placed it at the center of black peoples' struggle for sovereignty. Rastafari, in this view, appears as an expression of black knowledge and politics, a nexus of cultural autonomy and self-determination, in the face of persistent racial bias in the postcolonial era. Rastafari, for scholars and activists alike, tells us something about the faulty logic of the "Out of Many" basis for citizenship that characterized the 1962 moment of independence, and thus also about the excesses of the immediate postindependence security concerns as they related to black Jamaicans.

I am wondering, however, what would happen if we placed the livity of Rastafari in relation to a different set of concerns. Rather than positioning Rastafari as vanguardist in relation to liberal *nationalist* critiques of personhood, governance, and citizenship, what might we glean if we placed public and colonial discourses about Rastafari in relation to broader *imperial* transitions? It is my contention in this chapter that by foregrounding views of the colonial state toward Rastafari during the 1950s—views that were by no means unitary, based on information that was not always clearly circulated—we can see how centrally the Cold War—and in particular, U.S. anticommunism stemming from the Cold War—shaped the experiences of and possibilities for sovereignty during the 1960s. Witnessing 2.0, in this case, means mining early newspaper accounts and colonial records of the emergent movement, as well as later surveillance reports from the "migrated archives" in the United Kingdom, to elucidate a transition in the approach toward Rastafari on the part of the colonial government due to both local events (the "Henry Rebellion" of 1960), and conflicts elsewhere in the British Empire (the Malaya "Emergency" of 1948–60 and nationalist violence in Cyprus throughout the 1950s). Security concerns related to the effect of black radicalism on Jamaican nationalist consolidation became entangled with, and were eventually enlisted in the service of, security concerns related to the effect of communism on imperial control. Paranoia, palpably, became the dominant affective register for these concerns, and security and surveillance were the technologies through which it was circulated.

The Oxford English Dictionary defines paranoia first as a "mental condition characterized by delusions of persecution, unwarranted jealousy, or exaggerated self-importance, typically worked into an organized system," and second, as "unjustified suspicion and mistrust of other people." In the first case, paranoia is a psychological symptom of a chronic personality disorder, of drug abuse, or of a more serious mental illness such as schizophrenia. In the second, it is a more generalized problem of perception. In both cases, it marks an intensification of a state that might otherwise be identified as anxiety, which is defined as "a feeling of worry, nervousness, or unease about something with an uncertain outcome." While we can certainly read anxiety (in relation to specific events or people) throughout the colonial archives, what draws me to paranoia in considering the late colonial and early independent periods in Jamaica is the sense of infrastructure undergirding the first definition. The "organized system" here is one that was generated to uncover and diffuse potential solidarities along the lines of race (both intensified racial consciousness locally, and transnational alliances with African

Americans and others) and potential solidarities between radical labor politics and radical racial politics, as well as the potential "spread" of radical counterinsurgency movements from location to location throughout the empire. By the time bureaucratically managed British colonial paranoia gave way to its somewhat more disorganized and nervously reactive American version, the "organized system" was also meant to protect U.S. economic interests overseas through the active destabilization of anything resembling Marxist-inspired thought or action.[1]

Indeed, my attention to Rastafari in this chapter is mainly as a foil to discuss the effects of an intensifying concern with anticommunism that began in the late 1940s and grew throughout the 1950s, one that produced Rastafari no longer merely as a racialist nuisance to the local elite but as a primary threat to the security of the Jamaican state as the result of purported or potential alliances with leftist political organizations, alliances that were nevertheless often rejected by Rastafari themselves. As a result of this emergent paranoid preoccupation on the part of the colonial state, one supported by post-1952 U.S. foreign policy throughout the Western Hemisphere, neither nationalist organizers nor the progressive left in Jamaica were able to fully recognize the salience of the specificities of racial injustice to the majority of the population during the colonial period.[2] My agenda in this chapter, therefore, is to elucidate the pervasiveness of overt and covert external intervention as part of the infrastructure of decolonized sovereignty in order to make a case for paranoia as the dominant affective sphere characterizing this period. It should be said that this paranoia was not always unfounded, as it was true that alliances were being made, broken, and remade throughout this period among and between a variety of organizations as they sought to build political space for themselves within and against the logics of colonial dehumanization.

This story of the 1950s—as one in which security (in relation to communists, Soviet sympathizers, and agitators for racial justice) emerges as the paramount problem of late colonialism—is one to which we can now bear witness in part because of the public release of the "migrated archives" from the Foreign Commonwealth Office (FCO) at the National Archives at Kew. These archives, which were released in the third tranche in September 2012, contain, among other things, monthly reports from the Local Security and Intelligence Committee (LSIC) for Jamaica for the period 1957–62.[3] But this story of the 1950s is also available to us at this juncture precisely because of the "failures" of both official nationalism and the more radical and leftist alternatives to nationalism that were imagined and, to a degree, implemented after the 1960s moments of independence and Lewisian develop-mentalism. By using the word "failure" here, I do not mean to adhere to the tragic reading of our postcolonial present (though one surely could), but instead to redirect our attention away from the anticipatory, triumphalist, and teleological narratives that often pervade discussions of constitutional decolonization.[4] What I want to argue in this chapter is that, despite the many immediate pressures that influenced British imperial policy, we need to see the United States as fundamental to the reorganization of sovereignty in the British West Indies after World War II. In Jamaica, this reorganization was crucially located within two spheres—intelligence gathering, and labor mobilizing—and it necessitated a restructuring of both of them.

On one hand, then, this chapter's discussion of paranoia centers on the emergent intelligence infrastructure of the LSICs and the more organized communication of intelligence related to anticommunism more generally, including British surveillance of organizations such as the People's Educational Organization (PEO) and the People's Freedom Movement (PFM), both founded after the expulsion of the left from the People's National Party (PNP) in 1952. On the other hand, it explores how political developments in Jamaica were influenced by American intervention in the local trade union move-ment, which I chronicle through an investigation of archives developed by U.S. government agencies, such as the U.S. Agency for International Develop-ment (USAID), the National Security Council, and the Central Intelligence Agency (CIA). Trade union intervention was something that also occurred after the 1952 split in the PNP, and that was initially geared toward protect-ing the U.S. interests in the emergent bauxite industry, but it was framed in relation to the broader post–World War II U.S. labor ideology of promot-ing antitotalitarianism and anticolonialism (Windmuller 1963). Ultimately, this would lead to the appointment of a labor leader, William C. Doherty, as the first U.S. ambassador to independent Jamaica, and to the establishment of social programs—such as the construction of low-cost housing in Kings-ton slums—under the aegis of the American Institute of Free Labor Devel-opment (AIFLD), led by Doherty's son, William C. Doherty Jr. Of course, these two phenomena (the development of a more uniform and bureaucratic intelligence infrastructure and the intensifying influence of American labor on Jamaican politics) are not unrelated. Moreover, their entanglement fun-damentally shaped the way Jamaica was to emerge on the scene of indepen-dent nations as a country tightly harnessed not only to Britain through the Commonwealth, but also to the United States through the penetration of Jamaica's most important channel for political expression.

BEFORE HENRY, THERE WAS HOWELL. LEONARD PERCIVAL HOWELL began preaching the new doctrine of Ras Tafari in St. Thomas and downtown Kingston as early as 1933, after his return to Jamaica from New York.[5] Members of the press and of the Jamaica Constabulary Force (JCF) immediately took notice, asking "the authorities to bring the activities of those who preach Ras Tafari in Jamaica to an end."[6]

Local business and clerical elites soon also became concerned about the emergent "cult" of Rastafari. Here is an example: on 23 January 1937, Vivian Durham, writing on behalf of the Kingston and St. Andrew Civic League (KSACL), petitioned Governor Sir Edward Denham, urging him to take action against the "blasphemous and indeed sacrilegious movement" of Rastafari.[7] Durham's letter, which was also published in full in the *Daily Gleaner*, argued that the movement threatened "to resurrect the causes which led up to the unfortunate Incident of 1865 by the abominable doctrine of SKIN FOR SKIN AND COLOUR FOR COLOUR being inculcated in the minds of the Ignorant and hot-headed masses of this Colony who for the most part can be easily driven to any extremes at the present time oweing [*sic*] to the evils of unemployment and privations."[8] The letter continued by elucidating elements of the doctrine of Rastafari as the KSACL saw them, including the view of His Imperial Majesty (HIM) Haile Selassie as the returned Messiah, the "propagation of racial hatred and prejudice" as a result of the Italo-Ethiopian War, the condemnation of Christian practices, and "the wicked Idea that there is an unholy conspiracy between church and state and capitalists in the country which is responsible for their poor condition." This last point, Durham argued, was a teaching "as dangerous as that of Soviet Russia," and the view of the league was that this kind of ideology would harm the progress of the island and would produce mental illness among its followers who, in the opinion of the KSACL, were generally ignorant and susceptible to duping at the hands of charlatans attempting to exploit their vulnerability.

After the KSACL letter was published in the *Gleaner*, Altamount Reid, Philip Walker, and R. N. White, officers of the Ethiopian King of Kings Salvation that was founded by Reid in Jones Town in 1936, wrote a rebuttal on 4 February 1937.[9] Their letter was also written to Governor Denham, but in it they stated their desire for a public forum in the *Gleaner*, as well. (There is no indication it was ever published.) The Salvation was particularly exercised by the KSACL petition's reference to the Morant Bay Rebellion, and the letter writers took the opportunity to remind Governor Denham of the political outcome of that event: "We hate to recall the Morant Bay Rebellion of 1865, because as British citizens enjoying years of evolution we are looking forward to the time when the Governor, His Majesty's Representative, will be able to show more appropriate mannerism than that of Sir [Edward] John Eyre, who had to be recalled home."[10] Reid, Walker, and White continued by refuting the KSACL's determination that whatever racialism was being inculcated into the masses—"skin for skin" and "colour for colour"—was necessarily negative. "If this had been the case," they argued, "of the one million two hundred thousand people in Jamaica the approximately eight hundred thousand coloured, or darks or blacks, would be a menace to the minority white." They continued by turning a line of biological argumentation commonly used to buttress racial segregation on its head and by appealing to the Governor's duty to protect all citizens of empire:

> It is a self-evident proof that nature intended various species of things to associate, as to their kind. Hence for the sake of social instinct, the cow is always found with the cow, sheep with sheep, parrots with parrots, pigeons with pigeons, though they are all birds and beasts. Therefore the black or colored man as the white man, has no apology to make if he preaches ratial [sic] solidarity. What Englishman did not feel the onslaught of the Germans in the 1914 to 1918 War? What African whether at home or abroad would not feel the indignity of Italian atrocities in the recent Ethiopian conflict? It is utterly absurd to think that men must be made inmates of the Lunatic Asylum when they are taught to think in terms of themselves. Englishmen thought in terms of themselves hence the Great Empire. Japanese, Germans, Italians, Russians, Americans— all thought in terms of themselves. As British Citizens, we are hoping to have such legislation and laws enacted which will be compatible with our finer feelings as to prevent reprecussion [sic] within the state.[11]

While neither the Governor nor the colonial secretary seems to have responded to Reid, Walker, and White, in a letter dated 11 March 1937, Colonial Secretary J. D. Lucie-Smith did acknowledge receipt of Durham's January missive. He assured the KSACL that "the Government is considering the enactment of legislation to prohibit the practices of these curious cults."[12] However, no official action against Rastafari was taken at that time by the colonial government.

Here is a second example. In May 1936, Elder V. R. Cameron, pastor of the Church of God at Font Hill, complained to Governor Denham that "hard working and very law abiding" people in Cedar Valley, St. Thomas, were being pressured by the movement, echoing the concerns expressed in numerous newspaper reports throughout 1934 and 1935 regarding harassment, noise, children being removed from school, people abandoning their provision grounds to await the expected repatriation, and the cultivation of racial hatred.[13] In response, Acting Colonial Secretary A. R. Singham wrote, "The Government is not prepared to interfere in the matter."[14] In fact, despite Howell's sedition trial in March 1934 and his sentence to a two-year term in the asylum, despite ongoing coverage in the media of the activities of Ras Tafari in St. Thomas, Portland, and Kingston, and despite the continuous detaining of followers of Rastafari on charges of disorderly conduct and ganja possession, the colonial government maintained a position of noninterference during the early years. As far as the Colonial Office was concerned, extensive police action in St. Thomas had brought Rastafari activity "to a standstill in that parish," and therefore the "movement has lost very considerably in members and influence and at present need not be seriously regarded."[15] Moreover, the inspector general wrote, letters such as Cameron's and others within Kingston's corporate community were "merely the airing of imaginary grievances and fears by . . . high coloured folks. I feel certain that the white population have nothing whatever to fear."[16]

After the region-wide labor rebellions of 1937–1938, both reporting in the *Gleaner* regarding the activities of Rastafari and notices within the records of the Colonial Office became considerably less frequent, with a brief uptick of interest during the Moyne Commission's visit. This West India Royal Commission, named for its chair, Lord Moyne, was appointed to investigate the causes for the rebellions, and to make recommendations regarding social and economic reform. During their visit to Jamaica, they were invited to walk through the slums of western Kingston where many Rastafari were resident at the time, which is what generated journalists' attention.[17] By 1940, however, as Britain was attempting to get the United States to join the war effort against Nazi Germany, two new lines of attack against Howell and Rastafari were pursued.

The first was locally rooted. It was spurred by concerns from representatives of the Ministry of Health in St. Catherine whose attention was drawn to Howell's camp at Pinnacle in late November 1940 when nineteen adherents were sent to the Spanish Town Hospital for treatment and were admitted to the poorhouse. Three days later, two medical officers made a surprise visit to Pinnacle to examine the housing and sanitary conditions within the community. They reported that the wattle-and-daub dwellings of the two hundred-odd persons living in the area known as East Avenue were sufficient, that the four four-seater latrines were fly-free, that the water supply (taken from the Rio Cobre) was clean, that there was good drainage, that "light, ventilation and general sanitation are satisfactory," and that residents cultivated crops in the fields. "The discipline is excellent," they reported. "There were no complaints and all were willing to be examined and advised." This team, however, also noted that undernourishment prevailed and that "the need for food relief is urgent."[18] The "acute starvation" they noted was likely what prompted people to seek help at the hospital, and ultimately, eight of those nineteen who were admitted to the poorhouse died of malnutrition and complications related to it.[19]

This situation was publicized in the *Gleaner*, and by January 1941, the commissioner of police had been in touch with the director of medical services regarding sanitary conditions at Pinnacle.[20] The medical officer and inspector of police subsequently visited the camp, reporting that the living conditions "of the inmates" were unsatisfactory, that "when food was distributed, the stronger ones deprived the weaker," and that "they were all armed with sticks, obviously with the intention of scaring off visitors."[21] These observations, as well as the eight adherents' deaths, were used by the Parochial Board of St. Catherine to try to force the director of medical services to intervene by asking the government to charge Howell with criminal negligence. However, a solicitor sent to investigate the case responded that "no legal liability can be attached to the Ethiopian Salvation Society as far as your Board is concerned."[22] Malnutrition, it was argued, "might be result of ignorance and not neglect."[23]

The second line of attack against Rastafari, and in particular Howell, was rooted in the renewed attention to the group on the part of an "increasingly repressive" colonial state (Palmer 2014: 241).[24] In April 1940, the new Governor, Sir Arthur Frederick Richards, wrote to Secretary of State for the Colonies Malcolm MacDonald outlining continued activity on the part of the Ethiopian Salvation Society and his attempts to stop the group's meetings. He specifically detailed one meeting at Port Morant, which, he wrote, was attended by approximately five hundred people. Howell, Richards recounted, "informed the crowd that the white man's time was ended and that soon black men would sit on the throne of England; further that Hitler was in charge of Europe and that all European powers would be overthrown in 1940, and that at the end of this war the white nation would be utterly exterminated."[25] Richards was concerned about the "racial feeling" aroused during these meetings, and saw this as "prejudicial to the public safety." As a result, when he learned that Howell was planning another meeting, and upon hearing that men were to arrive armed with sticks and cutlasses, he resolved to prohibit that and any subsequent meeting in accordance with the state of war emergency that had been issued on 24 August 1939 by Colonial Secretary A. G. Grantham. It was ultimately the war, then, that generated a more sustained onslaught on Pinnacle, culminating in the raid on 14 July 1941 during which 115 police were dispatched to capture Howell and round up his followers.[26] During this raid, seventy people were arrested, and 101 ganja plants were removed from a field close to Howell's residence. The police commissioner reported that the raid "has undoubtedly had a good effect and was very popular with the surrounding inhabitants, and it would appear that a certain amount of terrorism which had been exercised by members of the Camp has been to a considerable extent broken."[27]

DURING THE WAR, NEW SECURITY MEASURES WERE FORMALLY OUTlined with the passage of the Defense Regulations Act in England in 1938, and its extension to the colonies in 1939. This act "allowed the arrest and detention of individuals who allegedly engaged in acts prejudicial to public safety or the security of the realm" (Palmer 2014: 231) and provided the grounds for censorship of the press. Governor Richards, who was brought from Fiji to take over from the deceased Governor Denham, mobilized these regulations enthusiastically, taking even more stringent measures in Jamaica than those being applied within Britain itself, even as the act was being decried by British citizens. In August 1939, for example, all street meetings were banned throughout downtown Kingston, a ban that was "directed at 'gatherings for singing and drum beating . . . with cult leaders in the front line'" (Palmer 2014: 240). Leaders of the nascent trade union were similarly being harassed during this time, and their meetings were attended by members of the JCF, who then reported the content of speeches and the reactions of the crowd to colonial authorities.

Nevertheless, outside of a four-part series on "Ras Tafarianism" in February and March 1943 in *Public Opinion*, the weekly newspaper published by the PNP between 1937 and 1974, there was limited reporting on Ras Tafari during or after World War II and up to the 1954 raid of Pinnacle, which ultimately devastated the commune and dispersed its members to Kingston and other areas of Jamaica.[28] There has been speculation as to why, after the considerable public anxiety concerning the movement in the early days, there would be such a dearth of interest as the country moved toward constitutional reform and the establishment of full internal self-government. That Pinnacle by that time had developed an industrial-scale trade in ganja would make the seeming decline in public interest even more baffling.[29] Frank Jan van Dijk has argued that while heightened suppression during the war may have been the primary cause of the reduced public activities of Rastafari, it is also possible that the rise of trade unions and political parties, as well as the achievement of universal adult suffrage in 1944, may have diminished the movement's political role among some lower-class Jamaicans.[30] "Rastafari," he writes, "had temporarily succumbed to repression and the rise of party politics" (Van Dijk 1995: 69).

Again, this proposition is especially important to consider if we understand Rastafari less as the purest and most powerfully resonant expression of a counterhegemonic worldview than as one among a number of alternative visions for the future that circulated among working-class and lumpen Jamaicans, articulated an analysis of their social position, and elaborated both the history behind it and a way out of it.[31] However, what I want to argue here is that the period between 1945 and 1954 marks a critical shift in approach to Rastafari on the part of the colonial government because it also marks the beginning of Jamaica's entrance into what would become its most crucial transnational commodity trade at the commercial level—bauxite—and therefore also an intensification of Jamaica's position within the U.S. sphere of interest during the early years of the Cold War.

IN DECEMBER 1942, A REPRESENTATIVE FROM THE DUTCH BILLITON company traveled to New York City and Washington, DC, to report that commercial quantities of bauxite had been discovered in St. Ann, Jamaica, on land belonging to Sir Alfred D'Costa, "from whom Billiton had obtained a concession of 3,900 acres" (Post 1981: 2:346). Walter Rice, the vice-president of Reynolds Metals, wrote to U.S. Secretary of State Cordell Hull to impress upon him that this discovery was "vitally important to the industrial future of our country and our national security" (quoted in Munroe and Bertram 2006: 79). Prior to 1940, the United States was purchasing bauxite from Alcoa, the Canadian company that had a monopoly on bauxite mining up to World War II. But because demand increased with the war, and with the establishment of antitrust legislation, R. J. Reynolds and Kaiser also entered the market (Sheller 2014). Reynolds had been mining in Arkansas, but the reserves there were buried deep into the ground and were of a relatively low grade compared with bauxite they were able to obtain through Alcoa from Guyana and Suriname. With German U-boats penetrating the Caribbean Sea, the United States had an interest in obtaining supplies of bauxite closer to the mainland; therefore, the discovery of six hundred million tons of reserves in Jamaica provided a convenient source for both Reynolds and Kaiser (Girvan 1971, 1976).[32]

I have already written in these pages about some of the vectors of U.S. engagement within Jamaica, which emerged with the United Fruit Company and the development of a global banana and tourism industry at the turn of the twentieth century and developed socially, economically, and politically throughout the twentieth century. We know that during World War II, the United States emerged from its Great Depression–era isolationism and developed anew its political stake in Caribbean futures by signing the Destroyers for Bases Agreement in September 1940. Through this deal, fifty U.S. destroyers were sent to Britain to assist that country in the war effort in exchange for ninety-nine-year leases on a range of military bases in the Western Hemisphere, including Trinidad and Bermuda (with smaller bases in Guyana, Jamaica, Antigua, St. Lucia, and the Bahamas).[33] As Steven High (2009: 11) has argued, these bases were represented by journalists as signs of American hypermodernity, in contrast to "picturesque British colonial outposts," and they gave material substance to the 1904 Corollary to the Monroe Doctrine. They were also targets of anti-imperialist agitation, in part because of the introduction of Jim Crow–style racism through employment and leisure practices, but also because the United States refused to recognize collective-bargaining rights and other forms of trade union activity. Within the context of intensifying leftist trade unionism in Jamaica after the war, as well as growing rumors that to forgive the war debt, the United States would annex the colonies where bases were located, the bases came to symbolize "everything that was wrong with colonization" (High 2009: 116.).[34]

The militarism of the U.S. bases was accompanied by the developmentalism of the Anglo-American Caribbean Commission (AACC), an advisory body that was established in March 1942 in order to coordinate and augment cooperation between the United States and the United Kingdom in relation to social welfare and economic growth. Charles Taussig, president of the American Molasses Company and "brain trust" adviser to President Franklin Delano Roosevelt, was the prime mover here. Having chaired the U.S. Commission to Study Social and Economic Conditions in the British West Indies after the labor riots of the 1930s, Taussig believed that the British colonial government's efforts to improve conditions throughout the islands were insufficient. While one million pounds had been allocated through the Colonial Development and Welfare Act per year, the Taussig Commission reported that only a fraction of the development project proposals submitted were actually pursued, and by July 1942, consuls were reporting "growing unrest in the colonies owing to food shortages and rapidly increasing unemployment" (Johnson 1984: 184). In an August 1944 meeting with Parliamentary Under-Secretary Richard Law of the British Foreign Office, who was visiting Washington, Taussig pointed out that the United States spent much more on social development in Puerto Rico and the Virgin Islands than did the British government in all of its colonies in the Western Hemisphere put together, and that American troops had been thrice invited to suppress riots throughout the region in the previous six months alone (Johnson 1984; see also Whitham 2002). The concern, of course, was that if riots resumed, the security of the U.S. bases throughout the region, as well as emergent economic interests in bauxite, would be compromised.

Hence, the AACC provided a means by which an anxious wartime United States sought to formally influence British colonial policy in the West Indies by pressuring the British government to implement the Moyne Commission's recommendations, especially those having to do with increasing and making more efficient expenditures through the Colonial Development and Welfare Act and—more obliquely—those regarding constitutional transformation. Through these critiques of colonial administration, U.S. representatives to the AACC hoped to alleviate unemployment and therefore prevent renewed outbursts of political unrest akin to the late 1930s labor riots, unrest that in their view might also encourage African Americans in the United States (see Johnson 1984: 182, 184). After 1943, when the Caribbean was no longer an active war theater, the AACC turned its attention to promoting industrialization, trade, and economic diversification, thereby laying "the foundations for the commercial penetration of the British Caribbean" by the United States (Johnson 1984: 192; see also Whitham 2002). And after 1947, with the articulation of the Truman Doctrine, anticommunism became the structuring principle through which this "penetration" occurred, and containment—through overt and covert means—became the central pillar of post-1945 American foreign policy (Fraser 1994).

American anxiety about potentially subversive activity, however, did not begin with World War II. Gerald Horne (2007) has shown that even before the late 1930s labor riots, the U.S. State Department was concerned about the mobilization of potential racial solidarities across borders, solidarities that would undermine not only British colonial security but also U.S. initiatives toward greater economic influence throughout the West Indies.[35] And High (2009) has revealed Americans' concern with a link between radical union politics and radical racial politics, one that would lead them to fire Jamaican union leaders who attempted to persuade the U.S. government to recognize trade unionism and collective bargaining on its bases. Nevertheless, it wasn't until 1943 that Paul Blanshard, consultant to the AACC, was deployed to Jamaica in order to "monitor the political situation" (Munroe and Bertram 2006: 83). The concern of the United States was that the British government wasn't "up to keeping a lid on a vast Empire" (Horne 2007: 33), and this would mean that between 1945 and 1959, the U.S. Consulate in Kingston sent regular dispatches—sometimes as often as three times a week—to Washington regarding Jamaican political developments (Munroe

1992). The United States thus exerted a fair amount of pressure on the British government to ramp up its intelligence and surveillance infrastructures. Calder Walton (2013: 124) has argued that after Winston Churchill's election in October 1951, "It was the special intelligence relationship between London and Washington that guided British colonial security in the early Cold War," both within Britain itself and across its empire. It is clear, however, that U.S. pressure was not the only incentive for the reorganization and intensification of British intelligence. Various insurgencies across the empire created the internal impetus for innovations in British colonial policy related to security.

ON 5 AUGUST 1948, SECRETARY OF STATE FOR THE COLONIES ARTHUR Creech Jones sent a circular dispatch from Church House to all colonial Governors regarding colonial police forces that read:

> You will be aware that in the Federation of Malaya and in Singapore the Governments are at present engaged in the defeat of a determined attempt by organized dissident elements, through a campaign of terrorism and murder, to overthrow established order. In the Gold Coast also public security was seriously threatened earlier this year, and, although the inspiration and motives of the disorders in that territory differed from those in Malaya, there were rioting and destruction of property on an appreciable scale. It is in my view essential that every possible means should be taken to prevent similar happenings in other Colonial territories, and there is much evidence that the sources which have inspired the outbreak in Malaya (and had some indirect responsibility for those in the Gold Coast) are on the look-out for similar opportunities elsewhere. I therefore consider it necessary to ask Governors to take into review the present state of efficiency, in numbers, organization, and equipment, of their Security forces, and to report as soon as possible, indicating any respects in which those forces are not considered to be fully adequate or efficient at present. Such a review should of course take into account the existence or otherwise of intelligence and special branches.[36]

Jones wrote separately to Jamaican Governor John Huggins on 20 August, stating that, while the specifics of guerrilla insurgencies might not be applicable to his context, he should still know what was going on in the larger territories. In this letter, Jones also requested that Huggins send monthly political intelligence reports "with specific reference to communism."[37] While there had been a senior defense security officer for the Caribbean area, this person was withdrawn late in 1947, which meant that the Governor was reliant on the Police Special Branch for political information through its weekly intelligence reports covering political meetings and other gatherings where speeches might be "inflammatory" or "seditious." Huggins's own sense, therefore, was that a British battalion should remain close to Jamaica, that the Special Branch should be bolstered, and that more generally there was a need to "strengthen the sources from which political intelligence is received."[38] The form this strengthening would take in Jamaica and throughout the empire was the establishment of LSICs and the appointment of security liaison officers (SLOs), as well as extensive training schemes for colonial police forces.

The LSICs marked a general expansion of the British Security Service (MI5) within the United Kingdom after 1945, and reports from the LSICs were submitted directly to MI5 headquarters in London (Walton 2013). They were headed by the SLOs, who were appointed by the British intelligence services and who would work with Police Special Branch, the armed forces, and representatives of the administration to generate monthly reports. These reports were to contain information about "typical points" of interest in territories "where no actual state of emergency exists," using headers such as "Communism," "Extremist Nationalism," "Labour and Agrarian Unrest," "Racial, Religious and Tribal Tension," and "Frontier and Border Incidents." Governors were also expected to provide regular intelligence reports to the Secretary of State for the Colonies, and the Colonial Office assumed that without notice to the contrary, the Governor endorsed the conclusions of the LSICs. Where constitutional decolonization was in process, the security and intelligence relationship would be one in which the SLO would manage the relationship between the United Kingdom's security service and the security service of the country in question.[39] Most often, these SLOs were asked to remain in place after independence by the new national governments (Walton 2013: 113).

While there were SLOs in the Caribbean as early as 1951, an LSIC was not officially established in Jamaica until January 1953. It is unclear who the first SLO was, but he was replaced temporarily by M. T. E. Clayton, who had been with the security services since 1939 and had had prior colonial experience in West Africa. Clayton was subsequently replaced in June 1951 by K. M. D. Mills, who had served four years as district security officer in Gibraltar. When Mills went on leave in 1953, Commander F. G. Johnstone stepped in. Johnstone had served in the Navy and also did a tour in security services in Gibraltar. His Jamaica tour lasted until 1956, at which point he was replaced by E. W. Battersby, who had served in the Burma Police, was then posted to the Security Corps Eastern Army, and served afterward in India and Malaya. In July 1957, W. F. Bell was appointed senior security representative in the Caribbean, but he was transferred to Trinidad in November 1957, which until 1960 was seen as the more important post due to its position as the headquarters of the incipient, though ultimately failed, federation. H. D. Eastwood, who had previously served in the Malayan Civil Service from 1946–48, was nominated to take over Jamaica's SLO position in March 1961.[40] What is clear from this list is that the SLOs, as well as Hugh Foot, perhaps Jamaica's most influential Governor, had all seen service in some of the empire's "hottest spots," which suggests that Jamaica was regarded as an area of concern—one imagines due to its proximity to the United States—that required experience with both communist insurgencies and ethnic/racial conflict.

In Jamaica, LSIC reports generally had three headers—"Communism," "Political/Trade Union Activity," and "Rastafari"—and at the end they would report emigration numbers for the month.[41] This was in line with their terms of reference, formally adopted in November 1957:

i   To advise the Governor and Minister of Home Affairs on all intelligence affecting the security of Jamaica, including communism, threats to public order and stability, espionage, sabotage, and subversion;

ii   To keep under review all matters of intelligence policy, including the development of efficiency of the intelligence organization in Jamaica;

iii To define intelligence objectives, as and when considered necessary;

iv   To prepare such intelligence reports and appreciations as may be required by the Governor and Minister of Home Affairs;

v   To prepare a monthly report and appreciation to be forwarded to the Minister of Home Affairs and Secretary of State through the Governor;

vi   To keep under review, in light of the current security appreciations, protective security measures.[42]

Not all Governors seem to have been on board with this new organization of intelligence. Governor Foot, for instance, raised concerns within MI5 by not submitting the LSIC report at the same time as he sent his Governor's monthly report, which included information on internal security concerns. Foot was admonished by representatives of the colonial government for not using "any of the material of the LSIC for the monthly intelligence report, whereas in other territories the LSIC report covers political and all other aspects of intelligence and appears to be either 'rubber stamped' or only slightly amended by the Governor."[43] In his defense, Governor Foot pointed out discrepancies between reality and the perception of the Colonial Office. He argued that there was a need for balanced reporting of internal security threats and that he felt the LSIC reports were overly anxious, that they would provoke the sense within the Colonial Office that there were communists everywhere in Jamaica. He suggested that his own report was more nuanced and could give more accurate contextual information that was needed: "I have previously said and I repeat that I think that the Local Intelligence Committee is a body performing a very useful service, but when it comes to attempting to give to the Colonial Office a balanced picture of the main developments of the month I think that the job should be done by the Governor rather than by a Committee of officials following up detailed lines of enquiry on particular subjects."[44] The colonial secretary appeared to take Foot's side in this matter, in principle, writing that Foot's reports were "in a class by themselves," and that he should not be antagonized. While assistant under-secretary Philip Rogers relayed Wallace's sentiments to Governor Foot, writing that his reports were always "exceedingly interesting, often entertaining, and invariably a pleasure to read," he nevertheless asked him send the reports at the same time from that period on.[45] The intense surveillance of and reporting on the activities of those thought or known to be communists, therefore, won the day, continuing the earlier intelligence concern that had developed during World War II.

BY NOVEMBER 1942, GOVERNOR RICHARDS WAS RECEIVING SURVEIL-lance reports from the police stating that the PNP "had fallen 'under the influence and control and domination of a group of men with avowed revolutionary aims'" (Palmer 2014: 254). Norman Manley himself had learned by 1940 that a segment of the PNP had become interested in Marxism, but he was not overly concerned at that point. The Governor, however, was, and as a result he ordered the Criminal Investigation Department (CID) to make a security list, to keep suspects under surveillance and otherwise follow their actions, and to "view them as enemies of the colonial state" (Palmer 2014: 254). It was this department that monitored political developments in Jamaica until an SLO was appointed.

Richard Hart (1989: 18–19) has written that Jamaica's first "active Marxist" was Hugh Buchanan—who, incidentally, knew Leonard Howell personally—and that Jamaica's first Marxist group, "loosely centered around Buchanan," began meeting in late 1937. Some of the original members of this group were Hart himself, Frank Hill (one of the founders in 1937 of *Public Opinion*), Henry Fowler (one of the founders of the Little Theatre Movement), Cecil Nelson, Wellesley McBean, and, after 1939, Arthur Henry. These men, according to Hart, were definitely anti-imperialist and nationalist, and though they were interested in Marxism as an analytic framework, they were not at that time promoting communism as a mode of economic and political organization. The 1938 labor rebellions encouraged them to imagine that trade unionism might be organized on a much broader scale, and they therefore contacted the Congress of Industrial Organizations (CIO) in the United States for literature. They saw trade union development as a commitment to collective participatory education, and recognizing that the struggle against imperialism had to precede the struggle for socialism, they agreed to mobilize through a multiclass PNP while maintaining their identity as a Marxist left wing within the party. "Members of the Marxist left played a leading part in organizing PNP groups all over the country," Hart (1989: 120) reflected, "but we nevertheless maintained our own organisations within the party." While originally working within one party (the PNP) and one union (the Bustamante Industrial Trade Union [BITU]), conflicts with Bustamante and his paternalistic and antidemocratic methods led them to develop a second union (the Trades Union Council [TUC]), through which they attempted to expand within BITU's strongholds.

The violence associated with these union conflicts, and particularly that accompanying a series of strikes between 1946 and 1948, is what ultimately set the stage for the formal split within the PNP. In part, this split was precipitated by pressure from the *Daily Gleaner*, which reported that the Marxist left had deliberately organized the violence in order to stage a communist coup after the 1949 elections (Munroe and Bertram 2006). Though this pressure was not new—indeed, segments of Jamaican society had always believed the PNP was a communist organization—it continued throughout 1949, and was ramped up after the American trade unions and British Trade Union Conference withdrew from the World Federation of Trade Unions (WFTU). In September 1949, the Jamaican TUC also disaffiliated from the WFTU. Nevertheless, the position of the left within the PNP was strengthened after the 1949 elections, particularly in West Kingston, as Ken Hill took over Bustamante's seat in West Kingston and became the mayor of Kingston. This trend would continue with the internal elections in 1951, at which point ten of the twenty-one members of the new PNP Executive Committee were TUC leaders, with Ken Hill becoming second vice-president of the party (Munroe and Bertram 2006).

These events are usually considered the background to the expulsion of the left from the PNP, as they brought to the fore the ideological conflicts within the leadership that came to a head in 1951 when Thossy Kelly and W. R. MacPherson were brought before a Committee of Enquiry organized by the PNP's Executive Committee. Kelly and MacPherson were under investigation for having announced to a meeting of bauxite workers in Manchester that they had left the TUC and were forming a new union, the National Labour Congress. The charges against Kelly and MacPherson were that, as members of the TUC leadership, they were not to weaken the trade union movement by competing for workers through a rival organization. Their lawyer, Vivien Blake (also a member of the PNP leadership), however, positioned Kelly and MacPherson's actions in relation to a longer frustration with the Marxist faction of the PNP, whom they accused of being engaged in "the dissemination of communist doctrines; the instruction and training of persons in the Party and TUC to follow and carry out the communist policy; and the discrediting of the PNP and its socialist policy in furtherance of communist doctrines," among other things.[46] In the end, Kelly and MacPherson were removed from their offices in the party, and the leaders of the Marxist left within the PNP—Ken Hill, Frank Hill, Richard Hart, and Arthur Henry—were expelled. These four men went on to form the People's Education Organization (PEO), which would become a Marxist body for education and study and would also operate a bookshop (Hart 1989; Munroe 1990). After a split between Richard Hart and Ken Hill in 1953, the former established the People's Freedom Movement (PFM) in 1954 as an election-period pressure group supporting and putting forward progressive candidates in important constituencies. After the 1955 elections, the PFM became a party and established a union, the Sugar and Agricultural Workers Union (SAWU), which was active in the central Jamaican sugar zone, from which many of Reverend Henry's followers came.

While Hugh Buchanan was a member of the PEO and, ultimately, the PFM, he does not appear in the available colonial surveillance records before 1956. In the early years, instead, the CID, in its coverage of purported communists, was preoccupied with Ferdinand Smith and William Strachan, organizers who had been deported from the United States in May 1952 and who began speaking regularly at public meetings in Kingston.[47] One public meeting, held on 11 May and attended by five hundred to six hundred people, called by the Caribbean Labour Congress to protest against a travel ban imposed by West Indian governments against Strachan and Smith, was deemed "the first public Communist meeting in Jamaica, whereat the people were addressed by avowed Communists."[48] In the CID's continued attention to meetings attended by crowds of up to one thousand persons, Strachan was reported to have discussed issues such as racism in the United States, Malaya's insurgency against the British, and the importance of the WFTU. With respect to the latter, he argued that the International Confederation of Free Trade Unions—the grouping formed in 1949 after the departure of Western trade unions from the left-leaning WFTU—"was not a Union for the working class but an organization born out of United States dollars," and that "Russia is the only country for working class people."[49]

Needless to say, the police followed Smith and Strachan closely, noting their communications with people such as Ken Hill and Richard Hart and speculating regarding the possibility of their establishing a Communist Party in Jamaica. The commissioner of police was particularly exercised about a Marxist study group that had been established in Clarendon, warning in a note to the colonial secretary at the end of the CID report of 28 July 1952 that it would take only "a dozen of such study groups to cover the Colony."[50] Later that year, the CID began intensive reporting on meetings of the PEO that took place at their headquarters, then at 64 Barry Street. Of great concern here was the fact that approximately a hundred people regularly attended, "most of whom appeared to be middle class people from St. Andrew and were unknown to our observer who is better acquainted with the residents of Kingston." Again, a note appears at the end of this CID report from the commissioner of police to the colonial secretary. This time, he wrote, "The propagating of the Marxist doctrine in Jamaica is gathering momentum. This is another example of the developing hard core for an all-out Communist effort later on. The persons attending this Occasion were not the driftwood of society, but of middle class stock and accepted intellectuals."[51] By the time Hart and Hill split, there was an SLO in Jamaica, and some of the CID reports suggest sharing the information with him.

There is a gap in the existing archives between October 1952 and January 1956.[52] As reports picked up, they were mainly focused on the weekly meetings of the PFM's Executive Committee, listing the names of those present; describing a pamphlet Hart presented that criticized the government and "pointed out the evils and the good of Socialism";[53] discussing leadership struggles within the PFM (Buchanan handed in his resignation as chairman at the meeting on 15 January 1956); contemplating how to secure funding for their endeavors from overseas; and outlining their not uncontroversial decision to "carry out a strong protest campaign throughout the Corporate area and country parts against the proposed West Indian Federation," or, more specifically, to "oppose Federation of the British West Indies without Dominion Status."[54] The level of detail in these reports would suggest that someone on the Executive Committee was actually working with the Special Branch of the colonial police force, a possibility of which the leadership was not unaware. In fact, in April 1956, there was a report that Hart had received a letter from Janet Jagan, the American wife of Cheddi Jagan, who was ousted from his position as chief minister of Guyana due to his Marxist-Leninist beliefs. Jagan wrote that "there was a supply of small arms and tear gas bombs in Mexico which was originally intended for use in Guatemala," and apparently offered this store of arms to the PFM "if only they could find a means of transporting it."[55] The Special Branch, while trusting its source, was suspicious of this intelligence. Why would Janet Jagan write "that sort of thing on an ordinary air letter card?" they wondered, while also acknowledging that "every effort is being made by the People's Freedom Movement leaders to discover any possible Police Agents amongst their ranks."[56]

After November 1957, Special Branch monthly reports focused on secret meetings of the PFM called by leading members, organizing work PFM members were doing in Hanover and Clarendon, and the arrival of "over 700 copies of various communist publications . . . addressed to the PEO/PFM and members."[57] The SLO began to prepare dossiers on each of the "known" communists in Jamaica, paying special attention to those attending international conferences that might be associated with Comintern or other anti-imperial organizations, to those traveling in and out of Cuba, and to those within progressive student organizations at the University College of the West Indies.[58] By midyear in 1958, LSIC reports documented a membership that was dwindling, a bookshop that was losing money, and the need for a reorganization of leadership. In June, the PEO met at Hart's office, where it was reported that he expressed concern "over the future of the organization which he thought should continue to function as an educational body, but separate and distinct from the People's Freedom Movement . . . , which would concentrate on its political activities."[59] And in August, the Special Branch reported that the PEO/PFM "reached a new level of inactivity." It continued by stating, "As usual this was caused by lack of interest and dissension between the leaders."[60] Something new did begin to attract notice, however, and this was the return of Claudius Henry to Jamaica in late 1957 and the links the Special Branch imagined he was developing with members of the PFM.

IN RESPONSE TO A QUERY BY GOVERNOR HUGH FOOT ABOUT WHETHER there was any intelligence regarding Rastafari, several handwritten and typed notes appear on one of the Colonial Office folders toward the end of 1956.[61] Foot's query was prompted by a letter from Francis Moncrieff Kerr-Jarrett, Custos of St. James, who was concerned about an uptick of Rastafari activity in Montego Bay. Kerr-Jarrett wanted the Governor to procure a denial, from HIM Haile Selassie, that he was the Rastafari Messiah and to ask the editors of the *New Times and Ethiopia News*, the organ of the Ethiopian World Federation (EWF), to stop sending their paper to Jamaica. Governor Foot consulted with advisers within the Colonial Office before addressing the secretary of state. Cecil Juxon Barton, a British colonial administrator who had served as Governor of Fiji in the late 1930s, expressed surprise at the Governor's ignorance and wrote a note to an "M. Phillips (Esq.)" explaining, "I think you will find an amount of material in the Jamaica Intelligence Reports on the Rastafaris."[62] Barton went on to discuss the position of HIM Haile Selassie, noting that he "became something of an emblem of Africa to people of African descent in Jamaica." He also mentioned the EWF and the news of the land grant, as well as the practice of smoking ganja. Both Barton and Phillips advised against banning the EWF's publication on the grounds that such an action would cause more trouble than it was worth, with Phillips expressing the expectation that "Miss Pankhurst [editor of the EWF organ] would relish an approach from the C[olonial] O[ffice] on such a matter and use it to her own ends."[63] Barton concluded his note by writing,

> I have been wondering of later [sic] whether there is not something below the surface in Jamaica, and you will recollect there have been mentions of Communism in the LIC [Local Intelligence Committee] reports which the Governor does not cover in his monthly reports. I do not suppose there is anything of Communism in these Rastafaris as yet, but surely the great wealth and abject poverty displayed in Jamaica are all that is needed for genuine trouble?—[W]e have been taken unawares before in other places. Would it be acceptable to WID [West Indies Department] ... to ask for the LIC to write a paper on these Rastafaris, their origin, objects, etc., as is done in other Colonies?[64]

After receiving the materials, the Governor's response to Phillips noted his agreement that banning the paper would do more harm than good and indicated that he would "explain the position to Kerr-Jarrett when I see him again." This perspective would be in line with Foot's generally measured approach to Jamaica's social and economic realities during his tenure as Governor. Indeed, we should view his assessment of Rastafari as a relatively nuanced, and even sympathetic, one. He concludes his letter to Phillips by writing,

> The Rastafaris have long been a source of some concern and anxiety and those who like to make use of violence have previously attempted to engage the Rastafaris for their own evil purposes. I remember hearing, for instance, that the Rastafaris were brought into the violent strikes which took place at the end of 1950 and early in 1951 just before I came back to Jamaica. Now that we know the local Communist clique is trying to make use of them it is all the more important to watch developments carefully. But it would be a mistake to assume that all Rastafaris are criminals. ... [M]any of them are good and regular workers who respond to fair treatment and sympathetic handling. On the other hand there are pockets of Rastafaris in the slums of Kingston and Montego Bay which seem to be centres of various forms of crime and vice. Certainly the

Rastafaris provide an interesting example of reaction against the normal conventions and they also illustrate a commendable desire to escape from squalor and poverty by evolving some new pattern of communal life. There may well be some good in the Rastafari cult as well as the obvious bad.[65]

Here, Foot, though himself militantly anticommunist, eschewed the unitary and paranoid views of Rastafari that circulated among some elites in Jamaica. In part, this may have been the result of his great respect for scholarship and the arts. Perhaps he had read the anthropologist George Eaton Simpson's pioneering essay published in *Social and Economic Studies* in 1955, which generally presented a sympathetic and functionalist view of Rastafari. Simpson, influenced by Herskovitsian retentionism, understood Rastafari as a "cult" that nonetheless satisfied broader ego needs in relation to the social, economic, and political situation in which practitioners found themselves. In this respect, he would have been influenced as well by the growing literature on messianic movements and "cargo cults" within anthropology.[66] At the time, Rastafari and movements like it were understood as responses to rapid modernization and colonialism and were thought to emerge in relation to the contradictions people experienced due to intensified inequality within moments of crisis, during which charismatic leaders would necessarily have a greater appeal among followers. Today we might understand so-called cargo cults and anticolonial guerrilla warfare as two sides of the same coin, though this was not widely articulated at the time. Nevertheless, while Simpson's early work sought mainly to outline the ideas and practices of Rastafari, he was clearly also interested in the extent to which we might see Rastafari as an example of how subordinate groups acculturated within a context of domination (see Simpson 1955a, 1995b, 1998).[67]

Though Foot may have understood Rastafari as a generally peaceful, millennial group, he was concerned with the possibility of alliances between the Rastafari, trade union leaders, and those oriented toward popular education—in other words, the "Communist clique" to which he referred in his letter to Phillips. Indeed, potential links between the PFM and Rastafari were reported in January 1957 by the police:

Various Trade Unions have used individual Rastafarites as professional pickets and dues collectors, this particularly applies to the Trade Union Congress (TUC) under the leadership of the Hills. . . . During the past year, it has been known that the Communist inspired People's Educational Organisation (PEO) bookshop has imported books for circulation amongst the Rastafarites and overtures to the Rastafarites have been made by the Communist People's Freedom Movement (PFM), both in Kingston and St. James. It is difficult to assess the extent, if any, of PFM success, but it is known that Richard Hart, a PFM leader, defended a Rastafarite leader in Montego Bay and won the case, no doubt gathering considerable prestige.[68]

Kenneth Blackburne, who replaced Foot as Governor in December 1957, followed up on the issue of potential alliances between Rastafari and leftist political activists, but this time as a result of a concern expressed to him by Norman Manley.

"The Chief Minister suggested today that [the] Special Branch should keep a careful eye on the activities of the communists (PFM) in relation to the Ras Tafarians," Blackburne wrote in a note to Secretary of State for the Colonies Alan Lennox-Boyd. "He said that the PFM had moved their headquarters to the proximity of the Ras Tafarian area," the note continued. "He also said, after the riot in the Coronation market, the first person to telephone to him was Mr. Richard Hart."[69] A month later, Blackburne wrote to the secretary again, this time asking him to pass on whatever information he had about the movement.[70] By 1958, the Special Branch had already reported on a 12 January meeting of Rastafarians "at the corner of Spanish Town Road and Chestnut Lane, Kingston" that was presided over by the Reverend Claudius Henry, "an executive of the Ethiopian Movement in New York, who is on a visit to the island." During this meeting, Henry apparently urged those present to continue their loyalty to HIM Haile Selassie and to continue to organize for repatriation.[71] In September 1958, they returned to the issue, reporting that "a man named Claudius V. Henry who sometimes calls himself 'Shepherd'" gave an address at 78 Rosalie Avenue and held a meeting near Mandeville during which "he made an inflamatory [sic] speech concerning racialism." At that point, the Special Branch addressed him as the leader of a new group, the "United Ethiopian Pilgrims Pioneer Movement established for the purpose of uniting all the Rastafarians in Jamaica under Henry's leadership."[72] The question raised was whether the Special Branch should ask the attorney-general to press charges for sedition and the use of inflammatory language.[73]

In his somewhat belated response to Governor Blackburne, Lennox-Boyd included a summary of previous intelligence on Rastafari. He concluded his June 1959 letter to Blackburne by writing,

> After the initial attempt by the People's Freedom Movement (PFM) in 1957 to infiltrate the ranks of the Rastafarites in St. James, Westmoreland and the Corporate Area—which met with little success—there has been little effort by the Movement to pursue its object. It is known that certain individual members of the Cult hold communist beliefs, but the Rastafarites as a group have shown no more interest in the PFM than in the other political parties. Since the

inauguration, in December 1958, of the Progressive Independence Party . . . by H. C. Buchanan, one-time Chairman of the PFM, 2 members of the Cult have been admitted into its ranks with the object of using them to stir the interest of the cultists in the new political party.[74]

It is important to note here that Buchanan, whom you will remember was a member of the PFM and a Marxist, emerges again, as his own individual connections with Rastafari would soon generate suspicion within the Special Branch and the LSIC.[75] It is also important to mention here not only that Lennox-Boyd served as secretary of state in Kenya during the Mau Mau Rebellion (1952–64), but also that the "migrated archives" reveal him as having denied violent abuses and torture of Mau Mau detainees in the rebellion's aftermath and denounced colonial officials who attempted to bring such abuses to light.[76] Given that the Mau Mau were an inspiration to some Rastafari, we might imagine his experience would have colored his view of the brethren.

Aside from this purported penetration into Rastafari by the Jamaican left, the events surrounding Claudius Henry of 1959 and 1960 attracted an intensified interest in the movement on the part of both the Colonial Office and the U.S. Federal Bureau of Investigation (Meeks 2000).[77] In large measure, this was the result of the discovery during the 1960 raid of Henry's compound in Red Hills of the letter addressed to Fidel Castro, stating the community's intention to overthrow the government of Jamaica and turn it over to him as they repatriated to an African colony to spur a liberation movement there.[78] The Governor's own internal security reports also began to focus on Henry during this period. In December 1960, Blackburne linked the "threat" of Rastafari to the intensifying inequalities within the colony. "The Premier and the Cabinet as a whole appear to be fully appreciative of the dangers of the present situation," he wrote:

> In particular, there is at last a general realization that the threat to internal security lies not solely in the Rastafarian movement, but rather in the fact that too many of the population have been "left behind" in the great upsurge of development of the past few years. Many people—from the ranks of artisans upwards—are now enjoying standards of life which were beyond their wildest dreams a few years ago. Middle class housing estates, hire purchase and higher wages have all contributed to an air of prosperity among some people. But, despite all the publicity attendant on the opening of every new factory, despite figures showing the growth in the national income, and despite a fantastic increase in the number of cars on the roads, a sizeable part of the population—particularly in Kingston—are still without jobs, without houses, and without prospects for the future. For many years this lower segment of

the population has based its hopes on political promises at the times of election campaigns; but they now see the gap widening between themselves and the more fortunate members of the community, and they are beginning to lose hope. The sad fact is that the development of industry and the import of capital for housing and other development projects has not kept pace with the rapidly increasing population; and the number of unemployed increases rather than decreases. It is from the ranks of these underprivileged people that C. V. Henry gained such support for his "Back to Africa" movement; it is from these people that the Rastafarians are now gaining recruits; and it is from these people that some minor incident could easily provoke a serious riot in Kingston at any time.[79]

For Blackburne, Rastafari only indexed a broader problem: that of the increased wealth gaps created by economic development measures—through bauxite and tourism—put into place by Norman Manley's PNP. This was a view widely shared among left-leaning Jamaicans, as became clear after the events at Coral Gardens in 1963, when a number of editorials in *Public Opinion* identified economic development as the solution to the millenarian "problem" of Rastafari.[80]

As early as April 1960, however, the Colonial Office recognized that Rastafari posed a more fundamental problem, as the Rastafari focus on repatriation made it more difficult to capture them with developmentalist promises. "They admit no future for themselves in Jamaica and vociferously wish to be sent to Africa," Blackburne wrote. "They have been unmoved by constitutional progress, and are violently opposed to the present Government—or indeed to any established authority."[81] Here, Blackburne clearly identified the issue: he could not diffuse Rastafari by "sociological means" (Van Dijk 1995)—or, in other words, through social development programs—because they were focused on returning to Africa and thus did not see themselves as having a stake in the development of the Jamaican nation. Instead, the government, in Blackburne's opinion, would have to convince the Rastafari "that their faith in a return to Africa is misconceived and that their belief that they will be welcomed on their return by the Emperor Haile Selassie is without foundation."[82]

After the April 1960 preemptive raid of Reverend Henry's compound in Red Hills, there was a long discussion in the LSIC report focused on the question of how the Reverend could have amassed the funds to develop the arsenal that was found during the raid, an arsenal that was "modern, purchased from the proceeds of a series of bank robberies which had been well organized by a black New York policeman" (Lacey 1977: 83):

There is a large question mark in all this—the source of funds to meet the cost of Henry's frequent journeys abroad and of the arms and uniforms with which usually poor people have been equipped. While it is not yet possible to pronounce finally on this it is fair to say that there is no evidence that any external source of these funds which there may be is communist-connected and, indeed, it is possible that this money represents the proceeds of the illicit sale of ganja. Such communist connection with these developments as has come to light has been limited to the fact that Richard Hart and a few other members of the local People's Freedom Movement, but not Ferdinand Smith himself, are known to have some association with Henry, that Henry is being defended at the preliminary enquiry into the charges against him by Peter Evans, a barrister of Irish descent once connected with the Communist Party who was required to leave Kenya some six or so years ago, and that rumour has it that D. N. Pritt will appear for the defence [sic] in a higher court.[83]

In May 1960, during a meeting of the PFM at which Janet Jagan was present, Hugh Buchanan explained the connection between Henry and the PFM. He said that Reverend Henry had come to him after seeing pamphlets regarding the Convention Independence Party (CIP), of which Buchanan was the president, in order to see whether the party would assist the Peacemakers. The LSIC reported that Buchanan said "he had guided HENRY on matters concerning the Church and on his advice HENRY collected £600 from his followers":

> Later, [Buchanan said,] he severed connection with HENRY as he realized that the latter's plans would come to the ears of the Police and there would be trouble. He assured the meeting that at no time did the PFM have any dealings with HENRY or the AFRICA REFORM CHURCH as SMITH had always regarded the Rastafarians as fanatics. BUCHANAN said he had in fact joined hands with HENRY in order to get support for the CIP. (Buchanan's explanation of his connections with Henry agrees with Special Branch reports received at the time.)[84]

While the LSIC seemed certain of the PFM's disavowal of Claudius Henry, it continued to report that "certain executive members of the PFM are of the opinion that the scattered members of the African Reform Church should be encouraged to join the PFM," and surmised that this idea was suggested to Buchanan by Peter Evans. Of additional concern was Ivy Harris, at one time a leading member of the PFM and PEO who was living with her sister in Clarendon, who, according to the LSIC, had developed "an interest in the Cultists."[85] In July, the LSIC report indicated that Ferdinand Smith, then the leader of the movement, stated during a meeting at his house that "the PFM would consider taking over the AFRICAN REFORM CHURCH if HENRY were imprisoned."[86] Governor Blackburne's report for January 1961 continued with this concern. In the report, he turned his attention to the attempt by the PFM to organize in the sugar areas of Clarendon and Westmoreland, the sites of two large estates and factories owned by the West Indies Sugar Company. He noted that a governmental survey confirmed that workers there were experiencing significant hardships, in part as a result of increased mechanization, and argued that this problem should be added "to the hard core of Rastafarians and others in the area, who have always presented a security problem, as representing a focal point of disaffection."[87] Henry, of course, had many followers from Vere and other sugar areas in southern Clarendon; they were part of the "hard core" to which the Governor referred.

In May and June 1961, there was additional communication back and forth about Reverend Henry's American connection, the individuals involved, and a more general concern regarding support from "terrorist" organizations in New York City. The head of the West India Regiment (WIR) also weighed in, discussing a worry about the potential of continued operations on the part of Reverend Henry's followers, and an anxiety that some of his men may have traveled to Cyprus, where Governor Foot had been relocated from Jamaica during a period of intense nationalist and communist struggle that culminated in independence from British rule in August 1960.[88] This communiqué reveals how generally anxious the Colonial Office and Intelligence Services were about insurgent activity throughout the empire at that time.

After the June raids, carried out by a combined force of the police and army, Henry was arrested and subsequently convicted of treason, and was sentenced to ten years in prison. In December, the WIR—having been revived in response to the push for West Indian federation—received intelligence that over the Christmas holidays, Reverend Henry's followers would attempt to carry out armed attacks on the prison to allow their leader to escape. To thwart this possibility, police were ordered to start a number of raids among Rastafari settlements in order to disrupt their plans, and there was discussion about whether Reverend Henry should be moved to Up Park Camp in order to be placed under military guard.[89] In addition, the head of the WIR wrote a letter to Colonel B. Wilson in the War Office, petitioning him for support with arms and other forms of weaponry. "One further point on which I should be most grateful if you could help," he wrote:

Toward the latter part of the Cyprus emergency a splendid new gas was issued under the name "792", now known as "CS." I should very much like to have a supply out here. There is no doubt that this Rastafarian trouble is with us for some time, and if we should be called upon to raid another Camp in circumstances similar to the June episode, then rather than risk injuries to our chaps who would inevitably be invited to accept the first volley, I should like to be in a position first to neutralize the opposition with "792." Could you please look into this and let me know what are the possibilities and how soon we could get supplies. I should like 500 cartridges 1½ inch Anti-Riot Irritant L2A2CS: we have sufficient pistols signal 1½ inch from which they are fired.[90]

The response to this letter came via telegram and stated simply: "First. Much regret unable send you 200 L2A2 CST (729) by air as no civilian company will carry and RAF [Royal Air Force] unable to help. Second. 500 [tear gas] cartridges being despatched by quickest sea route."[91] These cartridges were likely the ones used against Rastafari during the Coral Gardens incident of April 1963.

While there was not a significant and sustained connection between Rastafari and the Marxist left prior to 1960, by 1961 there *were* left-oriented Rastafari interested in Marxism and revolution within Jamaica, and these brethren often found themselves in opposition to those who were more spiritually oriented toward repatriation. The 1961 Mission to Africa strengthened the position of the latter group. However, halfway through that year Hugh Buchanan and Sam Brown worked to draw Rastafari more closely into local politics through Millard Johnson's People's Political Party (PPP). Colin Clarke (2016) has argued that Johnson's PPP eventually became "virtually a front for Richard Hart's PFM," citing a June 1961 LSIC report that chronicled a meeting between the two men, with Johnson asking Hart for advice on how to orient his followers toward Cuban-style socialism. Nevertheless, with the April 1962 elections, Johnson's PPP, which fielded candidates in sixteen constituencies, only won 2 percent of the national vote, and Johnson lost his own race to Minister of Home Affairs William Seivright (Clarke 2016). Brown received fewer than one hundred votes in the Kingston Western constituency he was contesting, and this began Edward Seaga's forty-three-year tenure as member of Parliament for West Kingston.

AS JAMAICA PROCEEDED WITH CONSTITUTIONAL DECOLONIZATION in 1955, a report by Deputy Security Intelligence Adviser C. A. Herbert outlined various new recommendations, such as the addition of a Special Branch representative to St. Elizabeth, Manchester, and Clarendon, parishes important not only to sugar production but also to bauxite mining and transporting.[92] "Labor trouble is not infrequent [in these areas]," Herbert wrote, "and several security suspects reside here."[93] Governor Foot agreed with the recommendations, and added that preparations were being made "for the continuance of the post of Security Liaison Officer at the next stage of constitutional reform."[94]

At that point, the local political leadership, including Chief Minister Norman Manley, had not yet been formally apprised either of the LSICs or of the SLOs. It was not until April 1956 that Governor Foot raised the issue with Eric Battersby, the SLO. He wrote, "We have in mind that well before these constitutional changes are made the Chief Minister should be formally told the functions of the Security Liaison Officer and invited to agree in writing" that the position should continue to exist. Foot's sense was that Manley would comply with this, and indeed he did, subsequently informing the new Minister of Home Affairs W. M. Seivright of the arrangement, but Manley seemed to have resented being pressured to put his concurrence in writing again as the governorship transitioned to Kenneth Blackburne just after the events related to Claudius Henry in 1959 and 1960 and just prior to independence.[95] However, Foot also stated, "We do not think that any reference to the functions and activities of the Security Liaison Officer need to be made in the new Constitutional Instruments." He continued:

> In regard to Police intelligence the situation will of course be different. There will be no question of the records of the Security Liaison Officer being accessible to any Minister (or indeed to the Governor) but the Minister responsible for internal security will be free to call for any Police records which he may wish to see. It is therefore important that the Police records should not include any material which should not be seen by Ministers and it follows that the Security Liaison Officer will not refer any document to the Police unless he is content for that document to be seen by a Minister. We agreed that, with this in mind, it is desirable that the Police in consultation with you should undertake a review of all intelligence and security documents held by the Police so that within coming months all documents which should not be seen by Ministers may be destroyed.[96]

By the time Norman Manley was voted out of office and Jamaica was moving more quickly toward formal decolonization, Governor Blackburne wrote in a memo to the Colonial Office that he had informed Premier Alexander Bustamante and Donald Sangster about the existence and functions of the SLO, and that he had outlined what the relationships would be between U.K. intelligence and the Jamaican Ministry of Home Affairs. He reported that Bustamante and Sangster "welcomed the help offered to Jamaica in this way and there is no question . . . that the S. L. O. will continue to receive the fullest possible cooperation from the new Government of Jamaica." At that point, Blackburne also informed Bustamante and Sangster of the recent appointment of a CIA representative to the U.S. Consulate General in Jamaica.[97]

LET US NOW RETURN TO THE STORY OF BAUXITE. PART OF THE BENefit to the United States of the 1940 Bases for Destroyers Agreement was that, in exchange for air bases in Britain's West Indian colonies, the United States would replace Britain's European suppliers of bauxite. Because aluminum had become crucial to modern warfare, government investment in the industry was substantial, both during World War II and after the Korean War began (Sheller 2014). In fact, with the outbreak of the Korean War, Norman Girvan (1971: 21) writes, "It was determined that national security required a doubling of America's capacity in primary aluminium and related material facilities." As a result, U.S. investment in the Jamaican economy through the mining industry, as well as the emergent tourism industry and older light manufacturing and service industries, grew exponentially after 1950, and foreign capital investment in the bauxite industry became the largest form of investment in the economy (Girvan 1976; Harrod 1972).

With the development of the bauxite industry, the kind of land monopolies that had been created with sugar production were exacerbated. By the late 1950s, transnational corporations had come to own as much as a quarter of the land in some parishes, in particular in St. Ann and Manchester. While Alcan, Alpart, Kaiser, and Reynolds initially purchased large estates or crown lands, they also acquired land from peasant farmers, and by the late 1970s the majority of new acquisitions were from small farms with fewer than twenty-five acres (Beckford 1987: 14). As a result, where some peasant farmers became tenants on land they previously owned, thousands were displaced, migrating either internally to urban areas (and eventually to Kingston) or overseas. This internal displacement was one of the factors in the growth of urban unemployment, slum-related violence and crime, and the development of gangs. Among these internal migrants, and especially after the 1941 raid of Pinnacle, were Rastafari, who by the end of the decade had quietly established a rural-urban circuit of ganja that also spanned national borders by the early 1950s. As I mentioned earlier, there has been some speculation about why this trade would have been allowed to flourish until 1954, when Pinnacle was ultimately raided again. Hélène Lee suggests that there must have been some political linkage between Bustamante, then chief minister, and Howell that would have allowed for the trade, and the businessmen involved in it, to be protected (Lee 2003).

Others support this idea. Jahlani Niaah, for example, drawing from his extensive interviews with Mortimo Planno, refers to Pinnacle as having been "an important site for responding to the needs of those British troops on the front line [during World War II] who were sent ganja cultivated in Jamaica," and that "the development and subsequent problem of Pinnacle was really based on this reputation."[98] According to Planno, as Jamaica was approaching full internal self-government, it was determined that Pinnacle, and the economy it supported, had to be demolished. Winston Churchill's visit to Jamaica in 1953, in this view, was one diplomatic step toward this agenda, which was to "remove traces of Howell's linkages, alignments, economy, his national and international stature . . . [and] evidence of the level of facilitation that Howell was able to provide during the war."[99] This, then, was ultimately the project of the 1954 raid, during which hundreds of thousands of ganja plants, trees, roots and seeds were removed from the compound, and after which the *Gleaner* reported that it was "estimated that it will take the police nearly a month to destroy the ganja cultivations at Pinnacle."[100]

This narrative may not seem plausible, particularly when we remember that German U-boats were ubiquitous in the Caribbean Sea from about 1940 to 1943. However, given the extent of the official silence regarding these kinds of relationships and patterns, it is not impossible to imagine that this interpretation, among so many others being "only historicized by members of the Rastafari movement," might contain some kernels of truth. What is also interesting about this interpretation is that it positions Howell, unwittingly, according to his son Monty, as a kind of "Jamaican don-type businessman, controlling the day to day common working class people, but connected to all of the power forces and the political movers and shakers at that time." And from this perspective, it was his links to the centers of power in Jamaica—"those kinds of untidy political networks"—that needed to be undone.[101]

Whatever the reason for the relative quiescence on the part of the Colonial Office toward Rastafari, and Howell in particular, a quiescence that extended from the end of World War II to the expulsion of the left from the PNP in 1952, what is clear is that the emergent global hegemony of the Cold War framework of the United States was worked out in Jamaica through the suppression or protection of new industries and the generation of new labor regimes. It is true, of course, that within a year after the Marxist left was purged from the PNP in 1952, "the first major shipment of bauxite left Jamaica for the United States of America" (Munroe and Bertram 2006: 175).[102] One trade, ganja, spearheaded by an unrepentantly anticolonial and antinationalist black man who advocated principles of economic self-determination, was shut down; another, bauxite, organized according to the logics of externally based transnational corporations and working through the emergent common sense of U.S. business unionism and its dissociation from a more radical form of syndicalism, was allowed to flourish. Indeed, it was bauxite that spurred U.S. intervention into Jamaican trade unionism.

WHILE TRADE UNION ORGANIZING BEGAN IN JAMAICA IN THE LAST years of the nineteenth century, all the unions that had formed during the early years were inoperative by World War I. Another period of organizing started toward the end of the war, but again, these unions were defunct by the early 1930s (Carnegie 1973; Hart 1989). Then, in 1936, Hugh Buchanan and Alan George St. Claver Coombs formed the Jamaica Workers and Tradesmen Union (JWTU), originally affiliated with the BITU, and this ushered in the period of union activity that would ultimately lead to the workers' rebellions of the late 1930s. As I mentioned earlier, while the left originally mobilized through the BITU, it later split off to form the Trades Union Congress of Jamaica (TUCJ), which was affiliated with the British TUC, whose Colonial Scholarship Scheme funded trade unionists such as Florizel Glasspole (then secretary of the TUCJ) to be trained in Britain.[103] The loss of the left from the PNP meant the loss of some of the most skilled trade unionists in the party, including Ken Hill, who continued to run the TUCJ after his expulsion from the party. The PNP therefore was faced with the prospect of developing a new union to compete not only with the TUCJ but also with the new National Labour Congress, the union that prompted Kelly and MacPherson's removal from office within the PNP. Glasspole and Noel Nethersole would become the leaders of the new PNP union, the National Workers' Union (NWU), and in the chaos of early 1952, all three of these unions petitioned the British TUC for recognition, financial assistance, and sponsorship for membership within the ICFTU. Finally, in September 1952, J. H. Oldenbroek, general secretary of the ICFTU, recommended to Sir Vincent Tewson, president of the TUC, that the NWU become affiliated with the ICFTU, and Assistant General Secretary George Woodcock of the TUC authorized the disbursement of five hundred pounds to the new group.[104]

Despite the party's formal recognition internationally, it took almost a year for the PNP "to recover from the loss of the left" (Munroe and Bertram 2006: 176). This recovery was jump-started by Michael Manley, whose father asked him to return from Britain in late 1951. Though Glasspole and Nethersole stood at the helm of the NWU, it was twenty-eight-year old Mi-

chael who gave the union its strength in mobilizing bauxite and sugar workers away from the TUCJ, and who generated the energy and strategic thinking needed for the NWU to become a force in relation to the BITU, then
led by Hugh Shearer. By 1953, the NWU had all but defeated the left-wing
TUC, whose membership dropped off dramatically, and it led the PNP to
victory in the 1955 elections (Gonsalves 1977; Munroe and Bertram 2006).
The British TUC was not the only overseas entity providing financial and institutional assistance to the NWU, however. The American labor movement,
through the United Steelworkers of America (USWA), also used the removal
of the left wing from the PNP to strengthen its hand in the global fight against
communism.

Prior to World War II, American trade unionism was not particularly
focused on foreign affairs, and where it was, it generally opposed emergent
American imperialism in Latin America and Asia. However, after the Spanish-
Cuban-American War began, leaders such as Samuel Gompers, founder of the
American Federation of Labor (AFL), shifted their position to support the
U.S. government. This prompted an involvement in intelligence gathering,
even before the September 1947 founding of the Central Intelligence Agency
(Morris 1967).[105] After World War I, as the left wing of American unions was
being suppressed, the AFL received government assistance for international
activities, and a $50,000 allocation from Woodrow Wilson financed the es-
tablishment of the Pan-American Labor Press, "a publication intended to advocate the establishment of the Pan-American Federation of Labor ... [and]
designed to extend U.S. economic and political influence throughout Latin
America" (Sims 1992: 37).

After World War II, the U.S. government continued to look to the labor movement "for assistance in its overseas activities" (Windmuller 1963:
112), in large part because of concerns related to Soviet influence over the
colonial world. In 1944, the AFL established the Free Trade Union Committee (FTUC) with an initial budget of $1 million to assist in the regeneration
of the labor movement throughout Europe and elsewhere and to counter
the influence of the CIO and the WFTU. Labor officers were sent to help
with the establishment of "free trade unions"; labor attachés were appointed
to major U.S. embassies overseas; and labor representatives became central
within the Foreign Service after 1946 and within emergent development organizations, such as USAID, during the 1960s. By 1950, the AFL was allocating about a half-million dollars for international affairs and was maintaining
fully staffed bureaus in Brussels, where the ICFTU was headquartered, and in
Latin America (Harrod 1972: 36). And by 1960, by which point the AFL and
CIO had merged, approximately fifty labor attachés were stationed through-

out the world, with an additional one hundred Foreign Service officers serving as part-time labor officers at smaller posts (Morris 1967: 32).[106] Through these channels, U.S. unions provided financial assistance and technical help to overseas trade unionists who were aligned with American economic and political interests.

This involvement culminated in a formal AFL-CIO foreign policy statement in 1962—which asserted, "The preservation of the security and freedom of the United States is the overriding concern of American labor" (Windmuller 1963: 105)—and in the appointment of labor leaders to United Nations delegations to the General Assembly, and, in the case of Jamaica, to the appointment of a labor leader as the first U.S. ambassador after independence. I return to this last, and critically important, point shortly, but for now I will merely state that the foreign policy position of American labor centered on antitotalitarianism, militant anticolonialism, advocacy for a strong defense establishment accompanied by economic and technical assistance, and bipartisanship (Windmuller 1963).[107]

This is this point at which the Italian-born Serafino Romualdi enters our story. Having fled Italian fascism (and a nascent career in journalism) for the United States in 1923, Romualdi landed his first job in 1933, working with the International Ladies Garment Workers Union (ILGWU) to organize Latin Americans of Italian descent against Mussolini. He was later placed on the payroll of the Office of Inter-American Affairs, the propaganda agency established in 1940 by Franklin D. Roosevelt to use radio, news, and film to counter Italian and German propaganda in Latin America (Radosh 1969). After a brief stint as an Office of Strategic Services (OSS) agent between May 1944 and April 1945, Romualdi returned to the ILGWU to establish contacts within Latin American labor unions and promote closer collaboration. By this point he was the Latin American representative for the AFL, a position that became full time in 1948 and that he held until 1965.

The Truman Doctrine in Latin America had several arms. While one was centered on opposing communism through military collaboration and the training of armed forces with the establishment of the School of the Americas in 1946 (Gill 2004), another was the strengthening of anticommunist labor federations. Romualdi laid out the rationale in his memoir, writing,

> As free trade unionists, we were convinced that our efforts to reach the millions of Latin Americans suffering under the yoke of military dictatorships would be futile unless and until the democratic nations of the hemisphere, particularly the United States, were willing to demonstrate through their actions and their friendship and alliance with the oppressed—not with the oppres-

sors. It was our contention that, in a world where isolationism had become an impossibility, there could be no such thing as a national policy of true nonintervention and that it was the responsibility of free nations to assist the people of every nation to mold the democratic institutions necessary for economic and social progress. (Romualdi 1967: 122)

After Romualdi's first tour of Latin America in 1946, he continued to travel throughout Central America, South America, and the Caribbean. This organizing work ultimately led to the 1951 establishment of the Inter-American Regional Organization of Workers (ORIT), which was founded to weaken left-leaning labor federations in the region, including the Confederation of Latin American Workers (CTAL), then headed by the Mexican communist Vincente Lombardo Toledano (Munroe 1992; Spaulding 1977).[108] After Romualdi's 1951 trip to British Guiana, during which he realized Cheddi Jagan was a communist (Munroe 1992), the Caribbean branch of ORIT, the CADORIT, was established in June 1952. According to Romualdi himself, "One of CADORIT's first organizational tasks was to assist in the development of the Jamaican NWU" (Romualdi 1967: 354).

Jamaica had perhaps come to Romualdi's attention after the events of 1951. He received a letter from a representative of the Jamaican TUC (presumably Ken Hill) that was written after the results of the enquiry but before the "4 Hs" had capitulated to the decision of their expulsion from the PNP, explaining the history of labor organizing in Jamaica and the split in the PNP leadership. It concluded with a plea for assistance with organizing in sugar areas and for two cars, since "only English cars are allowed into the island and they can't stand the strain of our rural roads."[109] By January 1953, Romualdi was receiving reports on the situation in Jamaica written by Robert J. Alexander, a pro-labor and anticommunist economist and professor at Rutgers University who had worked closely with ORIT after 1948 and with the AFL-CIO under Jay Lovestone's leadership.[110] Romualdi traveled to Jamaica himself on numerous occasions during the early 1950s to assist with negotiations for better working conditions in the bauxite industry and to attend annual conventions of the NWU. From his point of view, the NWU's growth was critical to the development of American-style unionism as Jamaica headed toward independence, at which point the three major issues, as he saw them, were "immigration policy; the allocation of a sugar quota to help Jamaica dispose of some of its 70,000-ton annual surplus; and the Island's desire for an increase in the number of British West Indies workers recruited for seasonal farm work in the United States" (Romualdi 1967: 354). Part of ORIT's agenda with the NWU was to weaken the link between the leadership of unions and that of the political parties, something that was seen as a holdover of British labor politics, and while Romualdi felt that much had been accomplished in this regard, "much still remains to be done" (Romualdi 1967: 342; see also Harrod 1972: 311–12).[111]

For Trevor Munroe, Romualdi's activity in Jamaica "formed part of a comprehensive intervention by American and British labour interests to weaken left unionism and build anticommunist, pro-American organizations" (Munroe 1992: 93). Direct assistance for this activity came through the USWA, originally a CIO union that resolved in 1950 to work with the U.S. government and unionists abroad to support the Truman Doctrine, having become active in Latin America after World War II. Prior to that time, as the Aluminum Workers of America (AWA), they mobilized bauxite workers at Alcan, the Aluminum Company of America's foreign subsidiary, in Canada. Under Charles Millard, then the executive director of the Steel Workers Organizing Committee (which would later become the USWA), the AWA registered the majority of bauxite workers at Alcan in Kingston, Ontario, forming Local 343 and "opening up the field for the USWA within the industry" (MacMillan 1995: 12). At that point, Alcan's corporate ideology linked the company's development—and that of its employees—to nation building and, therefore, to antifascism and anticommunism (MacMillan 1995). This ideology also permeated its overseas operations. In other words, the USWA got into the business of assisting workers internationally in order to strengthen the position of ICFTU unions vis-à-vis communist labor organizations (Munroe 1992).

In early 1953, David McDonald, the head of the USWA, sent Charles Millard to Jamaica at the request of ORIT to aid Jamaican trade unionists in organizing bauxite workers (MacMillan 1995: 25). Prior to Millard's visit, the American organizer Nicholas Zonarich, the original president of the AWA and eventually the director of the Industrial Section of the AFL-CIO, had traveled to Jamaica to participate with the NWU in negotiations with Alumina Jamaica and Sprostons Limited.[112] During this trip, Zonarich addressed a group of bauxite workers, referring to their wage rates as "the lousiest he had ever heard of," and declaring that "the bauxite royalties obtained from this wealthy company were a disgrace to the Jamaica Government and that working conditions in the industry were such that it was hard to believe there was a Government in Jamaica." Zonarich was reported to have continued to argue "that it was no wonder that communism was prevalent in the world when such conditions existed and that American workers had not obtained their present status without bloodshed and loss of life."[113] Needless to say, though the attorney-general advised that Zonarich had not opened himself up to criminal proceedings, the JLP government of the time did consider de-porting him for incitement to disorder before he left the country voluntarily. In addition, as a result of this speech, visa restrictions were imposed by British authorities that stipulated that visiting unionists should not have anything to do with labor-management relations and that they were not to hold discussions with union leaders. This was part of a more general attempt on the part of the British to thwart the USWA's efforts to penetrate the trade union movement in its colony.

When Millard accompanied Zonarich to Jamaica in March 1953, however, these new restrictions provoked embarrassment, consternation, and a bit of jurisdictional mayhem. Immediately on arrival, both men were detained by immigration authorities, and were presented with restraining orders signed by Colonial Secretary (and Acting Governor) Colville Deverell stipulating that they must not "at any time address any group of persons on any topic relating to political or trade union matters, or discuss such matters with any group of persons, or participate in any way in any negotiations arising out of any trade dispute."[114] They were both told that if they did not sign the order, they would be immediately deported.

Glasspole, by then the general secretary of the NWU, immediately sent a telegram to the secretary of state for the colonies protesting the detention of Millard and Zonarich. He wrote that the two men were there to provide "friendly technical advice on matters affecting bauxite mining workers and to offer educational and other facilities from [the] Canadian union" and argued that their arrival during a strike at Alumina Jamaica was pure coincidence. Glasspole reminded the Colonial Office that bauxite companies also brought in "foreign trained specialist advisers to deal with trade union negotiations" and lodged a strong protest on behalf of the NWU against "this unwarranted act calculated to undermine international influence by free trade union movement and contrary declared British policy." He concluded by entreating that the Colonial Office intervene and cancel the ban.[115] Less than a week after Millard and Zonarich were detained at the airport, *Public Opinion* published an article reporting that the NWU had charged the government with 'Fascist' interference," noting also that protest telegrams had been sent to "the Secretary of State for the Colonies in London; the State Department in Washington, USA; the Home Office, Ottawa, Canada; Headquarters of the International Confederation of Free Trade Unions in Brussels, Belgium, and to the Governor at King's House."[116] When Deverell got wind of the NWU protest, he sent a telegram to Assistant Colonial Under-Secretary Stephen Luke that outlined the issues and stated that Millard told him that McDonald had sent him to Jamaica in part "to keep an eye on Zonarich, whose previous activities in Jamaica had displeased the State Department, but that his main objective was to protect the standards of American and Canadian workers by raising the standard of Jamaica bauxite workers."[117]

After returning to Canada, Millard also wrote to Sir Vincent Tewson, the general secretary of the British TUC, to make a formal protest of his detention and the limitations placed upon him. Attaching the detention order to his letter, Millard explained that he had traveled to Jamaica on 22 March 1953 as part of a mission for the USWA that had the approval of the secretary general of ORIT. He continued that on 26 March he had received a visit from the same immigration officer saying the conditions of his landing had been withdrawn. "Though I asked for it," he wrote, "no explanation of either action was given me."[118] Millard sent a similar letter to the Hon. L. B. Pearson, Secretary of State for External Affairs, in which he also explained that there could have been no misunderstanding about the objective for his trip. "On the plane," he wrote, "I had refused a 'Tourist Entry Permit' and had signed a Business Entry Permit on which the purpose of my visit was given as to 'visit with and consult with certain trade unions.'"[119] Glasspole's and Millard's complaints prompted a series of discussions within the Colonial Office that lasted well into the summer of 1953. At issue were three problems: how to respond to Millard and the Canadian officials, given that by 6 May the lack of explanation for the detention and release of Millard raised a Parliamentary Question; how and when to respond to Glasspole, given that he was due to travel to the United Kingdom as a delegate to the ICFTU conference in early April; and how to deal with what they saw as U.S. interference in Jamaican politics.

Regarding the first issue, a typed note dated 27 March 1953 appears on the file folder from H. F. Heinemann, a lawyer working within the West Indian Department of the Colonial Office, addressed to a Miss Gaved, Mr. Barltrop, Mr. Biggs, Mr. Barton, and Mr. Luke. Heinemann explained that while the laws governing the immigration of aliens into Jamaica empower the Governor to attach conditions to permission to land, those governing the arrival of British subjects do not. As a result, "The restrictions attached to Mr. Millard's permission to land were therefore not legal and, presumably, ineffective."[120] Heinemann continued with the general opinion that "it is inadvisable to attach conditions to permission to land," except in exceptional and serious cases, because attempts to restrict activities "are likely to lead to more trouble than they are worth and to add to the prestige of the people concerned."[121] This was, indeed, the case with Millard, because the NWU happily took credit for having had the ban lifted. They did not know about the 24 March meeting with Colonial Secretary Sir Colville Deverell, during which Millard revealed that he was a Canadian citizen (not an American) and admitted that he had been sent to keep an eye on Zonarich. Ultimately, Heinemann argued that the response to the Parliamentary Question should be "that the matter is within the competence of the Government of Jamaica," but "the Secretary of State might offer advice to the Government of Jamaica if he thought that that would not affect the formal decision."[122] E. W. Barltrop, labor adviser to the secretary of state, added that while "some Member [of Parliament] may be expected to raise the issue of freedom of access to Colonial territories by bona fide representatives of the ICFTU or its affiliated unions, or that of the right of established colonial trade unions to seek advice and help from the free trade union movement," regardless of the private advice the secretary of state may offer to colonial governments, "we clearly can do no other in public than uphold the principle of the competence of Colonial Governments in this field."[123] When the Colonial Office finally responded in August to the query from the high commissioner in Ottawa, it stipulated that since the "technical error" in the restriction of Millard, and the reason for subsequently lifting it, had not been revealed to the involved parties, it "should be kept strictly confidential."[124]

This may look like the Colonial Office was passing the buck, and in a way, it was. In part, this is because it regarded Glasspole as having directed his appeal to the wrong office, which, because of the Parliamentary Question, then put the secretary of state for the colonies in an awkward position. Heinemann initially wrote that generally the Colonial Office wanted to see the ICFTU taking an interest in the British West Indies and that therefore it was disinclined to restrict international trade union activity.[125] He also noted that "Mr. Glasspole makes a good point when he says that the bauxite companies are allowed to bring in people from outside to advise them on question of labour relations and it seems to me unfortunate to place restrictions on a member of the International Executive Board of ICFTU."[126] However, after the notice of the Parliamentary Question, Heinemann became more cautious, arguing, "We should avoid giving Mr. Glasspole a formal interview on this matter." This was because "his representations were made on behalf of the National Workers' Union and were, improperly, addressed direct to the Secretary of State." The matter was "within the competence of the Government of Jamaica," he concluded, "and I think it would be a mistake for officials of the Colonial Office to try to explain the government of Jamaica's decision to Mr. Glasspole."[127]

Finally, Millard's assertions that the USWA was working with Jamaican workers primarily to protect the position of their own did not sit well with the Colonial Office. Some colonial officials remembered that encouraging Jamaicans to seek wages based on American standards was not new; it had also occurred during the war, both within England and on West Indian bases, "when we had to urge the American Government not to pay wages to civilians over the rates prevailing here."[128] Nevertheless, in a letter to Assistant Secretary W. I. J. Wallace, Governor Foot wrote, "What are the motives of these trade unionists in interfering in Jamaican affairs? As I have already reported, Millard quite frankly stated that his main objective was to protect the standard of wages of American and Canadian workers rather than concern for the Jamaican workers. Is it to be expected that those in authority in Jamaica will permit foreign trade unionists to interfere in Jamaican affairs in order that they may serve the interests of workers elsewhere?"[129]

N. D. (Duncan) Watson wrote to Assistant Secretary Wallace with additional context. He confirmed that what "really rankled with the Executive Council [in Jamaica] was that Zonarich's real aim . . . was to protect the interests of United States workers, without any regard to the problems and economics of Jamaica." This was all the more annoying when considering that they themselves, even those entirely unconnected with trade unionism, were obliged when visiting the United States "to sign declarations undertaking not to engage in political or trade union activity."[130] Watson was a trusted adviser who had previously been posted in the West Indies and was selected in 1947 as head of the private office of Secretary of State for the Colonies Creech-Jones. He later was posted to Kenya during the Mau Mau Rebellion, and then to Malaya, where he helped determine the political arrangements for independence in 1956. He was, incidentally, a big fan of Serafino Romualdi, whom he met in British Honduras and whom he described as "responsible" and "restrained" in relation to his trade unionism.

Watson's letter to Wallace also addressed broader issues related to ICFTU activities in the colony, issues he had discussed with Governor Foot. "On the one hand," he wrote, "we had openly and officially welcomed their activities in our territories in order to help colonial trade unions to stand up against communist infiltration. On the other hand, there was no doubt that the ICFTU were taking an increasing interest in Colonial affairs and that this interest was extending from the purely labour field into the political and social fields." In Watson's view, the problem here had to do with the fact that the British TUC did not always see eye to eye with the American unions, especially in the Caribbean, where the ICFTU had to work through ORIT, which did not appreciate the close link between unions and political parties in British West Indian contexts. "If American ICFTU unions were going to come in and help the NWU and to send them funds (as they propose to do)," he wrote, "the other unions would inevitably regard it as help to an opposition political party and would do all they could to stop it."

Watson expressed the same to Ernest Bell of the TUC, explaining that because of the intense rivalry between Bustamante's BITU and the NWU, when foreign trade unionists support the NWU financially and otherwise and at the same time attack the government, "their action can only be regarded locally as constituting interference in the party politics of Jamaica."[131] He apologized on behalf of the Governor for whatever complications this incident may have caused in international trade union circles, but also pointed out that "the train of events which Mr. Zonarich started has in fact done a grave disservice to the cause of the ICFTU in Jamaica at a time when he is most anxious to encourage Jamaican trade unions generally to recognize that their interests lie with the ICFTU and not the WFTU."[132] Because of Millard's and Zonarich's activities, he wrote, the ICFTU was being seen as a pro-Manley organization.

Despite the controversy attendant to the visit by Millard and Zonarich, the result was that Millard was able to persuade McDonald to allocate $3,000 in funding to the NWU and to provide financial support for a full-time organizer for the union. Ken Sterling, island supervisor of the NWU, was hired for this position. This received attention from the international media, as the *Telegram* reported that the move of the USWA to assist Jamaica's NWU is "believed to be the first of its kind by any labor group on the North American Continent," and the *Globe and Mail* revealed that "the entire services of the steel union—its legal, educational, and research departments—will be placed at the disposal of the workers in Jamaica under the arrangement cleared through the ICFTU."[133] After spending several months in the United States and Canada learning about the aluminum industry and trade unionism under the auspices of the USWA, Sterling, once back in Jamaica, continued organizing bauxite workers and generating broad working-class support for the PNP (R. Alexander [with Parker] 2004; Harrod 1972; MacMillan 1995). He remained on the USWA payroll at least until the end of 1956, "long after the NWU had acquired full bargaining rights for all the bauxite workers in Jamaica" (Harrod 1972: 265), and by mid-1957 he had become the executive secretary of CADORIT and the secretary of the Caribbean Aluminium Workers Federation, to which the NWU was affiliated.[134] Romualdi wrote to McDonald in praise of Millard, stating that his "work in helping the NWU establish a foothold in the bauxite industry greatly enhanced the prestige of U.S. unions and the organization of Alcan's bauxite workers would establish pattern bargaining in the industry" (MacMillan 1995: 26).

Millard and Zonarich both maintained a presence in Jamaica between 1953 and 1956 as advisers and negotiators for workers within the bauxite industry with the full support of the NWU, and of Michael Manley—first as sugar supervisor in 1952–53 and after 1955 as island supervisor and first vice-president. They also continued to attend the NWU's annual conventions, as well as ORIT and CADORIT conferences. Manley's recollection of the early moments of U.S. involvement in Jamaican trade unionism was that he "looked forward to working with them as allies" but "declared our firm intention to be the sole determinants of the goals which we would set for our members as Jamaican workers" (Manley [1975] 1991: 131). His sense was that their assistance was important with respect to organizing, but some workers felt that the foreign unionists didn't care for them outside their identity as workers. Again, this gets at the crux of the difference between American-style business unionism and more radical syndicalism, in which the former values the pulling together of labor and management and the disaffiliation of unions and political parties. "Labor in the United States does not subscribe to the concept of the class struggle," Romualdi (1967: 418) wrote. "It believes in the free enterprise system, subject to limitations and controls designed to prevent dangerous monopolies and abuses, but a free enterprise system nevertheless."

The involvement of the USWA in Jamaican trade unionism therefore generated a relationship between aluminum companies and the NWU, thereby guaranteeing bauxite supplies to the United States. By promoting anticommunism and business unionism, this partnership also increased possibilities for future investment in Jamaica (Spaulding 1977), with a survey of corporate executives revealing that they "viewed the NWU as 'a useful social institution serving a police function which is of value to the company'" (Spaulding 1977: 79). For these executives, a union interested in economic issues rather than local politics was "safe," and this was confirmed by the lack of industrial action in the Jamaican bauxite industry after the 1950s. By late 1956, reports to Romualdi were suggesting a trend toward unity in the Jamaican labor movement as the Jamaican TUC declined. In October of that year, Alexander wrote:

> The Communists are active, as one might expect. They maintain a political party now, the People's Freedom Movement, which was established something over a year ago, and a trade union group, the Jamaica Federation of Trade Unions. The government has told employers that it thinks that they should not negotiate with the Communist labor group, and the employers have unanimously accepted this advice. The Communists have some strength in the sugar industry, but have no collective bargaining rights.... My principal Communist contact there told me that for the time being they did not have much hope in building up their party as a mass organization, being buffaloed as they are by the two party system. However, he seemed relatively optimistic about making progress in the trade union field.[135]

And in December 1956, the decision was taken to channel all ICFTU financial assistance to Latin America and the Caribbean through ORIT beginning in January 1957, "including the expenses for the offices in Brazil, Chile, and Barbados."[136] Prior to that time, international activities were budgeted under the Research Department of the USWA, "which had a salary and expense budget ranging from approximately $61,000 in 1953 to over $100,000 in 1958" (Harrod 1972: 133). But by 1957, Charles Millard was the ICFTU's director of organization, and ORIT's budget had grown exponentially because of contributions from the AFL-CIO, the Cuban Confederation of Workers, and the ICFTU.

By 1959, the NWU had grown to be about the same size as the BITU, but its workers were in more remunerative industries, and by 1970 the NWU had a monopoly on the bauxite-alumina industry. This growth, however, came with a cost, which was the decline of the kind of participatory and deliberative political consciousness-raising that had been advocated by organizations such as the PFM and the TUC, and the intensification and institutionalization of bureaucratically oriented business unionism, which denies the role of organized labor as a political force (Harding and Spaulding 1976). The paradox here is that these are processes that occurred under Michael Manley's leadership during the twenty years prior to his own declaration of democratic socialism in 1974. As Munroe (1992: 199) has argued, "It is an historic irony that the consequences of this connivance by Michael Manley of the 1950s in the debilitation of working class political awareness, unity and democracy in the labour movement returned to haunt his efforts two decades later at radical reform of Jamaican society."

The collaboration between the USWA and the NWU would ultimately lay the groundwork for intensified American agitation within the trade union movement and, eventually, to the establishment in 1964 of the Trade Union Education Institute (TUEI) at the University of the West Indies, Mona. The TUEI was financed by the AIFLD, the CIA-supported, USAID-funded anti-communist "education" arm of AFL-CIO labor imperialism throughout Latin America and the Caribbean, Asia, and Africa. Elsewhere in Latin America, the AIFLD was involved in building housing enclaves for workers supporting business unionism. In Jamaica, the combination of USAID and AIFLD initiatives should prompt us to raise questions regarding the processes of garrisonization in Kingston.

WHEN NORMAN MANLEY WENT TO WASHINGTON, DC, TO MEET WITH President John F. Kennedy in April 1961, he could not have predicted the long-term effects of what was being set into motion by his appeal for assistance with housing construction. Prior to his trip, Manley had sent a memo to various senators, laying out the issues in Jamaica as he saw them at the time. In the memo, he wrote of his worries about Cuba, which he identified as a potential "menace": "We have positive evidence that Cuban money is flowing into Jamaica in an effort to build up left wing agitators. They have begun to preach the overthrow of the Government and link up their aims with the propagation of a vicious racist policy."[137] Here, Manley is undoubtedly referring to the recent events related to Reverend Claudius Henry and his son Ronald, knowing that the United States had definitely been paying attention.[138] By 1963, the U.S. government's Plan of Action for Jamaica listed Rastafari as the main group of "dissident elements," who, though "poorly organized," nevertheless numbered upward of twelve thousand. Dedicated to "Negro superiority," Rastafari were understood by U.S. policy makers to form "a potentially explosive group vulnerable to exploitation by any elements which might wish to precipitate violence against the government."[139]

Manley's main agenda for the visit, however, was not anticommunism or the suppression of Rastafari. Instead, it was to discuss various economic and social development initiatives, prospects for the lifting of the U.S. migration quota after independence, and the extension of the Farm Work Program. While in the United States, therefore, Manley also met with Senator J. William Fulbright and Secretary of Labor Arthur Goldberg; the directors of Food for Peace, the Development Loan Fund, and the Peace Corps; Representative Adam Clayton Powell (at the time the chair of the House Committee on Labor and Education) and Representative Francis Walters (then chair of the House Committee on Migration); and Allen Dulles, director of the CIA, who advised him "on important aspects of the development of communism in Latin America."[140] With President Kennedy, Manley reiterated concerns raised in his memo, noting that the Jamaican government would need to spend one million pounds on water supplies yearly for five years and five million pounds on housing. Because the government could afford only 20 percent of this amount, he asked for loans to cover the rest through Kennedy's new Alliance for Progress, which had been inaugurated in March 1961 to coordinate economic cooperation between the United States and Latin America.[141]

Housing development schemes were first initiated by the British after the region-wide labor rebellions of the late 1930s. At that point, as Don Robotham (2003: 121) has argued, "The British were seeking to divide the nationalist movement and the corruption of the delivery of social services was one way to achieve this." The first housing scheme emerged from the old colonial ghetto of Smith Village, one of the notorious slum areas near the market in

Western Kingston that developed after the collapse of the sugar industry in the mid-nineteenth century and the massive outmigration from rural areas after 1880. This scheme, Denham Town, was named after a deceased colonial Governor, and it was adjacent to Kingston Pen, what is now Tivoli Gardens.

The groundwork for Manley's particular request in 1961, however, had been laid the previous December at the West Indies Bases talks at King's House in Jamaica.[142] This series of talks was the result of the impending independence of the West Indies Federation and the need for the U.S. government to renegotiate base leases throughout the region. In Jamaica, the U.S. delegation, headed by U.S. Ambassador to the United Kingdom John Hay Whitney, agreed "to give special consideration in future fiscal years to a Low Cost Housing and Slum Clearance Program in Jamaica."[143] This stemmed from an understanding that slum conditions and overcrowding bred discontent and could therefore "furnish the motivation for anti-social action." While a Slum Clearance and Housing Law had been on the books in Jamaica since 1939 (coming out of the establishment of the Central Housing Authority in 1937), the development of new housing under the law was based on the provision of small government grants to individuals until Hurricane Charlie (1951), when relief housing was provided by the colonial government.[144] It wasn't until the new Housing Act of 1955 and its amendment in 1958 that provisions were made for private capital to finance the construction of new housing schemes. The agreement with Manley in 1961 marked another innovation, as the U.S. government agreed to undertake a pilot scheme through which the emergent USAID would provide Jamaica with experts in city planning, resettlement, and housing finance and construction, as well as urban community development.[145] These experts would "review the existing housing program and its problems" and would offer recommendations for both short- and long-term solutions.[146]

The report written by these experts outlined the issues they saw in relation to insufficient access to jobs, food, and water. "In Kingston Pen," they wrote, "there is no water to serve 493 families nor sanitary facilities of any kind. Similarly in Trench Town there are virtually no bathing or washing facilities." These living conditions, they argued, were hardly conducive to "social stability or to respect for authority." If, as they estimated, ten thousand persons lived in squatter settlements such as Back O'Wall and Trench Town— settlements that had been in existence since the 1920s (Lawton 2005)—then 2,500 new dwellings would be required. To build them, people first would have to be relocated and temporarily rehoused during the construction period in a series of three- to four-story walk-up units containing approximately forty-two one-room flats, each with a bathroom and kitchen sink. The hope was that these families would be moved into the new dwellings after redevelopment was completed.[147]

In July 1961, this proposal was accepted, and the U.S. publicly committed to finance the foreign exchange and local currency costs of the urban housing project through USAID in the initial amount of $1.9 million (this was later raised to $2.8 million).[148] The USAID country team in Jamaica strongly urged approval and early disbursement of the loan. The loan was approved, but as late as 1966 funds still had not been fully disbursed.[149] Nevertheless, construction began in Trench Town, Briggs Park, Long Mountain Pen, and Rennock Lodge. With the increased funding, Elletson Flats and Twickenham Park, St. Catherine, were added to the list. It is worth mentioning that all of these areas targeted for USAID-financed slum clearance and housing redevelopment were in PNP constituencies, with one (Twickenham Park) having switched from the PNP to the JLP in the 1959 elections by an extremely small margin (Munroe and Bertram 2006). Kingston Pen, which would ultimately become Tivoli Gardens, was not included on this roster, despite the observations of the USAID committee, and we can assume this was because these lands were privately, rather than publicly, owned. The team did report, however, that although residents there were "'hosed-out' a few years ago, they moved right back on to the same land again."[150]

Between 1963 and 1971, the USAID allocated £719,000–£1,584,000 pounds annually in loans to Jamaica, with the bulk of these funds being directed toward the housing program. The funds were supplemented by a loan special investment of £443,718 per year from 1961 to 1970.[151] The USAID housing development project marked the beginnings of a more comprehensive U.S. policy toward Jamaica at a time when independence—either as a West Indies Federation or as a singular nation-state—was imminent. This policy was driven by a recognition of the region's strategic location five hundred miles from southern Florida (and the existing military installations); the significance of U.S. economic interests in the region, especially in bauxite and oil; and an interest in maintaining a staunchly anticommunist ally, given Cuba's position in the region.[152] The expectation, on the part of the U.S. government, was that the United States would engage the West Indies as a federation; that this federation would maintain strong ties with the Commonwealth while also entering into "constructive relationship" with other nations in the Western Hemisphere and with the Organization of American States, and that the United Kingdom would provide the necessary external capital for the West Indies as a whole, with the U.S. providing "technical assistance and modest economic assistance on a grant or loan basis."[153]

In 1960, the United States was concerned with population pressure in most of the territories, and the extent to which economic conditions in the federation "could be exploited by the Communists should the Soviet Union undertake a concerted drive in the federation or should economic conditions seriously deteriorate."[154] They were also concerned with the effect of the pre-1965 immigration quota system on perceptions of the United States and with an "*anti-white sentiment*" on the part of West Indians, one they acknowledged was due to West Indians' awareness of racial discrimination in the United States and their own experience of "indignities during visits here." Finally, they were watching potential separatism within the federation, and they noted that "Jamaica, the largest unit, is currently opposed to surrendering to the central government those powers which the federation needs to function effectively."[155] When federation indeed failed, the political objectives with respect to Jamaica remained grounded in Jamaica's strategic location (and the presence of U.S. military bases); its position as the world's largest bauxite producer; and the desire to maintain a pro-Western, anticommunist ally within the region, in part through participation in regional organizations, which they saw as a bulwark against communism.[156] As we have already seen, trade union activity was another critical pillar of this agenda.

IN FEBRUARY 1963, WILLIAM DOHERTY SR. SENT AN AIRGRAM TO THE U.S. State Department requesting that a Task Order or contract be allocated to the Social Projects Department of the American Institute for Free Labor Development. The airgram proposed that the AIFLD provide two experts to travel to Jamaica for two months to "research and establish a trade union-sponsored Cooperative Low-Cost Housing Scheme based on revolving capital investment utilizing workers' savings through a worker-oriented National Housing Cooperative" and "to analyze the possibility of utilizing seed capital loans to said National Housing Cooperative, to be provided by the AID and possibly AFL/CIO guaranteed investment funds."[157] While one of these experts, an architect or engineer, would provide a financial and technical feasibility study for the establishment of the housing cooperative, the trade union's financial and cooperative expert would explore the financial capabilities of "generating workers' savings and the legal aspects of establishing a National Workers Cooperative."[158] He would also be tasked with working closely with the trade union movement to provide structure and guidelines for a cooperative. Doherty framed this proposal in relation to existing USAID housing assistance in Jamaica, and felt that it "would serve in an important way to supplement present [government of Jamaica] efforts to plan for and implement a national housing program involving the construction of approximately 125,000 low-cost and medium-cost homes during the next ten years."[159] Doherty also argued that the proposal conformed with USAID policies encouraging cooperative housing schemes, as well as the broader rationale and goals of the USAID programs in Jamaica for fiscal years 1963 and 1964 geared toward "improving the health, contentment and productivity of the individual worker as an essential of economic growth and political stability."[160] In July 1963, Doherty was given authority to "negotiate and execute on behalf of the Agency for International Development" an amendment to the original loan agreement with the government of Jamaica, increasing the disbursement to $2.8 million to assist with the financing of owner-occupied, low-cost family dwelling units in accordance with the amended Loan Authorization dated 29 June 1963.[161]

William C. Doherty Sr. was President Kennedy's appointment as the first U.S. ambassador to independent Jamaica in 1962. At the end of World War II, while serving as president of the Mail Carriers Union (a post he held from 1941 to 1962), Doherty was chosen to help develop a free trade union movement in West Germany, and he became one of the organizers of the ICFTU in London. In 1950, the National Association of Letter Carriers joined the Postal, Telephone, and Telegraph International (PTTI), and Doherty ultimately became a vice-president of the AFL-CIO. When he was named the ambassador to Jamaica, his son, William C. Doherty Jr., assumed the position of director of social projects for the AIFLD before becoming executive director in 1965 when Romualdi retired.[162]

The AIFLD was created in 1962 "to oppose communism and other totalitarian forms of government in Latin America and to assist the growth of 'democratic trade unions,' principally through trade union educational activities and assistance to trade unionists in raising their standard of living." The AIFLD was backed by the AFL-CIO, business organizations with interests in Latin America and the Caribbean, and the U.S. government. In 1962, the AFL-CIO contributed more than $200,000 to the AIFLD's activities overseas, which was supplemented by $150,000–$160,000 from business groups and $3 million from the U.S. government (Harrod 1972: 288).

The AIFLD grew out of a training program that was established in the late 1950s for Peruvian communications workers by Joseph Beirne, then president of the Communications Workers of America (CWA), affiliated with the PTTI. Through this program, union leaders were funded to attend a three-month course in "democratic unionism" at the CWA's training center in Fort Royal, Virginia. The expectation was that these leaders would subsequently return to their home countries and receive an additional nine-month stipend to promote "free" anticommunist and pro-business trade unionism (Radosh 1969;

Sims 1992; Spaulding 1977). As Beirne expanded this program throughout Latin America, he received a $20,000 grant from the AFL-CIO, which was disbursed through the National Institute of Labor Education via the Union Research and Education Project Center at the University of Chicago, then directed by John McCollum (Romualdi 1967). After McCollum resigned in early 1962, Romualdi took the leadership of the AIFLD, by then the AFL-CIO's conduit for U.S. government funds for labor projects established through the Alliance for Progress. "We made it clear to President Kennedy that we had a part to play," George Meany has explained, "and that some of the Alliance for Progress funds, instead of being spent through business institutions or banks or government, should be channeled through free trade unions and for their projects to advance their living standards" (U.S. Government 1969: 8). It is at this point that the AIFLD also began constructing low-cost housing.[163] The alliance's first labor loan consisted of a $400,000 grant to an anticommunist Honduran union for a housing project (Spaulding 1977), and this kind of activity became one of the cornerstones of the AIFLD's work.

This is the context in which we must assess Doherty's airgram proposal. The real question thus materializes: since the existing USAID contract was earmarked for PNP constituencies, did the AIFLD jump in after independence to help Edward Seaga develop Tivoli Gardens? In fact, there is a much longer and more complicated history of ownership and slum clearance attempts for Kingston Pen, the area that would become Tivoli Gardens. Shortly after the land was purchased by Allan Blissett and others in 1945, the Jamaican government declared it a slum area inhabited by a total of 3,752 people, 1,252 of whom were squatters, and plans for clearance were announced.[164] By September 1947, the government had agreed to finance the construction of alternative housing for the Kingston Pen dwellers in Cockburn Pen. Remember that many of Reverend Henry's early followers came from that neighborhood, which should signal to us that they had likely been removed from Kingston Pen in these clearance efforts. During the summer of 1950, the government was still attempting to resettle those squatters remaining in Kingston Pen as deadlines for removal continued to pass, and in July 1958, Blissett wrote an extremely frustrated letter to the editor of the *Gleaner*, outlining the history of the land and the consortium members' financial losses because of damages and their inability to develop the Industrial Terrace area because tenants were still not removed.[165]

By February 1961, Minister of Agriculture and Lands K. A. Munn had asked for an assessment from the Commissioner of Lands, and the government began negotiating with Blissett to acquire Kingston Pen for £110,900.[166] In January 1962, Blissett accepted the government's offer on behalf of the consortium of owners, and after the government changed, plans were drawn to develop the area. In a submission to the cabinet, new Minister of Housing D. C. Tavares outlined his construction and development timetable:

> The first step in the development of the area will be the construction of a road along the eastern side of the lands followed by a road running diagonally across the lands from east to west in order to open up the area, which is, at present, no man's land, and make easy access possible for the police, who, quite likely, will have to be called in from time to time and who will have to police the area vigilantly during development and construction. When these roads have been constructed the subdivision of the land and the construction of houses will be carried out on a phased basis. This programme of development has been devised because it has been ascertained that to move all the people in Kingston Pen into temporary accommodation would be much too expensive.[167]

Tavares concluded by asking that the cabinet agree to give squatters two months' notice to quit; that development take place according to the proposed plan; and that, should squatters interfere with construction, all would be removed without alternative accommodation. Ultimately, with the first phase of construction, the forty-two original lots would be subdivided into 173.[168] On 2 August 1963, the *Gleaner* reported on the plan to construct 751 units (470 for sale and 228 for rental), keeping fifty-three lots for sale. Eviction notices had been issued the day before.[169] In July 1964, construction finally began.[170]

In his memoir, Seaga (2009: 154) writes about the "unique" funding structure for Tivoli Gardens:

> The project was to be financed in a unique manner. Instructors for the programme [the community center and its educational training programs] were provided by government, and the housing units would, as was usual, be constructed by government for rent and sale but, unusually, private funding was sought for the construction of the community centre and the Mother and Child complex. This was made possible by earnings from community projects and donations from businesses in the area which had done well over the years. The Chin Loy family contributed to the basic school, which would bear its name, and George Fong Yee [financed] the nutrition centre for the complex. The Kiwanis club of Kingston donated the Maternity Centre.

While parliamentary budget records do not clearly disaggregate the sources of funds for the Tivoli Gardens housing project, Cabinet Submissions reveal that some Housing Trust funds were allocated to the construction, and by Phase III of the development (1967–69), the government had received both hard loans totaling approximately £500,000 and Canadian loans in the amount of £14,000. Seaga also received a loan from the World Bank, which was used for the construction of a secondary school and for at least two hundred of the housing units (Bryan 2009: 151). Annual reports from the Jamaican Department of Housing indicate that government spending on the Tivoli Gardens schemes constituted the largest government housing expenditure by far, excepting the USAID projects. In the 1964–65 fiscal year, £235,740 was authorized for Tivoli Gardens, and in the following year, houses completed or under construction in Tivoli Gardens totaled slightly more than half of the new units built, with a new authorization of capital expenditure of £437,390.[171] This was in addition to the amount allocated for the previously authorized scheme, and again, it represents the highest housing allocation by a factor of almost seven.[172]

Seaga also writes in his memoir that while the government made a provision of £10,000 to assist those Back O' Wall residents who were displaced by the bulldozing, many did not return to populate the new housing units. For Seaga (2009: 158), this was the result of political activists' being "too fearful of potential harm to live among persons of other political persuasions," but Colin Clarke (2006a: 253) has argued that the new housing in Tivoli Gardens was "not intended for the inhabitants of the original squatter camps, despite oral promises to the squatters by officials who visited them."[173]

MEANWHILE, THE AIFLD CONTINUED TO OFFER ITS THREE-MONTH training courses at Fort Royal and worked to establish similar training centers in countries in which the institute had a presence, such as Jamaica. With William Doherty Jr. at the helm of social projects for the AIFLD after independence, Doherty Sr. continued conversations begun in August 1962 with Norman Manley about the possibility of establishing a Trade Union Education Institute on the University of the West Indies campus. While this kind of institute had originally been proposed by the NWU, Manley offered his willing agreement that it should move forward, "notwithstanding that it may go down to the credit of the present [JLP] Government."[174] Doherty Sr. confirmed that the project, which would involve an outlay of approximately $183,000 over four years, was being championed by George Meany, chairman of the AIFLD, and was only awaiting final authorization in Washington.[175] Indeed, on 21 May 1963, an agreement was signed by Sir Alexander Bustamante and William C. Doherty establishing the institute, which would offer one-month residential courses, weekend seminars, and a number of one- to two-week courses in outlying, rural areas, the latter with the assistance of a mobile film unit. The AIFLD was scheduled to administer $141,000 of the $183,000 USAID grant.[176]

In April 1964, the TUEI was officially opened by Donald Sangster, hosting its first month-long course in May with the participation of thirty-four people from Jamaica, the Bahamas, Trinidad and Tobago, Barbados, St. Vincent, Antigua, and British Honduras.[177] By the end of 1964, 115 students had come through the TUEI, and a total of 485 people had participated in all of the educational activities offered across the island.[178] Between 1965 and 1966, seven trade union workers traveled from Jamaica to complete advanced courses in Washington, and in April 1968, the Jamaican Lindel Lawrence, an organizer with the TUC, attended the training at Front Royal, returning home afterward for his nine-month internship. By the late 1960s, the AIFLD's attention had shifted from the Caribbean to Central America, Guyana, and Peru, and its activities in Jamaica seem to have slowed to a trickle, coming to a complete standstill by the late 1970s.[179]

By 1966, concerns were being raised regarding CIA influence on the labor movement. In May of that year, Victor Reuther, international affairs director of the United Auto Workers' Union, charged that the AFL-CIO's International Affairs Department was involved with the CIA (Morris 1967: 7). Several journalists began probing links among USAID, the AIFLD, and the CIA, and in the aftermath of the 1967 exposure of CIA involvement through dummy foundations in overseas work by the American Newspaper Guild, public anger led Senator Fulbright to convene congressional hearings on the AIFLD in August 1969.[180]

During these hearings, Fulbright asked Meany to respond to charges that "in a number of countries the AIFLD labor institutes have been closed down by the host country for meddling in internal politics" (U.S. Government 1969: 2) and to explain the history and funding of the institute. Meany explained that the AFL-CIO, committed to spending 20 percent of its income on international activities geared toward maintaining "free governments" in the Western Hemisphere (U.S. Government 1969: 6), began to recruit businessmen to contribute to the work of the AIFLD, including Peter Grace, president of the W. R. Grace Company and an ally of Chile's Augusto Pinochet.[181] Grace ultimately became the chair of the AIFLD's board, whose members also included William Hickey, president of the United Corporation; U. W. Balgooyen, director of Ebasco Industries; Brent Friele of the SVP American International Association for Economic and Social Development; and Juan Trippe, founder and executive director of Pan-American Airlines. Between 1962 and 1968, upward of fifty corporations—many of which had consistently fought unionization at home and overseas—also contributed funds to the AIFLD, including American Standard, American Telephone and Telegraph, Chase Manhattan Bank, Bacardi Corporation, Bristol Myers, Coca-Cola, First National Bank of Boston, General Foods Corporation, Gillette, IBM, ITT, Johnson and Johnson, Kimberly-Clark, Merck, Mobil Oil Company, Monsanto, National Biscuit Company, Otis Elevator Company, PanAm, Pfizer, Reader's Digest, Rockefeller Brothers Fund, Shell, Standard Fruit Company, Standard Oil, 3M, and United Fruit (U.S. Government 1969: 21). These contributions totaled $2.3 million for Latin America alone; the AIFLD and private investors also committed $31 million for low-cost worker housing (U.S. Government 1969: 7). By 1967, the AIFLD budget was more than $6 million, three times the annual AFL-CIO budget (Hirsch 1974).

When Senator Fulbright asked whether the AFL-CIO had known affiliation with the CIA, Meany replied, "The AFL-CIO has never received any money in any form from the CIA. This is an accusation which had been made by certain representatives of certain unions, widespread around the world. It has never been established as being true, and I can say to you categorically now that it is not true and under no circumstances have we ever received or solicited any money from the CIA. We do not spend CIA money" (U.S. Government 1969: 23). Fulbright followed up to state that the concern was not with a direct disbursement of CIA funds to the AFL-CIO, but with funding channeled to the AFL-CIO through USAID to the AIFLD.[182] He further suggested that the funding the AIFLD received was a "payoff" for supporting the Vietnam War. "It certainly is more . . . than purely coincidental," Fulbright challenged, "that this very intimate relationship existed between you and the former administration and the large amount of moneys that have been contributed by the Government to your activity" (U.S. Government 1969: 46). Indeed, the general question prompting the hearings was whether the massive investment in the AIFLD on the government's part was justified, given the extremely limited oversight that had been imposed to that point. This was also the issue ultimately taken up by the U.S. General Accounting Office in 1975, when it recommended that overseas embassies, USAID, and the State Department take a much more active role in formulating AIFLD program objectives, developing timelines for the turnover of programs to local unions, and evaluating the institute's performance (Comptroller General of the United States 1975).

Workers themselves had additional critiques. Fred Hirsch, chairman pro tem of the Emergency Committee to Defend Democracy in Chile and a member of the Plumbers and Steamfitters Local 393, argued in a self-published pamphlet that, although there are "more than 60 million workers in this country who are unorganized, the AFL-CIO has never asked for government funds to use here in the U.S. for organizing a 'democratic labor movement'" (Hirsch 1974: 7). Hirsch continued to explain that the actions of AFL-CIO leadership in Latin American affairs have an enormous impact on U.S. unions and those they represent:

> Through alliance with the major multinationals and U.S. government representatives bought and paid for by those corporations, only one thing has been gained: top men in the AFL-CIO are able to sit down with the men who run our government and deal as junior partners. This amounts to less than nothing at all on the paycheck or in the dignity of the working people of our country. In exchange for such favors, our name is used as a front for the State Department and the CIA, whose invisible tentacles wrap around the vital functioning parts of the labor movement. (Hirsch 1974: 42)

Hirsch concluded by insisting that the AIFLD should be abolished and that Latin American working people should be able to organize in their own interests.

While the PTTI was eventually identified as the first union to accept CIA funds in order to channel them through the AIFLD for anticommunist activity in Latin America, William Doherty Sr., like George Meany during the congressional hearings, denied having ever received CIA funds or having participated in CIA operations (Kwitny 1984). In his 1975 memoir, the former CIA agent Philip Agee, who often worked with the AIFLD as his chief cover, exposed the AIFLD as having been created and run by the CIA and its leaders, including Romualdi and Doherty Jr., as some of its most important operatives (Harrod 1972; Hirsch 1974; Kwitny 1984; Sims 1992; Spaulding 1977).[183] While it is important to understand the AIFLD in terms of its usefulness to the CIA—Agee and others have also revealed the involvement of its trainees in coups throughout Latin America, including Brazil, Chile, the Dominican Republic, and Guyana—it is equally important to understand its function in relation to the crushing of radical workers' movements through the spreading of business unionism, which means also the spreading of the ideology of class collaboration. Thus, a process that began in Jamaica with the discovery of commercial quantities of bauxite and the assistance of North American unionists to the fledgling NWU eventually created the conditions not only for the incredible, though incredibly uneven, economic growth of the first decade after independence, but also for the sharpening of the partisan political divides that would ultimately lead to the phenomenal proliferation of election-related violence.

THERE IS ONE ADDITIONAL PIECE TO THE PUZZLE I AM PUTTING together here, and that is the role of Rastafari in West Kingston as gangs were being formed. Douglas Mack (1999: 62) reminds us that while the major exodus of Rastafari from rural St. Catherine occurred with the destruction of Pinnacle in 1954, "Rastafarian brethren began to establish camps all over the corporate areas by the mid-1940s."[184] That some of these brethren were involved in emergent gangs coalescing in West Kingston between 1955 and 1963, therefore, should not be surprising (Chevannes 1981). The first of these gangs, the Vikings, was established near what is now Newport East, a community of fishermen and hustlers who worked the ships docking in the harbor. The Vikings, Barry Chevannes reported, were influenced by the Rastafari movement *and* the socialist movement. The defeat of the latter in 1952 with the purging of the left from the PNP, he argued, "left an ideological vacuum in semi-lumpen Viking community which was partially filled by the dreadlocks, who by 1960 could be identified as the leading trend throughout the Rastafari movement" (Chevannes 1981: 393). The Vikings became a dominant force among urban youth not only through their winning football team (that was, not incidentally, composed of all dreadlocks), but also because of their ability to secure valuable commodities—such as pistols—from the ships.

The second gang was the Park, or "Culbut" (Culvert), men, who met in a park in Denham Town at the top of Wellington Street. Park men, Chevannes wrote, were known to be petty thieves, but they were also involved in more dangerous crimes that involved weapons, so they were "on good and friendly terms with the Vikings." The third gang was the Salt City group, who were "famous for their use of knives and cutlasses, and for riding around on their bicycles in large numbers" (Chevannes 1981: 393). Chevannes also mentioned a group of youth, friendly with the Vikings, who followed Duke Reid and hung out on the corner of Regent and Charles Streets. This group's activities, he argued, were not based in crime, but the group was drawn into political affiliation when the PNP constituency headquarters moved to their corner and they "found themselves also the object of attacks" (Chevannes 1981: 394). They became known as the Spanglers.

Chevannes argued that these gangs coexisted relatively peacefully until 1963, when the JLP, through West Kingston MP Edward Seaga, who was also the minister of community development and welfare, began to organize youth toward social development goals through the Youth Development Agency (YDA).[185] Chevannes recounted that the Park gang formed a club, Wellington United, which became affiliated to the YDA, which afforded the club access to sports gear and equipment but also subjected it to intense pressure to affiliate with the JLP. It was not long until YDA affiliation became "regarded as tantamount to JLP affiliation," which generated physical boundaries and fissures between groups that previously had operated on friendly terms. "Inter-gang hostilities," Chevannes (1981: 394–95) wrote, "became at the same time inter-party hostilities," with the Salt City gang (now renamed Phoenix City) and other smaller groups based in youth clubs allied to the JLP and the Vikings and Spanglers maintaining a PNP affiliation. The Park gang was split and eventually became a target of violence from both sides. With the slum clearance project that began in 1963 and culminated in 1966, the communities of Back O'Wall and Ackee Walk were completely wiped out, and the Vikings were dispersed from the area that would become the new housing estate of Tivoli Gardens. As a result, the JLP developed its most notorious stronghold in the Kingston ghetto areas, thereby reversing the long-standing dominance, enjoyed since 1949, of the PNP.

This brings us right back to where we started.

The point I am making is that by the time the 1960s began, there was an established ground for linking security, Rastafari, and the trade in ganja with trade unionism and political partisanship, itself generated through an intensifying anticommunist paranoia throughout the 1950s on the part of the United Kingdom and the United States. Bearing witness through these surveillance archives shows that as Jamaican nationalists were envisioning the constitutional changes that would lead to self-government, they were envisioning them within the paranoid parameters—violently maintained—that were established by the Cold War and growing U.S. hegemony and covert action. These parameters also provided the ground upon which territory in downtown Kingston would be linked to the provision of services; thus, the vectors of what would become intense political violence and penetration by the United States (politically and economically) were established by the beginning of the decade. That we still feel the effects of these entanglements today should be obvious. How to dismantle them is less so.

Coda

The END *of the* WORLD
as WE KNOW IT

I HAVE WRITTEN IT BEFORE, BUT I WILL WRITE IT AGAIN. BEFORE I was an anthropologist I was a dancer. Or perhaps it is more accurate to say that before I knew I was an anthropologist I was doing the sort of "deep hanging out" one might understand as fieldwork with concert and popular dancers, learning about politics, economy, and social and cultural histories—my own and others'—through the kind of collaborative relationships dance requires. For me, knowledge was embodied before it was text-based, and methods were participatory before they were anything else. Once I learned there was something called anthropology during my first semester in graduate school, I saw myself following in the footsteps of Katherine Dunham and Zora Neale Hurston—other artists who became anthropologists—because I had always entered new communities through dance. Moreover, I had always been interested in how theatrical and dance performance could not only *express* a political worldview but also *enact* it. We *knew* and became conscious by doing something—with our bodies—together, and in this way, we also became human. In her exploration of Afro-diasporic sacred, secular, martial, and touristic dance forms, Yvonne Daniel has articulated this phenomenon this way:

As diaspora dance travels in translocal and transnational performances, transcendent experiences are shared . . . such that the corporeal becomes the ecstatic, so that the ancestral world joins the present, and transformational states of being preside. . . . Repeated transcendent experiences over time give the dancing community form and solidarity, and dancing itself encourages a virtual journey that makes the ephemeral moments of the dance usual, normal, the ideal. . . . While dancing cannot confer legal citizenship, it does ignite feelings surrounding commitment to the group, bonds of solidarity, and communal connections within the dancing community. . . . In the moments of the dance, feelings of belonging are generated and solidarity is affirmed, even if temporarily; in the moments of the dance, feelings of fierce self-worth, strength, and rebellion are also activated. (Daniel 2011: 190, 193; see also Daniel 2018)

Here, sovereignty *feels* like a kind of self-naming, a responsibility for others to whom we are attached, an embodied practice that counters a history of dispossession, culminating in forms of transcendence—personally, spiritually, and communally (see also Ellis 2015; Henriques 2011; Stanley 2010). In this affective state, body becomes spirit becomes something more than the sum of its parts, resonating far beyond the domain of arts practice.

My own complicities in this story do not end with dance, however. As the Destroyers for Bases Agreement was being signed, my maternal grandfather, a machinist, began working at the Kohler Company just outside Sheboygan, Wisconsin, where my mother was born and raised. Because he had a baby and a skill, my grandfather received an exemption from the draft and could serve the war effort locally, working the second shift at Kohler in addition to his day job. During the war, torpedo manufacturing replaced that of bathroom fixtures on the production floor, and the small engines, generators, artillery shells, and piston rings they made were shipped to troops in every war theater. After the war, my grandfather was asked whether he wanted to stay on at Kohler, but instead he went to work for my great-grandfather, Grandpa Rusch. Grandpa Rusch was one of thirteen children in a family that had migrated from Germany, seeking a better life in the Midwestern woods. After his mother died, he was raised by his older sister. He left school in the fourth grade, became a logger and eventually a blacksmith, and opened his own shop on Sheboygan's south side. This eventually became the auto body repair shop my cousin now owns and manages, and Grandpa Rusch's old blacksmith anvil still holds pride of place in the back.

Twelve years after my grandfather began his brief tenure at Kohler, as U.S.-based unions were beginning to mobilize bauxite workers in Jamaica through the National Workers Union (NWU), unions also attempted—ultimately unsuccessfully—to organize at Kohler. This led to the longest workers' strike in U.S. history. As a company town, Kohler employed hundreds of people throughout the area, and the father of one of my mother's grade-school friends was involved in the organizing. For my mother and many others, the strike was divisive and devastating. Workers were brought in from Detroit because so many people locally refused to cross the picket lines. "A lot of families split up," she remembered, "because some were for the union and some were not. They picketed at our church because we were putting Kohler fixtures in when we rebuilt the church. It was really kind of a scary thing for Sheboygan, demonstrating a lot, threatening, paint-bombing houses, destruction. . . . It affected the community a great deal."

In 1962, when Katrin Norris published her incisive critique of Jamaican socioeconomic and political realities on the eve of Jamaica's independence, my German-Dutch-American mother met my Jamaican father in a church choir in Milwaukee. Sixteen years after Hugh Macmillan attended the Priory School during the year his father, William Macmillan, served as interim head of the Department of History at the University College of the West Indies (1954–55), I began primary school there. The year before Michael Manley declared "democratic socialism" in 1974, my mother, father, and I left Jamaica for the United States, thus ending their vision of return and contribution to newly independent Jamaica.

My father is not particularly compelled by the substance of my work, only really by the fact that I am working and that, for the most part, I am *happy* working. In his view of things, Jamaica betrayed him. Unlike so many others, he managed to advance from a technical secondary school in rural St. Catherine to a job in the sales technical department at Shell. From there he had the opportunity to travel to other parts of the Caribbean, where he encountered worlds unimaginable in rural Jamaica. One kind Jesuit priest he met at a bar in Venezuela offered to obtain an application form for Marquette University, where, the priest told my father, he'd be able to work and go to school, and more important, where the Jesuits would make sure he *stayed* in school. He sent off the application and was accepted, but he deferred a semester in order to earn enough money to satisfy the requirements of the university and the U.S. Immigration Office.

With the exception of marrying my mother, which at the time was traumatic for all parties concerned, my father did what he was supposed to do. He got an undergraduate degree in business. He stayed on for the master's. He made his plans to return. He landed a job at GraceKennedy. But being from rural St. Catherine and growing up without a father, he didn't have a "name."

Thanks to the genetic input of my mother, people I meet outside my usual circles in Jamaica assume *I* have a "name." They ask me "which Thomases" I belong to, and they blush with shame when I tell them I have no idea, that my father never knew his father, that I am not a generations-deep member of the professional educated brown middle class.

I, in turn, marvel at those whose families' status goes *way* back, before my grandmother migrated from Troja to Kingston to work as a seamstress, before she met my father's father near the Kingston docks, before her parents migrated to Cuba when she was a baby, before her father—the son of an enslaved woman and her owner—became a tailor. Those are families, educated and "cultured," whose ties to one another span worlds from Kingston to Oxford to America and back again. Always back again. My father went back again, with his American wife and hybrid daughter, and could move only so far within the systems in which the kinds of networks created in and through those ties were essential. Disenchanted and broke, he returned to the United States. As someone who had campaigned for Norman Manley in rural St. Catherine before the 1955 elections, he would have felt the promise of that moment.

Indeed, in Troja, where he grew up, those seeking political office would usually end up at his grandfather's house. Mr. Fergie, as he was known by people in the community, was a tailor who had owned a shop in Cuba early in the twentieth century and who, upon returning to Jamaica, worked with several hotels in Kingston, in addition to opening his own shop in Spanish Town. He was, as my father has said, "recognized as a force," as someone with some intellectual ability and some "reasonableness." "When we would go to community meetings," he remembered, "people would listen to him when he spoke, and he didn't speak a lot." Mr. Fergie was also a Justice of the Peace and a member of the Anglican cathedral in Spanish Town, and, as my father recalled, "People knew about that so they would come and talk to him on weekends." Between these informal meetings and accompanying his mother and aunt who worked at the polling booths in 1949, my father developed a level of awareness of politics in Jamaica, which for most people in rural St. Catherine at the time was oriented toward how the different candidates would affect the price of coffee and sugar.

By the time my father was twelve or thirteen, he had begun to visit his aunties in Kingston during the summers. Aunt Viola had a bar and brothel on Hanover Street just east of Parade, and Aunt Olga ran a bar on Spanish Town Road between Oxford Street and Rose Lane, near Coronation Market. Because politicians would give speeches in the market, they often ended up in Aunt Olga's bar afterward to meet with people. This is how my father came to be familiar with the West Kingston politicians. Through Aunt Olga's husband, Beres, who boxed in a gym on North Street but was known best as Batmo the Cyclist, he became involved in running sound trucks, and by the time he was at Dint Hill Technical High School, he had met Norman Manley at the bar. "We knew Manley and Busta were related, and that Manley was the more educated of the two," he remembered, "and we thought it was time for a change, and the PNP embodied that change."[1]

At that time, from his perspective, there was really no movement for independence, but people in Troja were aware of the support for federation within Kingston. My father developed an affinity for Ben Cox, and he became involved in campaigning for him and Norman Manley. He pulled out of politics, however, once he graduated from Dint Hill and started his job at Shell, around 1958. It wasn't until my father began his studies at Marquette that he became aware of U.S. trade unions' involvement in Jamaica. At Marquette, he also became engaged in the attempts to eradicate McCarthyism and to admit China to the United Nations, an involvement, he would later find out, that opened an FBI file with his name on it. For my father, and doubtless others like him, his inability to make his own aspirations dovetail with those of the newly independent Jamaica upon his return would have chafed painfully. He naturalized as a U.S. citizen in 1975 and never looked back. It is complicated, therefore, that I do.

"America made you!" a friend recently exclaimed to me. We were discussing our complicated relationships to the class, color, and gender normativities in Jamaica, coming to the conclusion that those who see themselves fitting within these norms are the ones who find it easier to stay. The rest of us live in the worlds of diaspora, multiply. There are always at least two worlds in my head, and I am happy in both, never quite complete in either, always slightly peripatetic. As an American, I am fully confident in my blackness, though I would never be recognized as such in Jamaica. As a Jamaican, I am fully confident in my worldliness, though I am sometimes playfully chastised for having "exercised my options," as it were. As an academic anthropologist, I revel in the privilege of deep reflection and research, of the periods of blissful solitude punctuated by the intensities of fieldwork, teaching, and traveling with students. As an artist and former dancer, I long for creative embodied collaboration. As someone with activist inclinations, I wonder whether any of this matters, is useful, lights a fire, creates change.

Michelle Stephens (2014) has reminded us that approaching racial politics through the lens of performance—just as thinking sovereignty in relation to affect—requires us to think explicitly in terms of audience. The audiences for the story of post-plantation political life that I have rendered here are complexly organized, and what I have offered in these pages will also be complexly consumed. Some West Indian academics may have less patience for the theoretical musings regarding temporality and affect, seeing them perhaps as an imposition of "foreign" preoccupations irrelevant to the fierce urgencies of the neoliberal now, but Jamaicans at home and in diaspora may appreciate the specificities of the historical revisitations here. African American Studies scholars may feel bogged down by the minutiae of a context that does not necessarily seem immediately germane, but thinking relationally about what Jamaica teaches us about general twentieth-century processes should be useful for scholars theorizing diaspora. Mainstream anthropologists, I hope, will be interested in the conceptual interventions related to sovereignty and affect, but historically the field has been largely uninterested in processes that concern "New World" black folk, as the black people who have mattered in the discipline tend to be located in Africa, and there they somehow seem to exist outside global discourses regarding raciality (see Pierre 2008; Thomas and Clarke 2013). Human rights workers will likely be interested in the narratives of Tivoli Gardens residents but may be frustrated by my resistance to producing them as transparent testimonies.

While I have wanted, in these pages, to identify the forms of political life that have been possible at particular junctures, to parse what sovereignty has felt like at specific moments, and to think through the technologies that have circulated these affects and the archives they have generated, it seems also worth asking what repair would feel like. I have said repair here rather than reparation in order to mark a shift in orientation, a shift similar to the one marked by a move from resistance to refusal.[2] Repair, like refusal, is practice-oriented and quotidian; it is non-eventful and deeply historical and relational. Like its nominal counterpart, repair urges us to interrogate the multiple scales of entanglement that have led us to where we are now. But where reparation seeks justice through the naming of names, the exposure of public secrets, and the articulation of chains of causality, repair looks for something else. It demands an active listening, a mutual recognizing, an acknowledging of complicity at all levels—behavioral evidence of profound interior transformations that are ongoing.[3]

The shift from reparation to repair indexes another, from justice to "affectability." This is Denise Ferreira da Silva's (2013) term, one that she uses to think through the ways popular responses to antiblack state violence—such as riots, such as fires—demand a different kind of understanding, "knowing" in her words, than those usually pursued juridically. "Knowing at the limits of justice," she writes, "as an ethico-political praxis, requires ontoepistemological accounts that begin and end with relationality (affectability)—that do no

more [than] to anticipate what is to be announced, perhaps, a horizon of radical exteriority, where knowing demands affection, intention, and attention"
(Ferreira da Silva 2013: 44). It is an unsettled horizon, this knowing—not a
blueprint—where futures uncertainly cotch, and where civil society is resitu-
ated through a recognition of the limits of justice within the contextual terrain of liberal post-Enlightenment humanism. And so we return to the questions animating this book: What does it mean to be human—politically—in
the wake of the plantation? What kind of revolution would have had to have
happened for processes of repair to be meaningful? How might we think of
repair affectively, without evacuating the possibility of politics? How are we
implicated in the perpetuation of sovereign violence, and to whom are we
accountable?

WHILE THE WEST KINGSTON COMMISSION OF ENQUIRY HAS BEEN
critical to a national (and diasporic) discussion of how sovereign violence
has been generated and the institutions through which it is and has been enacted, it has not ultimately repaired the lives of those who lost loved ones or
were themselves injured within Tivoli Gardens, even if they were compensated monetarily for damage to property. It did not suddenly enable Annette
to revel in the company of her nephews, whom she avoids because they remind her of her own loss. Nor was it what eventually stopped Shawn Bowen
from beginning his morning with white rum. It did not, as community members say, "bring back life," either literally or metaphorically. In part, this is
because this Commission, and others like it, was a juridical solution that, as
many have critiqued within other contexts, was rooted in a liberal human-
ist conception of rights and morality attendant to a universal human that
does not recognize the gendered, sexual, racial, and civilizational inequalities
that have sedimented over centuries and that therefore merely (re)produces
the undifferentiated juridical and economic subjects it presupposes without
fundamentally transforming the material, social, or symbolic circumstances
through which they emerged.[4] It is also because truth commissions and other
enquiries require for their realization that we imagine ourselves to exist in a
post-violence, post-conflict moment rather than encouraging us to interrogate the forms of historical and everyday violence that co-relate to create the
conditions for spectacular enactments.

If a shift from reparation to repair rescues us from the hegemony of liberalism, it must also foreground a more robust sense of ethics and justice. The
real question, therefore, arrives: *Is the political the sphere through which ethical
relations can meaningfully emerge?* Of course, Rastafari have long answered

this question in the negative, grounding ethical life instead in *marronage*, a state of being in which "agents struggle psychologically, socially, metaphysically, and politically to exit slavery, maintain freedom, and assert a lived social space while existing in a liminal position" (Roberts 2015: 10).[5] I want to argue that it is in conditions of marronage that repair is possible.

Reparation, as David Eng (2011, 2016) has noted, is not only a political concept but also a psychoanalytic one. Eng reads Melanie Klein's account of child development to note that in its singular form, reparation refers to the repairing of harm at the psychic level. For Eng (2011:168), Klein's immediate post–World War II context of global war and genocide prompted her to posit love as the means through which to address the "negative psychic forces associated with Freud's death drive: paranoia, hate, projection, and aggression." Love, for Klein, was the mediating element in psychic processes, the mechanism through which an infant would mitigate the psychic violence of loving and then hating the mother. Eng (2011) explains this way: Klein believed that infants carry unconscious guilt for this hatred, and this guilt propels the infant to seek a reparative process in order to preserve the object of love (the mother) and, therefore, love itself. Drawing from Judith Butler's *Frames of War* (2009), Eng continues by arguing that because this process is ultimately rooted in self-preservation, it is self- rather than other-interested, making reparation not a process of justice or an ethical responsibility toward another who has been harmed—reparations, in its plural form—but instead a means by which to stave off precarity. He concludes, therefore, that where Klein's theory *could* help us "describe reparation as the psychic condition of possibility for the precipitation of both the (m)other and the social world" (Eng 2011: 172), it ultimately stops short of this realization.

For Eng, this is because Klein's own intellectual and sociopolitical orientation—as she surprisingly scales up to discuss these processes in relation to European colonization of the New World—leads her to understand the colonizer as the infant in the reparative relationship, with this infant seeking to repair a relationship with the mother(land) in Europe. "With Hegelian echoes of lord and bondsman," he argues, "psychic reparation is transformed into an alibi for war and aggression by displacing the actual, external violence of colonial conquest and genocide into an internal struggle of European family and nation" (Eng 2011: 178). In this way, Klein differentiates the human into those who deserve care and redress (overseas colonists) from those who do not (natives, and later, African slaves), and the preservation of love through reparation becomes the perpetuation of colonial violence, which is later transmuted (within the U.S. context) through nationalist processes (Eng 2016). The leap from psychic to political reparation in Klein, then, enables us to see how racist and genocidal violence becomes foundational to U.S. nationalism, and by extension, to understand how "colonial modernity frames not only the material development but also the psychic emergence of liberal subjectivity" (Eng 2016: 2–3). Here, reparation circumscribes love. *Real* love thus requires something else. It requires deep affective recognition.

This is not the recognition of Hegel, the antagonistic process through which the subject recognizes itself in opposition to that which is different and thus comes into being by defending itself against that difference, thereby resolving difference into a form of sameness.[6] The problem here is that if subjectivity is the result of hostile conflict, then recognition must inevitably exist as a relation of domination. It is this domination that, for Frantz Fanon, makes mutual recognition impossible within a colonial context. As he famously argued, the abolition of slavery and emancipation did not give the enslaved person what was urgently needed: a reciprocal intersubjective relation that would create a mutual sense of responsibility for the other's being-in-itself. Instead, the historically specific structure of racism required the colonized to seek recognition on the colonizer's terms, what the philosopher Kelly Oliver (2001: 26) has called a "double bind."[7] Put another way, if racism entails denying an "Other" those qualities of being so central to the self, as Lewis Gordon (2015: 69) has written, then intersubjective relations between whites and blacks "are such that blacks, in their effort to rise out of the zone of nonbeing, struggle to achieve Otherness (to get into Self-Other relations); it is a struggle to be in a position, in effect, *for the ethical to emerge.*" Colonial recognition therefore could entail one's apprehension only as "an object in the midst of other objects," and any effective dis-alienation would require a fundamental transformation of the social, political, and economic worlds that undergird this psychic objectification. Of this, Fanon ([1952] 1967: 109) wrote:

> Sealed into that crushing objecthood, I turned beseechingly to others. Their attention was a liberation, running over my body suddenly abraded into nonbeing, endowing me once more with an agility that I had thought lost, and by taking me out of the world, restoring me to it. But just as I reached the other side, I stumbled, and the movements, the attitudes, the glances of the other fixed me there, in the sense in which a chemical solution is fixed by a dye.

Note here Fanon's attention to physicality and to the realm of the sensual. Liberation washes over the body; it endows it with agility. We leap out of the world, but then stumble and become stuck in place.[8]

Jessica Benjamin's wrestling with Hegel led her to develop the concept of the "intersubjective third," a literal and metaphorical space outside the traditional power dynamics of the therapist-analysand dyad, but one that is still grounded in language.[9] For Kaja Silverman (1996: 41), this third is the textual or visual material that can generate a reparative process of idealization, the "radical redistribution of value" that destabilizes the misrecognition of the mirror and potentially produces the generous and active gift of love she sees as necessary for genuine relation to another. My sense is that the space of the "third"—that space that also emerged for Homi Bhabha (1994) as the hybrid location where new structures of authority and new forms of political engagement were possible—is closer to Silverman's. That is to say that the space of recognition is not best realized through language but is emergent through affect. Or perhaps it is more accurate to say that narrative has value only insofar as it engenders—verbally or otherwise—a structure of feeling that is dependent on relationality.

Michael Jackson's (2013) exegesis of Hannah Arendt's view of storytelling as a modality of politics is useful here. From Jackson, we know that Arendt understood storytelling as purposeful action linking individuals to the collectivity, and both to the histories that have created the world as it is and that have shaped our places within it. For Arendt, intersubjectivity was the intentional result of a process of communication that, through the relating of individual experience, "brings the social into being" (Jackson 2013: 16), by which she really meant the ideal of a democratic community of equals. Storytelling, moreover, "is a form of restorative praxis," a way to "act in the face of forces that render us inactive and silent" (Jackson 2013: 23). It is a mechanism through which to create the ethical discursive space in which answers to problems are not juridically proscribed but are open-ended and contingent. "Rather than supporting the status quo," Jackson (2013: 29) writes, "stories open up for discussion the ethical dilemmas not of perpetuating a given social order but of creating a more viable life." In this way, narratives are neither transparent nor the property of individuals, though they may describe an individual's experience. Instead, in creating a field of intersubjective recognition through dialogue, the relating of narratives is a form of Witnessing 2.0, a witnessing beyond human rights whose purpose is not merely to document tragedy, suffering, and abuse for an audience elsewhere but is geared toward materializing a transformation in the very relation between narrator and audience. This, of course, is how we have approached the narratives of those West Kingston community members whose stories became the backbone of the multimedia installation "Bearing Witness," the film *Four Days in May*, and this book.

The affective recognition I am striving toward here is akin to the embodied hapticality Stefano Harney and Fred Moten (2013: 98) identify as "the capacity to feel through others, for others to feel through you, for you to feel them feeling you." Yet this is not the "affective recognition" Axel Honneth (2008) describes, despite his more recent move toward a theory of primary, social affective ontology preceding love, law, and achievement, the three forms of recognition he considers the basis of ethical life. Honneth's theory of recognition has been understood by philosophers as more anthropological than most, grounded as it is in a "phenomenology of social suffering" (Petherbridge 2013: 3). As someone who is interested in the move within Marxism toward a Habermasian paradigm of communicative action, Honneth (1995) sees intersubjectivity as something more than a linguistic phenomenon and as a process that is situated within particular power relations. He's therefore interested in the normative conditions, and the broader social and institutional structures, within which people attempt to relate and, potentially, to self-realize.[10]

Yet Honneth's recognition, for me, remains too tethered to object relations theory, too dependent on a notion of stages of intersubjectivity that radiate out from the infant-caregiver relationship (constituted through love, which for him is the basis for all forms of self-realization, ethics, and, eventually, political action), and, ultimately, too grounded in the language of law and rights. As such, it is still dominated by a subject-other relation grounded in binary notions of freedom and unfreedom. Recognition here is still something to be given rather than felt; by the time we get to love, law, and achievement, we have already perceived, we have already theorized our bodily relation and come up short.[11] This is because quite apart from his interest in the local dynamics of power relations and his early interest in ethical intersubjectivity and social change, Honneth tends toward the presumption of a universal subject that can expect recognition rather than thinking through the implications of an inaugural condition of possibility that can never be available for particular members of a social group. Individuals, thus, must strive for recognition within normative ideals and existing forms of social organization rather than seeing recognition as a process of intersubjectively developing new ideals and institutional forms.

Emmanuel Levinas's ideas about recognition come closer to the affective technologies I am imagining. Levinas privileges an understanding of recognition as preobjective, as an ontology that has to be grounded in ethics. For him, the other is a "placeholder for an infinite ethical relation" (see Butler 2005: x) that rejects both domination and synthesis. Levinas eschews recognition as a struggle between antagonists whereby the other is maintained primarily as a mediator (which is what the self needs) in order to create a universal "We" through which intersubjectivity is realized (Pöykkö 2016: 641).

Instead, mutual recognition yields affirmation in difference through which two parties are not joined, because the other resists the self's claim to knowledge and identification (Levinas 1985, 1969). For Levinas (1969), the "face of the other" is irreducible to knowledge, and communication should not have the goal of making the interior knowable and legible.[12] He therefore does not accept ontological reckonings of intersubjectivity because they are based on knowledge processes designed to categorize (and therefore neutralize) others. He rejects this kind of representation as imperialist and suggests instead that the face of the other demands responsibility, which is the ethical imperative of unknowability. This is what Édouard Glissant (1997) would have called "opacity," a resistance to Western imperial knowledge projects in which we become objects among other objects. For Levinas, the embodied self holds priority over the intentional "I," and ethical recognition must therefore be prior to ontological recognition (Pöykkö 2016).

This takes us again back to embodiment. At an earlier anthropological moment, importantly and tellingly one that is now also making a comeback, the affective recognition I want to call into being might indeed have been understood through the language of phenomenology, or the kinds of "somatic modes of attention" Thomas Csordas (1993) has advanced over the years.[13] Csordas has understood embodiment as both a methodological and theoretical paradigm through which the body is the starting point for human investigation:

> Because attention implies both sensory engagement and an object, we must emphasize that our working definition refers both to attending "with" and attending "to" the body. To a certain extent it *must* be both. To attend to a bodily sensation is not to attend to the body as an isolated object, but to attend to the body's situation in the world. . . . Attention *to* a bodily sensation can thus become a mode of attending to the intersubjective milieu that gave rise to that sensation. Thus, one is paying attention *with* one's body. (Csordas 1993: 138)

This attention also requires *attending to* the bodies of others, yet understanding bodily experience beyond the self requires an embrace of a radical principle of indeterminacy, one "that undermines dualities between subject and object, mind and body, self and other" (Csordas 1993: 152). This indeterminacy stems from the "preobjective and prereflective experience of the body" (Csordas 1990: 6). Csordas uses Maurice Merleau-Ponty's notion of the *preobjective* here not to suggest that bodily movement or apprehension is precultural but, instead, to "capture that moment of transcendence in which perception begins, and, in the midst of arbitrariness and indeterminacy, constitutes and is constituted by culture" (Csordas 1990: 9). The subject here comes into being through embodied relation, not through language, which continually reenacts the subject-object binary. For Csordas (1990: 40), collapsing these binaries "allows us to investigate how cultural objects (including selves) are constituted or objectified, not in the processes of ontogenesis and child socialization, but in the ongoing indeterminacy and flux of adult cultural life."

It is my contention that this indeterminacy—one that allows us to develop an intersubjectivity grounded in "intercorporeal immediacy" (Csordas 2008: 118)—is the only way to appreciably move outside the Self-Other binary, and all of the dualisms that emerge from (and that are reproduced through) this binary, that still so suffuse psychoanalytic readings of recognition and intersubjectivity. If archives of affect are to generate technologies of deep recognition, then this recognition must occur at the site of precognitive (which, again, is not to say precultural or presocial) experience, an experience that is embodied before it is grasped through reflection.

The deep affective recognition I desire is therefore an embodied psychic recognition that decimates modernist imperial dualisms. It is the basis for new socialities, not the visual interpellation insisted on by the phrase "Look, a Negro!"; an interpellation still so reliant on flesh and skin, as Stephens (2014) has so magnificently theorized. It is, instead, Fanon's ([1952] 1967: 222) more hopeful *Yes!*: "*Yes* to life. *Yes* to love. *Yes* to generosity." Fanon's love is not love as a private affair—the eros Slavoj Žižek disdains as impatient, intolerant, and violent—nor is it the love of imperial control and liberal development, the claims to improvement and holds on populations as objects. It is not the "political love" Michael Hardt (2011: 677) advocates, though this love, too, moves across scales, "betraying the conventional divisions between personal and political, and grasping the power to create bonds that are once intimate and social."[14] It is, instead, "authentic love," that form of legitimating recognition, that "wishing for others what one postulates for oneself, when that postulation unites the permanent values of human reality" (Fanon [1952] 1967: 41). It is the agape love Martin Luther King Jr. advanced in his sermon delivered at the Ebenezer Baptist Church in September 1962; that love that is unmotivated, spontaneous, and overflowing. It is the love of Lauren Berlant's (2011b: 685, 687) "attachment to the world," an "affective binding that allows us to iron things out, or to be elastic, or to try a new incoherence." And finally, it is John Jackson's (2005: 226) real love of "opaque, interiorized, nervous, dark" sincerity, a sincerity that takes risks, that takes for granted the incompleteness and partiality of knowledge of both others and self. This love is a commitment to an attention that while not *grounded* in a search for certain recognizable accountabilities still makes our complicity in the matters at hand unavoidable and incontrovertible, and therefore our response-ability imperative.

This brings me back to Avery Gordon (2008: 205) and her insistence that "when you know in a way you did not know before, then you have been notified of your involvement. You are *already* involved, implicated, in one way or another." For Gordon (2008: 183), this implication requires "something to be done"; it demands an affective reckoning with the way the past haunts the present.[15] What violence produces, therefore, is the need for an ethical disposition beyond the political, one that seeks to probe and acknowledge the extent to which we are complicit in its reproduction and therefore obligated to its transformation. This is also Oliver's (2001) position, one grounded in the assertion that to get beyond binaries and toward relationality we must traverse the terrain of responsibility. This is Witnessing 2.0, and it can take many forms, but in its broadest sense, for Oliver (2001: 143), it "is a commitment to embrace the responsibility of constituting communities, the responsibility inherent in subjectivity itself." Having thus dispensed with the antagonistic and binaristic model of recognition as the basis for a sincere love and attention, we can now contend that real subjectivity requires a responsible—indeed, response-able—witness, and that this creates the terrain for being human.

I have attempted, throughout this book, to show how the disavowal of the continued relationship between coloniality and contemporary state violence has created a condition in which the constant state of injury inhibits the recognition of a shared history and thus a collective humanity, and in which we must therefore constantly enact forms of counter-narration that are supported by other kinds of archives. I have also sought to limn the affective dimensions of post-plantation sovereignty at three moments in Jamaica and, by doing so, to suggest something about the relationship between Romanticist poets and developmentalist pragmatists within broader projects of social and political transformation.

We have seen that during the late 1960s and early 1970s, these two versions of social change came into a more intimate relation (though sometimes in unexpected ways), creating the possibility for *expectancy* as a dominant affective sociopolitical field. Nevertheless, the late colonial moment of the 1950s and the late liberal moment of the early twenty-first century produced affective hegemonies—*paranoia* and *doubt*, respectively—that revealed the vast chasm between the developmentalist and, later, neoliberal dictates of the state and the aspirations of citizens to be recognized as human. In part, this has had to do with the centrality of security to both moments, a centrality that endlessly reproduces social worlds in which an Other must constantly be identified and kept out of a Self. What we might learn, however, from the archives I have assembled here is a way to cultivate new and loving terrains through which we might bring new social worlds into being.

THERE WERE NO JAMAICAN SONGS ABOUT THE "INCURSION" IN ITS aftermath (Page 2017).[16] In a cultural context in which every event is instantaneously memorialized, debated, and mined for social and political significance within the lyrics and spaces of the dancehall, this absence—this failure of language—is significant. Two songs have been insistently running across my mind throughout the process of writing about Tivoli and editing our footage—Mos Def's "Umi Says" and Talib Kweli's "I Try." That these are both songs by American hip hop artists who once recorded as a duo called Black Star also says something about this material and my relationship to it. Both these songs, though in different ways, hypnotize and hail through repetition. I recognize these repetitions like the chants, thumps, or dances of Revival, Kumina, and other Afro-diasporic spiritual traditions in which repetition is intended to produce a state of trance. In this state, we communicate with beings and things unseen; we exceed our physicality; we time-travel. Our bodies are delivered into sound. It is this state that enables affective recognition, that gives us a sense of how, when, and why embodied freedom can actually counteract the constraints of historical violence in the present, that helps create the conditions of response-ability through real love, and that urges us to work through the complex entanglements of accountability in order to act reparatively, in concert, as humans.

Acknowledgments

This project, like all projects, has been years in the making, but it wouldn't have happened at all had Deanne Bell not approached me in New York after a screening of our film, *Bad Friday*, and suggested we start a similar project about the 2010 "Tivoli Incursion" in West Kingston. Her insistence on doing something, and her approach as a community psychologist, has influenced my thinking enormously, and has taken me down paths (reluctantly, at times) that I otherwise wouldn't have gone. Because she is responsible for initiating this project, I begin my acknowledgments with her. Our interlocutors in Tivoli Gardens and the members of the International Peacemakers Association so generously gave of their time and insights so that their experiences might be known to, and felt by, others.

Many, many other people have contributed ideas, arguments, and artistic talents to what is presented here. Listing them seems so inadequate in the face of our deep conversations, arguments, and discoveries, but it will have to do. Several students in the United States and in Jamaica worked in various capacities to bring this project to completion. Ken Lum, the director of Fine Arts at Penn's Design School selected three undergraduate students to conduct photography workshops with a youth group in Tivoli Gardens while we were also recording narratives during the summer of 2013: Bonnie Arbittier, Levi Gikander, and Evan Robinson. Three Annenberg graduate students were also integrally involved with aspects of this work. Lindsey Beutin helped me develop visual and historical archives on state-led housing initiatives (among other topics), and Corrina Laughlin and Emily Ladue came to Jamaica to assist our cinematographer while we did a landscape shoot in January 2015. Josslyn Luckett was my Research Assistant during the fall 2013 semester, and she developed annotated bibliographies about affect, visual culture, and other topics. Josslyn was also one of three graduate students—the other two were Mariam Durrani and Arjun Shankar—who accompanied us to South Africa, where we also screened *Bad Friday* and presented early versions of aspects of the analysis of the Incursion that appears in these pages. Mariam and Arjun also produced "filmlets" documenting that trip, and Josslyn produced a blog. Three undergraduate students were also on that South African journey—Debi Ogunrinde, Melanie White, and Nicole Cone. I am grateful for all their insights, and have been thrilled to see them graduate and continue with their interests in anthropology and media. Three additional graduate students were helpful with various steps of this project, even when the work they were doing did not seem immediately relevant to it: Ethiraj Dattatreyan, Diego Arispe Bazan, and Krystal Smalls. And special thanks are due to three students from the Cultural Studies Program at the Mona campus of the University of the West Indies—Shelley Ann Morgan, Trojean Burrell, and Michael Lewis—who conducted interviews for me throughout the fall of 2014, and to Sonjah Stanley, who suggested these students as research assistants.

The graduate students in anthropology whom I have supervised have pushed my thinking forward in so many ways—it is inspiring to work with such wonderful intellects who are also such stellar human beings. Here, I want to recognize Osei Alleyne, Celina de Sa, Khwezi Mkhize, Negar Razavi, Michelle Munyikwa, Amber Henry, Amrey Mathurin, and Leniqueca Welcome, and also Tali Ziv and Sara Rendell, to whom I feel a close kinship though I am not their primary advisor. Negar also conducted archival research for me at the U.S. Department of State and the Central Intelligence Agency, and Leniqueca was also involved in curatorial assistance for the exhibit at the Penn Museum (alongside David Chavannes, a doctoral student in Africana studies) and in building the website, which is beautiful because of her designer's eye (https: //www.tivolistories.com). As always, my Race, Nation, Empire graduate seminar was formative and thrilling, and I thank all the students who make that space so generative and generous.

My analysis of the questions and problems that animate this book has been deeply influenced not only by my students, but by my participation in a number of sustained working groups: the Gendering Archives group at

Columbia University, the working group I'll call Rethinking the Making of Modern Jamaica (organized by David Scott and Donette Francis), and the Practicing Refusal group (organized by Saidiya Hartman and Tina Campt). So many colleagues in these spaces have offered important food for thought and intellectual comradeship, including Hazel Carby (who read and commented on the entire manuscript), Inderpal Grewal, Marianne Hirsch, Jennifer Tucker, Christina Sharpe, Alex Weheliye, Kaiama Glover, Derrieck Scott, Arthur Jafa, Denise Ferreira da Silva, Tavia Nyong'o, Phil Harper, David Scott, Donette Francis, Faith Smith (who also read and commented on the entire manuscript), Wayne Modest, Maziki Thame, Val Carnegie, Michelle Stephens (to whom I owe a great debt for pushing me toward psychoanalytic frameworks for thinking), and Don Robotham (who read and commented on most of the manuscript and who offered important comments about the film, *Four Days in May*, at a critical moment). My annual "workations" with Tina Campt have been spaces of expansive intellectuality and incredible adventure, and I could not survive academia without them.

Additional colleagues intervened at important moments, provided sounding boards, and otherwise enacted forms of loving collaboration, including Yanique Hume, Kamala Kempadoo, Kamari Clarke, Honor Ford-Smith, Deborah Anzinger, Charles Campbell, Nicole Smythe-Johnson, Melinda Brown, Linden Lewis, Dave Ramsaran, Anton Allahar; Bea Jaregui, Karen Redrobe and others who participated in the Humanities Forum 2013 year on "Violence"; Keith McNeal, Shalini Puri, Danny Hoffman, Nikhil Anand, Adriana Petryna, Rebecca Stein, Rivke Jaffe, Alex Fattal, Lisa Stevenson, Yarimar Bonilla, Harvey Neptune, Vince Brown, Herman Bennett, Judith Casselberry, Jessica Cattelino, Stephen McIsaac, Laurie Lambert, Nadia Ellis, and two powerful women whose absence from this planet is so sorely and constantly felt—Donna MacFarlane and Sonia Harris. Special thanks are also due to Danilyn Rutherford, who read and provided comments on the entire manuscript and whose orientation to a different archipelago proved incredibly generative. Tony Harriott offered important assistance at a number of points; Matthew Smith suggested I reach out to Sir Roy Augier to find out more about William Macmillan's second stay in Jamaica in the 1950s, and Augier himself was willing to sit for an interview; Hugh Small and Jerry Small are constant touchpoints and important co-thinkers, and special thanks are due to Jerry for introducing me to Sidney Ricketts; Carol Narcisse supported this project from the beginning, and put us in touch with Mattathias Schwartz, the *New Yorker* journalist who urged an American reading public to be concerned with the actions of the Jamaican security forces during the "Tivoli Incursion," and who also passed on his contacts and the Freedom of

Information Act materials he received from the U.S. Government regarding the incursion, including the footage from the U.S. drone that was overhead during the operation; Hugh Macmillan generously shared his mother's and father's archives with me, and assisted me at the Bodleian Library (Oxford); Bobby Hill put me in touch with both Brother Ruddy and Brother Slim during an early phase of my research, and made himself available for conversation about what I was gleaning from that community, as did Mark Figueroa, Clinton Hutton, Rupert Lewis, and Trevor Munroe; and Katrin (Norris) Fitzherbert responded to my letters and emails, and agreed to meet with me in her home in Western London.

Audiences at Penn (in the Anthropology Department, the Humanities Forum, and the Digital Humanities Forum); York University; the University of the West Indies, Mona and Cave Hill; Indiana University, the University of Washington; New York University; Bard College; the University of Chicago; Wesleyan University; the University of Illinois, Chicago; Princeton University; Syracuse University; Dartmouth College; the University of California, Irvine; Cornell University; and Swarthmore College provided stimulating reflections and questions. I am also incredibly indebted to Robert Simpson and Jason Smith at the National Library of Jamaica; Sheree Rhoden at the Gleaner Company; Oneil Hall and his team at CO Research Consultancy, who were able to unearth parliamentary and budgetary records pertaining to the purchase of Kingston Pen by the government prior to and in service of the development of Tivoli Gardens, as well as potential funding sources, including the U.S. Agency for International Development, for the development of the housing scheme; and to the incredibly amazing archivists and librarians at New York University's Bobst Library (Tamiment Collection) and Cornell University's Kheel Center for Labor Management Documentation and Archives, and at the National Archives in Jamaica, the United States and the United Kingdom.

I also owe an enormous debt to Julian Siggers, Dan Rahimi, and Kate Quinn of the Penn Museum for agreeing to mount (and fund) the exhibition *Bearing Witness: Four Days in West Kingston*, and to the incredibly talented and thoughtful exhibitions team for attending so empathetically to its realization. Jessica Bicknell, Josh Lessard, Michael Barker, Yuan Yao, Benjamin Neiditz, and Anne Brancati met weekly for six months to plan, discuss, evaluate fake fruit, and otherwise provide guidance for the theoretical and pragmatic framework for the exhibit. The opening of the exhibit was enormously enhanced by the panel, "Feminists Tackling State Violence," which was supported by the Alice Paul Center for Research in Gender, Sexuality and Women's Studies. The assistance of Kathy Brown, Anne Esacove, Gwendolyn Beetham, Luz Marin, and Osei Alleyne was crucial to developing this discussion; and an enormous thank you is due to Junior Wedderburn, without whose initiative we wouldn't have had the participation of revival singers from Jamaica and Jamaican drummers from New York, especially Rocky, Bishop Bailey, Jenese, and Congo Billy. Thanks also to Varun Baker, whose incredibly beautiful and sensitive portraits of our interlocutors now circle the walls of the exhibit space, and to Antonio Rossi, who allowed me to take advantage of our friendship to mobilize his Oscar-nominated cinematography skills for the price of the ticket to Kingston. And many thanks to Storm Saulter and Justine Henzell for the feedback, support, and contacts that helped to make the film better at every step.

Ken Wissoker has always stood by me in the face of what sometimes seemed like insurmountable issues, and I am grateful for his loyalty and friendship over the years. The two readers for Duke University Press offered up such useful and moving assessments of this text, and I am so thankful also for the support of Sean Mallin, my managing editor at *American Anthropologist*, who agreed to develop his skills as an indexer.

Many people offered up their homes during the years of my obsession with this project. My auntie Jean was my home away from home in London, and she welcomed me back to the east side after long days at Kew with the best braised lamb on the planet. Annie Paul, as always, provided my home away from home in Kingston, and I am always thankful for the ease of our conversations and laughter. Vanessa Spence and Carol Lawes have always been generous with their friendship and support, and my two Brown besties, Angela Mitchell and Dawn Crossland, always remind me of the ground I walk on. Shelley Smith, as well, remains my "person" in Philadelphia, even though I now travel way too much to cook Sunday dinner every week.

Something way beyond gratitude is due to my mother and father, both of whom allowed themselves to be more exposed than they normally would in these pages. Their unfaltering and principled love buoys me, even when they don't fully understand why I keep returning to these questions. My dad, and my mom by proxy, has particularly enjoyed being reentangled into family as other diasporic kin in New York and Florida made it their project almost twenty years ago to track him down. I know it has been gratifying to realize that so many people who came from so little in such a small corner of Jamaica left for "America" and did well for themselves. Junior Wedderburn, as always, has been my partner in the adventures, sorrows, amusements, and surprises that animate this book. He is my sounding board, co-thinker, and alter-ego, and none of this work could move in the world the way it does without his hands and heart. John Jackson still makes the world turn for me. At the end of the day, when I turn around, it's his example that I see, his voice that I hear, his smile that engages me, and his spirit that I strive to emulate. There may be "nothing new under the sun," but if we believe that one decides every day to walk abreast, then there is abiding contentment in the circling of the wind and the flow of the rivers to the sea. We are, still, more than the sum of our parts, until the day that eight times eight times eight is four. And finally, this book is for Oliver and Marleigh, who are no longer "small people" but are slowly coming into their own personhood. Even though they will never really be more than well-connected "tourists" in Jamaica, I hope that one day they will see the entanglements that fill these pages as their inheritance, one they will have to both inhabit and transform.

AN EARLIER DRAFT OF SOME SECTIONS FROM CHAPTER 1 WAS PRE-viously published in "Time and the Otherwise: Plantations, Garrisons, and Being Human in the Caribbean," *Anthropological Theory* 16, nos. 2–3 (2016): 177–200; an earlier exploration of the issues raised in chapter 2 was published in "What Development Feels Like: Politics, Prophecy, and the International Peacemakers in Jamaica," in *Contradictory Existence: Neoliberalism and Democracy in the Caribbean*, ed. Dave Ramsaran (Kingston, Jamaica: Ian Randle Press, 2015); and an earlier draft of part of chapter 3 was published in "Rastafari, Communism, and Surveillance in Late Colonial Jamaica," *Small Axe* 54 (2017): 63–84.

Notes

1 At his trial, Coke pled guilty to charges of racketeering and distribution of marijuana and cocaine on 30 August 2011, and he was sentenced in June 2012 to twenty-three years, which he is currently serving in a medium-security prison in South Carolina.

2 The overarching rubric of this attempt is "Tivoli Stories," a collaborative practice that has been the basis for a film (*Four Days in May*) and a multimedia installation (which was mounted in November 2017 at the Penn Museum). See https://www.tivolistories.com.

3 I have also heard through the convoluted networks that embrace Rastafari, tourists, and other lovers of Jamaica, and through the diasporic channels that link spaces within Brooklyn and the Bronx with media productions originating in Jamaica, that *Bad Friday* has screened on television in Germany, and that almost immediately after we released the film, bootlegged copies were on sale in the "bend down plazas" in Flatbush. For an analysis of the perils of visual ethnography and bootlegging, see Stout 2014.

4 By this, I do not mean to invoke an agreement with those who have argued that affect is prelinguistic or precultural, of whom Brian Massumi (2002) has been the most celebrated proponent. I have more to say about this in chapter 1 and the coda.

1   Michel-Rolph Trouillot gave us some of our most significant insights regarding archives, evidence, and the multiple roles, conceptions, and uses of history as they bear on anthropological research. His work continually asked us to position archives not just as static sources of information but as dynamic spaces of knowledge production. His argument was that both the materiality of history and the interpretations of that materiality are constructed, and that they exist as part of the scaffolding of a discursive frame of belonging and mattering vis-à-vis political and social communities. Trouillot talked about this frame mostly in terms of effects, and in relation to particular forms of silencing, but I engage this frame in relation to its affective productions and to plumb the multiple dimensions of these productions.

2   Sylvia Wynter has elaborated this tension in a number of publications (see esp. Wynter 2003), but I am thinking here of her iteration of it in Scott 2000.

3   Achille Mbembe (2011: 1) reminds us that "the task of the witness is to reopen the emancipatory possibilities which, as a consequence of the structured blindness and collective self-deception of the age, are in danger of foreclosing the future." See also Ahmed 2004 on witnessing and the ways individual pain, when witnessed, becomes a social and embodied affect; Cvetkovich 2003 on the ambivalence of witnessing; and Berlant 2011a on the affective attachments we develop to formations of inequality and injustice. I address the forms of recognition these scholars are implicitly calling for more fully in the coda.

4   One way to think about the limits of TRCs and human rights tribunals is offered by Sharon Sliwinski (2011: 56), who argues that they arise because the judgments of moral action these tribunals generate "are only afforded to those of us who are removed from the immediate action, those of us whose flesh has not been wounded directly, but whose imagination has been aroused by such images." For additional critiques of TRCs, witnessing, and testimony, see Fassin 2008; Feldman 2004; Hinton 2010; Redfield 2006; Ross 2003; Shaw et al. 2010; Theidon 2012; Ticktin 2011; Wilson 2001; Wilson and Brown 2011. And for a critique of "reconciliation" in relation to Native North American populations, see Coulthard 2014.

5   For a discussion of the issues raised by an insistence on "shared temporality," see Rifkin 2017.

6   Tait distinguishes "bearing witness" from what Paul Frosh and Amit Pinchevski (2014) have discussed as "media witnessing," a form of witnessing that has emerged from the ubiquity of smart phones. Their argument is that collective and egalitarian media witnessing has destabilized the temporal gaps between experience and discourse, bringing them into a state of "permanent simultaneity" (Frosh and Pinchevski 2014: 595). The effect of this is a kind of millenarian relationship to temporality in which each moment is experienced in terms of potentiality—"ripeness" in their account—that creates a sense of both shared vulnerability and political possibility. Media witnessing, in this context, challenges the ontological centrality of the event, instead configuring

it as repeatable and thus as shared. Events, in this formulation, can only always already be co-constituted with their repetitions, and witnessing these events exceeds the immediate experience of them, creating an embodied and material relationship to witnessing, but it does not necessarily create an imperative for meaningful action.

7 For more on the importance of developing new critical archives, see Robert Reid-Pharr's (2016) analysis of humanism and modernity through an exploration of African American engagements with Spain. Reid-Pharr (2016: 156) has called for "a radical Black Studies and an invigorated Critical Archive Studies as parts of broad-based efforts to disrupt the Man/anthropophorous animal binary." For Reid-Pharr, the development and critical reading of archives of affect also has the potential to reframe the grounds of humanism and the definition of the human.

8 There are many scholars to whom we are indebted for the certainty of this assertion. The list would include, but is not limited to, Lloyd Best (1968), Sidney Mintz ([1966] 1971, 1996), Cedric Robinson ([1983] 2000), Michel-Rolph Trouillot (1992), Eric Williams (1944), and Sylvia Wynter (2003).

9 On racial projects, see Omi and Winant 1986. For scholarship on the diverse legislative twists and turns that emerged to govern the forms of political, economic, and intimate relations throughout the long histories of Spanish, Dutch, French, and British colonial rule, see Chatterjee (1986) 1991, 1989, 1993; Cohn and Dirks 1988; Cooper 1996; Hansen and Stepputat 2006; Mignolo 2001; Stoler 2007; Taussig 1992.

10 See, e.g., Christen Smith (2016a), who has outlined the ways racialized violence against black bodies has been institutionalized through legal codes and the development of various levels of the police force in Brazil and has therefore been part and parcel of state formation during the colonial and republican periods.

11 But for examples of anthropological analyses of sovereignty that take affect seriously, see Bonilla 2015; Masco 2014; Navaro-Yashin 2012; Rutherford 2012a. Other ethnographers have striven to focus on the everyday to render the experience and expression of affective states at a variety of levels of scale through various realms of labor and public culture (see, e.g., Chalfin 2012; Mankekar 2015; Riles 2000; Stewart 2007). For an excellent review of empirical studies of affect within anthropology, see Rutherford 2016.

12 The obvious references, here and earlier, are to W. E. B. Du Bois and his classic question underpinning *The Souls of Black Folk* ([1903] 1996) and Frantz Fanon and his exploration of the psychic dimensions of colonialism in *Black Skin, White Masks* ([1952] 1967). On disavowal, see Fischer 2004.

13 While state violence has often been a focus of scholarship, sovereignty claims are also produced from the ground up. Bonilla's (2015) analysis of the syndicalist strikes in Guadeloupe demonstrates that her interlocutors' activism was not only about the constitution of new labor relations, but also about an engagement with histories of slavery and *marronage*, the development of a broader critical sociopolitical consciousness, and the generation of affective intimacies

and conceptual spaces in which new—and, in this case, nonsovereign—political forms might be imagined. In Bonilla's text, intensities of feeling are also spawned through the materialities of particular places, as is also the case in Yael Navaro-Yashin's (2012) exploration of affective geographies in Northern Cyprus. Navaro-Yashin (2012: 8), like Bonilla, argues that dates and places have "affective properties"; they are phantoms that haunt—in the Derridean sense—the contemporary actions and imaginations of people who feel them.

14 Joseph Masco (2014: 20) has argued that in the post–World War II security state, we are affectively "coordinated as subjects through felt intensities rather than [through] reason at a mass level." Daniel Goldstein's (2012) analysis of vigilante justice in Bolivia exists, in many ways, as the B side of Masco's rendering of counterterrorist paranoia, as for him mob violence is a way for people to produce security within an institutional, infrastructural, and affective context defined by insecurity. See also the "Post-Fordist Affect" special collection of *Anthropological Quarterly* (2012) for analyses of the ways insecurity is affectively rendered within a variety of neoliberal contexts. Where for Masco insecurity is a quintessentially modern affect, Ulla Berg and Ana Ramos-Zayas (2015) have argued that modernity produced additional (though related) affects, such as rationality, disenchantment, and vulnerability.

15 In a posthumously published essay in the *Annual Review of Anthropology*, Begoña Aretzaga argued that to explore everyday subject making in relation to states, one must "ask about bodily excitations and sensualities, powerful identifications, and unconscious desires of state officials; about performances and public representations of statehood; and about discourses, narratives, and fantasies generated around the idea of the state" (Aretzaga 2003: 395). Aretzaga's formulation here echoes the eighteenth-century philosopher David Hume's assertions that reason and rational thought are driven in and through bodily passions, which Rutherford engages in her discussion of state building in West Papua. What is useful for Rutherford is Hume's materialist linking of behavior and passions and his argument that "the 'force and vivacity' of the idea leads one to feel what one thinks the other feels" (Rutherford 2009: 5). Of course, scholarship on affect is not the first time the body emerges on the stage of critical thinking about governance, feeling, and knowing. There is a mass of feminist scholarship from anthropology, philosophy, and allied fields that has been oriented toward critiquing the body-mind dualism as one of several related binaries on which hierarchies of nature and culture, material and ideological, and subject and object have been grounded (see, e.g., Alexander 1994, 1997, 2005; Chatterjee 1989; Kaplan et al. 1999; Lewis 2003; Ong 1990; Parker et al. 1991; Stoler 1989, 2002). For an excellent early review essay on gender and state formation, see Silverblatt 1991. More recent work includes Abu-Lughod 2004; Navaro-Yashin 2012; Rofel 1999.

16 But on how the affective relation might also seek to connect a conservative sense of territorial homeland to a structure of feeling, see Kuntsman and Stein 2015.

17 Purnima Mankekar (2015: 19) has argued that temporalization is an "affective

process that is constantly produced through everyday life"; she draws from Henri Bergson's notion of *durée* to think through the ways time "crisscrosses, transects, articulates, and, equally importantly, disarticulates the lives of [her] informants with the temporalizing processes through which nations are made and unmade." Mankekar's context is India, but this framing of the relationship between temporality and affect is also useful in my own.

18 See Harvey Neptune's (2014) retrospective on the ways Trouillot's work was geared toward creating an anthropological and historical archive of the West (and specifically, the "North Atlantic"), and sought to deconstruct the epistemological categories that created these archives in the first place. It is also interesting to note that groups such as the African Hebrew Israelites of Jerusalem also have challenged this spatializing and periodizing of modernity by relocating the "New World," for example, in Israel (newly conceptualized as Northeast Africa) and the "Old World" in the Americas (J. Jackson 2013). The question of creating presences from absences has also been explored by those interrogating queer archives (see Agard-Jones 2012; Ellis 2016). Finally, archivists themselves have also become interested in the affective turn, thinking through the ways researchers affectively experience archives themselves (see *Affect and the Archive, Archives and Their Affects* in *Archival Science*, special issue [November 2015]).

19 I discuss the counter-archive in relation to Caribbeanist scholarship elsewhere (see Thomas 2013).

20 Quoted in Patterson (1967: 75); the original can be found in the National Archives of the United Kingdom, Kew Gardens, Colonial Office Records (henceforth "CO") 139/8.

21 For discussions of land tenure and inheritance, see Besson 2002; Carnegie 1987. On the relationship of land during slavery and patterns of political authority, see Burnard 2004; Thomas 2011. On authoritarianism and patronage, see Munroe 1972; Singham 1968.

22 Slavery was abolished throughout the British West Indies in 1834 and was to be followed by a six-year "apprenticeship" period, during which time formerly enslaved people would continue to work for their former masters for a wage, thereby becoming socialized into a new relationship between labor and value. This system failed, and "full free" was declared in 1838. During the period of slavery, it should also be noted, judicial authority rested in the hands of the slaveholder or estate manager and was transferred after emancipation to the state. Diana Paton has written extensively about the forms of punishment and new legislation that emerged after emancipation, arguing that these legal mechanisms were tools of social control over urban space and that they in effect criminalized laborers through the proliferation of "small charges" (Paton 2004, 2014).

23 Michael Manley to Norman Manley, letter, 8 September 1966, Jamaica National Archives, Spanish Town, Norman Manley Papers 4/60/2A/71.

24 Trevor Munroe and Arnold Bertram (2006: 322) have demonstrated that, while in 1962 "there were 37 casualties caused by firearms, in the year of the

1967 elections, this number had increased to 202." These arms were entering the country illegally in conjunction with the growing trade of ganja between Jamaica and the United States, and the accusation was that politicians were arming criminals (Lacey 1977; Senior 1972).

25 For an analysis of representational practices related to these phenomena, see Gray 2011; Jaffe 2013. For an analysis of their gendered dimensions, see Ulysse 2007. For more on the history of these polarizations, see Clarke 2006a and 2006b; Howard 2005. For a description of the role of dons as arbitrators and purveyors of justice and social welfare within their communities, see Charles 2002. For a somewhat more popular academic exegesis of garrisons, see Gunst 1995.

26 For a longer discussion of racial categories in Jamaica and the ways these index class identities, see chapter 1 in this volume. While my focus is Jamaica, there are clear commonalities throughout the region. For example, for the Brazilian context, see Perry 2013; Smith 2016a.

27 For a few examples of the relationships among gendered class, kinship norms, and nationalist respectability, see Barrow 1988; Edmondson 1999; Reddock 1994; Thomas 2004.

28 For an insightful analysis of how organized crime becomes a mode of governance in and through the implementation of community development projects, see Galvin 2014. Ultimately, her argument is that the development programs "do not successfully weaken the need for informal community governance, crime, or vigilantism and, in fact, reinforce undemocratic community hierarchies" (Galvin 2014: 145). Instead, they reproduce garrisons as ministates within the Jamaican nation.

29 On the critique of Kantian and Lockean liberalism, see, e.g., Fischer 2004; Mahmood 2011; Povinelli 2011. These critiques are trenchant but have not necessarily explicitly addressed the foundational racism of Enlightenment theorists. For a primer on the development of philosophical views on racial and geographical hierarchies, and the ways these came to inform an emergent anthropology, see Eze 1997.

30 See, classically, Weber 1946. I have more to say about the relationship between charisma and notions of power and politics in chapter 2.

31 David Scott (2014: 63) has argued similarly in his exploration of the aftermath of the Grenada Revolution: "In undertaking to uproot the institutions and practices of the status quo, in daring to interrupt the necessity by which we are ruled and therefore to be otherwise than we have been obliged to be by the powers that have control over our lives, revolution is almost *purely* a matter of action, of intervention, of initiatives without precedent. Therefore, revolution entails a permanent exposure to risk and reversal. By the same token, nowhere is the price of freedom more dearly paid than in the collapse or failure of revolution when *everything* has been risked in action—and *everything* has been lost to it."

32 For an accounting of the sensory relations being heralded here, see Campt 2017.

33 For an analysis of the relationships among technology, archive, and the psychic domain, see Smith and Sliwinski 2017.

34 This differs from David Scott's interpretation of Derrida, whose notion of "messianic time" leads to a kind of "waiting without expectation" (quoted in Scott 2014: 10). For Scott, Derrida is turning our eyes through an *atemporal futurity*" (Scott 2014: 10), one that is not reducible to any particular ontology of time.

35 On *surveillance*, see Masco 2014; on *inaction*, see Ngai 2005; and on *conspiracy*, see Jackson 2008; Marcus 1999.

36 Anthony Harriott, personal communication, 24 October 2014.

1. DOUBT

1 Here, I am referencing Alfredo González-Ruibal (2008) and Jane Guyer (2007). I have more to say about endurance in chapter 2.

2 The Commission of Enquiry's report provides some additional details on Chineyman's brother's death (Government of Jamaica 2016: 236–38), at the end of which the Commissioners note that his stepfather received three gunshot wounds in his back, and that Dashan (Dashard in the report) sustained four gunshots in his chest. The Commissioners concluded that "inferences are compelling that they must have died at the hands of the security forces" (Government of Jamaica 2016: 238). They therefore suggest additional investigations.

3 An investigation by Amnesty International of the 2001 West Kingston Commission of Enquiry found that the inquiry "failed to fulfill its obligations under international law to fully investigate the deaths of at least 25 people," who were likely killed extrajudicially, because it found no one responsible and failed "to consider the possibility of criminal proceedings, in violation of international standards" (Amnesty International 2003: 4). See also Amnesty International, "Jamaica 2017/2018," https://www.amnesty.org/en/countries /americas/jamaica/report-jamaica.

4 For an elaboration of these points, see Paton 2017. In particular, she discusses the simultaneous growth of state activity under Crown Colony rule at the same time that populations were being denied access to the political system and as the state was continually enhancing its capacity to suppress opposition. See also Paton 2004.

5 W. G. Johnson, Police Adviser to the Secretary of State, to Colonial Secretary, letter, 18 April 1950, National Archives of the United Kingdom, Kew Gardens, Colonial Office Records (CO) 537/5435.

6 For an analysis of this event, as well as additional sources, see Thomas 2011.

7 Holding a public Commission of Enquiry was one of the recommendations made by the Office of the Public Defender in its interim report to Parliament (Witter 2013). The Commission was ultimately convened in mid-2014. It held public hearings on the following dates (they were broadcast live on local television and were recorded by the Jamaica Information Service): 1–12 Decem-

ber 2014; 9–20 February 2015; 10–24 April 2015; 26 May–4 June 2015; 7–23 September 2015; 20 October–5 November 2015; 23 November–4 December 2015; 8–19 February 2016. Ninety-four persons came forward to give evidence publicly, and several others provided witness statements (between civilians and members of the security forces, there were approximately 1,138 witness statements). The Terms of Reference for the Commission are listed in the report (Government of Jamaica 2016).

8 Of course, there is nothing new about the U.S. government training Latin American police, initially as part of U.S. imperialist expansion overseas and later as a key vector of U.S. anticommunism and international security policy. For extended discussions of this phenomenon, see Gill 2004; Huggins 1991. For an analysis of "post-Dudus" policing strategies that places them in relation to circulations both across geographic locations and among different actors and institutions, see Meikle and Jaffe 2015. They argue that in the aftermath of the 2010 State of Emergency, police began mobilizing strategies long used by dons to maintain security in garrison communities, thereby becoming a kind of "new don."

9 I have more to say about this speech in chapter 2 and much more to say about the intensification of U.S. interest in Jamaica after independence in the second interlude and chapter 3.

10 "Extradition Treaty with Jamaica," treaty doc. 98-18 (1984).

11 For the indictment against Coke, see Sealed Indictment at 1, *United States v. Coke*, no. S15 07 Cr. 971 (RPP) (SDNY), accessed 13 June 2014, http://amlaw daily.typepad.com/files/coke-christopher-michael-s15-indictment-1.pdf.

12 These emails, as well as several hours of footage from the two cameras attached to the drone, were obtained through the Freedom of Information Act by the journalist Mattathias Schwartz, in collaboration with a Yale University law clinic. I am grateful to him for sharing these materials with me.

13 In this way we might understand footage from the drone, as Andrew Herscher (2014: 473) does, as a form of "'surveillant witnessing': a hybrid visual practice that has emerged at the intersection of satellite surveillance and human rights witnessing" and the extension of human rights witnessing from on the ground humanitarianism to "extraterrestrial surveillance machines."

14 For a more detailed, minute-by-minute report of what the security forces were facing based on police logs, see, e.g., Government of Jamaica 2016: 61–63.

15 Kilcullen's (2013: 102) conclusion is that, "as the planet urbanizes, as populations centralize in coastal cities, and as increasing international connectivity enables globalized communication and population movement, this kind of local/transnational, criminal/military hybrid threat—which John P. Sullivan has insightfully labeled criminal insurgency, 'a global form of neo-feudalism linked together by cyberspace, globalization, and a series of concrete ungoverned zones'—may affect vastly more cities on the planet as it already does." For a better-informed and somewhat more nuanced accounting of these issues, see McDavid et al. 2011. I thank Danny Hoffman for making me aware of Kilcullen's reference to Tivoli Gardens.

16 For more on the so-called culture of violence, see Gray 2011; Thomas 2011. Within the United States, this kind of discourse is usually expressed in relation to a "culture of poverty" (Glazer and Moynihan 1963; Lewis [1959] 1975, 1965), but for the seminal critique of this position, see Stack 1974), which views it as a result of deindustrialization and black middle-class flight from inner cities, see also Wilson 1987.

17 I thank Honor Ford Smith for this reminder: Honor Ford Smith, personal communication, 2 June 2017.

18 "Brown," within a Jamaican racial lexicon, means lighter skinned, with the connotation also of belonging to a "higher" class.

19 I have analyzed this point at length elsewhere (see Thomas 2002a, 2002b, 2004).

20 This is what is meant by Alex Weheliye's (2014: 4) concept of "racializing assemblages," the "set of sociopolitical processes that discipline humanity into full humans, not-quite-humans, and nonhumans."

21 The reference to technologies and processes comes from Pat Saunders's discussion with NourbeSe Philip (Saunders 2008).

22 The obvious references here are to Du Bois (1903) 1966 and Fanon (1952) 1967.

23 By using the term "raciality" here, I mean to invoke Jackson's (2005) attempt to denaturalize and defamiliarize what we imagine when we hear the word "race." This approach also destabilizes Fanon's claim that "the black cannot be an other for another black" and thus brings us to a different apprehension of ontological realities (see Moten 2008 and the discussion of Keeling and Snead in Thomas 2016). For additional important work on place, landscape, and subjectivity, see Brown 2005; Navaro-Yashin 2012; Ramos-Zayas 2012.

24 Here I am drawing from Berg and Ramos-Zayas 2015 and the ethnography of antiblack police violence in Salvador, Brazil, in Smith 2016a.

25 Seaga would take over the leadership of the JLP in 1974 and would later be elected Prime Minister of the country, serving in that role from 1980 to 1989.

26 I thank Don Robotham for pointing me in these important directions.

27 In probing the history of how human rights activists have used satellite images, Herscher (2014) notes that where once these images stood as one form of evidence among others, increasingly they have stood on their own, creating a complex relationship between state surveillance and human rights witnessing. "For the surveillance state," he argues, "the development of this geo-witness has allowed a politicized practice of surveillance to be publicly presented as a witnessing of human rights abuses; for human rights advocates, it has allowed human rights witnessing to be extended from on-the-ground victims and survivors to extraterrestrial machines" (Herscher 2014: 473). In the Israeli context, Rebecca Stein (2017: 18) has argued, this complexity "tempers a resilient popular investment in the capacity of photographic technologies, in ever greater hands, to catalyze justice by making injustice *ever more* visible."

28 Hugh Gusterson has argued that drone warfare creates a kind of "remote intimacy" for the pilots, one that encourages them to identify with their sub-

jects and to narrativize—sometimes over-narrativize—the lives of those they are surveilling day after day, week after week. Pilots' sense of time and space becomes discombobulated—"simultaneously more elongated and more compressed" (Gusterson 2016: 47)—and they experience a sense of "distanced voyeurism" and "immersive intimacy" simultaneously (Gusterson 2016: 64). See also Kaplan 2018; Parks and Kaplan 2017.

29 E. Valentine Daniel (1996: 3) wrote the most classic formulation of the pornography of violence within anthropology, asking, "How to give an account of these shocking events without giving in to a desire to shock? And more important, what does it mean to give such an account?"

30 These kinds of visual archives share some similarities with those identified by Stein, both in her own work (Stein 2017) and in her collaboration with Adi Kuntsman (Kuntsman and Stein 2015). For Stein, the Israeli military's adoption of the camera as a "public relations technology" marks a shift in the long-standing relationship between visual technology and war in that it is now geared toward generating affective connections with the public at large, harnessing support for its war effort against Palestinians (Stein 2017; Kuntsman and Stein 2015). The forms of "mapping" she describes, during which Israeli soldiers go house to house in Palestinian territories to collect a "photographic history" of each household (Kuntsman and Stein 2015), bears resemblance to the census taking of youth at the National Stadium as a kind of "military disciplining of the visual field" (Kuntsman and Stein 2015: 12). And the human rights organizations' use of footage from Israeli cameras certainly resonates, even though the images broadcast by one Israeli nongovernmental organization (NGO) concerned about documenting human rights abuses in the occupied territories regularly fails to persuade its target audience, who publicly debate the veracity of the claims being made, even sharing their own images to refute the NGO's claims. However, it is in the Israeli military's more recent use of social media (Kuntsman and Stein 2015) that the connection between the use of visual technology and the justification of extrajudicial violence differs somewhat from the case I am exploring here, and this is largely because in the Jamaican context there was no intended audience for the drone footage, not even secondarily. This raises the question: Without the intention of public viewing, is the footage itself somehow less tainted by its origin? Is this a way to "derange the archive" (Hartman 2008)?

31 Joan McCarthy's story appears in the Commissioners' report (Government of Jamaica 2016: 179–80), where the death of her daughter's boyfriend (Dwayne Edwards) and her grandnephew (Andre Smith) is detailed. The post mortem report on Ms. McCarthy's grandnephew "records that he sustained two gunshot wounds—one in the abdomen, the other to his right forearm continuing into his chest" (Government of Jamaica 2016: 224). Dwayne Edwards's body, the one carried out wrapped in a sheet, still has not been identified. In this case, the Commissioners found "that a criminal offence may have been committed" (Government of Jamaica 2016: 225), and they therefore recommended further investigation into the deaths of Edwards and Smith.

32 I am referring here to a march that was held on 20 May 2010, designed to protest the extradition of Coke. Women dressed in white carried signs that read:
"Without Dudus, there will be no Jamaica"; "Next to God, Dudus"; "Jesus die
for us, we will die for Dudus" (Government of Jamaica 2016: 44). For an excellent theoretical discussion of this march as it resonated in the register of what
she calls "spiritual warfare," see Bloomfield 2018.

Before the West Kingston Commission of Enquiry, representatives of the
JCF and the JDF gave the following evidence: "Intelligence available to the JCF
and JDF on a continuing basis was to the effect that, in the days leading up to
24 May, some 300 gunmen from all over Jamaica and loyal to Coke, had migrated into Tivoli Gardens and other parts of West Kingston. They had come
to assist Coke and local gang members in resisting any attempt by the security
forces to enter the Tivoli Gardens' community and arrest Coke" (Government
of Jamaica 2016: 47). These gunmen, some of whom may also have returned to
Jamaica from overseas, were also involved in coordinated attacks against members of the JCF and their facilities (the Hannah Town and Darling Town police stations were burned down), and had reportedly also planned to attack the
power station at Hunts Bay and the oil facility Petrojam (Government of Jamaica 2016: 50, 56). Representatives of both the police and the military stated
that these mercenaries were paid anywhere between J$30,000 to J$100,000
to come to Tivoli, where they erected barricades, and established lookout
points and shooting positions (Government of Jamaica 2016: 60). One of the
findings of the West Kingston Commissioners was that the officers who gave
evidence during the Commission of Enquiry "were clearly surprised by and
unprepared for the magnitude and coordination of the onslaught directed
at assets of the JCF" (Government of Jamaica 2016: 70). Only three Tivoli
Gardens residents who gave evidence at the Commission of Enquiry acknowledged the presence of gunmen in the community, admitted people were erect-
ing roadblocks, and stated that the area was fortified to protect Coke.

33 For Mary Douglas (1966), of course, ritual avoidance indexed both sacrality
and defilement, and taboo generally was once a central construct within social
anthropology relating to strong ritual prohibitions (see, e.g., Radcliffe-Brown
1965) and within psychoanalytic theory and structuralism (Freud [1913] 1989;
Lévi-Strauss [1949] 1969) to think through societal norms and how they are
embodied. The conceptual framework of "taboo" has generally fallen out
of contemporary anthropological scholarship due to its association, among
earlier scholars, with an irrational Otherness irreconcilably different from
Western, rational modes of behavior, practice, and societal organization. However, I find it provocative to think a bit through this rubric here in relation to
Douglas's original assertion that taboos about the physical body mirror those
about the social body, and that therefore the fear of pollution is a moral fear.
For Douglas, ritual avoidance and notions of pollution are strongest in societies marked by the subordination of the individual to authority, which is what
we find in garrison governance scenarios.

34 Many, including representatives of the Peace Management Initiative (the civil

society group working toward gang demobilization and other interventions into violence and crime), counter-argue that the guns are still in the community: "The real situation on the ground in these communities is that there are thousands of guns buried and waiting to be used by thousands of at-risk youth who are not actively engaged in gang activity, who are not wanted by the police and who are quite prepared for the next round of gun battles at the community level" (Hutchinson 2016: 34).

35 Marjorie Williams also gave evidence at the West Kingston Commission of Enquiry (a discussion of her testimony appears in the report [Government of Jamaica 2016: 230–36], and it provides some additional details). As in the case of Joan McCarthy, the Commissioners found Marjorie to be truthful, and wrote that the evidence she and her neighbors gave regarding the death of her two sons was "suggestive of deliberate murder by unidentified police officers" (Government of Jamaica 2016: 236). They therefore recommended further investigation.

36 The public defender at the time reported that during this visit to Tivoli Gardens, he received innumerable complaints of excessive abuse at the hands of the security forces, and he saw the hundreds of detainees at Seprod. Regarding the detainees, he wrote that they were "mainly men of mature years" and that "younger detainees were tightly bunched up behind a fence of razor wire, many kneeling in gravel. They were all being 'processed.' There were no sanitary conveniences" (Witter 2013: 37). The public defender and the other visitors also went to Maddens, the local funeral parlor, where they "viewed three large mounds of tagged corpses, most in varying stages of decomposition, many nude or scantily clad, piled up on the bare concrete floor" (Witter 2013: 38). Witter's sense was that "the high incidence of removal of clothing from relevant corpses raises reasonable suspicion that there was an intention to conceal, contaminate or destroy vital evidentiary material capable of yielding up important forensic data, e.g., gunshot primer residue or gunpowder burns" (Witter 2013: 63).

37 Marjorie's neighbor, Ms. Muirhead, also gave evidence at the Commission of Enquiry that another young man was enlisted to throw Marjorie's dead sons into the back of a police truck, and that the police killed him as well after he did so. Ms. Muirhead also said she could identify the police officer who killed Marjorie's sons: "I see him at Denham Town station. I see him more than 5 times," she stated (Government of Jamaica 2016: 234).

38 This announcement was issued over the radio on the evening of 23 May by the JCF, and aired as follows: "'The security forces are asking all decent and law abiding residents of Tivoli Gardens and Denham Town to leave those respective communities immediately. They are being asked to leave the areas via the corridors of Industrial Terrace onto Marcus Garvey Drive where buses will be waiting at the intersection of Marcus Garvey Drive and Industrial Terrace to transport them to a secure location. Those persons opting the be evacuated are being asked, if possible, to bring food and clothing to last them for at least 24 hours" (Government of Jamaica 2016: 147). While the "secure location" ended

up being the National Arena, the statement aired over the radio did not make this clear.

39 The Commissioners' report also lists many instances of houses being completely ransacked by the security forces during the state of emergency, both while residents were present and after they had been removed from the community. They argue in their conclusion that too many members of the JCF exhibited "inadequate, internal discipline" and that this pointed to "weak unit leadership" and "weak supervision" on the part of the JCF" (Government of Jamaica 2016: 376–77). They also found that the JDF caused most of the property damage (Government of Jamaica 2016: 203), arguing that "the force used by the JDF in carrying out searches was disproportionate to the circumstances existing in West Kingston at the time of those searches" (Government of Jamaica 2016: 204). In fact, a team of assessors convened by the Ministry of Labour and Social Security carried out an assessment using USAID standards in summer 2010 that revealed that ninety-four dwellings were totally destroyed, two hundred were severely damaged, and 1,505 more suffered minor damage (Government of Jamaica 2016: 207). Some of these residents had been compensated by the Ministry of Labour in 2010, but the Commission recommended continued investigation into numerous cases of property damage, arguing that that compensation was far from sufficient.

40 Marjorie Hinds's case was also taken up by the Commissioners and is detailed in their report (Government of Jamaica 2016: 244–45). With respect to her fiancé, they found "that there might be something very perverse about the circumstances of his death. It is highly probable that criminal offences may have been committed" (Government of Jamaica 2016: 245), and they recommended further investigations.

41 On the impossibility of black mothering in the aftermath of slavery in the New World, see Ain-Davis 2016; Carby 1987; Hartman 1997; Mullings 1995; Mullings and Wali 2000; Spillers 1987. But see Gumbs 2016.

42 For more on the development of political and intimate affective voice within the context of postwar Nepal, see Kunreuther 2014.

43 For a discussion of North African critics, including Albert Memmi and Kateb Yacine, who also articulated this problematic, see Keller 2007. (Similarly, for a somewhat different slant, see Mannoni 1990). The argument about the relationship between colonialism and madness is also, of course, a biopolitical one (see Foucault 1988). However, as with Foucault's *History of Sexuality* (1978), he neglects the centrality of geopolitics—in particular, colonialism—to modern European constructions and experiences of mental illness (Stoler 1995). For a broader discussion of work on the psychology of colonial domination and its imbrication within processes of racialization, see also Keller 2001.

44 For a nuanced discussion of this position found in *Wretched*, see Gordon 2015.

45 For a discussion of the relation between representations and repetitions of madness and the processes of formal decolonization, see Josephs 2013.

46 For critiques of this paradigm, see, among others, Feldman 2004; Posel 2008; Ross 2003; Trouillot 2000.

47 While this may be a hegemonic position within Tivoli Gardens circa 2012–14, we also know it is subject to change, and, moreover, that there are institutionalized spaces within the community (such as churches) that are encouraging alternative stances by, for instance, supporting the development of youth and women's leadership (personal communication with Kijan Bloomfield, 27 May 2015, a doctoral student in the Department of Religious Studies at Princeton University whose dissertation focused on the ways spirituality operates within conditions of violence (see Bloomfield 2018).

48 This is something with which David Scott has also long been concerned, and he has addressed it eloquently in his recent analysis of temporality vis-à-vis the collapse of the Grenada Revolution (Scott 2014). Scott's argument here is that temporal disjunctures live on in the aftermaths of political catastrophe and that these disjunctures dislodge what had been, for the revolutionary generation, a taken-for-granted relationship between history and time. No longer is time experienced as linear and redemptive—itself, as many have noted, a product of liberal modernity—where more perfect futures are brought into being through the realization of a political project that would, ironically, mark the end of history. Instead, in the wake of revolutionary failure, that generation experiences time traumatically as stalled in the present, as a cyclical loop without promise of change. For them, as Scott (2014: 13) writes, "the past is a wound that will not heal." The new hegemony of neoliberalism, however, has produced a "post"-revolutionary generation that is less enmeshed in the liberal temporalities that organized political time before them and therefore more immune to the sense of vulnerable longing that characterizes their parents' sense of time. This means that their histories of the present are "disconnected," as Scott writes (2014: 123), "from the temporal structure of revolutionary desire." For Scott, the younger generation of Grenadians about whom he is writing could interrogate the silences surrounding the revolution, because they were unfettered by the expectations of a global left and a politics of non-alignment. In a context like Tivoli Gardens, however, this seems significantly trickier.

49 A team of assessors from ECLAC were invited by the Jamaican government, through the Planning Institute of Jamaica, to quantify the cost of physical assets damaged; the loss of resources due to intensified expenditure on security (as well as the loss of security forces infrastructure due to burning, etc.); the loss of productivity "as a result of death, injury and social distancing" (ECLAC 2010: 5); ongoing problems in relation to school attendance and school functioning; loss of tourism, wholesale and retail trades (including vendors from the country who sell at Coronation Market, as well as damage to the physical infrastructure of the market); and health costs. They found that "the total effect of the unrest on the economy of Jamaica was estimated at J$22,515.80, equivalent to US$258.8 million. The total impact represented some 2.1% of 2009 current GDP and 50% of tourism GDP" (ECLAC 2010: v).

50 The model for these last recommendations is Trench Town's I-SEE program, and its "Culture Yard." The public defender supported ECLAC's conclusions, arguing that a "model of self-sustainable social and economic development of

Tivoli Gardens and West Kingston, i.e., which is not patronage-based, would quite probably help to reverse chronic stagnation" (Witter 2013: 180).

51 I thank Joseph Masco for the phrase "condition of our condition." He was referencing the counterculture-era song "Just Dropped In (to See what Condition My Condition Was In)." The song was written by Mickey Newbury and recorded in 1967 by Teddy Hill and the Southern Soul, but it became a hit for Kenny Rogers and the First Edition in 1968. It was said to capture the experience of being on LSD while also warning against the danger of using the drug.

52 Kezia Page has explored this through her analysis of what many observers (and participants) have identified as a "reggae revival" (Page 2017). This revival, she notes, is one that should be understood as a social movement led by artists— not only musicians, but also theatrical performers, and those working in the realm of visual culture. For Page, the reggae revival is not a unified movement in the particularities of its expressions by any means, yet it is one that signals a new epistemological and ontological principle of community. Consciousness of the "condition of our condition," as has so often been the case, rests at the popular level and is expressed through arts practices that reach toward recognition on affective domains.

53 "Historical responsibility," Michel-Rolph Trouillot (2000: 183) writes, "cannot hark back to an original sin that the collective-individual supposedly committed. Rather," he continues, "it needs to take into account the structures of privilege unleashed by a history of power and domination and to evaluate the current losses induced by the reproduction of these structures." See also Nelson 2015.

INTERLUDE I: INTERROGATING IMPERIALISM

1 Froude 1897; Thomas 1889; and see Smith 2002 for a discussion of Thomas's response to Froude. See also Pullen-Burry 1903 and 1905.

2 Raymond Buell, the first U.S. political scientist to conduct fieldwork in Africa, was an instructor of comparative colonial administration at Harvard University during the early 1920s. For more on his position within the burgeoning field of international relations and his relationship to the political scientists at Howard University, see Vitalis 2015. The *Jamaica Gleaner* is the oldest consistently published newspaper in the Western Hemisphere, having begun publication in 1834 upon the abolition of slavery in the British West Indies. Its morning edition was known as the *Daily Gleaner* until 1992.

3 This sense that Jamaica was an exemplar of peaceful multiracial coexistence was expressed not only by local officials such as Lord Sydney Olivier, but also by representatives of the colonial service such as former Governor Hugh Foot, who, on the occasion of the extension of his term as Governor in 1956, argued in a public address that West Indians could "lead the world" in "showing that people of different races can live and work together freely and equally, respecting each other, trusting each other, defending each other, helping each other" (Foot 1964: 121).

4 The interest in peasant practices was also elaborated in the folklore and ethnography of the period (see Beckwith [1929] 1969; Dunham 1946; Hurston 1938; Jekyll 1907).

5 Bruce Murray (2013) argues that the breakup of Macmillan's marriage and his courtship of (and subsequent marriage to) Mona Tweedie, who was half his age and the daughter of the British vice-admiral at Simon's Town, contributed to the pressure exerted on him to resign from his position at Wits, which he ultimately did in 1934.

6 In London, William Macmillan encouraged Mona to attend Malinowski's seminar in social anthropology at the London School of Economics, and she was in class with Audrey Richards, Meyer Fortes, Margaret Read, Margaret Wrong, and Jack Simons (Macmillan and Macmillan 2008: 131).

7 Macmillan notes, Jamaica, William Macmillan Papers, Courtesy of Hugh Macmillan.

8 William Macmillan to Mona Macmillan, letter, 5 January 1935, Macmillan Papers.

9 William Macmillan to Mona Macmillan, letter, 31 December 1934, Macmillan Papers.

10 William Macmillan to Mona Macmillan, letter, 11 January 1935, Macmillan Papers.

11 William Macmillan to Mona Macmillan, letter, 24 January 1935, Macmillan Papers.

12 Again, the exception to this claim was St. Kitts, where there existed a more politically aware proletariat with connections to the United States.

13 Here, of course, I am referring to Trouillot's use of the term in describing the attitude toward the Haitian Revolution just prior to its occurrence.

14 W. M. Macmillan, (1936) 1938, 12. Macmillan would go on to write an even more trenchant tract against imperial neglect and supporting the move toward self-government for the colonies as World War II began (Macmillan 1941). While *Warning* was not favorably received by local government administrators in Jamaica upon its original publication, the text is now acknowledged as the primary catalyst for a change in colonial policy toward the West Indies. Macmillan eventually returned to Jamaica in 1954 for a yearlong post as a visiting professor in the History Department at the University of the West Indies.

15 Roy Augier, interview by the author, Kingston, 9 January 2015. Mona Macmillan, however, did write a book based on this period (see Macmillan 1957).

16 The complexities of this period for Afro-Germans is beautifully documented in Campt 2004.

17 "Jamaica Can Industrialize Graciously," *Daily Gleaner*, 19 September 1960, 8; "Handicrafts—Potential Big Business," *Daily Gleaner*, 29 October 1960, 14; "Let the Accent Be on Things Jamaican," *Daily Gleaner*, 1 February 1961, 10.

18 "Castro Is No Russian Puppet," *Sunday Gleaner*, 15 January 1961, 7; "Cuba's Controversial Economy," *Sunday Gleaner*, 12 February 1961, 7.

19 "Cuba's Year of Education: For Every Child a Place in School," *Sunday Gleaner*, 22 January 1961, 5.

20 "Cuba's Year of Education."

21 "Cuba's Controversial Economy."

22 "Cuba's Controversial Economy."

23 "Cuba's Controversial Economy."

24 "Castro Is No Russian Puppet"; "Cuba's Year of Education."

25 Philip Rogers to Kenneth Blackburne, note, 20 October 1958, National Archives of the United Kingdom, Kew Gardens (TNA), Colonial Office Records (CO) 1031/2754.

26 John Vickers accompanied Hugh Buchanan, then a member of the People's Freedom Movement (PFM), to Cuba as the Jamaican Federation of Trade Unions delegate to the Cuban Conference, and he invited two visitors from England who had spent six weeks in Cuba to a meeting of the PFM on 28 September 1960 gathering at Richard Hart's home of the PFM. In chapter 3 I discuss the PFM at length.

27 Kenneth Blackburne to Philip Rogers, letter regarding Kirkvine strikes, 29 September 1958, TNA, CO 1031/2754.

28 Blackburne to Rogers. The reference could be to David Lowenthal, who had left his position as assistant professor of geography at Vassar in 1956 to work as a Fulbright Scholar at the University of the West Indies, where he stayed until 1960, after which point he took a position at the Institute of Race Relations in London until 1972, when he became a faculty member at University College, London.

29 "Bauxite Workers Move to Form Own Union," *Daily Gleaner*, 8 August 1957, 13; "Catspaw," *Gleaner*, September 9, 1957, 10.

30 "Ex-Union Delegate Fined £10 for Having Prohibited Organ," *Daily Gleaner*, 17 May 1961, 5.

31 "Undesirable Literature Charge on Two," *Daily Gleaner*, 12 April 1961, 1; "Undesirable Literature Trial May 2," *Daily Gleaner*, 19 April 1961, 4; "Undesirable Literature Trial Put Off," *Daily Gleaner*, 3 May 1961, 4; "Ex-Union Delegate Fined £10 for Having Prohibited Organ."

32 "Report from Jamaican Constabulary Force," April 5, 1961, TNA, Foreign Commonwealth Office Records (FCO) 141/5312.

33 "Report from Jamaican Constabulary Force."

34 Interview with author, 3 November 2014.

35 Local Security and Intelligence Committee report, September 1961, TNA, FCO 141/5432.

36 Norris's critique of the organization of the bauxite industry echoes those by George Beckford (1987), Norman Girvan (1976), and Owen Jefferson (1972).

37 Norris's text received a positive review from Frank Hill (1963: 89), who wrote that it stood as a reliable "mirror in which our society can take a good look at itself." Hill noted, however, that "many won't like what they see in the mirror, for the very reason that forms the theme running through Miss Norris' book: the facility of Jamaicans to live apart from each other in varied groups that spin around themselves artificial ideas of themselves that bear little relation to reality" (Hill 1963: 89). David Lowenthal (1963) also called the book a "tour

de force," praising it for illuminating the official version of Jamaica, which, he argued, has been wrongfully cited as a model of economic, social, and political development within a multiracial context.

38 In a review of this book in *Race and Class*, Richard Hart lauds the book as an "unpretentious study" of the particular problems West Indian migrants pose for child welfare services in the United Kingdom. "Uninhibited by professional attachment to welfare procedures perfected in dealing with native Britons," he writes, "she appreciates the flexibility necessary when catering to the needs of people who have been accustomed to a very different way of life" (Hart 1967: 269). He draws special attention to Fitzherbert's argumentation regarding "the advantages to be gained if child welfare officers working with migrant cases adopt an approach based on an understanding of the enlarged West Indian family structure and of the flexible role of the father within it" (Hart 1967: 270).

39 For a compelling and nuanced memoir of colonial service and of the forms of knowledge and collaboration that were to emerge from it, see Foot 1964.

2. EXPECTANCY

1 While Singham's case study was Grenada under Eric Gairy, his framework has been picked up by analysts of Jamaican political society. For classic examples, see Eaton 1995; Munroe 1972; Stone 1980. For a more contemporary assessment of a number of Caribbean political leaders, see also Allahar 2001.

2 Saba Mahmood (2009) has also argued for a relational historical view of secularity and religiosity in order to better understand ongoing contemporary political and cultural conflicts.

3 Robert Hill is currently also conducting research on the early period of Henry's activities, which will revise many of our insights into his vision at that point.

4 Jamaica Constabulary Force (JCF), "Report on Activities of Claudius V. Henry," 9 April 1959, National Archives of the United Kingdom, Colonial Office Records (CO) 1031/2767.

5 JCF, "Report on Activities of Claudius V. Henry," 7 May 1959, TNA-PRO, CO 1031/2767.

6 Alan Lennox-Boyd to Claudius V. Henry, letter, 2 September 1959, TNA-PRO, CO 1031/2768.

7. Alan Lennox-Boyd to Kenneth Blackburne, letter, June 1959, TNA-PRO, CO 1031/2767.

8 "Extracts from Personal Intelligence Report of the Governor of Jamaica for August–September 1960, Original on WIS 185/55/01," TNA-PRO, CO 1031/3995.

9 "Extract from Governor of Jamaica's Intelligence Report for November–December, 1960, Original WIS 472/1025/01," TNA-PRO, CO 1031/3995.

10 Post (1981: 1:15) has also noted that by 1939 "wage labour was central to peasant existence," in part because previous attempts at land reform had failed

and the subsequent rural-to-urban migration that began after World War II resulted in the swelling of Kingston's slums, which held upward of fourteen thousand unemployed.

11 For more on the history of Jamaica Welfare, see D. Girvan 1949; N. Girvan 1993; Marier 1953; Midgley and Piachaud 2011. Charles Carnegie is also currently conducting important research into this area.

12 Woodville Marshall (1985), among others, has shown that after emancipation, planters attempted to curtail the development of an independent peasantry as a result of their fear that this would dampen profits from sugar. He lays out the various strategies planters used, including refusing to conduct surveys of Crown lands, prohibiting squatting on Crown land, refusing to sell "surplus and marginal estate land," requiring that small scale producers of sugar and coffee purchase licenses, and levying exorbitant land taxes (Marshall 1985: 5). After the Morant Bay Rebellion, these kinds of repressive policies continued, now through the Governorship of John Peter Grant, who implemented taxation measures that disproportionately affected the poor.

For additional exegeses of the relationship between respectability and citizenship, see Austin-Broos 1992; Hall 1995. See also the authors of *Jamaica's Jubilee* (1888).

13 Hart (1989: 27–28), in his own retrospective of leftist labor organizing in Jamaica, argued, "Given the close identification of the peasantry with the working class and the considerable over-lapping that existed in Jamaica, forms of joint worker-peasant activity were a natural development."

14 Indeed, this was one of Hart's regrets, as expressed during an interview with Trevor Munroe when he stated, "I think this was the basic weakness of the Left. It was urban based" (Munroe 1990: 125).

15 This is also the argument put forward by Trevor Munroe in his classic *The Politics of Constitutional Decolonization* (1972: 184) in which he tracks for each electoral period the choices and decisions made that consistently led to a scenario in which "participation among the masses could be confined to elections and such other occasions as the ruling circle held political audience." Indeed, most political observers today lament the "voting machine" dimension of electoral politics.

16 In response to an assertion by Edward Seaga that by 1962 Rastafari numbered about 10,000, Terry Lacey (1977: 39) estimated that by 1970, "the number of Rastafarians *and* their sympathizers was probably nearer to one hundred thousand."

17 Brother Douglas McHayle, interview by author, 11 March 2015.

18 Brother Burnett Hall, interview by Shelley Ann Morgan and Michael Lewis, 19 October 2014.

19 Christine "Lovey" Gordon, interview by author, 19 October 2014.

20 Post (1981: 1:190) has argued, in fact, that one of the characteristic tendencies regarding Rastafari has been "its tendency to separate its followers from other poor peasants and thus isolate itself." He makes this statement in relation to the conflicts among Rastafari at Pinnacle after 1940 and peasants within the

area who were not Rastafari and discusses how the peasants' complaints, coupled with those of members of the middle and upper classes, opened the door for the state to take a stand regarding Leonard and Pinnacle.

21 Brother Lester Lindo, interview by Shelley Ann Morgan and Michael Lewis, 12 October 2014.

22 "Four Held in Raids on Churches," *Daily Gleaner*, 24 January 1968, 1–2.

23 "Protests Raids on Claudius Henry," *Daily Gleaner*, 15 July 1968, 14.

24 "Protests Raids on Claudius Henry."

25 "Protests Raids on Claudius Henry."

26 *Daily Gleaner*, 22 February 1972, 28, 24 February 1972, 19, 27 February 1972, 18.

27 *Daily Gleaner*, 26 February 1972, 5.

28 Robert Hill, personal communication, 3 August 2012. The *Gleaner* also reports on the Peacemakers providing music for Manley's political rallies: "Past Labour Leaders, *Daily Gleaner*, 25 May 1971, 5. See also Munroe and Bertram (2006: 375), who argue that the PNP was significantly strengthened by Henry's participation: "As Manley toured the country, Henry would be seen on his platform, with his corps of African drummers performing in the cultural presentations as an integral part of Manley's campaign."

29 Brother Kiddie Thompson, interview by author, 31 July 2012. Indeed, after his deportation, Rodney wrote a "Message to Afro-Jamaican Associations," in which he extolled Henry's development initiatives. The full text concerning Reverend Henry is available in Lewis 1998: 95–96.

30 Mark Figueroa, personal communication, 15 September 2015. He also remembered that that period was one during which leftist groups, unhappy with the two-party system, were attempting to decide whether they would support Manley's PNP or remain independent.

31 Trevor Munroe, personal communication, 8 January 2015. What is also revealed in this comment is the division within the left between those more concerned with class transformation and those more explicitly concerned with racial revolution.

32 "Claudius Henry: 'Communism Must Be Stopped in 1978,'" *Daily Gleaner*, 8 January 1978, 16, 22.

33 Michael Manley visited Ethiopia in September 1969 and returned with what he identified as a "Rod of Correction," purportedly a gift from HIM Haile Selassie. After his return, he began to call himself Joshua, the Old Testament figure who led the enslaved Jews out of Jericho, and this is what caused Reverend Henry to take notice, and to publish the pamphlet "Michael Manley Is Our Political Leader," 25 September 1969. However, the only letter from then candidate Manley to the Peacemakers that I have been able to find that addresses political campaigning was dated 14 June 1971, in which he states he was following up on previous correspondence and asks Reverend Henry whether he can "have the Peacemakers [band] all day" for the Central Kingston Annual Conference.

34 McHayle interview.

35 Brother South, interview by Shelley Ann Morgan and Michael Lewis, 5 October 2014.

36 Brother Kiddie Thompson, interview by author, 3 January 2013.

37 Thompson interview (3 January 2013).

38 Brother Slim, interview by author, 7 August 2012.

39 International Peacemakers Association (no signatures) to Prime Minister Michael Manley, letter, 25 April 1972, 3.

40 International Peacemakers Association to Manley, 2.

41 This sentiment recalls earlier speeches by Leonard Howell in which he stated that "'the white man's time was ended and that soon black men would sit on the throne of England; further that Hitler was in charge of Europe and that all European powers would be overthrown in 1940, and that at the end of the war the white nation would be utterly exterminated'" (quoted in Post 1981: 1:95).

42 At that time, the Master Bakers Association controlled the wheat coming into Jamaica, milled it, and then distributed to the various bakeries in Jamaica.

43 Although there was no formal ongoing relationship, the Peacemakers could count on Manley to provide them with the flour and other items they needed, even when these items were scarce for the general consumer during the second half of the 1970s.

44 Bertram Henry, interview by author, 24 August 2012.

45 "The Study of Cladius [sic] Henry's Property," *Daily Gleaner*, 30 October 1977, 7.

46 Ken Jones, personal communication, 19 August 2012.

47 "Report on Idle Land Said Misleading," *Daily Gleaner*, 27 October 1977, 1, in which is referenced the article on 22 October headlined "Property with Livestock, Crops, to Be Declared Idle."

48 "A New World Created in Man," *Daily Gleaner*, 16 April 1978, 22. Reverend Henry invited Michael Manley to this opening in a letter dated February 26, 1973, but Manley had to decline due to a previous commitment: Michael Manley to Reverend Claudius Henry, letter, 5 March 1973, held by Peacemakers.

49 "A Child . . . yet a Prophet," *Daily Gleaner*, 30 July 1978, 7.

50 Sadly, Brother Ruddy and Brother Slim both died in 2013.

51 Transcribed from author's audio recording.

52 Nelson Mandela Thompson, interview by Shelley Ann Morgan and Michael Lewis, 6 November 2014.

53 Here, I am thinking through Elizabeth Povinelli's (2011) engagement with how the problems and effects of liberalism draw our attention to the generation of alternative forms of life. She argues that the diffusely institutional social projects of late liberalism generate spaces in which non-teleological "alternative projects of embodied sociality" might emerge.

54 For insights into these positions, see Meeks 2014; Puri 2014; Scott 2004, 2014.

55 See also Maragh (1935) 2007; Pettersburgh (1926) 2003.

56 "Assist the Police, Tackle Criminals with Courage—no Beatitudes," *Daily Gleaner*, 12 May 1967, 1, 3. This speech also got Shearer into hot water with the Jamaican Council for Human Rights, which published a report in May 1968,

during the United Nations International Human Rights Year (which Jamaica had proposed), that named the government "'the chief perpetrator of violence in Jamaica'" (Jensen 2016: 202). This led to a parliamentary proposal (by Michael Manley) for the establishment of a National Human Rights Commission in Jamaica, which Shearer unequivocally opposed. This, in turn, led to the abandonment of the central role Jamaica had played in the development of international human rights within the United Nations from 1962 to 1968 (Jensen 2016).

57 Mark Figueroa, interview by author, 15 September 2014.

58 This photographic archive, as well as a set of interviews with early members of the community, will soon be available as a repository through the University of Pennsylvania library.

59 Bobby Hill reported hearing the same story at the time, and felt Brother Kiddie and Miss B were worried Ruddy was trying to stir something up, just prior to his own death.

60 Junior "Gabu" Wedderburn accompanied me during this interview, which took place on 11 March 2015.

INTERLUDE II: NAMING NAMES

1 According to Wolf, this press conference, on 2 July 1980, was organized by Trevor Munroe: Louis Wolf, interview with author, Washington, DC, 7 December 2014.

2 In the October 1979 issue of *CAIB*, the editors announced that Dean Almy, who had been outed as a CIA agent by Agee, had been replaced by Kinsman. They also reported that Kinsman was born on 17 August 1936, received his bachelor's degree from Syracuse University in 1958, spent a year in the U.S. Army, then spent five years in unspecified "government experience." From 1965 to 1967, Kinsman was a "program officer" with USAID, and in early 1968 he was stationed at the U.S. Embassy in Colombia as a political officer. In 1971, he was transferred to Caracas, and in August 1977 he was moved to Lima, where he was deputy chief of station ("Naming Names" 1979: 25).

3 Jo Thomas, "Gunmen in Jamaica Hit Home of U.S. Aide," *New York Times*, 5 July 1980, A1.

4 Jeff Stein, "The Trenchcoats Retrench," *Mother Jones*, February–March 1981, 55.

5 "Naming Names," *CAIB*, no. 1, July 1978, 23.

6 Philip Agee, "Destabilization in Jamaica," July 1980, 5–6, Tamiment Library and Robert F. Wagner Labor Archives, Elmer Holmes Bobst Library, New York University, Philip Agee Papers (hereafter, Agee Papers), box 17, folder 32.

7 Ellen Ray, "The Cuban Ambassador to Jamaica: A Case Study in Media Manipulation and Destabilization, *CAIB*, December 1979–January 1980, 4–5.

8 Fred Landis, "The CIA and the Media: IAPA and the Jamaica *Daily Gleaner*," *CAIB*, December 1979–January 1980, 10.

9 Landis, "The CIA and the Media," 11.

10 Landis, "The CIA and the Media," 12.

11 Ellen Ray and Bill Schaap, "Chile All Over Again? Massive Destabilization in Jamaica, 1976, with a New Twist," *CAIB*, August–September 1980, 9.

12 Ernest Volkman and John Cummings, "Murder as Usual," *Penthouse*, December 1977, 112.

13 Volkman and Cummings, "Murder as Usual," 182.

14 Volkman and Cummings, "Murder as Usual," 182–83. See also Agee, "Destabilization in Jamaica," 32.

15 Agee, "Destabilization in Jamaica," 4.

16 Volkman and Cummings, "Murder as Usual," 190.

17 Agee, "Destabilization in Jamaica," 24. See also Manley 1982.

18 Agee, "Destabilization in Jamaica," 32.

19 Agee, "Destabilization in Jamaica," 35.

20 Wikileaks, Public Library of U.S. Diplomacy, cable from U.S. Embassy in Kingston to U.S. Department of State, 4 November 1977, "Reuters-CANA Story on 'Penthouse' Destabilization," https://wikileaks.org/plusd/cables /1977KINGSTO6550_c.html.

21 "Kissinger Forces Reporter's Ouster," *Executive Intelligence Review*, vol. 4, no. 50, December 13, 1977, 6.

22 "Briefing Paper for Vice President's Attendance of Jamaica Independence Celebrations," NARA, FRUS, Kennedy Library, National Security Files, Countries Series, Jamaica, 1961–62.

23 "Jamaica: Plan of Action for the Period Beginning 1 June 1963," 15 February 1963, approved by Latin American Policy Committee, 29 May 1963, FRUS, NARA, Kennedy Library, National Security Files, Countries Series, Jamaica, 1962–63.

24 Telegram no. 1938, 9 March 1967, NARA, Classified Central Subject Files, 1963–75, RG 84/4713723, HMS no. P 406, box 2.

25 "Interdepartmental Regional Group for Inter-American Affairs, Country Analysis and Strategy Paper, Jamaica," 31 May 1967, NARA, Classified Central Subject Files, 1963–75, RG 84/4713723, HMS no. P 406, box 1.

26 In 1971, they would report that "Seaga admits privately that he would like to be Prime Minister—a worthy ambition—in about ten years, but he feels that it is impractical for a white man to attempt to be Prime Minister of a black country in the foreseeable future": U.S. Embassy (Roberts) to State Department, "General Intelligence Reporting List for Jamaica" (in response to a request for intelligence from Latin America), 13 June 1971, NARA, Classified Central Subject Files, 1963–75, RG 84/4713723, HMS no. P 406, box 5.

27 U.S. Embassy (Beale) to State Department, "The Question of Government Leadership in Jamaica," memorandum, 25 March 1967, NARA, Classified Central Subject Files, 1963–75, RG 84/4713723, HMS no. P 406, box 1.

28 U.S. Embassy (Wilken) to Secretary of State, telegram no. 715, 13 October 1967, NARA, Classified Central Subject Files, 1963–75, RG 84/4713723, HMS no. P 406, box 1.

29 U.S. Embassy (Wilken) to State Department, "The PNP—A Status Report,"

airgram, 7 October 1967, NARA, Classified Central Subject Files, 1963–75, RG 84/4713723, HMS no. P 406, box 1.

30 "Interdepartmental Regional Group for Inter-American Affairs."

31 "Interdepartmental Regional Group for Inter-American Affairs."

32 There is quite a bit of literature on the extent to which black leaders were surveilled by the police and FBI, but see, e.g., Blackstock 1988; Brown 1993; Garrow 1981. See also the Senate Select Committee to Study Governmental Operations with Respect to Intelligence Activities, U.S. Senate Historical Office, Washington D.C., 1976, otherwise known as the Church Committee Report.

33 "Internal Security Review of Walter Rodney," November 1968, NARA, Classified Central Subject Files, 1963–75, RG 84/4713723, HMS no. P 406, box 1.

34 "Internal Security Review of Walter Rodney."

35 "Internal Security Review of Walter Rodney."

36 "Internal Security Review of Walter Rodney."

37 "Internal Security Review of Walter Rodney."

38 "Internal Security Review of Walter Rodney."

39 See, e.g., U.S. Embassy (Wilken) to State Department, "Country Analysis and Strategy Paper, Jamaica, FY 1971, referring to CA-12727 of December 17, 1968," airgram, 24 January 1969, NARA, FRUS, RG 59, Central Files 1967–69, POL 1 JAM-UP.

40 "Jamaica and Guyana: Caribbean Alternatives?" intelligence memorandum, 23 February 1971, NARA, CIA Archives, CIA/OCI/IM-1268/71, 11. See also John Irwin to Richard Nixon, "U.S Bauxite Investment in the Caribbean," memorandum for the president, 9 June 1971, NARA, FRUS, Nixon Presidential Materials, National Security Council Files, Country Files, Latin America, Latin America General, vol. 4, January–June 1971, box 798.

41 Viron Vaky to Henry Kissinger, "Ambassador de Roulet's Proposal re Jamaican Prime Minister," memorandum, 20 July 1970, NARA, FRUS, Nixon Presidential Materials, National Security Council Files, Country Flies, Latin America, Jamaica, vol. 1, box 786. While Vaky believed that the ambassador was probably right, he felt the companies were becoming annoyed by the ambassador's persistence in this matter.

42 Viron Vaky to Henry Kissinger, "Ambassador de Roulet's Proposal re Jamaican Prime Minister," memorandum, 20 July 1970, NARA, FRUS, Nixon Presidential Materials, National Security Council Files, Country Flies, Latin America, Jamaica, vol. 1, box 786.

43 Viron Vaky to Henry Kissinger, "Ambassador de Roulet's Proposal re Jamaican Prime Minister," memorandum, 20 July 1970, NARA, FRUS, Nixon Presidential Materials, National Security Council Files, Country Flies, Latin America, Jamaica, vol. 1, box 786.

44 Embassy to State Department, "General Intelligence Reporting List for Jamaica."

45 U.S. Embassy to State Department, "Likely Attitudes of the People's National Party If Elected," airgram, 17 November 1971, NARA, FRUS, RG 59, Central Files 1970–73, POL 12 JAM.

46 U.S. Embassy to Secretary of State, "On Your Mark, Get Set, Don't Go (For Now)," telegram, 9 August 1972, NARA, FRUS, RG 59, Central Files 1970–73, POL 17 JAM-CUBA.

47 "U.S. Leverage on Guyana and Jamaica," memorandum, 2 January 1974, NARA, CIA Archives, CIA/OER/S-05789-74, 1.

48 "U.S. Leverage on Guyana and Jamaica," 7.

49 "U.S. Leverage on Guyana and Jamaica," 1.

50 "U.S. Leverage on Guyana and Jamaica," 4.

51 "Jamaica: Implications of the Tax Increase on Bauxite, Key Judgments," n.d. (but before 30 September 1974, the date of the cover letter), NARA, CIA Archives, CIA/OER/S-06512-74, 8.

52 "Jamaica: In Pursuit of Its National Identity," intelligence memorandum, 28 April 1976, NARA, CIA Archives, CIA-70-10110C, i.

53 "Jamaica at the Crossroads," memorandum, 5 March 1976, NARA, CIA Archives, CIA-M 7610081, no. 0748-76, 1.

54 "Jamaica at the Crossroads."

55 "Jamaica at the Crossroads," 2.

56 "Jamaica at the Crossroads," 4.

57 "Jamaica: In Pursuit of Its National Identity," 4.

58 "Jamaica: In Pursuit of Its National Identity," 5; "Jamaica: Current Economic Situation and Implications for U.S. Interests," intelligence memorandum, 5 June 1977, NARA, CIA Archives, CIA/OER 77-10433; U.S. Embassy (Gerard) to Secretary of State, "Attacks on 'CIA and U.S. Imperialism,'" telegram no. 4947, 17 December 1975, NARA, Classified Central Subject Files, 1963–75, RG 84/4713723, HMS no. P 406, box 8.

59 U.S. Embassy (Irving) to Secretary of State, "Aid Message," telegram no. 2029, 21 February 1976, NARA, Central Subject Files, 1971–83, ARC 6088029, HMS no. P 533, box 1.

60 U.S. Agency for International Development (USAID), "Multiyear Country Strategy—Jamaica," 12 September 1978, NARA, Central Subject Files, 1971–83, ARC 6088029, HMS no. P 533, box 1.

61 USAID, "Multiyear Country Strategy."

62 "Jamaica: Pre-Election Violence," *Latin America Review*, 15 August 1980, 1–4, NARA, CIA Archives.

63 National Security Act of 1947, Title VI, sect. 601.

64 The counterpart to the Church Committee in the House of Representatives was the Pike Committee.

65 Wolf argues that Welch had been warned that living in that home would identify him as a CIA agent but that he refused to move.

66 Public Law 97-200, 97th Congress, sec. 401[c], https://www.govinfo.gov/content/pkg/STATUTE-96/pdf/STATUTE-96-Pg122.pdf.

67 Joseph Biden, "A Spy Law That Harms National Security," *Christian Science Monitor*, 6 April 1982, 27.

68 Stein, "The Trenchcoats Retrench."

69 Galley proofs dated 12 August 1980, Agee Papers, box 18, folder 53.

70 Joseph Lerner, "Company Secrets: An Interview with Louis Wolf," *Washington Book Review*, vol. 1, no. 1, August–September 1981, 2, in Agee Papers. See also Grayson 1981; Lessne 1981–82.

71 Joseph Lerner, "Company Secrets: An Interview with Louis Wolf," *Washington Book Review*, vol. 1, no. 1, August–September 1981, 7.

72 Lerner, "Company Secrets," 9; *CAIB*, nos. 14–15, October 1981, 5.

73 "Lou Wolf Testimony," *Council on Hemispheric Affairs*, 24 June 2009, accessed 14 January 2019, http://www.coha.org/lou-wolf-testimony/.

74 "Lou Wolf Testimony."

75 Horace Campbell (1987) provides extensive documentation of shifts in the ganja business over the course of the twentieth century and the changing place of small-scale cultivators within it. He also gives a comprehensive account of Operation Buccaneer, which I draw from later. See also U.S. Government 1975.

3. PARANOIA

1 In an incredibly influential essay published in *Harper's* magazine in 1964 which was reprinted in a book later that year, Richard Hofstadter (1964) identified paranoia as the structuring principle of conservative American politics, and traced its historical lineage. In a more contemporary assessment of the post-9/11 security apparatus, Joseph Masco (2014: 20) has argued, "the inability to perfectly predict and counter terror creates in the American security system the opportunity to constitute nearly every domain and object of everyday life as a potential vector of attack, creating a national security project that performs as a nearly perfect paranoid system, but one with planetary reach."

2 Indeed, Manley's assignment of a Mission to Africa following the publication of *The Ras Tafari Movement in Kingston, Jamaica* (Smith et al. 1960) positioned the possibility for repatriation as one among many migration opportunities of which Jamaicans had long taken advantage, rather than as a racial reparation or repatriation. Ken Post has offered the most sustained critique of the left's insufficient analysis and understanding of the ways racial discrimination (and pride) affected political subjectivity among the peasantry and working classes in Jamaica (see Post 1978, 1981). Colin Clarke has also revisited his own field notes from this period, and argues that what characterized late colonial politics in Jamaica "were the failure of the black and Marxist dissident elements to fill the vacuum they believed was being created in 1961–62 by British decolonization and federation; and, by contrast, the self-confident seizure of the period of transition after the referendum by the two major parties, the JLP and the PNP, under the leadership of Bustamante and Manley" (Clarke 2016: 23).

3 Unfortunately, there is a gap in these records from November 1958 to September 1961. As these were crucial years, I was eager to see whether there was another way to gain access to them. However, my Freedom of Information Act (FOIA) request resulted in confirmation that the "cannot identify any other LSIC reports from Jamaica in the information that we hold" (letter, 27 May

2015, National Archives of the United Kingdom, Kew Gardens [TNA], Foreign Commonwealth Office Records [FCO]).

4   For a more extended discussion of the productive dimensions of "failure" (and therefore of why we must not see purported failure as an endpoint, but rather as a lens through which we might become privy to other processes), see, for example, Yarimar Bonilla's (2015) exploration of the sociopolitical agitation among union activists in Guadeloupe. Incidentally, this 1950s story might also promote new insights into how federation (and its failure) were viewed, not only by the colonial government but also by the United States, as a few State Department documents express a distinct sense of trepidation about the results of the referendum, having preferred Manley's statesmanship to Bustamante's.

5   Howell was deported from New York (see Hill 1983; see also Dunkley 2013; Lee 2003; Price 2009.

6   "It Is Not a Joke," *Daily Gleaner*, 27 December 1933, 13.

7   Vivian Durham, KSACL, to Governor Sir Edward Denham, letter, 23 January 1937, Jamaica National Archives, Spanish Town, 18/5/77/283, Pinnacle Papers, Colonial Secretary's Office (hereafter, PP-CSO) 5073/34.

8   "Petition re Ras Tafarian Cult Movement: Officers of the Kingston and St. Andrew Civic League Send Protest to His Excellency the Governor, Incident of 1865," *Daily Gleaner*, 26 January 1937, 31; Durham to Denham, letter.

9   Reid would go on to become involved in the riots of 1938; by 1940 he had become Norman Manley's bodyguard (see Lee 2003: 207).

10 Ethiopian King of Kings Salvation to Governor Sir Edward Denham, letter, 4 February 1937, PP-CSO 5073/34.

11 Ethiopian King of Kings Salvation to Denham, letter.

12 J. D. Lucie-Smith to Vivian Durham, letter, 11 March 1937; PP-CSO 5073/34.

13 "Deluded Creatures," *Daily Gleaner*, 9 July 1934, 12; "Alleged Members of Ras Tafari Cult Held by St. Thomas Police," *Daily Gleaner*, 13 July 1934, 2; "A Meeting of the Kingston School Board," *Daily Gleaner*, 7 September 1934, 8; "Matters of Interest Dealt with by Education Board," *Daily Gleaner*, 29 April 1935, 8; "Current Items," *Daily Gleaner*, 20 May 1935, 3; "Harm 'Ras Tafari' Advocates Are Doing in Eastern Parish," *Daily Gleaner*, 23 May 1935, 1; "Ras Tafari Cults Excite Portlanders," *Daily Gleaner*, 30 July 1935, 4; "Danger Signals," *Daily Gleaner*, 31 July 1935, 12.

14 A. R. Singham to V. R. Cameron, letter 30 June 1936; PP-CSO 5073/34.

15 "Sequel to Ras-Tafari Cult in Districts of St. Thomas Parish," *Daily Gleaner*, 19 August 1935, 19; Acting Inspector General to "Private Secretary," letter, 18 July 1936, PP-CSO 5073/34.

16 Acting Inspector General to "Private Secretary." For a more detailed discussion of the complaints against and surveillance of Leonard Howell, see Dunkley 2013.

17 For more on the visit of the Moyne Commission to Jamaica, see Palmer 2014: esp. 93–117.

18 Report by F. W. Avis, Minister of Health, St. Catherine, 29 November 1940, PP-CSO 5073/34.

19 Report of the Clerk of the Parochial Board of St. Catherine, 22 March 1941, PP-CSO 5073/34.

20 "Plight of Ras Tafarians at Camp Pinnacle in Saint Catherine: Disease Said to be Rampant Among Poverty Stricken People," *Daily Gleaner*, 22 December 1940, 1.

21 J. M. Hall, "Report of Medical Officer and Inspector of Police," 16 January 1941, PP-CSO 5073/34.

22 Director of Medical Services to Parochial Board, letter, 28 March 1941, PP-CSO 5073/34.

23 Letter from Director of Medical Services to Colonial Secretary, 15 April 1941; PP-CSO 5073/34.

24 Palmer argues that surveillance and repression of union activity (by the police) intensified after 1938 as part of a more general concern with wartime security.

25 Governor Arthur Richards to Malcolm MacDonald, letter, 9 April 1940, PP-CSO 5073/34.

26 Report of Commissioner of Police to Acting Colonial Secretary, 17 July 1941, PP-CSO 5073/34. See also "Police Raid 'Pinnacle,' Ras Tafarian Den, Seize Seventy, but Miss Chief," *Daily Gleaner*, 15 July 1941, 1, 14. A full pictorial of the police raid also was published in the *Gleaner* on 16 July 1941.

27 Report of Commissioner of Police to Acting Colonial Secretary, 17 July 1941, PP-CSO 5073/34.

28 R. A. Leevy, "Ras Tafarianism," *Public Opinion*, 13 February, 20 February, 27 February, 13 March 1943, all 3.

29 For an interesting take on the role of the 1948 amendment of the Dangerous Drugs Act in colonial attention to (and suppression of) Howell's activities, and for a somewhat different take on the period between the raids of Pinnacle in 1941 and 1954, see Dunkley 2013.

30 Ken Post, however, has argued that Jamaican communists never succeeded in creating a worker-peasant alliance because they focused on the development of trade unions (and therefore to a large degree excluded peasants from their organizing techniques). "In so far as any of its members moved towards political protest," Post (1981: 2:542) writes, "it was indirectly, through the medium of Rastafarianism, and often then as migrants to urban centres."

31 The overlap and movement back and forth among these various visions would perhaps become most obvious during the late 1960s and 1970s when various left-leaning groups centered at the University of the West Indies, and especially the WPJ, would combine forces with particular groups of Rastafari.

32 By late January 1943, with other deposits reported in St. Catherine, St. Elizabeth, and Manchester, the colonial government took over the properties involved and granted concession to the Aluminum Company of Canada (Alcan), seeking to maintain imperial control over the new commodity. When Reynolds Metals petitioned to have a stake in the trade, the Governor decided to put a decision off until World War II was over. By December 1943, concerns about relations between the United States and Jamaica resulted in renewed

negotiations, which ultimately resulted in Reynolds getting a foothold in 1944 (Girvan 1976; Harrod 1972; Jefferson 1972; Post 1981).

33 For historical analyses of the Bases for Destroyers arrangement and its effects, see High 2009; Neptune 2007; Post 1981.

34 On the rumors of a U.S. political takeover of West Indian colonies, see Fraser 1994; Johnson 1984; Whitham 2002.

35 See also Palmer (2014:244), which reports that during World War II, the British colonial government was exceedingly "sensitive to the invocation of a racialized language against it" that it forbade "newspapers to carry stories relating to racial strife anywhere."

36 Arthur Creech Jones, Church House, to Colonial Governors, circular dispatch, 5 August 1948, TNA, Colonial Office Records (CO) 537/2795.

37 Arthur Creech Jones to Governor John Huggins, letter, 20 August 1948, TNA, CO 537/2795.

38 Governor John Huggins to Arthur Creech Jones, letter, 25 November 1948, TNA, CO 537/2795.

39 Secretary of State Alan Lennox-Boyd, "Organisation of Intelligence," Colonial Office dispatch, 28 April 1956, TNA, CO 1035/43.

40 Savingrams, 20 February 1951, 13 June 1951, 10 April 1953; for additional memos, see TNA, FCO 141/5316.

41 Special Branch Monthly Report, 28 November 1957, TNA, FCO 141/5434.

42 "Terms of Reference of the Jamaica Local Standing Intelligence Committee," November 1957, TNA, FCO 141/5418.

43 Colonial Secretary to Governor Foot, memorandum, 16 July 1956, TNA, FCO 141/5393.

44 Governor Foot to Secretary of State Philip Rogers, letter, 20 July 1956, TNA, CO 1035/43.

45 N. D. Watson, Secretary of State; Philip Rogers, Colonial Office; Governor Hugh Foot; I. Wallace; and Alan Lennox-Boyd, Secretary of State for the Colonies, correspondence,16 July– 11 September 1956, TNA, CO 1035/43, FCO 141/5393.

46 "Report of Committee of Enquiry Set Up by Executive Committee of PNP," Jamaica National Archives, Norman Manley Papers (hereafter, Manley Papers), 4/60/2A/5.

47 Criminal Investigation Department (CID) reports, 12 May 1952, 15 May 1952, 21 May 1952, 28 May 1952, TNA, FCO 141/5418.

48 Commissioner of Police to Colonial Secretary, handwritten note, CID report, 12 May 1952, TNA, FCO 141/5418.

49 CID report, 21 May 1952, TNA, FCO 141/5418. Strachan would again discuss Malaya as a war against imperialism at a public meeting of the TUC in Coronation Market on 3 June 1951, which concerns local security forces greatly (CID Report, 4 June 1952, TNA, FCO 141/5418).

50 CID report, 28 July 1952, TNA, FCO 141/5418.

51 CID report, 8 August 1952, TNA, FCO 141/5418.

52 Unfortunately, there is another gap in the records from November 1958 to September 1961. See note 3 in this chapter.

53 CID report, 10 January 1956, TNA, FCO 141/5295.

54 CID reports, 16 January 1956, 24 January 1956, 31 January 1956, TNA, FCO 141/5295.

55 CID report, 5 April 1956, TNA, FCO 141/5295.

56 CID report (5 April 1956).

57 CID report, 28 November 1957, TNA, FCO 141/5434.

58 Lord Hailes to Governor Blackburne, letter, 22 May 1958, TNA, FCO 141/5361.

59 Local Security and Intelligence Committee (LSIC) report, June 1958, TNA, FCO 141/5434.

60 Special Branch report to the LSIC, August 1958, TNA, FCO 141/5434.

61 See TNA, CO 1031/1958.

62 Marginalia on folder, TNA, CO 1031/1958.

63 Handwritten note from Phillips, 13 October 1956, TNA, CO 1031/1958.

64 (Cecil) Juxon Barton, typewritten note, 26 October 1956, TNA, CO 1031/1958. Barton was colonial secretary in Fiji from 1936 to 1941 and Chief Secretary in Nyasaland from 1941 to 1945.

65 Typewritten letter to Phillips, 19 November 1956, TNA, CO 1031/1958. This correspondence is also detailed in Van Dijk 1995.

66 The literature here is vast, but I am thinking especially of Linton 1943 and Worsley 1957.

67 A more developed consideration of the influence of North American anthropologists on public perceptions of Rastafari is beyond the scope of this book, although I discuss the scholarship on Rastafari at greater length elsewhere (see Thomas 2011). But this would be a fascinating and critically important exercise.

68 Jamaica Constabulary Force, "The Rastafari Cult," report, 5 January 1957, TNA, CO 1031/2767.

69 Kenneth Blackburne to Alan Lennox-Boyd, letter, 11 May 1959, TNA, FCO 141/5295.

70 This concern on the part of Norman Manley would apparently grow during the years Claudius Henry returned to Jamaica and began actively recruiting people to the faith. Robert A. Hill, who has recently constructed a more detailed picture of the Claudius Henry events of 1959 and 1960, has controversially argued that the *Ras Tafari Movement in Kingston, Jamaica* (Smith et al. 1960) was actually an intelligence document posing as an academic study and that it was written entirely by the anthropologist M. G. Smith, who had been tasked by Prime Minister Norman Manley to conduct surveillance research on the Rastafari communities in West Kingston. The goal of the report, for Hill, was pacification of the movement through the political cooptation of its members. Nettleford's own accounting of the story of the report, however, has Planno and others visiting him at the Extramural Department at the University of the West Indies asking that a study be done "to let Jamaica understand what they're about" (Scott and Nettleford 2006: 164). Nettleford reports

that he sent the group of Rastafari to Sir Arthur Lewis, who then made arrangements to sponsor a six-week study of the movement, concentrating in downtown Kingston, conducted by Nettleford, Roy Augier, and M. S. Smith. The report was serialized in the *Gleaner* and sold out its initial printing of ten thousand copies in one day (Scott and Nettleford 2006: 167).

71 Special Branch report to the LSIC, 27 January 1958, TNA, FCO 141/5434.

72 Special Branch report to the LSIC, September 1958, TNA, FCO 141/5434.

73 In the meeting at which the Special Branch report of September 1958 was discussed, it was reported that the attorney-general advised against pressing charges for sedition, but that if he continued these kinds of public pronouncements he should be charged with using indecent language (LSIC Meeting Notes, 6 November 1958, TNA, FCO 141/5434).

74 Secretary of State for the Colonies Alan Lennox-Boyd to Governor Sir Kenneth Blackburne, letter, appendix I(2), 10 June 1959, TNA, CO 1031/2767.

75 When asked about links between the left and Rastafari in an interview with Trevor Munroe, Richard Hart remembered that Buchanan knew Leonard Howell personally, but the two movements did not work together in the early days. "I don't recall really being close to Rastas before the '50s," he replied (Munroe 1990: 130). Although Hart sometimes gave public lectures about black history and black leadership within struggles for social change, race was not an organizing principle for the left. As Munroe put it, "It is clear that there was no real analysis of Rastafarianism within the communist Left and no systematic effort at organizational relationship." This was true despite the fact that, as Munroe further points out, there was significant "overlap between Rastafarian and communist working people and unemployed, particularly in Western Kingston" (Munroe 1992: 46). The assertion of a link between Rastafari and Marxism was also made in the report *The Ras Tafari Movement in Kingston, Jamaica* (Smith et al. 1960: 25–26). Of course, this concern would also emerge with Walter Rodney's forays downtown and reasoning with Rastafari.

76 Ian Cobain and Peter Walker, "Secret Memo Gave Guidelines on Abuse of Mau Mau in 1950s," *The Guardian*, 11 April 2011, accessed 14 November 2014, https://www.theguardian.com/world/2011/apr/11/mau-mau-high-court-foreign-office-documents.

77 See also Special Branch Reports, TNA, CO 1031/2767, CO 1031/2768, CO 1031/3994, FCO 141/5434.

78 According to followers who were with Henry at the time, this letter was written but never sent, and it was written not by Henry but by an undercover police informer.

79 "Extract from Governor of Jamaica's Intelligence Report for November–December 1960, Original on WIS 472/1025/01," TNA, CO 1031/3995.

80 For discussion of this, see Thomas 2011: chap. 5.

81 Monthly Intelligence Report, April 1960, TNA, CO 1031/3995.

82 Kenneth Blackburne to Secretary of State for the Colonies Allan Lennox-Boyd, letter, 10 June 1959, TNA, CO 1031/2767.

83 Report of the Local Standing Intelligence Committee, April 1960, TNA, CO

1031/3994. D. N. Pritt was an English barrister who was ultimately expelled from the Labour Party because of his pro-Soviet stance.

84 Report of the Local Standing Intelligence Committee, May 1960, TNA, CO 1031/3994.

85 LSIC reports, June 1960, July 1960, TNA, CO 1031/3994.

86 Report of the Local Standing Intelligence Committee, July 1960, TNA, CO 1031/3994.

87 "Extract from Governor of Jamaica's Intelligence Report for January 1961," TNA, CO 1031/3995.

88 "Extract from Governor of Jamaica's Intelligence Report for January 1961."

89 Major St. J. C. Brooke-Johnson, War Office, to G. P. Lloyd, West Indian Department, Colonial Office, confidential letter, 15 December 1960, TNA, CO 1031/3995.

90 "D.W.L." [Brigadier-General D. W. Lister] to Colonel B. Wilson, letter, 15 December 1960, TNA, War Office Records (WO) 336/26.

91 "Troopers" to "General Jamaica," "Rastafarian Movement: Your G2061 of 152220 Z December," telegram, 21 December 1960, TNA, WO 336/26.

92 C. A. Herbert, "Report on the Intelligence Organization in Jamaica," 11 July 1956, TNA, CO 1035/103.

93 D. A. Herbert to Governor Hugh Foot, letter, 11 July 1956, TNA, CO 1035/103.

94 Governor Hugh Foot to C. A. Herbert, letter, 18 September 1956, TNA, CO 1035/103.

95 Governor Hugh Foot to Norman Manley, letters, 19 November 1956, 18 April 1957; Norman Manley to Governor Hugh Foot, letter, 21 November 1956; Norman Manley to A. Crasswell, letter, 8 November 1957; Governor Kenneth Blackburne to Norman Manley, letters, 31 March 1959, 18 August 1959; Norman Manley to Governor Kenneth Blackburne, letter, 1 April 1959; Norman Manley to W. M. Seivright, letter, 17 May 1960; "Internal Security and Planning," memorandum, 17 May 1960, all in Manley Papers, 4/60/2A/20.

96 Hugh Foot to Eric Battersby, letter, 16 April 1956, TNA, CO 1031/10.

97 Governor Kenneth Blackburne to Colonial Office, memorandum, 30 April 1962, TNA, FCO 141/5316.

98 Jahlani Niaah, interview by author, Kingston, Jamaica, 11 March 2014.

99 Niaah interview.

100 "Police Raid Pinnacle Again: Nine Thousand More Ganja Trees Destroyed," *Daily Gleaner*, 25 May 1954, 1; "Police Burn More Ganja at Pinnacle," *Daily Gleaner*, 28 May 1954, 1.

101 Niaah interview.

102 The headline of the *Gleaner* on 29 December 1952 was "Alumina: First Shipment Leaves Shortly" (100 tons from Kaiser in St. Bess).

103 Glasspole participated in the TUC Scholarship Scheme in 1946–47.

104 Thossy Kelly and W. M MacPherson, letter, 3 January 1952; George Woodcock to Sir Vincent Tewson, letter, 14 March 1952; letter to NWU, TUCJ, National Labour Commission, 7 May 1952; letter to J. H. Oldenbroek, 5 June 1952; Noel Nethersole, letter, 3 April 1952; Florizel Glasspole, letter, 2 April 1952;

J. H. Oldenbroek to Sir Vincent Tewson, letter, 17 September 1952, all in Trades Unions Congress Archives, Modern Record Centre, University of Warwick, Warwick, U.K., file 972–1, 1947–52.

105 Jeffrey Harrod (1972: 57) also argues that trade unions were involved with the CIA, with the agency using the unions' facilities, sometimes without the knowledge of leaders.

106 The merger between the AFL and CIO occurred in 1955, at which point their policy toward less-developed countries was to oppose communism by supporting anticolonialism and providing assistance with food security and the development of health and irrigation infrastructure (Harrod 1972: 123).

107 It is interesting to note that as these foreign policy positions were being publicly articulated, John Windmuller's (1963: 113) ultimate argument is that labor is not an equal partner in foreign policy because representatives are not sufficiently experienced to effectively take on the positions they are given, distrust between AFL and CIO principals stymies unified action, and labor "contributes practically no new ideas to the policy-making process."

108 The precursor to ORIT was the Inter-American Confederation of Labor, founded in Lima in 1948, just before the British, American, and Dutch members of the WFTU withdrew and formed the ICFTU.

109 Serafino Romualdi Papers, Kheel Center for Labor-Management Documentation and Archives (Collection 5459), Cornell University Library (hereafter, Romualdi Papers), box 5, folder 9.

110 It is possible that Alexander's reports in Romualdi's papers were actually those he had written for Lovestone under the auspices of the International Department of the AFL, as many of his trips to Latin America between 1952 and 1959 were made with both government and CIA funds received through Lovestone (Romualdi 1967).

111 This sensibility was reiterated by William Doherty Sr., the new U.S. ambassador to independent Jamaica, in his speech during the independence ceremonies. I have much more to say about Doherty later.

112 "U.S. Union Man in Alumina Labor Talks," *Daily Gleaner*, 8 January 1953, 1.

113 N. D. Watson to Ernest Bell, letter regarding Zonarich's visit to Jamaica in January 1953, 1 July 1953, TUC, TNA, CO 1031/7.

114 Restraining orders, TUC Archives, 972.1(2), 1953–60.

115 Florizel Glasspole to Oliver Lyttleton, Secretary of State for the Colonies, Telegram, 27 March 1953, TNA, CO 1031/7.

116 "Top Int[ernationa]l Unionists 'Silenced' during Stay," *Public Opinion*, 28 March 1953, 1.

117 Colville Deverell to Stephen Luke, telegram, 28 March 1953, TNA, CO 1031/7.

118 Charles Millard to Sir Vincent Tewson, letter, 8 April 1953; TUC Archives, 972.1(2), 1953–60.

119 Charles Millard to L. B. Pearson, letter, 8 April 1953, TNA, CO 1031/7.

120 H. F. Heinemann to a Miss Gaved, Mr. Barltrop, Mr. Biggs, Mr. Barton, and Mr. Luke, note on file, 27 March 1953, TNA, CO 1031/7.

121 Heinemann to Gaved et al., note on file (27 March 1953).

122 Heinemann to Gaved et al., note on file (30 March 1953).

123 E. W. Barltrop to H. F. Heinemann, Miss Gaved, Mr. Biggs, Mr. Barton, and Mr. Luke, note on file, 30 March 1953, TNA, CO 1031/7.

124 C. Costley-White to James Thomson, Esq., letter, 21 August 1953, TNA, CO 1031/7.

125 Costley-White to Thomson, letter.

126 Heinemann to Gaved et al., note on file (27 March 1953).

127 H. F. Heinemann to Miss Gaved, Mr. Barltrop, and Mr. Wallace, letter, 29 April 1953, TNA, CO 1031/7.

128 Miss Gaved to H. F. Heinemann, Mr. Barltrop, Mr. Biggs, Mr. Barton, and Mr. Luke, note on file, 27 March 1953, TNA, CO 1031/7.

129 Governor Hugh Foot to Assistant Colonial Secretary W. I. J. Wallace, letter, 22 June 1953, TNA, CO 1031/7.

130 N. D. Watson to W. I. J. Wallace, letter, 2 May 1953, TNA, CO 1031/7.

131 N. D. Watson to Ernest Bell, letter, 1 July 1953, TNA, CO 1031/7.

132 Watson to Bell, letter.

133 "USW Aid to Needy Jamaica Steel Men," *Telegram*, 9 June 1953; "Jamaican Named to Union Position by Steelworkers," *Globe and Mail*, 9 June 1953, both in TNA, CO 1031/1105.

134 "Bauxite Workers Move to Form Own Union," *Daily Gleaner*, 8 August 1957, 13.

135 Robert J. Alexander, report, 7 October 1956, Romualdi Papers, box 9, folder 3.

136 George Meany to Serafino Romualdi, memorandum, December 18, 1956, Romualdi Papers, box 9, folder 3.

137 Report on visit to Washington, DC, Manley Papers, 4/60/2A/40.

138 For a discussion of the FBI records related to this event, see Meeks 2000.

139 "Jamaica: Plan of Action for the Period Beginning 1 June 1963," U.S. National Archives and Records Administration, College Park, MD (NARA), John F. Kennedy Presidential Library and Museum, National Security Council Files (hereafter, JFK-NSC), Country Series: Jamaica, 1962–63, 11.

140 "Jamaica: Plan of Action for the Period Beginning 1 June 1963."

141 American universities were also enlisted to support Alliance for Progress projects. Cornell University's School of Industrial and Labor Relations, for example, trained Latin American labor leaders and established departments of labor relations at universities overseas (Spaulding 1977: 65).

142 "Bases Talks Open Here today," *Jamaica Gleaner*, 13 December 1960, 1.

143 "Proposal and Recommendations for the Review of the Latin American Executive Committee on Capital Development: Jamaica—Low Cost Housing and Redevelopment," U.S. State Department, Agency for International Development, 30 January 1963, NARA, Unclassified Central Subject Files, ARC 4125766, HMS P 405, box 212.

144 Don Robotham (2003) has argued that this housing was made available on a partisan basis.

145 USAID was not formally established until November 1961 as the U.S. government agency responsible for administering civilian aid overseas.

146 "Development Financing Memorandum; Jamaica—Low Cost Housing and Redevelopment, Detailed Description of the Project," paper attached to State Department, Agency for International Development, "Proposal and Recommendations for the Review of the Latin American Executive Committee on Capital Development: Jamaica—Low Cost Housing and Redevelopment," 30 January 1963, NARA, Unclassified Central Subject Files, ARC 4125766, HMS P 405, box 212.

147 "Report of Housing Team of the International Cooperation Administration to the United States Operations Mission—Jamaica," n.d., NARA, Unclassified Central Subject Files, ARC 4125766, HMS P 405, box 212.

148 "Report of Housing Team of the International Cooperation Administration to the United States Operations Mission—Jamaica" and press release no. 521, 21 July 1961, Unclassified Central Subject Files, ARC 4125766, HMS P 405, box 212. For documentation of the increase, see Philip Glaessner, Deputy Assistant Administrator for Capital Development, AID[USAID], "Delegation of Authority to Negotiate and Sign Agreements," 22 July 1963, NARA, Unclassified Central Subject Files, ARC 4125766, HMS P 405, box 212.

149 This delay was attributed to changes in USAID policy and inefficiency within the USAID bureaucracy and to a balance of payments problem between Jamaica and the United States (see USAID, Kingston, to U.S. State Department, airgram, 5 October 1962; Warren Wolff to Stanley Grand, "Jamaica Low-Cost Housing Loan," memorandum, 14 January 1964; Acting Permanent Secretary of Ministry of Housing to USAID Mission to Jamaica, memorandum, 20 October 1966, all in NARA, Unclassified Central Subject Files, ARC 4125766, HMS P 405, boxes 211–12. In the January 1964 memo, Wolff argues against blaming administrative inefficiency at USAID for the delay in disbursement, instead stating that the delay was due to the need for implementation letters and the selection of an appropriate architectural engineer from the United States by the Government of Jamaica.

150 "Report of Housing Team of the International Cooperation Administration to the United States Operations Mission—Jamaica" and press release no. 521, 21 July 1961, Unclassified Central Subject Files, ARC 4125766, HMS P 405, box 212.

151 Government of Jamaica, Parliamentary Budget Records, 1960–70.

152 National Security Council (NSC), "Statement of U.S. Policy toward the West Indies," memorandum, 21 March 1960, NARA, Foreign Relations of the United States Papers (FRUS), NSC 6002/1, lot 62D1.

153 NSC, "Statement of U.S. Policy toward the West Indies."

154 NSC, "Statement of U.S. Policy toward the West Indies," in annex to a memo titled "General Conditions."

155 NSC, "Statement of U.S. Policy toward the West Indies."

156 "Briefing Paper for Vice President's Attendance of Jamaica Independence Celebrations," 1962; "Jamaica Scope Paper"; "Jamaica: Plan of Action for the Period Beginning 1 June 1963," all in NARA, JFK-NSC, Country Series: Jamaica, 1962–63.

157 William Doherty to John R. Kanline, U.S. State Department, "AIFLD," air-gram, 26 February 1963, NARA, Unclassified Central Subject Files, ARC 4125766, HMS P 405, box 212.

158 Doherty to Kanline, "AIFLD."

159 Doherty to Kanline, "AIFLD."

160 Doherty to Kanline, "AIFLD."

161 Glaessner, "Delegation of Authority to Negotiate and Sign Agreements."

162 William Doherty Jr. received his degree in philosophy from Catholic University in 1949 and moved from there to work as an assistant administrator for the Marshall Plan. However, within a year he was voted president of the American Federation of Government Employees. After that posting, he worked in Europe as the assistant director of regional activities for the ICFTU and later in South America as the inter-American representative for the PTTI (Sims 1992).

163 This was also a program of the PTTI. Doherty's editorial "PTTI Progress in 1960," in *Inter-American Information Bulletin*, lists a housing program among the PTTI's accomplishments. He writes, "From a mere idea proceeding from the April 1960 meeting of the Inter-American Advisory Committee in Sao Paulo we have progressed to the point of joining with international housing teams in recommending concrete solutions to the complex problems of inadequate housing. We are confident that as our union cooperatives are successfully organized in Ecuador and elsewhere that 1961 will not pass before the first section of PTTI union-sponsored homes is dedicated": William C. Doherty Jr., "PTTI Progress in 1960," *Inter-American Information Bulletin*, vol. 5, no. 1, 1960, 3–4, in Postal, Telephone, and Telegraph International (PTTI) Archives, Tamiment Library and Robert F. Wagner Labor Archives, Elmer Holmes Bobst Library, New York University.

164 "Thirty New Houses to Go Up at Cockburn Pen for Kingston Pen Settlers," *Daily Gleaner*, 16 September 1947, 1; "Squatters on Kingston Pen," *Daily Gleaner*, 3 October 1947, 7; "Settlement of West Kingston Squatters," *Daily Gleaner*, 8 August 1950, 11.

165 "Squatters Given Two Weeks More at Kingston Pen," *Daily Gleaner*, 17 August 1950, 1; "Notice to Quit," *Daily Gleaner*, 12 September 1950, 14; "Extra Sum Sanctioned for Housing Project," *Daily Gleaner*, 13 September 1950, 3; Alan Blissett, "Kingston Pen," letter to the editor, *Daily Gleaner*, 3 July 1958, 12.

166 "Acquisition of Tivoli Gardens (formerly Kingston Pen)," 8 February 1961, Government of Jamaica (GOJ), Cabinet Submissions, 1B/31/198–961; land commissioner's report with cover letter from Ken Sterling, Minister of Housing, GOJ, Cabinet Submissions, 1B/31/1030–1962.

167 "Kingston Pen, Eviction of Squatters," GOJ, Cabinet Submissions, 1B/31/426–1963.

168 GOJ, Cabinet Submissions, 1B/31/178/1964.

169 "Housing Scheme for Kingston Pen," *Daily Gleaner*, 2 August 1963, 1.

170 "Kingston Pen: Construction of Houses Starts," *Daily Gleaner*, 30 July 1964, 12.

171 In 1964–65, £254,267 was authorized for slum clearance and rehousing in Trench Town: GOJ, Department of Housing Annual Reports, Year ended 31 March 1965, app. IVA, 13; GOJ, Department of Housing Annual Reports, Year ended 31 March 1966, 2, app. A, 11.

172 An additional £232,603 was allocated to phase I of Tivoli Gardens. In comparison, a total of £66,347 was authorized for construction at Glendevon/ Norwood: GOJ, Department of Housing Annual Reports, Year ended 31 March 1966, 2, app. A, 11.

173 Clarke builds this conclusion from "Survey of Trench Town and Victoria Town: A Preliminary Report" (Barham et al. 1965). These authors compared present and previous accommodation of residents in the housing projects and found that current residents did not have a squatter background (Barham et al. 1965: 29).

174 Norman Manley to Ambassador William Doherty, letter, 28 January 1963, Manley Papers, 4/60/2A/71.

175 Ambassador William C. Doherty to Norman Manley, letter, 29 January 1963, Manley Papers, 4/60/2A/71.

176 "New Jamaican Center Will Be Established," *AIFLD Report*, July 1963, 1, 4.

177 "Jamaica Labor School Opens," *AIFLD Report*, July–August 1964, 6.

178 "1965 – Summary of AIFLD Education," *AIFLD Report*, January 1965, 3.

179 "AIFLD in Action," *AIFLD Report*, March 1966, 6–7 (table); "Interns Active in Caribbean," *AIFLD Report*, April 1968, 1; Roy T. Havercamp to Secretary of State, "Relations with USAID and Embassies," telegram no. 1311, 20 February 1979, NARA, Classified Subject Files (Correspondence), 1978-1979; ARC 6171543, Boxes 1-2; HMS P 66.

180 Richard Dudman, "AID Funds for CIA Projects," *St. Louis Post-Dispatch*, 13 April 1969; Richard Dudman, "Channel to Overseas Labor," *St. Louis Post-Dispatch*, 4 April 1969, William Greider, "Unions Turn to AID after CIA Pullout," *Washington Post*, 21 April 1969; Henry Berger, "Labor and State," *The Nation*, 13 January 1969; Henry Berger, "Lovestone, Meany and State," *The Nation*, 16 January 1967; Susan Bodenheimer, "U.S. Labor's Conservative Role in Latin America," *The Progressive*, November 1967; Stanley Meisler, "Dubious Role of AFL-CIO," *The Nation*, 10 February 1964; Sidney Lens, "Latin America IV," *The Nation*, 19 September 1966; Sidney Lens, "American Labor Abroad," *The Nation*, 5 July 1965; Dan Kurzman, "Lovestone's Cold War," *New Republic*, 25 June 1966; Eugene Methvin, "Labor's New Weapon for Democracy," *Reader's Digest*, October 1966; "Labor's Establishment—Stop the World," *The Commonweal*, 21 March 1969, all reprinted in U.S. Government 1969.

181 For more on Peter Grace's engagement with Latin America, see "Amazing Grace" 1976.

182 Beth Sims (1992: 23) has also argued that AID funding was channeled directly to the institutes, "bypassing the international affairs department of the AFL-

CIO," and in her book she discusses at length how difficult it is to track funding through AID.

183 See also the "CIA Target: Labor" special issue of *Counterspy* (Fall 1974).

184 See also Ken Post, who in the second volume of *Strike the Iron* notes that the squatter settlements in the Corporate Area of Kingston were the centers of the Rastafari by mid-1945 (Post 1981: 2:537), and Frank Jan van Dijk (1995: 75), who argues that "given their relatively small numbers, it is improbable that the dispersal of the Howellites had such a major impact on an already well-established movement in Kingston."

185 Amanda Sives disputes Chevannes's claim that prior to 1963, inter-gang rivalry was unknown. She argues that newspaper reports as early as 1959 document politically motivated violence by organized groups, occurring "at the sites of political meetings, outside party and trade union headquarters, against candidates and between rival party supporters" (Sives 2010: 47).

CODA

1 For additional perspectives on why rural Jamaicans would have supported Manley over Bustamante during this period, see Scott 2013.

2 For an elaboration of the frame of "refusal" I am referencing here, one that has come out of an ongoing working group in which I have been involved at Barnard called "Practices of Refusal," see Campt 2017. For additional perspectives, see also "Theorizing Refusal," a special issue of *Cultural Anthropology* (31[3] [2016]) edited by Carole McGranahan, and Simpson 2007.

3 Aimee Cox (2015: 33–35) has a discussion of complicity in her introduction.

4 For analyses of the evacuation of structural-historical perspectives in tribunals related to violence, see Clarke 2009; Englund 2006. See also the numerous critiques of the juridical limitations of truth and reconciliation commissions, esp. Feldman 2004; Ferreira da Silva 2013; McAllister 2013; Posel 2008; Ross 2003; Scott 2014; Trouillot 2000; Weheliye 2014.

5 For an analysis of *marronage* in relation to social movements in Guadeloupe that were geared toward reimagining sovereignty absent the struggle for control over the nation-state, see also Bonilla 2015.

6 This kind of recognition also undergirds Johannes Fabian's discussion of moments in which European explorers saw themselves (or others they knew, or think they could know) in the Africans they were encountering. For Fabian (1999: 54, 59), recognition among these European explorers was an involuntary embodied sensibility generated by "some form of reaching out," but it was also inherently limited in that the Europeans understood that "any appeal to *mutual* recognition would undermine [their] authority and be incompatible with the European's mission as the emissary of a superior race."

7 Indigenous recognition has also been discussed in terms of a "double bind" in which indigenous persons must perform a particular version of native-ness to the state (and often to each other) in order to access juridical and socio-economic "goods," while also negotiating the realities of modern economic

life and geopolitics (see, e.g., Cattelino 2008, 2010; Hale 2005; Hooker 2005; Povinelli 2002, 2006). But for a useful discussion of the ways the racialization of Native Americans serves to obscure the dynamics of settler colonialism and erases Native claims to priorness, turning them instead into internal ethnic minorities, see Byrd 2011. For his advocacy of a strategic politics of recognition rooted in what he calls "grounded normativity," anticolonial struggle rooted in the question of land, not only as materiality but as the relations between people, space, ritual practice, and things, see Coulthard 2014. Finally, for a discussion of recognition that refuses external assessment, and focuses on intra-community "affection and care, outside of the logics of colonial and imperial rule," see Simpson 2007: 76.

8   Fred Moten has usefully reread Fanon's ontological rendering of blackness, particularly his assertion that blackness is an impossibility in relation to humanness within the context of colonialism. Moten (2008: 185) is interested instead in how, when, and where we see "the case blackness makes for itself in spite and by way of every interdiction." For him, these moments refuse and disrupt the ontologies of social life, and therefore rely on other forms of historical consciousness (see also Judy 1996).

9   Jessica Benjamin (1988) is perhaps the earliest psychoanalyst and social theorist who sought to challenge this Hegelian form of recognition through psychoanalytic practice. Her concern was the relationship between the therapist and the analysand, and her aim was to disturb the position of the analyst as the all-knowing party in the relationship, encouraging therapists instead to surrender to the experiences of the analysand, at least momentarily (Benjamin 2004). This process, Benjamin believed, would lead to a form of intersubjectivity based on mutual recognition through a relational system built on what she called "thirdness," a position outside the dyad (Benjamin 2004). Benjamin's critique here is a feminist one, an excoriation of classic psychoanalytic theory's focus on a normative movement away from the mother (rather than mutual recognition and attachment), and of the Euro-centricity and linearity of post-Freudian object relations theory (Benjamin 1990). See also the critique of Benjamin by Judith Butler in which she argues that Benjamin seems to be holding up an ideal model of recognition in which "destruction is an occasional and lamentable occurrence" (Butler 2000: 273) rather than a constitutive force. Butler's skepticism is rooted in the idea that the Other will inevitably "lapse" into the category of object unless there is a more profound recognition of history, and an apprehension of historical process that does not always have oneself at the center. Like Fanon, she proposes that the humility of recognition must be grounded in love.

10 Sara Ahmed's conceptualization of this relation is rather more robust: "Encounters between embodied subjects always hesitate between the domain of the particular—the face to face of this encounter—and the general—the framing of the encounter by broader relationships of power and antagonism. The particular encounter hence always carries *traces* of those broader relationships. Differences, as markers of power, are not determined in the 'space' of

the particular *or* the general, but in the very determination of their historical relation (a determination that is never final or complete, as it involves strange encounters)" (Ahmed 2000: 9).

11 For excellent exegeses of Honneth's work, see Petherbridge 2011, 2013.

12 For an interesting discussion of how technologies influence an ethics of recognition as grounded in the face and of a "radical ethics of nonindexical facehood," see Pearl 2017: 156.

13 This earlier phenomenological anthropology has also recently been taken up by Kevin Groark (2013: 279) in his analysis of Tzotzil Maya "intersomatic processes." I thank Erika Hoffmann-Dilloway for bringing this article to my attention.

14 But see the critique of Hardt's position by Lauren Berlant in which she reminds him that feminists have long theorized a politics that joins political interests and affective life ("the personal is political"), and who takes him to task for separating "bad love" from "good love," the latter of which is open to transformation, arguing instead that "love is not entirely ethical, if it has any relation to desire" (Berlant 2011b: 684–85).

15 It is this sense of ethics that suffuses Jacques Derrida's "future anterior," the time that will have been in the process of becoming (Derrida [1967] 1997: 5). For Derrida, time cannot be anteriorized merely through memory—the methodological basis of many truth commissions or commissions of enquiry—because memory does not exhaust the relationships of obligation, causality, and accountability created through entanglement.

16 Kezia Page (2017) points out that there was only one song that directly recounted the incursion, and it was written by the Trinidadian artist Ataklan ("Kingston Town").

References

ARCHIVES

Bodleian Library, Oxford University
  Mona Macmillan Papers
Government of Jamaica (GOJ), Kingston
  Cabinet Submissions
  Parliamentary Budget Records, 1960–70
  Department of Housing Annual Reports, 1963–69
Jamaica National Archives, Spanish Town
  Norman Manley Papers
  Pinnacle Papers, Colonial Secretary's Office (PP-CSO)
Kheel Center for Labor-Management Documentation and Archives, Cornell
    University Library, Ithaca, NY
  Serafino Romualdi Papers, Collection 5459
National Archives of the United Kingdom (TNA), Kew Gardens
  Colonial Office Records (CO)
  Foreign Commonwealth Office Records (FCO)
  War Office Records (WO)
Tamiment Library and Robert F. Wagner Labor Archives, Elmer Holmes Bobst
    Library, New York University
  Philip Agee Papers
  Postal, Telephone, and Telegraph International (PTTI) Archives

Trades Unions Congress (TUC) Archives, Modern Record Centre, University of
Warwick, Warwick, U.K.
U.S. National Archives and Records Administration, College Park, MD
Central Subject Files, 1971–83
CIA Archives
Classified Central Subject Files, 1963–75
Classified Subject Files (Correspondence), 1978–79
Foreign Relations of the United States Papers, Office of the Historian
John F. Kennedy Presidential Library and Museum, National Security Council
Files
Records Relating to Jamaican Affairs, 1960–63
Unclassified Central Subject Files, 1962–75
USAID Project Files Pertaining to Housing Guaranty Program, 1963–95
William Macmillan Papers, Courtesy of Hugh Macmillan

NEWSPAPERS

Covert Action Information Bulletin
Jamaica Daily Gleaner
Jamaica Sunday Gleaner

SECONDARY WORKS

Abu-Lughod, Lila. 2004. *Dramas of Nationhood: The Politics of Television in Egypt.*
Chicago: University of Chicago Press.
Agard-Jones, Vanessa. 2012. "What the Sands Remember." *GLQ* 18(2): 325–46.
Agee, Philip. 1975. *Inside the Company: CIA Diary.* New York: Stonehill.
Agha, Asif. 2004. "Registers of Language." In *A Companion to Linguistic Anthro-pology*, ed. Alessandro Duranti, 23–45. Malden, MA: Blackwell.
Ahmed, Sara. 2000. *Strange Encounters: Embodied Others in Post-Coloniality.* New
York: Routledge.
Ahmed, Sara. 2004. *The Cultural Politics of Emotion.* Edinburgh: Edinburgh University Press.
Ain-Davis, Dana. 2016. "'The Bone Collectors' Comments for Sorrow as Artifact:
Black Radical Mothering in Times of Terror." *Transforming Anthropology*
24(1): 8–16.
Alexander, Jack. 1977. "The Culture of Race in Middle-Class Kingston, Jamaica."
American Ethnologist 4(3): 413–35.
Alexander, M. Jacqui. 1994. "Not Just (Any) Body Can Be a Citizen: The Politics of
Law, Sexuality, and Postcoloniality in Trinidad and Tobago and the Bahamas."
Feminist Review 48: 5–23.
Alexander, M. Jacqui. 1997. "Erotic Autonomy as a Politics of Decolonization: An
Anatomy of Feminist and State Practice in the Bahamas Tourist Economy." In
Feminist Genealogies, Colonial Legacies, Democratic Futures, ed. Chandra Talpade Mohanty and M. Jacqui Alexander, 63–100. New York: Routledge.

Alexander, M. Jacqui. 2005. *Pedagogies of Crossing: Meditations on Feminism, Sexual Politics, Memory and the Sacred.* Durham, NC: Duke University Press.

Alexander, Robert J., with Eldon M. Parker. 2004. *A History of Organized Labor in the English-Speaking West Indies.* Westport, CT: Praeger.

Allahar, Anton, ed. 2001. *Caribbean Charisma: Reflections on Leadership, Legitimacy, and Populist Politics.* Boulder, CO: Lynne Rienner.

"Amazing Grace: The W. R. Grace Corporation." 1976. *NACLA Latin America and Empire Report* 10(3): 3–14.

Amnesty International. 2003. *Jamaica: "... Until Their Voices Are Heard...,"* the West Kingston Commission of Inquiry, AMR 38/010/2003, July. Accessed 14 November 2011. https://www.refworld.org/docid/3f12f2c34.html.

Anderson, Benedict. (1990) 2006. *Language and Power: Exploring Political Cultures in Indonesia.* Jakarta, Indonesia: PT Equinox.

Aretzaga, Begoña. 2003. "Maddening States." *Annual Review of Anthropology* 32: 393–410.

Austin, Diane. 1984. *Urban Life in Kingston, Jamaica: The Culture and Class Ideology of Two Neighborhoods.* New York: Gordon and Breach Science.

Austin-Broos, Diane. 1992. "Redefining the Moral Order: Interpretations of Christianity in Post-Emancipation Jamaica." In *The Meaning of Freedom: Economics, Politics, and Culture after Slavery*, ed. Frank McGlynn and Seymour Drescher, 221–44. Pittsburgh: University of Pittsburgh Press.

Azoulay, Ariella. 2008. *The Civil Contract of Photography.* New York: Zone.

Baer, Ulrich. 2002. *Spectral Evidence: The Photography of Trauma.* Cambridge, MA: MIT Press.

Bair, Madeleine. 2011. "The Impact of the War on Drugs on Security, Legitimacy, and Sovereignty in Jamaica: A Case Study of the 2010 Extradition of Christopher 'Dudus' Coke." Master's thesis, International and Area Studies, University of California, Berkeley.

Barham, A., E. Davis, S. Graham, and H. McKenzie. 1965. "Survey of Trench Town and Victoria Town: A Preliminary Report." Mona, Jamaica: Department of Sociology, University of the West Indies.

Barrett, Livern. 2015. "'Dudus' Gang Invested in Weapons and Explosives, Says Former Commish." *Jamaica Gleaner*, 15 April, http://jamaica-gleaner.com/article/lead-stories/20150415/dudus-gang-invested-weapons-and-explosives-says-former-commish.

Barrow, Christine. 1988. "Men, Women and the Family in the Caribbean: A Review." In *Gender in Caribbean Development*, ed. Patricia Mohammed and Catherine Shepherd, 149–63. Mona, Jamaica: Women and Development Studies Project, University of the West Indies.

Basch, Linda, Nina Glick Schiller, and Cristina Szanton-Blanc. 1994. *Nations Unbound: Transnational Projects, Postcolonial Predicaments, and Deterritorialized Nation-States.* Langhorne, PA: Gordon and Breach.

Beckford, George. 1987. "The Social Economy of Bauxite in the Jamaican Man-Space." *Social and Economic Studies* 36(1): 1–55.

Beckwith, Martha. (1929) 1969. *Black Roadways: A Study of Jamaican Folk Life.* New York: Negro Universities Press.

Benjamin, Jessica. 1988. *The Bonds of Love: Psychoanalysis, Feminism, and the Problem of Domination.* New York: Pantheon.

Benjamin, Jessica. 1990. "Recognition and Destruction: An Outline of Intersubjectivity." *Psychoanalytic Psychology* 7 (supp.): 33–47.

Benjamin, Jessica. 2004. "Beyond Doer and Done To: An Intersubjective View of Thirdness." *Psychoanalytic Quarterly* 73: 5–46.

Benjamin, Walter. 2005. "Little History of Photography." In *Selected Writings: Volume 2, Part 2, 1931–1934,* 508–30. Cambridge, MA: Harvard University Press.

Berg, Ulla, and Ana Ramos-Zayas. 2015. "Racializing Affect: A Theoretical Proposition." *Current Anthropology* 56(5): 654–77.

Berlant, Lauren. 2011a. *Cruel Optimism.* Durham, NC: Duke University Press.

Berlant, Lauren. 2011b. "A Properly Political Concept of Love: Three Approaches in Ten Pages." *Cultural Anthropology* 26(4): 683–91.

Besson, Jean. 2002. *Martha Brae's Two Histories: European Expansion and Caribbean Culture-Building in Jamaica.* Chapel Hill: University of North Carolina Press.

Best, Lloyd. 1968. "Outlines of a Model of the Pure Plantation Economy." *Social and Economic Studies* 17(3): 283–323.

Bhabha, Homi. 1994. *The Location of Culture.* New York: Routledge.

Biehl, João. 2005. *Vita: Life in a Zone of Social Abandonment.* Berkeley: University of California Press.

Bigelow, John. 1851. *Jamaica in 1850.* New York: G. P. Putnam.

Blackstock, Nelson. 1988. *Cointelpro: The FBI's Secret War on Political Freedom.* New York: Pathfinder.

Bloomfield, Kijan. 2018. "Refuge and Deliverance." Ph.D. diss., Department of Religious Studies, Princeton University, Princeton, NJ.

Bogues, Anthony. 2002. "Politics, Nation and PostColony: Caribbean Inflections," *Small Axe* 11: 1–30.

Bogues, Anthony. 2003. *Black Heretics, Black Prophets: Radical Political Intellectuals.* New York: Routledge.

Bonilla, Yarimar. 2015. *Non-Sovereign Futures: French Caribbean Politics in the Wake of Disenchantment.* Chicago: University of Chicago Press.

Bourdieu, Pierre. 1994. "Rethinking the State: Genesis and Structure of the Bureaucratic Field." *Sociological Theory* 12(1): 1–18.

Brown, Elaine. 1993. *A Taste of Power: A Black Woman's Story.* New York: Anchor.

Brown, Jacqueline Nassy. 2005. *Dropping Anchor, Setting Sail: Geographies of Race in Black Liverpool.* Princeton, NJ: Princeton University Press.

Brown-Glaude, Winnifred. 2007. "The Fact of Blackness? The Bleached Body in Contemporary Jamaica." *Small Axe* 11(3): 34–51.

Browne, Simone. 2015. *Dark Matters: On the Surveillance of Blackness.* Durham, NC: Duke University Press.

Bryan, Patrick E. 2009. *Edward Seaga and the Challenges of Modern Jamaica*. Mona, Jamaica: University of the West Indies Press.

Buck-Morss, Susan. 2000. "Hegel and Haiti." *Critical Inquiry* 26(4): 821–65.

Buck-Morss, Susan. 2009. *Hegel, Haiti, and Universal History*. Pittsburgh, PA: University of Pittsburgh Press.

Buell, Raymond. 1931. "Jamaica: A Racial Mosaic." *Opportunity* (June): 180–83.

Burnard, Trevor. 2004. *Mastery, Tyranny and Desire: Thomas Thistlewood and His Slaves in the Anglo-Jamaican World*. Chapel Hill: University of North Carolina Press.

Butler, Judith. 2000. "Longing for Recognition: Commentary on the Work of Jessica Benjamin." *Studies in Gender and Sexuality* 1(3): 271–90.

Butler, Judith. 2005. *Giving an Account of Oneself*. New York: Fordham University Press.

Butler, Judith. 2009. *Frames of War: When Is Life Grievable*. New York: Verso.

Byrd, Jodi. 2011. *The Transit of Empire: Indigenous Critiques of Colonialism*. Minneapolis: University of Minnesota Press.

Campbell, Horace. 1987. *Rasta and Resistance: From Marcus Garvey to Walter Rodney*. Trenton, NJ: Africa World Press.

Campt, Tina. 2004. *Other Germans: Black Germans and the Politics of Race and Memory in the Third Reich*. Ann Arbor: University of Michigan Press.

Campt, Tina. 2012. *Image Matters: Archive, Photography, and the African Diaspora in Europe*. Durham, NC: Duke University Press.

Campt, Tina. 2017. *Listening to Images*. Durham, NC: Duke University Press.

Carby, Hazel. 1987. *Reconstructing Womanhood: The Emergence of the Afro-American Woman Novelist*. New York: Oxford University Press.

Carlyle, Thomas. 1849. "Occasional Discourse on the Negro Question." *Fraser's Magazine for Town and Country* 40: 670–79.

Carnegie, Charles, ed. 1987. *Afro-Caribbean Villages in Historical Perspective*. Kingston: African-Caribbean Institute of Jamaica.

Carnegie, Charles. 1996. "The Dundus and the Nation." *Cultural Anthropology* 11(4): 470–509.

Carnegie, Charles. 2014. "The Loss of the Verandah: Kingston's Constricted Postcolonial Geographies." *Social and Economic Studies* (63(2): 59–85.

Carnegie, Charles. 2015. "Yearning for Community in Late-Colonial Jamaica." Paper presented at the meetings of the Caribbean Studies Association, New Orleans, 27 May.

Carnegie, James. 1973. *Some Aspects of Jamaica's Politics: 1918–1938*. Kingston: Institute of Jamaica.

Caruth, Cathy. 1995. "Introduction (Part II)." In *Trauma: Explorations in Memory*, ed. Cathy Caruth, 151–57. Baltimore: Johns Hopkins University Press.

Cattelino, Jessica. 2008. *High Stakes: Florida Seminole Gaming and Sovereignty*. Durham, NC: Duke University Press.

Cattelino, Jessica. 2010. "The Double Bind of American Indian Need-Based Sovereignty." *Cultural Anthropology* 25(2): 235–62.

Chalfin, Brenda. 2012. *Neoliberal Frontiers: An Ethnography of Sovereignty in West Africa*. Chicago: University of Chicago Press.

Charles, Christopher. 2002. "Garrison Communities as Counter Societies: The Case of the 1998 Zeeks' Riot in Jamaica." *Ideaz* 1(1): 29–43.

Chatterjee, Partha. (1986) 1991. *Nationalism: A Derivative Discourse?* Minneapolis: University of Minnesota Press.

Chatterjee, Partha. 1989. "Colonialism, Nationalism, and Colonized Women: The Contest in India." *American Ethnologist* 16(4): 622–33.

Chatterjee, Partha. 1993. *The Nation and Its Fragments: Colonial and Postcolonial Histories*. Princeton, NJ: Princeton University Press.

Cheng, Anne. 2001. *The Melancholy of Race: Psychoanalysis, Assimilation, and Hidden Grief*. New York: Oxford University Press.

Chevannes, Barry. 1976. "The Repairer of the Breach: Reverend Claudius Henry and Jamaican Society." In *Ethnicity in the Americas*, ed. Frances Henry, 263–89. The Hague: Mouton.

Chevannes, Barry. 1981. "The Rastafari and the Urban Youth." In *Perspectives on Jamaica in the Seventies*, ed. Carl Stone and Aggrey Brown, 392–422. Kingston: Jamaica Publishing House.

Clarke, Colin. 2006a. *Decolonizing the Colonial City: Urbanization and Stratification in Kingston, Jamaica*. Oxford: Oxford University Press.

Clarke, Colin. 2006b. "Politics, Violence and Drugs in Kingston, Jamaica." *Bulletin of Latin American Research* 25(3): 420–40.

Clarke, Colin. 2016. *Race, Class, and the Politics of Decolonization: Jamaica Journals 1961 and 1968*. New York: Palgrave Macmillan.

Clarke, M. Kamari. 2009. *Fictions of Justice: The International Criminal Court and the Challenge of Legal Pluralism in Sub-Saharan Africa*. New York: Cambridge University Press.

Cohn, Bernard, and Nicholas Dirks. 1988. "Beyond the Fringe: The Nation State, Colonialism, and the Technologies of Power." *Journal of Historical Sociology* 1(2): 224–29.

Comptroller General of the United States. 1975. *How to Improve Management of U.S.-Financed Programs to Develop Free Labor Movements in Less Developed Countries*. Report to the Congress by the U.S. Department of State, Agency for International Development. Washington, DC: U.S. General Accounting Office.

Cooper, Frederick. 1996. *Decolonization and African Society: The Labor Question in French and British Africa*. New York: Cambridge University Press.

Coulthard, Glen Sean. 2014. *Red Skin, White Masks: Rejecting the Colonial Politics of Recognition*. Minneapolis: University of Minnesota Press.

Cox, Aimee. 2015. *Shapeshifters: Black Girls and the Choreography of Citizenship*. Durham, NC: Duke University Press.

Crapanzano, Vincent. 2000. *Serving the Word: Literalism in America from the Pulpit to the Bench*. New York: New Press.

Crichlow, Michaeline. 2005. *Negotiating Caribbean Freedom: Peasants and the State in Development*. Lanham, MD: Lexington.

Cross, Jason. 2017. "We Are Sorry—Gov[ernmen]t Apologises to Rastas for Coral Gardens Incident." *Jamaica Gleaner*, April. Accessed April 5, 2017. http://jamaica-gleaner.com/article/lead-stories/20170405/we-are-sorry-govt -apologises-rastas-coral-gardens-incident.

Csordas, Thomas. 1990. "Embodiment as a Paradigm for Anthropology." *Ethos* 18(1): 5–47.

Csordas, Thomas. 1993. "Somatic Modes of Attention." *Cultural Anthropology* 8: 135–56.

Csordas, Thomas. 2008. "Intersubjectivity and Intercorporeality." *Subjectivity* 22: 110–21.

Cvetkovich, Ann. 2003. *An Archive of Feelings: Trauma, Sexuality, and Lesbian Public Cultures*. Durham, NC: Duke University Press.

Daniel, E. Valentine. 1996. *Charred Lullabies: Chapters in an Anthropography of Violence*. Princeton, NJ: Princeton University Press.

Daniel, Yvonne. 2011. *Igniting Citizenship: Caribbean and Atlantic Diaspora Dance*. Urbana: University of Illinois Press.

Daniel, Yvonne. 2018. "Dance Artistry and Bahian Cultural Citizenship just before and after 1985: Isaura Oliveira and *Malinké*." In *Dancing Bahia: Essays on Afro-Brazilian Dance, Education, Memory, and Race*, ed. Lucía M. Suárez, Amélia Conrado, and Yvonne Daniel. Chicago: University of Chicago Press.

Das, Veena. 2007. *Life and Words: Violence and the Descent into the Ordinary*. Berkeley: University of California Press.

Derrida, Jacques. (1967) 1997. *Of Grammatology*. Baltimore, MD: Johns Hopkins University Press.

Douglas, Mary. 1966. *Purity and Danger: An Analysis of Concepts of Pollution and Taboo*. New York: Frederick A. Praeger.

Du Bois, W. E. B. (1903) 1996. *The Souls of Black Folk*. New York: Penguin.

Dunham, Katherine. 1946. *Katherine Dunham's Journey to Accompong*. New York: Henry Holt.

Dunkley, Daive. 2013. "The Suppression of Leonard Howell in Late Colonial Jamaica, 1932–1954." *New West Indian Guide* 87: 62–93.

Economic Commission for Latin America and the Caribbean (ECLAC). 2010. *Jamaica: Report of the Macro Socio-Economic Effects of the Events in Western Kingston Area, 22 May–7 June 2010*, October 27. Port-of-Spain: ECLAC, Subregional Headquarters for the Caribbean.

Eaton, George. 1995. *Alexander Bustamante and Modern Jamaica*. Kingston: LMH.

Edie, Carlene J. 1994. "Jamaica: Clientelism, Dependency, and Democratic Stability." In *Democracy in the Caribbean: Myths and Realities*, ed. Carlene Edie, 25–41. Westport, CT: Praeger.

Edmondson, Belinda. 1999. *Making Men: Gender, Literary Authority, and Women's Writing in Caribbean Narrative*. Durham, NC: Duke University Press.

Edwards, Erica. 2012. *Charisma and the Fictions of Black Leadership*. Minneapolis: University of Minnesota Press.

Ellis, Nadia. 2015. *Territories of the Soul: Queered Belonging in the Black Diaspora*. Durham, NC: Duke University Press.

Ellis, Nadia. 2016. "Splay: Moving from Incursion in New Orleans and Kingston." *Genders* 1(2). http://www.colorado.edu/genders/2016/05/19/splay-moving-incursion-new-orleans-and-kingston.

Eng, David. 2011. "Reparations and the Human." *Columbia Journal of Gender and the Law* 21(2): 561–83.

Eng, David. 2016. "Colonial Object Relations." *Social Text* 34(1): 1–19.

Englund, H. 2006. *Prisoners of Freedom: Human Rights and the African Poor.* Berkeley: University of California Press.

Eze, Emmanuel Chukwudi. 1997. *Race and the Enlightenment: A Reader.* Malden, MA: Blackwell.

Fabian, Johannes. 1999. "Remembering the Other: Knowledge and Recognition in the Exploration of Central Africa." *Critical Inquiry* 26: 49–69.

Fanon, Frantz. (1952) 1967. *Black Skin, White Masks.* New York: Grove Weidenfeld.

Fanon, Frantz. 1963. *The Wretched of the Earth.* New York: Grove.

Fassin, Didier. 2008. "The Humanitarian Politics of Testimony: Subjectification through Trauma in the Israeli-Palestinian Conflict." *Cultural Anthropology* 23(3): 531–58.

Fassin, Didier. 2012. *Humanitarian Reason: A Moral History of the Present.* Berkeley: University of California Press.

Fassin, Didier, and R. Rechtman. 2009. *The Empire of Trauma: An Inquiry into the Condition of Victimhood.* Princeton, NJ: Princeton University Press.

Feldman, Allen. 2004. "Memory Theaters, Virtual Witnessing, and the Trauma-Aesthetic." *Biography* 27(1): 163–202.

Felman, Shoshana, and Dori Laub. 1992. *Testimony: Crises of Witnessing in Literature, Psychoanalysis, and History.* New York: Routledge.

Ferreira da Silva, Denise. 2007. *Toward a Global Idea of Race.* Minneapolis: University of Minnesota Press.

Ferreira da Silva, Denise. 2013. "To Be Announced: Radical Praxis or Knowing (at) the Limits of Justice." *Social Text* 31(1): 43–62.

Fischer, Sibylle. 2004. *Modernity Disavowed: Haiti and the Cultures of Slavery in the Age of Revolution.* Durham, NC: Duke University Press.

Fischer, Sibylle. 2015. "Atlantic Ontologies: On Violence and Being Human." *Caribbean Rasanblaj* 12(1). Accessed February 15, 2016. http://hemisphericinstitute.org/hemi/fr/emisferica-121-caribbean-rasanblaj/fischer.

Flint, John E. 1989. "Macmillan as a Critic of Empire: The Impact of an Historian on Colonial Policy." In *Africa and Empire: W. M. Macmillan, Historian and Social Critic,* ed. Hugh Macmillan, 212–31. Aldershot, U.K.: Institute of Commonwealth Studies.

Foot, Hugh. 1964. *A Start in Freedom,* New York: Harper and Row.

Foucault, Michel. 1978. *The History of Sexuality,* Vol I. New York: Pantheon Books.

Foucault, Michel. 1988. *Madness and Civilization: A History of Insanity in the Age of Reason.* New York: Vintage.

Franck, Harry A. 1920. *Roaming through the West Indies.* New York: Blue Ribbon.

Fraser, Cary. 1994. *Ambivalent Anti-colonialism: The United States and the Genesis of West Indian Independence, 1940–1964.* Westport, CT: Greenwood.

Freud, Sigmund. (1913) 1989. *Totem and Taboo*. London: W. W. Norton.

Frosh, Paul, and Amit Pinchevski. 2014. "Media Witnessing and the Ripeness of Time." *Cultural Studies* 28(4): 594–610.

Froude, James Anthony. 1897. *The English in the West Indies; or, the Bow of Ulysses*. New York: Scribner.

Galvin, Anne M. 2014. *Sounds of the Citizens: Dancehall and Community in Jamaica*. Nashville, TN: Vanderbilt University Press.

Garrow, David. 1981. *The FBI and Martin Luther King Jr*. New York: Penguin.

Gill, Leslie. 2004. *The School of the Americas: Military Training and Political Violence in the Americas*. Durham, NC: Duke University Press.

Ginsburg, Faye. 1995. "The Parallax Effect: The Impact of Aboriginal Media." *Visual Anthropology Review* 11(2): 64–76.

Ginsburg, Faye, Lila Abu-Lughod, and Brian Larkin, eds. 2002. *Media Worlds*. Berkeley: University of California Press.

Girvan, D. T. M. 1949. "Social Welfare Developments in Jamaica and the Jamaica Social Welfare Commission." In *Educational Approaches to Rural Welfare*, 11–37. Washington, DC: United Nations Food and Agricultural Organization.

Girvan, Norman. 1971. *Foreign Capital and Economic Underdevelopment in Jamaica*. Mona, Jamaica: Institute of Social and Economic Research, University of the West Indies.

Girvan, Norman. 1976. *Transnational Corporations and Economic Nationalism in the Third World*. New York: Monthly Review.

Girvan, Norman. 1993. *Working Together for Development: D. T. M. Girvan on Cooperatives and Community Development*. Kingston: Institute of Jamaica.

Glazer, Nathan, and Daniel Moynihan. 1963. *Beyond the Melting Pot: The Negroes, Puerto Ricans, Jews, Italians, and Irish of New York City*. Cambridge, MA: MIT Press.

Glick Schiller, Nina, Linda Basch, and Cristina Blanc-Szanton, eds. 1992. *Towards a Transnational Perspective on Migration: Race, Class, Ethnicity, and Nationalism Reconsidered*. New York: New York Academy of Sciences.

Glissant, Édouard. 1997. *The Poetics of Relation*. Ann Arbor: University of Michigan Press.

Goldstein, Daniel. 2012. *Outlawed: Between Security and Rights in a Bolivian City*. Durham, NC: Duke University Press.

Gonsalves, Ralph. 1977. "The Trade Union Movement in Jamaica: Its Growth and Some Resultant Problems." In *Essays on Power and Change in Jamaica*, ed. Carl Stone and Aggrey Brown, 89–105. Kingston: Jamaican Publishing.

González-Ruibal, Alfredo. 2008. "Time to Destroy: An Archaeology of Supermodernity." *Current Anthropology* 49(2): 247–79.

Gordon, Avery. 2008. *Ghostly Matters: Haunting and the Sociological Imagination*. Minneapolis: University of Minnesota Press.

Gordon, Lewis R. 2015. *What Fanon Said: A Philosophical Introduction to His Life and Thought*. New York: Fordham University Press.

Government of Jamaica. 2016. *Report of the Commission of Enquiry, Appointed to*

Enquire into Events which Occurred in Western Kingston and Related Areas in May 2010. Kingston: Government of Jamaica.

Gray, Obika. 1991. *Radicalism and Social Change in Jamaica, 1960–1972*. Knoxville: University of Tennessee Press.

Gray, Obika. 2011. *Demeaned but Empowered: The Social Power of the Urban Poor in Jamaica*. Kingston: University of the West Indies Press.

Grayson, M-P McCouch. 1981. "'Naming Names': Unauthorized Disclosure of Intelligence Agents' Identities." *Stanford Law Review* 33(4): 693–713.

Groark, Kevin P. 2013. "Toward a Cultural Phenomenology of Intersubjectivity: The Extended Relational Field of the Tzotzil Maya of Highland Chiapas, Mexico." *Language and Communication* 33: 278–91.

Gumbs, Alexis Pauline. 2016. *Revolutionary Mothering: Love on the Front Lines*. Oakland, CA: PM Press.

Gunst, Laurie. 1995. *Born fi' Dead: A Journey through the Jamaican Posse Underworld*. New York: Henry Holt.

Gusterson, Hugh. 2016. *Drone: Remote Control Warfare*. Cambridge, MA: MIT Press.

Guyer, Jane. 2007. "Prophecy and the Near Future: Thoughts on Macroeconomic, Evangelical, and Punctuated Time." *American Ethnologist* 34(3): 409–21.

Hale, Charles. 2005. "Neoliberal Multiculturalism: The Remaking of Cultural Rights and Racial Dominance in Central America." *Political and Legal Anthropology Review* 28(1): 10–28.

Hall, Catherine. 1995. "Gender Politics and Imperial Politics: Rethinking the Histories of Empire." In *Engendering History: Caribbean Women in Historical Perspective*, ed. Verene Shepherd, Bridget Brereton, and Barbara Bailey, 48–59. Kingston: Ian Randle.

Hanchard, Michael. 1999. "Afro-Modernity: Temporality, Politics, and the African Diaspora." *Public Culture* 11(1): 245–68.

Hansen, Thomas Blom, and Finn Stepputat. 2006. "Sovereignty Revisited." *Annual Reviews of Anthropology* 35: 295–315.

Harding, Timothy F., and Hobart A. Spaulding Jr. 1976. "The Struggle Sharpens: Workers, Imperialism and the State in Latin America, Common Themes and New Directions." *Latin American Perspectives* 3(1): 3–14.

Hardt, Michael. 2011. "For Love or Money." *Cultural Anthropology* 26(4): 676–82.

Harney, Stefano, and Fred Moten. 2013. *The Undercommons: Fugitive Planning and Black Study*. New York: Minor Compositions.

Harriott, Anthony, ed. 2004. *Understanding Crime in Jamaica: New Challenges for Public Policy*. Mona, Jamaica: University of the West Indies Press.

Harriott, Anthony. 2008. *Organized Crime and Politics in Jamaica: Breaking the Nexus*. Kingston: Canoe.

Harriott, Anthony. 2009. "Controlling Violent Crime: Models and Policy Options." Kingston: GraceKennedy Foundation.

Harrod, Jeffrey. 1972. *Trade Union Foreign Policy: A Study of British and American Trade Union Activities in Jamaica*. New York: Doubleday.

Hart, Richard. 1967. "Review: Katrin Norris *West Indian Children in London.*" *Race and Class* 9(2): 269–71.

Hart, Richard. 1989. *Rise and Organise: The Birth of the Workers and National Movements in Jamaica (1936–39)*. London: Karia.

Hartman, Saidiya. 1997. *Scenes of Subjection: Terror, Slavery, and Self-Making in Nineteenth Century America*. New York: Oxford University Press.

Hartman, Saidiya. 2008. "Venus in Two Acts." *Small Axe* 12(2): 1–14.

Haughton, Suzette. 2014. "The 2009 Jamaica-USA Extradition Affair: A 'Securitized' Response to Jamaica's Drug Problem." *Caribbean Journal of International Relations and Diplomacy* 2(3): 15–41.

Henriques, Julian. 2011. *Sonic Bodies: Reggae Sound Systems, Performance Techniques, and Ways of Knowing*. London: Bloomsbury Academic.

Herscher, Andrew. 2014. "Surveillant Witnessing: Satellite Imagery and the Visual Politics of Human Rights." *Public Culture* 26(3): 469–500.

High, Steven. 2009. *Base Colonies in the Western Hemisphere, 1940–1967*. New York: Palgrave Macmillan.

Hill, Frank. 1963. "Review: *Jamaica – the Search for an Identity*, by Katrin Norris." *Caribbean Quarterly* 9 (1–2): 89–90.

Hill, Robert. 1983. "Leonard P. Howell and the Millenarian Visions in Early Rastafari." *Jamaica Journal* 16(1): 26–28.

Hinton, Alex. 2010. *Transitional Justice: Global Mechanisms and Local Realities after Genocide and Mass Violence*. New Brunswick, NJ: Rutgers University Press.

Hirsch, Fred. 1974. *An Analysis of Our AFL-CIO Role in Latin America, or Under the Covers with the CIA*. Pamphlet. San Jose, CA. Self-published.

Hirsch, Marianne. 1997. *Family Frames: Photography, Narrative and Postmemory*. Cambridge, MA: Harvard University Press.

Holt, Thomas. 1992. *The Problem of Freedom: Race, Labor, and Politics in Jamaica and Britain, 1832–1938*. Baltimore: Johns Hopkins University Press.

Honneth, Axel. 1995. *The Struggle for Recognition: The Moral Grammar of Social Conflicts*. Cambridge: Polity.

Honneth, Axel. 2008. "*Reification: A New Look at an Old Idea*. New York: Oxford University Press.

Hooker, Juliet. 2005. "Indigenous Inclusion/Black Exclusion: Race, Ethnicity, and Multicultural Citizenship in Latin America." *Journal of Latin American Studies* 37(2): 285–310.

Horne, Gerald. 2007. *Cold War in a Hot Zone: The United States Confronts Labor and Independence Struggles in the British West Indies*. Philadelphia: Temple University Press.

Howard, David. 2005. *Kingston: A Cultural and Literary History*. Oxford: Signal.

Huggins, Martha. 1991. "U. S. Supported State Terror: A History of Police Training in Latin America." In *Vigilantism and the State in Modern Latin America: Essays on Extralegal Violence*, ed. Martha Huggins, 219–42. New York: Praeger.

Hurston, Zora Neale. 1938. *Tell My Horse: Voodoo and Life in Haiti and Jamaica*. New York: Harper and Row.

Hussain, Nasser. 2013. "The Sound of Terror: Phenomenology of a Drone Strike." *Boston Review*, October 2013. Accessed 17 November 2014. http://boston review.net/world/hussain-drone-phenomenology.

Hutchinson, Damian. 2016. *The Peace Management Initiative: Interrupting Violence, Mainstreaming High Risk Youth, Empowering and Re-building Communities.* Kingston: Pear Tree.

Iton, Richard. 2008. *In Search of the Black Fantastic: Politics and Popular Culture in the Post–Civil Rights Era.* New York: Oxford University Press.

Jackson, John. 2001. *Harlemworld: Doing Race and Class in Contemporary America.* Chicago: University of Chicago Press.

Jackson, John. 2004. "An Ethnographic FilmFlam: Giving Gifts, Doing Research, and Videotaping the Native Subject/Object." *American Anthropologist* 106(1): 32–42.

Jackson, John. 2005. *Real Black: Adventures in Racial Sincerity.* Chicago: University of Chicago Press.

Jackson, John. 2008. *Racial Paranoia: The Unintended Consequences of Political Correctness.* New York: Basic.

Jackson, John. 2013. *Thin Description.* Cambridge, MA: Harvard University Press.

Jackson, Michael. 2013. *The Politics of Storytelling: Variations on a Theme by Hannah Arendt,* 2d ed. Copenhagen: Museum Musculanum.

Jackson, Shona. 2012. *Creole Indigeneity: Between Myth and Nation in the Caribbean.* Minneapolis: University of Minnesota Press.

Jaffe, Rivke. 2013. "The Hybrid State: Crime and Citizenship in Urban Jamaica." *American Ethnologist* 40(4): 734–48.

Jamaica's Jubilee; or, What We Are and What We Hope to Be. 1888. London: S. W. Partridge.

Jefferson, Owen. 1972. *The Post-war Economic Development of Jamaica.* Mona, Jamaica: Institute for Social and Economic Research, University of the West Indies.

Jekyll, Walter. 1907. *Jamaica Song and Story.* London: Folklore Society.

Jensen, Steven L. B. 2016. *The Making of International Human Rights: The 1960s, Decolonization, and the Reconstruction of Global Values.* New York: Cambridge University Press.

Johnson, Howard. 1984. "The Anglo-American Caribbean Commission and the Extension of American Influence in the British Caribbean, 1942–1945." *Journal of Commonwealth and Comparative Politics* 22(2): 180–203.

Jonas, Susanne. 1975. "Trade Union Imperialism in the Dominican Republic." NACLA *Latin America and Empire Report* 9 (April): 13–30.

Jones, Marilyn J. 2002. "Policy Paradox: Implications of U. S. Drug Control Policy for Jamaica." *Annals of the American Academy of Political and Social Science* 582: 117–33.

Josephs, Kelly Baker. 2013. *Disturbers of the Peace: Representations of Madness in Anglophone Caribbean Literature.* Charlottesville: University of Virginia Press.

Judy, Ronald. 1996. "Fanon's Body of Black Experience." In *Fanon: A Critical*

Reader, ed. Lewis Gordon, T. Denean Sharpley-Whiting, and Renee T. White. Malden, MA: Wiley Blackwell.

Kaplan, Caren. 2018. *Aerial Aftermaths: Wartime from Above*. Durham, NC: Duke University Press.

Kaplan, Caren, Norma Alarcón, and Minoo Moallem, eds. 1999. *Between Woman and Nation: Nationalisms, Transnational Feminisms, and the State*. Durham, NC: Duke University Press.

Keeling, Kara. 2005. "Passing for Human: *Bamboozled* and Digital Humanism." *Women and Performance* 15(1): 237–50.

Keller, Richard. 2001. "Madness and Colonization: Psychiatry in the British and French Empires, 1800–1962." *Journal of Social History* 35(2): 295–324.

Keller, Richard. 2007. *Colonial Madness: Psychiatry in French North Africa*. Chicago: University of Chicago Press.

Kelley, Robin. 1990. *Hammer and Hoe: Alabama Communists during the Great Depression*. Chapel Hill: University of North Carolina Press.

Kilcullen, David. 2013. *Out of the Mountains: The Coming Age of the Urban Guerrilla*. New York: Oxford University Press.

Kunreuther, Laura. 2014. *Voicing Subjects: Public Intimacy and Mediation in Kathmandu*. Berkeley: University of California Press.

Kuntsman, Adi, and Rebecca Stein. 2015. *Digital Militarism: Israel's Occupation in the Social Media Age*. Stanford, CA: Stanford University Press.

Kwitny, Jonathan. 1984. *Endless Enemies: The Making of an Unfriendly World*. New York: Penguin.

Lacey, Terry. 1977. *Violence and Politics in Jamaica, 1960–1970: Internal Security in a Developing Country*. Totowa, NJ: Frank Cass.

Lawton, Jacquiann. 2005. "Social and Public Architecture in Kingston, Jamaica." *Docommo* 33 (September): 58–64.

Lee, Hélène. 2003. *The First Rasta: Leonard Howell and the Rise of Rastafarianism* Chicago: Lawrence Hill.

Lessne, Scott A. 1981–82. "Constitutional Law—International Travel Restrictions and the First Amendment: To Speak or Not to Speak? *Haig v. Agee*, 453 U.S. 280 (1981)." *Western New England Law Review* 44(3): 449–78.

Levinas, Emmanual. 1969. *Totality and Infinity: An Essay on Exteriority*. Pittsburgh: Duquesne University Press.

Levinas, Emmanual. 1985. *Ethics and Infinity*. Pittsburgh: Duquesne University Press.

Lévi-Strauss, Claude. (1949) 1969. *The Elementary Structures of Kinship*. Boston: Beacon.

Lewis, Linden, ed. 2003. *The Culture of Gender and Sexuality in the Caribbean*. Gainesville: University Press of Florida.

Lewis, Oscar. (1959) 1975. *Five Families: Mexican Case Studies in the Culture of Poverty*. New York: Basic.

Lewis, Oscar. 1965. *La Vida: A Puerto Rican Family in the Culture of Poverty—San Juan and New York*. New York: Random House.

Lewis, Rupert. 1998. *Walter Rodney's Intellectual and Political Thought*. Mona, Jamaica: University of the West Indies Press.

Lewis, Rupert. 2012. "Party Politics in Jamaica and the Extradition of Christopher 'Dudus' Coke." *Global South* 6(1): 38–54.

Lewis, Rupert. 2014. "Jamaican Black Power in the 1960s." In *Black Power in the Caribbean*, ed. Kate Quinn, 53–75. Gainesville: University Press of Florida.

Linton, Ralph. 1943. "Nativistic Movements." *American Anthropologist* 45: 230–40.

Lowenthal, David. 1963. "Review: *Jamaica: The Search for an Identity*, by Katrin Norris." *Race and Class* 4(2): 77.

Löwy, Michael, and Robert Sayre. 2001. *Romanticism against the Tide of Modernity*. Durham, NC: Duke University Press.

Mack, Douglas. 1999. *From Babylon to Rastafari: Origin and History of the Rastafarian Movement*. Chicago: Research Associated School Times.

MacMillan, Ian. 1995. *Making the Difference: 50 Years of Local 343*. Kingston, ON: USWA Local 343. Accessed 13 May 2013. http://www.oocities.org/local343 /343history.html.

Macmillan, Mona. 1957. *The Land of Look Behind: A Study of Jamaica*. London: Faber and Faber.

Macmillan, Mona. 1980. "The Making of Warning from the West Indies: Extract from a Projected Memoir of W. M. Macmillan." *Journal of Commonwealth and Comparative Politics* 18(2): 207–19.

Macmillan, Mona. 1985. *Champion of Africa: The Second Phase of the work of W. M. Macmillan, 1934–1974*. London: Greta Ilott and Swindon.

Macmillan, Mona, and Hugh Macmillan, eds. 2008. *Mona's Story: An Admiral's Daughter in England, Scotland and Africa, 1908–51*. Oxford: Oxford Publishing Services.

Macmillan, W. M. (1936) 1938. *Warning from the West Indies*. London: Penguin.

Macmillan, W. M. 1941. *Democratise the Empire! A Policy for Colonial Change*. London: Kegan Paul, Trench, Trubner.

Madison, Soyini. 2007. "Co-Performative Witnessing." *Cultural Studies* 21(6): 826–31.

Mahmood, Saba. 2009. "Religious Reason and Secular Affect: An Incommensurable Divide?" *Critical Inquiry* 35: 836–62.

Mahmood, Saba. 2011. *The Politics of Piety: The Islamic Revival and the Feminist Subject*. Princeton, NJ: Princeton University Press.

Mankekar, Purnima. 2015. *Unsettling India: Affect, Transnationality, Temporality*. Durham, NC: Duke University Press.

Manley, Michael. (1975) 1991. *Voice at the Workplace: Reflections on Colonialism and the Jamaican Worker*. Washington, DC: Howard University Press.

Manley, Michael. 1982. *Jamaica: Struggle in the Periphery*. London: Third World Media.

Mannoni, Octavio. 1990. *Prospero and Caliban: The Psychology of Colonization*. Ann Arbor: University of Michigan Press.

Maragh, G. G. (Leonard Howell). (1935) 2007. *The Promised Key*. N.p.: Forgotten Books.

Marcus, George, ed. 1999. *Paranoia within Reason: A Casebook on Conspiracy as Explanation*. Chicago: University of Chicago Press.

Marier, Roger. 1953. *Social Welfare Work in Jamaica: A Study of the Jamaica Social Welfare Commission*. Paris: United Nations Educational, Scientific, and Cultural Organization.

Marshall, Woodville. 1985. "Peasant Development in the West Indies since 1838." In *Rural Development in the Caribbean*, ed. P. I. Gomes, 1–14. New York: St. Martin's.

Masco, Joseph. 2014. *The Theater of Operations: National Security Affect from the Cold War to the War on Terror*. Durham, NC: Duke University Press.

Massumi, Brian. 2002. *Parables of the Virtual: Movement, Affect, Sensation*. Durham, NC: Duke University Press.

Mazzarella, William. 2009. "Affect: What Is It Good for?" In *Enchantments of Modernity: Empire, Nation, Globalization*, ed. Saurabh Dube, 291–309. New York: Routledge.

Mbembe, Achille. 2003. "Necropolitics." *Public Culture* 15(1): 11–40.

Mbembe, Achille. 2011. "Democracy as a Community of Life." *The Salon* 4: 1.

M'Charek, Amade. 2013. "Beyond Fact or Fiction: On the Materiality of Race in Practice." *Cultural Anthropology* 28(3): 420–42.

McAllister, Carlota. 2013. "Testimonial Truths and Revolutionary Mysteries." In *War by Other Means: Aftermath in Post-Genocide Guatemala*, by Carlota McAllister, 93–116. Durham, NC: Duke University Press.

McDavid, Hilton, Anthony Clayton, and Noel Cowell. 2011. "The Difference between the Constabulary Force and the Military: An Analysis of the Differing Roles and Functions in the Context of the Current Security Environment in the Caribbean (The Case of Jamaica)." *Journal of Eastern Caribbean Studies* 36(3): 40–71.

Meeks, Brian. 2000. *Narratives of Resistance: Jamaica, Trinidad, the Caribbean*. Mona, Jamaica: University of the West Indies Press.

Meeks, Brian. 2014. *Critical Interventions in Caribbean Politics and Theory*. Jackson: University Press of Mississippi.

Meikle, Tracian, and Rivke Jaffe. 2015. "'Police as the New Don? An Assessment of Post-Dudus Policing Strategies in Jamaica." *Caribbean Journal of Criminology* 1(2): 75–100.

Midgley, James and David Piachaud, eds. 2011. *Colonialism and Welfare: Social Policy and the British Imperial Legacy*. Cheltenham, U.K.: Edward Elgar.

Mignolo, Walter. 2001. "Coloniality at Large: The Western Hemisphere in the Colonial Horizon of Modernity." *CR: The New Centennial Review* 1(2): 19–54.

Mintz, Sidney. (1966) 1971. "The Caribbean as a Socio-Cultural Area." In *Peoples and Cultures of the Caribbean: An Anthropological Reader*, ed. Michael Horowitz, 17–46. Garden City, NY: Natural History Press.

Mintz, Sidney. (1974) 1989. *Caribbean Transformations*. New York: Columbia University Press.

Mintz, Sidney. 1996. "Enduring Substances, Trying Theories: The Caribbean Region as Oikoumene." *Journal of the Royal Anthropological Institute* 2(2): 289–311.

Miyazaki, Hirokazu. 2004. *Method of Hope: Anthropology, Philosophy, and Fijian Knowledge*. Stanford, CA: Stanford University Press.

Morris, George. 1967. *CIA and American Labor: The Subversion of the AFL-CIO's Foreign Policy*. New York: International Publishers.

Moten, Fred. 2008. "The Case of Blackness." *Criticism* 50(2): 177–218.

Mullings, Leith. 1995. "Households Headed by Women: The Politics of Race, Class, and Gender." In *Conceiving the New World Order: The Global Politics of Reproduction*, ed. Faye Ginsburg and Rayna Rapp, 122–39. Berkeley: University of California Press.

Mullings, Leith, and Alaka Wali. 2000. *Stress and Resilience: The Social Context of Reproduction in Central Harlem*, New York: Kluwer Academic/Plenum.

Munn, Nancy. 1992. "The Cultural Anthropology of Time: A Critical Essay." *Annual Reviews of Anthropology* 21: 93–123.

Munroe, Trevor. 1972. *The Politics of Constitutional Democratization, 1944–1962*. Mona, Jamaica: Institute for Social and Economic Research, University of the West Indies.

Munroe, Trevor. 1990. *Jamaican Politics: A Marxist Perspective in Transition*. Kingston: Heinemann.

Munroe, Trevor. 1992. *The Cold War and the Jamaican Left, 1950–55: Reopening the Files*. Kingston: Kingston Publishers.

Munroe, Trevor, and Arnold Bertram. 2006. *Adult Suffrage and Political Administrations in Jamaica, 1944–2002*. Kingston: Ian Randle.

Murray, Bruce. 2013. "W. M. Macmillan: The Wits Years and Resignation, 1917–1933." *South African Historical Journal* 65(2): 317–31.

Navaro-Yashin, Yael. 2012. *The Make-Believe Space: Affective Geography in a Postwar Polity*. Durham, NC: Duke University Press.

Nelson, Diane. 2009. *Reckoning: The Ends of War in Guatemala*. Durham, NC: Duke University Press.

Nelson, Diane. 2015. *Who Counts? The Mathematics of Death and Life after Genocide*. Durham, NC: Duke University Press.

Neptune, Harvey. 2007. *Caliban and the Yankees: Trinidad and the United States Occupation*. Chapel Hill: University of North Carolina Press.

Neptune, Harvey. 2014. "Savaging Civilization: Michel-Rolph Trouillot and the Anthropology of the West." *Cultural Dynamics* 26: 219–34.

Nettleford, Rex. 1970. *Mirror, Mirror: Identity, Race and Protest in Jamaica*. Kingston: William Collins and Sangster.

Ngai, Sianne. 2005. *Ugly Feelings*. Cambridge, MA: Harvard University Press.

Norris, Katrin. 1962. *Jamaica: The Search for an Identity*. London: Institute of Race Relations, Oxford University Press.

Norris, Katrin. 1967. *West Indian Children in London*. Occasional Papers on Social Administration, no. 19. London: G. Bell and Sons.

Norris, Katrin. 1997. *True to Both My Selves*. London: Virago.

Oliver, Kelly. 2001. *Witnessing: Beyond Recognition*. Minneapolis: University of Minnesota Press.

Olivier, Lord Sydney. 1936. *Jamaica: The Blessed Island*. London: Faber and Faber.

Omi, Michael, and Howard Winant. 1986. *Racial Formation in the United States: From the 1960s to the 1980s*. New York: Routledge.

Ong, Aihwa. 1990. "State versus Islam: Malay Families, Women's Bodies, and the Body Politic in Malaysia." *American Ethnologist* 17(2): 258–76.

Page, Kezia. 2017. "Bongo Futures: The Reggae Revival and its Genealogies." *Small Axe* 21(1): 1–16.

Palmer, Colin A. 2014. *Freedom's Children: The 1938 Labor Rebellion and the Birth of Modern Jamaica.* Chapel Hill: University of North Carolina Press.

Parker, Andrew, Mary Russo, Doris Sommer, and Patricia Yaeger, eds. 1991. *Nationalisms and Sexualities.* New York: Routledge.

Parks, Lisa, and Caren Kaplan, eds. 2017. *Life in the Age of Drone Warfare.* Durham, NC: Duke University Press.

Paton, Diana. 2004. *No Bond but the Law: Punishment, Race, and Gender in Jamaican State Formation, 1780–1870.* Durham, NC: Duke University Press.

Paton, Diana. 2014. "Small Charges: Law and the Regulation of Conduct in the Post-Slavery Caribbean." Elsa Goveia Memorial Lecture, delivered to the Department of History and Archaeology, University of the West Indies, Mona, April 1.

Paton, Diana. 2017. "State Formation in Victorian Jamaica." In *Victorian Jamaica,* ed. Tim Barringer and Wayne Modest, 125–38. Durham, NC: Duke University Press.

Patterson, Orlando. 1967. *The Sociology of Slavery: An Analysis of the Origins, Development, and Structure of Negro Slave Society in Jamaica.* Vancouver, BC: Fairleigh Dickinson University Press.

Pearl, Sharrona. 2017. *Face/On: Face Transplants and the Ethics of the Other.* Chicago: University of Chicago Press.

Perry, Keisha-Khan. 2013. *Black Women against the Land Grab: The Fight for Racial Justice in Brazil.* Minneapolis: University of Minnesota Press.

Petherbridge, Danielle, ed. 2011. *Axel Honneth: Critical Essays.* Boston: Brill.

Petherbridge, Danielle. 2013. *The Critical Theory of Axel Honneth.* Lanham, MD: Lexington.

Pettersburgh, Rev. F. B. (1926) 2003. *The Royal Parchment Scroll of Black Supremacy.* Chicago: Frontline.

Philippo, James. 1843. *Jamaica, its Past and Present State.* London: J. Snow.

Pierre, Jemima. 2008. "'I Like Your Color!' Skin Bleaching and the Geographies of Race in Ghana." *Feminist Review* 90: 9–29.

Posel, Deborah. 2008. "History as Confession: The Case of the South African Truth and Reconciliation Commission." *Public Culture* 20(1): 119–41.

Post, Ken. 1978. *Arise Ye Starvelings: The Jamaican Labour Rebellion of 1938 and Its Aftermath.* The Hague: Martinus Nijhoff.

Post, Ken. 1981. *Strike the Iron: A Colony at War, Jamaica 1939–1945,* vols. 1–2. The Hague: Institute of Social Studies.

Povinelli, Elizabeth. 2002. *The Cunning of Recognition: Indigenous Alterities and the Making of Australian Multiculturalism.* Durham, NC: Duke University Press.

Povinelli, Elizabeth. 2006. *The Empire of Love: Toward a Theory of Intimacy, Genealogy, and Carnality.* Durham, NC: Duke University Press.

Povinelli, Elizabeth. 2011. *Economies of Abandonment: Social Belonging and Endurance in Late Liberalism*. Durham, NC: Duke University Press.

Pöykkö, Panu-Matti. 2016. "Levinas and the Ambivalence of Recognition." *Open Theology* 2: 636–52.

Price, Charles. 2009. *Becoming Rasta: Origins of Rastafari Identity in Jamaica*. New York: New York University Press.

Pullen-Burry, Elizabeth. 1903. *Jamaica as It Is, 1903*. London: T. F. Unwin.

Pullen-Burry, Elizabeth. 1905. *Ethiopia in Exile: Jamaica Revisited*. London: T. F. Unwin.

Puri, Shalini. 2014. *The Grenada Revolution in the Caribbean Present: Operation Urgent Memory*. New York: Palgrave.

Radcliffe-Brown, Alfred R. 1965. "Taboo." In *Structure and Function in Primitive Society*, by Alfred R. Radcliffe-Brown, 133–52. New York: Free Press.

Radosh, Ronald. 1969. *American Labor and United States Foreign Policy*. New York: Random House.

Ralph, Laurence. 2015. "Becoming Aggrieved: An Alternative Framework of Care in Black Chicago." *Russell Sage Foundation Journal of Social Sciences* 1(2): 31–41.

Ramos-Zayas, Ana Yolanda. 2012. *Street Therapists: Race, Affect, and Neoliberal Personhood in Latino Newark*. Chicago: University of Chicago Press.

Reddock, Rhoda. 1994. *Women, Labour and Politics in Trinidad and Tobago: A History*. London: Zed.

Redfield, Peter. 2006. "A Less Modest Witness." *American Ethnologist* 33(1): 3–26.

Reid-Pharr, Robert. 2016. *Archives of Flesh: African America, Spain, and Post-Humanist Critique*. New York: New York University Press.

Rich, Paul. 1988. "Sydney Olivier, Jamaica and the Debate on British Colonial Policy in the West Indies." In *Labour in the Caribbean from Emancipation to Independence*, ed. Malcolm Cross and Gad Heuman, 208–33. London: Macmillan Caribbean.

Rifkin, Mark. 2017. *Beyond Settler Time: Temporal Sovereignty and Indigenous Self-Determination*. Durham, NC: Duke University Press.

Riles, Annelise. 2000. *The Network Inside/Out*. Ann Arbor: University of Michigan Press.

Roberts, Neil. 2015. *Freedom as Marronage*. Chicago: University of Chicago Press.

Robinson, Cedric. (1983) 2000. *Black Marxism: The Making of the Black Radical Tradition*. Chapel Hill: University of North Carolina Press.

Robotham, Don. 2003. "How Kingston Was Wounded." In *Wounded Cities: Destruction and Reconstruction in a Globalized World*, ed. Jane Schneider and Ida Susser, 111–28. Oxford: Berg.

Rofel, Lisa. 1999. *Other Modernities: Gendered Yearnings in China after Socialism*. Berkeley: University of California Press.

Romualdi, Serafino. 1967. *Presidents and Peons: Recollections of a Labor Ambassador in Latin America*. New York: Funk and Wagnalls.

Ross, Fiona. 2003. *Bearing Witness: Women and the Truth and Reconciliation Commission in South Africa*. London: Pluto.

Rutherford, Danilyn. 2009. "Sympathy, State Building, and the Experience of Empire." *Cultural Anthropology* 24(1): 1–32.

Rutherford, Danilyn. 2012a. *Laughing at Leviathan: Sovereignty and Audience in West Papua*. Chicago: University of Chicago Press.

Rutherford, Danilyn. 2012b. "Kinky Empiricism." *Cultural Anthropology* 27(3): 465–79.

Rutherford, Danilyn. 2016. "Affect Theory and the Empirical." *Annual Review of Anthropology* 45: 285–300.

Samuels, K. C. 2011. *Jamaica's First President: 1992–2010: His Rise, His Reign, His Demise, a Chronology of Lawlessness*. Kingston: Page Turner.

Saunders, Patricia. 2008. "Defending the Dead, Confronting the Archive: A Conversation with M. NourbeSe Philip." *Small Axe* 12(2): 63–79.

Schwartz, Mattathias. 2011. "A Massacre in Jamaica." *New Yorker*, December 12. Accessed 15 February 2012. http://www.newyorker.com/magazine/2011/12/12/a-massacre-in-jamaica.

Scott, David. 1999. *Refashioning Futures: Criticism after Postcoloniality*. Princeton, NJ: Princeton University Press.

Scott, David. 2000. "The Re-enchantment of Humanism: An Interview with Sylvia Wynter." *Small Axe* 4(2): 119–207.

Scott, David. 2004. *Conscripts of Modernity: The Tragedy of Colonial Enlightenment*. Durham, NC: Duke University Press.

Scott, David. 2013. "The Paradox of Freedom: An Interview with Orlando Patterson." *Small Axe* 17(1): 96–242.

Scott, David. 2014. *Omens of Adversity: Tragedy, Time, Memory, Justice*. Durham, NC: Duke University Press.

Scott, David, and Rex Nettleford. 2006. "'To Be Liberated from the Obscurity of Themselves': An Interview with Rex Nettleford." *Small Axe* 19(2): 97–246.

Seaga, Edward. 2009. *My Life and Leadership, Volume I: Clash of Ideologies, 1930–1980*. Oxford: Macmillan.

Sears, Walter E. 1975. "Operation Buccaneer." *Drug Enforcement* (Winter): 6–15.

Senior, Olive. 1972. *The Message Is Change: A Perspective on the 1972 General Elections*. Kingston: Kingston Publishers.

Sexton, Jared. 2007. "Racial Profiling and the Societies of Control." In *Warfare in the American Homeland*, ed. Joy James, 197–218. Durham, NC: Duke University Press.

Sexton, Jared. 2011. "The Social Life of Social Death." *In*Tensions 5. Accessed 24 November 2014. http://www.yorku.ca/intent/issue5/articles/jaredsexton.php.

Sharpe, Christina. 2016. *In the Wake: On Blackness and Being*. Durham, NC: Duke University Press.

Shaw, Rosalind, and Lars Waldorf, with Pierre Hazan. 2010. *Localizing Transitional Justice: Interventions and Priorities after Mass Violence*. Stanford, CA: Stanford University Press.

Sheller, Mimi. 2002. *Consuming the Caribbean: From Arawaks to Zombies*. New York: Routledge.

Sheller, Mimi. 2014. *Aluminum Dreams: The Making of Light Modernity*. Cambridge, MA: MIT Press.

Silverblatt, Irene. 1991. "Interpreting Women in States: New Feminist Ethnohistories." In *Gender at the Crossroads of Knowledge: Feminist Anthropology in the Postmodern Era*, ed. Micaela di Leonardo, 140–71. Berkeley: University of California Press.

Silverblatt, Irene. 2004. *Modern Inquisitions: Peru and the Colonial Origins of the Civilized World*. Durham, NC: Duke University Press.

Silverman, Kaja. 1996. *The Threshold of the Visible World*. New York: Routledge.

Simpson, Audra. 2007. "On Ethnographic Refusal: Indigeneity, 'Voice,' and Colonial Citizenship." *Junctures* 9: 67–80.

Simpson, George Eaton. 1955a. "Political Cultism in West Kingston, Jamaica." *Social and Economic Studies* 4(2): 133–49.

Simpson, George Eaton. 1955b. "The Ras Tafari Movement in Jamaica: A Study of Race and Class Conflict." *Social Forces* 34(2): 167–71.

Simpson, George Eaton. 1998. "Personal Reflections on Rastafari in West Kingston in the Early 1950s." In *Chanting Down Babylon: The Rastafari Reader*, ed. Nathaniel Samuel Murrell, William David Spencer, and Adrian Anthony McFarlane, 217–28. Philadelphia: Temple University Press.

Sims, Beth. 1992. *Workers of the World Undermined: American Labor's Role in U.S. Foreign Policy*. Boston: South End.

Singham, A. W. 1968. *The Hero and the Crowd in a Colonial Polity*. New Haven, CT: Yale University Press.

Sives, Amanda. 2010. *Elections, Violence, and the Democratic Process in Jamaica, 1944–2007*. Kingston: Ian Randle.

Sliwinski, Sharon. 2011. *Human Rights in Camera*. Chicago: University of Chicago Press.

Smith, Christen. 2016a. Afro-Paradise: *Blackness, Violence, and Performance in Brazil*. Urbana: University of Illinois Press.

Smith, Christen. 2016b. "Facing the Dragon: Black Mothering, Sequelae, and Gendered Necropolitics in the Americas." *Transforming Anthropology* 24(1): 31–48.

Smith, Faith. 2002. *Creole Recitations: John Jacob Thomas and Colonial Formations in the Late 19th Century Caribbean*. Charlottesville: University of Virginia Press.

Smith, M. G., R. Augier, and R. M. Nettleford. 1960. *The Ras Tafari Movement in Kingston, Jamaica*. Mona, Jamaica: Institute of Social and Economic Research, University College of the West Indies.

Smith, Shawn Michelle and Sharon Sliwinski, eds. 2017. *Photography and the Optical Unconscious*. Durham, NC: Duke University Press.

Snead, James. 1981. "On Repetition in Black Culture." *Black American Literature Forum* 15(4): 146–54.

Spaulding, Hobart A. 1977. "U.S. and Latin American Labor: The Dynamics of Imperialist Control." In *Ideology and Social Change in Latin America*, ed. June Nash, Juan Corradi, and Hobart Spaulding, 55–91. New York: Gordon and Breach.

Spillers, Hortense. 1987. "Mama's Baby, Papa's Maybe: An American Grammar Book." *Diacritics* 17(2): 65–81.

Stack, Carol. 1974. *All Our Kin: Strategies for Survival in a Black Community.* New York: Basic.

Stanley, Sonjah. 2010. *Dancehall from Slaveship to Ghetto.* Ottawa: University of Ottawa Press.

Stein, Rebecca. 2017. "GoPro Occupation: Networked Cameras, Israeli Military Rule and the Digital Promise." *Current Anthropology* 58(S15): S56–S64.

Stephens, Michelle. 2005. *Black Empire: The Masculine Global Imaginary of Caribbean Intellectuals in the United States, 1914–1962.* Durham, NC: Duke University Press.

Stephens, Michelle. 2014. *Skin Acts: Psychoanalysis and the Black Male Performer.* Durham, NC: Duke University Press.

Stevenson, Lisa. 2014. *Life beside Itself: Imagining Care in the Canadian Arctic.* Berkeley: University of California Press.

Stewart, Kathleen. 2007. *Ordinary Affects.* Durham, NC: Duke University Press.

Stoler, Ann Laura. 1989. "Making Empire Respectable: The Politics of Race and Sexuality in Twentieth Century Colonial Cultures." *American Ethnologist* 16(4): 634–60.

Stoler, Ann Laura. 1995. *Race and the Education of Desire: Foucault's History of Sexuality and the Colonial Order of Things.* Durham, NC: Duke University Press.

Stoler, Ann Laura. 2002. *Carnal Knowledge and Imperial Power: Race and the Intimate in Colonial Rule.* Berkeley: University of California Press.

Stoler, Ann Laura, ed. 2007. *Affective States: A Companion to the Anthropology of Politics.* Malden, MA: Wiley Blackwell Publishing.

Stone, Carl. 1980. *Democracy and Clientelism in Jamaica.* New Brunswick, NJ: Transaction.

Stout, Noelle. 2014. "Bootlegged: Unauthorized Circulation and the Dilemmas of Collaboration in the Digital Age." *Visual Anthropology Review* 30(2): 177–87.

Sutton, Constance, and Elsa Chaney, eds. 1987. *Caribbean Life in New York City: Sociocultural Dimensions.* Staten Island, NY: Center for Migration Studies.

Szilagyi, Andrew M. 2010. "Blowing Its Cover: How the Intelligence Identities Protection Act Has Masqueraded as an Effective Law and Why It Must Be Amended." *William and Mary Law Review* 51(6): 2269–312.

Tait, Sue. 2011. "Bearing Witness, Journalism and Moral Responsibility." *Media, Culture, and Society* 33(8): 1220–35.

Tanna, Laura. 2006. "Why I Haven't Written." *Daily Gleaner*, February 27, B7.

Tate, Winnifred. 2015. *Drugs, Thugs, and Diplomats: U.S. Policymaking in Colombia.* Stanford, CA: Stanford University Press.

Taylor, Diana. 2003. *The Archive and the Repertoire: Performing Cultural Memory in the Americas.* Durham, NC: Duke University Press.

Taussig, Michael. 1992. *The Nervous System.* New York: Routledge.

Taussig, Michael. 1999. *Defacement: Public Secrecy and the Labor of the Negative.* Stanford, CA: Stanford University Press.

Thame, Maziki. 2011. "Reading Violence and Postcolonial Decolonization through Fanon: The Case of Jamaica." *Journal of Pan African Studies* 4(7): 75–93.

Theidon, Kimberly. 2012. *Intimate Enemies: Violence and Reconciliation in Peru.* Philadelphia: University of Pennsylvania Press.

Thomas, John Jacob. 1889. *Froudacity: West Indian Fables by James Anthony Froude.* London: T. Fischer & Unwin.

Thomas, Deborah A. 2002a. "Democratizing Dance: Institutional Transformation and Hegemonic Re-ordering in Postcolonial Jamaica." *Cultural Anthropology* 17(4): 512–50.

Thomas, Deborah A. 2002b. "Modern Blackness: 'What We Are and What We Hope to Be.'" *Small Axe* 6(2): 25–48.

Thomas, Deborah A. 2004. *Modern Blackness: Nationalism, Globalization, and the Politics of Culture in Jamaica.* Durham, NC: Duke University Press.

Thomas, Deborah A. 2011. *Exceptional Violence: Embodied Citizenship in Transnational Jamaica.* Durham, NC: Duke University Press.

Thomas, Deborah A. 2013. "Caribbean Studies, Archive Building, and the Problem of Violence." *Small Axe* 17(2): 27–42.

Thomas, Deborah A. 2016. "Time and the Otherwise: Plantations, Garrisons and Being Human in the Caribbean." *Anthropological Theory* 16(2–3): 177–200.

Thomas, Deborah, and Kamari Clarke. 2013. "Globalization and Race: Structures of Inequality, New Sovereignties, and Citizenship in a Neoliberal Era." *Annual Review of Anthropology* 42: 305–25.

Thomas, Deborah, John Jackson, and Junior "Gabu" Wedderburn, dirs. 2011. *Bad Friday: Rastafari after Coral Gardens.* Documentary film, Third World Newsreel, New York, NY.

Thompson, Krista. 2015. *Shine.* Durham, NC: Duke University Press.

Ticktin, Miriam. 2006. "Where Ethics and Politics Meet: The Violence of Humanitarianism in France." *American Ethnologist* 33(1): 33–49.

Ticktin, Miriam. 2011. *Casualties of Care: Immigration and the Politics of Humanitarianism in France.* Berkeley: University of California Press.

Trollope, Anthony. 1859. *The West Indies and the Spanish Main.* London: Chapman and Hall.

Trouillot, Michel-Rolph. 1992. "The Caribbean Region: An Open Frontier in Anthropological Theory." *Annual Reviews of Anthropology* 21: 19–42.

Trouillot, Michel-Rolph. 1995. *Silencing the Past: Power and the Production of History.* Boston: Beacon.

Trouillot, Michel-Rolph. 2000. "Abortive Rituals: Historical Apologies in the Global Era." *Interventions* 2(2): 171–86.

Ulysse, Gina. 2007. *Downtown Ladies: Informal Commercial Importers, a Haitian Anthropologist, and Self-Making in Jamaica.* Chicago: University of Chicago Press.

U.S. Government. 1969. *American Institute for Free Labor Development, Hearing, 91st Congress, First Session, with George Meany, President, AFL-CIO, 1 August.* Washington, DC: U.S. Government Printing Office.

U.S. Government. 1975. "Marijuana-Hashish Epidemic and Its Impact on United

States Security: The Continuing Escalation." In *Hearings before the Subcommittee to Investigate the Administration of the Internal Security Act and other Internal Security Laws of the Committee on the Judiciary, United States Senate, 94th Congress, First Session, Part 2, 8 May 1975*. Washington, DC: U. S. Government Printing Office.

Van Dijk, Frank Jan. 1995. "Sociological Means: Colonial Reactions to the Radicalization of Rastafari in Jamaica, 1956–1959." *New West Indian Guide* 69(1–2): 67–101.

Vance, Sheldon B. 1975. "The International Narcotics Control Program." *Drug Enforcement* (Winter 1975): 2–5.

Vitalis, Robert. 2015. *White World Order, Black Power Politics: The Birth of American International Relations*. Ithaca: Cornell University Press.

Wald, Gayle. 2015. *"It's Been Beautiful!": Soul and Black Power TV*. Durham, NC: Duke University Press.

Walley, Christine. 2015. "Transmedia as Experimental Ethnography: The *Exit Zero* Project, Deindustrialization, and the Politics of Nostalgia." *American Ethnologist* 42(4): 624–39.

Walton, Calder. 2013. *Empire of Secrets: British Intelligence, the Cold War and the Twilight of Empire*. New York: Overlook.

Weber, Max. 1946. "Politics as a Vocation." In *Max Weber: Essays in Sociology*, ed. H. H. Gerth and C. Wright Mills, 77–128. New York: Oxford University Press.

Weheliye, Alexander G. 2014. *Habeas Viscus: Racializing Assemblages, Biopolitics, and Black Feminist Theories of the Human*. Durham, NC: Duke University Press.

Whitham, Charlie. 2002. *Bitter Rehearsal: British and American Planning for a Post-war West Indies*. Westport, CT: Praeger.

Whitten, Norman. 2007. "The *Longue Durée* of Racial Fixity and the Transformative Conjunctures of Racial Blending." *Journal of Latin American and Caribbean Anthropology* 12(2): 356–83.

Wilderson, Frank. 2008. "Biko and the Problematic of Presence." In *Biko Lives! Contesting the Legacies of Steve Biko*, ed. Andile Mngxitama, Amanda Alexander, and Nigel C. Gibson, 95–114. New York: Palgrave Macmillan.

Wilderson, Frank. 2010. *Red, White and Black: Cinema and the Structure of U.S. Antagonisms*. Durham, NC: Duke University Press.

Williams, Eric. 1944. *Capitalism and Slavery*. Chapel Hill: University of North Carolina Press.

Williams, Rhaisa. 2016. "Toward a Theorization of Black Maternal Grief as Analytic." *Transforming Anthropology* 24(1): 17–30.

Wilson, Richard. 2001. *The Politics of Truth and Reconciliation in South Africa: Legitimizing the Post-Apartheid State*. New York: Cambridge University Press.

Wilson, Richard, and Richard Brown. 2011. *Humanitarianism and Suffering: The Mobilization of Empathy*. New York: Cambridge University Press.

Wilson, William Julius. 1987. *The Truly Disadvantaged: The Inner City, the Underclass, and Public Policy*. Chicago: University of Chicago Press.

Windmuller, John P. 1963. "Labor: A Partner in American Foreign Policy?" *Annals of the American Academy of Political and Social Science* 350: 104–14.

Witter, Errol. 2013. *Interim Report to Parliament Concerning Investigations into the Conduct of the Security Forces during the State of Emergency Declared May, 2010*, April 29. Kingston: Office of the Public Defender.

Worsley, Peter. 1957. *The Trumpet Shall Sound: A Study of "Cargo" Cults in Melanesia*. London: MacGibbon and Key.

Wynter, Sylvia. 1960. "A Dream Deferred: Will the Condemned Rasta Far Ever Return to Africa?" *Tropic* (October): 50–51.

Wynter, Sylvia. 2003. "Unsettling the Coloniality of Being/Power/Truth/Freedom: Towards the Human, After Man, Its Overrepresentation—an Argument." *CR: New Centennial Review* 3(3): 257–338.

Zelizer, Barbie. 1998. *Remembering to Forget: Holocaust Memory through the Camera's Eye*. Chicago: University of Chicago Press.

Zelizer, Barbie. 2002. "Finding Aids to the Past: Bearing Personal Witness to Traumatic Public Events." *Media, Culture and Society* 24(5): 697–714.

Index

Narrative, 23, 24, 57, 59–60, 216. *See also* Witnessing 2.0

Nationalism: citizenship and, 5, 101–2; economic development and, 21, 98–101, 117, 175; garrisons and, 9–10, 63; Jamaicans and, 63, 84, 95, 100, 153–54; race and, 14, 41, 43, 69; slavery and, 1, 13, 151; trade unions and, 127. *See also* Black Power movement; Rastafari; Sovereignty

National Labour Congress, 167, 182

National Workers Union (NWU), 10–11, 80–82, 182–87, 191–93, 201–4. *See also* Manley, Michael

Navaro-Yashin, Yael, 231n13

Nelson, Diane, 37, 64

Neptune, Harvey, 233n18

Niaah, Jahlani, 181

Nixon, Richard, 149

Norris (Fitzherbert), Katrin (Kay), 76–80, 82–86, 235n36, 245n37, 246n38

Oliver, Kelly, 215, 220

Olivier, Sidney, 69–71, 74–75

Omi, Michael, 231n9

Operation Buccaneer, 149

Operation Garden Parish. *See* Tivoli Incursion

Page, Kezia, 243n52, 268n16

Palmer, Colin A., 159

Paranoia, 20, 29, 90, 150, 152–54, 172, 206, 220, 254n1

Paton, Diana, 233n22, 235n4

Patterson, Orlando, 7–8

Peacemakers. *See* International Peacemakers' Association

Peasantry, 98–101, 243n4; developmentalism and, 64, 69; disenfranchisement of, 180, 247n12; landownership and, 69, 73–74, 80, 180; plantations and, 9, 13; Rastafari and, 151; United Fruit Company and, 13, 70; urban communities and, 107

People's Educational Organization (PEO), 154, 168–70

People's Freedom Movement (PFM), 154, 168–70, 172–78, 193

People's National Party (PNP), 166–68, 181–85, 196, 199; Henry and, 109–11, 116, 122; Jamaica Labour Party versus, 10–11, 29, 38, 102, 110–11, 140, 143–46, 196, 206; left wing of, 100, 205; Rastafari and, 107, 159, 175; slum clearance and, 12, 42; trade unions and, 10–11, 99, 154, 191; U.S. government and, 139–40, 143–45. *See also* Manley, Michael; Manley, Norman; National Workers Union; Romualdi, Serafino

People's Political Party (PPP), 85, 178

Pinchevski, Amit, 230n6

Pinnacle, 76, 157–59, 180–81, 247n20, 256n29

Planno, Mortimo, 181, 258n70

Plantations, 1, 3–4, 7, 8–10, 13; critiques of, 17, 84, 86–87; doubt and, 23–24; economic production on, 69, 84, 98–99; legacy of, 84–86, 90, 92; modernity and, 17, 41, 151; race and, 41, 57, 211–12; social organization of, 84; sovereignty and, 220; violence and, 14, 45. *See also* Slavery

Policing, 14–15, 27, 29–31, 39, 128–29, 131–32, 155–60, 177–78, 236n8. *See also* Jamaica Constabulary Force; Jamaica Defense Force

Post, Ken, 100–102, 246n10, 247n20, 254n2, 256n30, 266n184

Povinelli, Elizabeth, 24, 249n53

Prophecy, 2, 61, 89–91, 120–29; black radical politics and, 95, 98; Henry and, 95, 109, 115–17; Manley and, 111, 117; Rastafari and, 17, 20

Public Safety Program, 30

Public secret, 49

Race, 3–5, 13–15, 40–43, 141–42, 151–53, 155–59; browns and, 101, 210; citizenship and, 63; class and, 248n31; colonialism and, 72, 141, 231n10; definition of humanity and, 237n20; economic development and, 126; garrisons and, 9, 63; narratives of racial harmony and, 68, 70–71, 74, 84–86, 95, 243n3; nationalism and, 69;

Vaky, Viron, 143
Van Dijk, Frank Jan, 159–60, 266n184
Vickers, John, 80–83
Violence, 1–4, 13–15; abolition of, 88–89; affect and, 24, 38–39, 46, 59, 63–64, 214, 220; colonialism and, 45, 57, 63, 152, 214–15; culture of, 6, 39, 237n16; ethical response to, 21, 219; garrisons and, 38–40, 46, 61–62, 101; Henry on, 88, 108–10; modernity and, 127; party politics and, 30, 39, 110, 138–39, 145, 204; plantations and, 7, 45; policing and, 30, 39, 128–29; race and, 42, 57, 142, 153, 212, 231n10; Rastafari and, 171; sovereignty and, 6, 21, 24, 38–39, 92, 213, 220; trade unions and, 167. *See also* Gangs
Volkman, Ernest, 137–38

Wald, Gayle, 6
Walker, Philip, 155–56
Walton, Calder, 163
Watson, N. D., 190
Weber, Max, 16, 18, 89–91, 129
Weheliye, Alexander G., 4, 237n20
West India Department of the Colonial Office: economic development and 75; Henry and, 95–96, 174–77; LSIC reports and, 164–70; Rastafari and, 96, 157,

174–75, 181; trade unions and, 81–84, 187–89. *See also* British colonial government; Local Security and Intelligence Committee
West Kingston Commission of Enquiry, 20, 29, 32–38, 44, 48–54, 56–62, 213, 235n2. *See also* Tivoli Incursion
White, R. N., 155–56
Wilderson, Frank, 5
Williams, Mahatma, 36
Winant, Howard, 231n9
Windmuller, John P., 183, 261n107
Witnessing 2.0, 2–3, 18–19, 37, 152–53, 216, 220, 230n3; as bearing witness, 23, 45, 60, 92, 108, 230n6; as relating narratives, 46, 59–60, 216; surveillance and, 23, 45, 206
Wolf, Louis, 133–35, 147–48, 150
Workers Party of Jamaica (WPJ), 113
Working class, 10, 14–15, 18, 169, 181, 191–93, 247n13. *See also* Rastafari
World Federation of Trade Unions (WFTU), 167–68, 183
Worsley, Peter, 120
Wynter, Sylvia, 1, 4, 16, 97, 129, 230n2

Zelizer, Barbie, 2
Zonarich, Nicholas, 186–91